The Emergence
of American Zionism

The Emergence of American Zionism

Mark A. Raider

NEW YORK UNIVERSITY PRESS

New York and London

NEW YORK UNIVERSITY PRESS
New York and London

Library of Congress Cataloging-in-Publication Data
Raider, Mark A.
The emergence of American Zionism / Mark A. Raider.
p.   cm.
Includes bibliographical references and index.
ISBN 0-8147-7498-9 (hardcover : alk. paper).—ISBN 0-8147-7499-7
(pbk. : alk. paper)
1. Zionism—United States—History.   I. Title.
DS149.5.U6R35   1998
320.54'095694'0973—dc21   98-23089
CIP

New York University Press books are printed on acid-free paper,
and their binding materials are chosen for strength and durability.

Manufactured in the United States of America

10 9 8 7 6 5 4 3 2 1

Contents

List of Illustrations

Preface

The image of Zionist pioneers in the late nineteenth and early twentieth centuries—hardworking, brawny, and living off the land—sprang from Labor Zionism, the ascendant socialist Zionist movement in Palestine. The building of the Yishuv, the new Jewish society in Palestine, was accompanied by the rapid growth of Zionism worldwide.

How did Zionism take shape in the United States? How did Labor Zionism and the Yishuv influence American Jews? This book argues that Zionism and Labor Zionism had a much greater impact on the American Jewish scene than has been recognized. It traces Labor Zionism's dramatic transformation in the United States from a marginal immigrant party into a significant political force. It shows how and why Labor Zionism in the United States—the voice of Labor Palestine on American soil—played a role disproportionate to its size in formulating the program and outlook of American Zionism. It also examines more generally the impact of Zionism on American Jews, making the case that Zionism's cultural vitality, intellectual diversity, and unparalleled ability to rally public opinion in times of crisis were central to the American Jewish experience.

This book, which originally was my doctoral dissertation at Brandeis University, would not have been possible without the steadfast support of my mentors: Jehuda Reinharz, Jonathan D. Sarna, and Stephen J. Whitfield. Since I began my graduate studies, they have persistently challenged and inspired me, leaving an indelible impression on my work as a modern Jewish historian. It is my hope that this book justifies their extraordinary investment in time and energy on my behalf.

In the course of my research, I also benefited from the reservoir of human talent associated with the Brandeis community. A special word of thanks must go to Sylvia Fuks Fried, who labored through multiple drafts of the manuscript and made numerous valuable suggestions for its revision and improvement. For their scholarly expertise, I am grateful to Joyce

Antler, Sylvia Barack Fishman, Michael Brenner, Marc Brettler, the late Marvin Fox, Antony Polonsky, Benjamin C. I. Ravid, Shulamit Reinharz, Bernard Reisman, the late Marshall Sklare, Daniel J. Tichenor, and Bernard Wasserstein. Lawrence H. Fuchs and Leon A. Jick were particularly gracious, generous, and inspiring tutors. Joanna Gould went out of her way to offer much needed computer assistance. Janet Webber of the Tauber Institute for the Study of European Jewry was exceptionally helpful. In the Judaica Division of the University Libraries, Jim Rosenbloom, Charles Cutter, and Nancy Zibman were an unflagging source of research support. Julian Brown provided expert photographic assistance.

Over the years, several other people have guided and encouraged my research efforts. I am deeply grateful to Aharon Appelfeld, Murray Baumgarten, Michael Brown, Mitchell Cohen, the late Moshe Davis, Sidra DeKoven Ezrahi, Leonard Fein, Henry Feingold, Evyatar Friesel, Allon Gal, Lloyd P. Gartner, Aryeh Goren, Gerd Korman, Eli Lederhendler, Paul Mendes-Flohr, Derek J. Penslar, Robert M. Seltzer, Anita Shapira, Gideon Shimoni, Shelly Tenenbaum, Melvin I. Urofsky, Chaim Waxman, and Robert Wistrich. At the University at Albany, State University of New York, where I completed this book, I have enjoyed the collegiality of Judith R. Baskin, Jerome Eckstein, Daniel Grossberg, and Stanley Isser. Special thanks are also due Muki Tsur of Kibbutz Ein Gev, Israel, who nurtured my interest in the cultural history of the Yishuv. Mishael M. Caspi, currently of Bates College, is a devoted teacher and friend. He and his wife Gila have played an inestimable role in my personal and professional growth.

A remarkable group of Zionist movement veterans shared their oral histories with me. I am grateful to David Breslau, Abe Cohen, Saadia Gelb, Nahum and Miriam Guttman, Haim Gvati, Gertrude Halpern, the late Jacob Katzman, and the late Kieve Skidell. Thanks are also due Ben Barlas for alerting me to several useful historical documents.

For archival assistance, I wish to thank the staffs of the American Jewish Archives, the Central Zionist Archives, the Lavon Institute for Labor Research, the National Center for Jewish Film, the Yad Tabenkin–United Kibbutz Movement Archives (especially Roni Azati), and the YIVO Institute for Jewish Research. Furthermore, I have been privileged to enjoy the warm support of friends and colleagues at the American Jewish Historical Society. Michael Feldberg, the society's executive director, has been an unwavering source of encouragement. I owe a special debt of gratitude to Ellen Smith, the society's curator, who read and commented on the manuscript and offered expert assistance concerning the illustrations. At each of the foregoing institutions, I was extended every possible courtesy.

Generous financial support of my work was provided by the American Jewish Historical Society; the National Foundation for Jewish Culture; the Tauber Institute for the Study of European Jewry, Brandeis University; and the YIVO Institute for Jewish Research. I also thank the Lucius N. Littauer Foundation for generously underwriting the publication costs associated with this book.

Portions of chapters 2 and 3 previously appeared in, respectively, "From Immigrant Party to American Movement: American Labor Zionism in the Pre-State Period," *American Jewish History* 82 (1994): 159–194; and in "Pioneers and Pacesetters: Boston Jews and American Zionism," *The Jews of Boston*, ed. Jonathan D. Sarna and Ellen Smith (Boston: Combined Jewish Philanthropies of Boston and Northeastern University Press, 1995): 241–275.

It has been a pleasure working with New York University Press. I am particularly thankful to my editors Jennifer Hammer and Despina Papazoglou Gimbel for seeing this project through to publication.

I conclude with heartfelt gratitude to my family. My parents, David and Elizabeth Raider, my siblings, Daniel and Elana, and my grandparents, Alfred and Estelle Raider, provided crucial moral support. My in-laws, Walter and Chaya Roth, showed keen interest in every stage of writing this book. For their warm encouragement, I thank Ari Roth, Kate Schecter, Judy Roth, and Stephen P. Zeldes as well as Isabel, Sophie, and Miko.

My children Jonah and Emma fill my days with joy and are constant reminders of life's immeasurable blessings. I happily dedicate this study to Miriam, my best friend, partner, and beloved, who makes my path possible and rewarding.

Author's Note

Throughout this book, I have modified somewhat the orthography and transliteration of Hebrew and Yiddish, to give English-speaking readers as clear a phonetic equivalent as possible without introducing complex diacritical marks and special linguistic values. Exceptions in this regard are terms and names for which a different usage is highly familiar (e.g., Eretz Israel, *yiddishkeit*, and Chaim Arlosoroff). In a few instances, the original English spelling of publications and groups has been retained (e.g., *Hechalutz* and Hadassah). In addition, although the glossary attempts to be fairly comprehensive, it does not include phraseology and terms that appear infrequently in the book. Rather, to assist the reader, this information has been inserted throughout the text. All translations, unless otherwise noted, are my own. Last, the synonymous place-names Palestine, Yishuv, and Jewish national home have been used interchangeably in accordance with the appropriate cultural-political context.

Glossary of Terms

aliyah (pl. *aliyot*, Hebrew for "ascent"): a term used to indicate immigration to the Land of Israel. The First Aliyah is usually dated 1881–1903; the Second Aliyah, 1903/4–1914; the Third Aliyah, 1919–1923; the Fourth Aliyah, 1924–1928; and the Fifth Aliyah, 1929–1939.

Aliyah Bet: the Hebrew term for the Zionist movement's program of "illegal Jewish immigration to Palestine" that was conducted in defiance of the British Mandate.

Bund: a term shortened from the Yiddish Der Algemeyner Yidisher Arbeter Bund (General Jewish Labor Union), the American wing of the east European mother organization active in Russia, Poland, and Lithuania.

dunam: Hebrew for one thousand square meters, approximately a quarter of an acre.

Eretz Israel (in Yiddish, Eretz Yisroel): Hebrew for the "Land of Israel," both a geographic and a spiritual designation.

galut: Hebrew for "exile," used to describe both spiritual and geographic conditions.

Gegenwartsarbeit: a German term used to denote "Zionist work in the diaspora" or "Zionist work in the present."

goldene medine: Yiddish for "golden land," used by east European Jewish immigrants to describe the United States.

golus: Yiddish for "exile" (see *galut*).

hagshamah azmit: Hebrew for "self-fulfillment."

haluz (pl. *haluzim*, Hebrew for "pioneer"): a term used to describe the Labor Zionist pioneers of Palestine.

haluzah (pl. *haluzot*): Hebrew for "young woman worker and settler."

haluziut: Hebrew for "pioneering."

Hapoel Hazair: Hebrew for The Young Worker, a non-Marxist Labor Zionist party established in Palestine in 1905 and the Palestinian sister organization of Zeirei Zion Hitahdut.

Hashomer: Hebrew for The Watchman, an organization formed in the Galilee in 1909 to guard the Jewish colonies of Palestine.

Haskalah: Hebrew for "enlightenment," the Jewish enlightenment movement in Europe, particularly that using the Hebrew language.

Hibbat Zion: Hebrew for Lovers of Zion, a philanthropic, proto-Zionist organization that originated in eastern Europe; used interchangeably with the name Hovevei Zion.

Histadrut: a shortened form of Histadrut Haovdim Haivrim be-Eretz Israel, Hebrew for General Federation of Jewish Workers in the Land of Israel, the umbrella framework of the Labor Zionist movement in Palestine.

Hovevei Zion (see Hibbat Zion).

kibbutz (pl. *kibbutzim*): Hebrew term for a cooperative rural settlement in Palestine.

kvuzah (pl. *kvuzot*): Hebrew term for a communal rural colony in Palestine.

landsmanshaftn: Yiddish for "mutual aid societies" formed for the purposes of welfare, burial, and the like; composed of immigrants from the same town or area in eastern Europe.

Mapai: an acronym for the Hebrew Mifleget Poalei Eretz Israel (Workers Party of the Land of Israel), established in Palestine in 1930; the party dominated Labor Zionism in the Mandatory and early state periods.

maskil (pl. *maskilim*): Hebrew for "enlightened Jew," referring to an adherent of the Jewish enlightenment movement (see Haskalah).

menorah: Hebrew for "candelabrum."

Mizrahi: an acronym for the Hebrew phrase *merkaz ruhani,* "spiritual center," and also "eastward"; the name of the religious Zionist party established in eastern Europe in 1902.

Moezet Hapoalot: Hebrew for the Working Women's Council, established in Palestine in 1922 as part of the Histadrut, and the sister organization of Pioneer Women in the United States.

moshav ovdim: Hebrew for "workers settlement," a rural Jewish colony in Palestine incorporating some cooperative principles.

Ostjuden: German for "eastern Jews," used by central European Jews to describe Polish Jewish immigrants to Germany.

Poalei Zion: Hebrew for Workers of Zion, a Marxist Zionist party that originated in Russia in 1901–1903 and subsequently established branches in other countries, including Palestine and the United States.

shaliah (pl. *shlihim*): Hebrew term for an emissary sent from Palestine, especially by the Labor Zionist movement.

shomer (pl. *shomrim*): Hebrew for "watchman, guard."

Talmud Torah: the Yiddish term for a traditional school, usually supported by the community, that taught boys the basics of biblical and rabbinic literature.

yahudim: pejorative Yiddish term used by east European Jews to describe Westernized German-speaking Jews.

yeshivah (pl. *yeshivot*): the Yiddish term for a school for advanced Talmudic study.

yidn: a pejorative Yiddish term used by German Jews to describe seemingly uncouth east European Jewish immigrants.

Yidish Nazionaler Arbeter Farband: Yiddish for the Jewish National Workers' Alliance, also known as the Farband, the fraternal order of the Labor Zionist movement in the United States.

Yidishe Nazional Radikale Shuln: Yiddish for Jewish National Radical Schools, also known as the Folkshuln, community schools of the American Labor Zionist movement that also served as the loci of cultural and party activities.

yiddishkeit: a Yiddish term for Jewishness.

Yishuv: the Jewish community in Palestine before the creation of the State of Israel in 1948.

yugnt: Yiddish for "youth."

Zeirei Zion Hitahdut of America: Hebrew for United Youth of Zion, established in the United States in 1920, an offshoot of the European non-Marxist Labor Zionist party and affiliated with the moderate Palestinian labor party Hapoel Hazair.

The Emergence
of American Zionism

Introduction

A political movement, like a living organism, is a dynamic and complex unity, a myriad of elements that evolve, change, and adapt over time. Zionism in the United States, initially an east European transplant, was shaped not only by developments in the New World but also by the turbulent social and political forces that transformed Jewish life in Europe and Palestine in the late nineteenth and early twentieth centuries.

The salient factor in the emergence of American Zionism, as was true of Zionism worldwide, was the rapid development of the Yishuv. This creation of a new Jewish society in Palestine had an impact on Zionist affairs that is difficult to overestimate. It was accompanied by the concomitant rise of Labor Zionism, the colonizing movement of socialist Zionist pioneers. At the center of this pioneering enterprise stood the Histadrut, the General Federation of Jewish Workers in the Land of Israel. The Histadrut created an intricate countrywide network of social, economic, and political institutions. As a result, the Palestinian labor movement determined much of the infrastructure of the Jewish state-in-the-making.

In the decades after World War I, Labor Zionism quickly rose to a position of political dominance in the World Zionist Organization, the Jewish Agency for Palestine, and the Vaad Leumi (the Yishuv's elected assembly). Accordingly, the Labor Zionist movement, with its base in Palestine and satellite organizations in Europe and the United States, played an increasingly significant role in Zionist affairs worldwide.

The complex relationship of American Jews, Labor Zionism, and the Yishuv invites close examination. American Jewry's rapid upward mobility and tendency toward professionalization and small entrepreneurship—a pattern that distinguished Jewish life in the United States from the austere socialist lifestyle and economic conditions of the Yishuv—would seem to have naturally militated against such a triad. After all, only a minority of American Jews officially belonged to the Zionist movement, and American Labor Zionism itself was never more than half the size of Mizrahi, the religious Zionist party.[1] Against this backdrop, Labor Zionism's disproportionate influence raises the question why, if the movement was so institutionally and numerically weak, it was so ideologically important and influential. How did Labor Zionism transform American Zionism? Who were the leaders that galvanized American Jewish support for Zionism and the Yishuv? What kind of impact did Zionism have on American Jewish life? The answers to these questions, this book contends, stem from the fact that Labor Zionism, unlike other Zionist variants, resonated not only with the Jewish experience but also with the American ideals of democracy, pluralism, and social justice.

The American scene was temperamentally and structurally different from that of Europe or Palestine. In Germany and Poland, for example, Zionist parties were characterized by their specifically nationalist orientation and generally negative appraisal of Jewish life in Europe. They formed political blocs and, in the case of the Polish Zionists, even played a short-lived role in national politics.[2] In Palestine, Zionists rejected the possibility of Jewish survival outside the Land of Israel. They also dominated the social and political life of the nascent Yishuv. By contrast, Zionist groups in the United States—despite their nationalist proclivities and attachment to Palestine—did not reject the New World. Moreover, they frequently found their philosophical and cultural positions to be consonant with those of mainstream Jewish groups. This hybrid character of American Jewry was perhaps nowhere more visible than in the east European Jewish immigrant milieu of the late nineteenth and early twentieth centuries, in which there often was no apparent conflict among belonging to a trade union, sending one's child to a Talmud Torah, and identifying as a card-carrying Zionist. In the American context, therefore, a practical alternative to the separatism of European Jewish politics was the creation of alliances that allowed numerically small groups like the Zionists to exert their influence from within.

Such was the case, for example, when Labor Zionist leaders spearheaded the campaign for the American Jewish Congress during World War I. The congress convened in December 1918 under the stewardship of Louis D. Brandeis, American Zionism's premier leader and an associate justice of the U.S. Supreme Court. This unprecedented representative democratic assembly brought working-class Yiddish-speaking immigrants into the mainstream of organized American Jewish life. With the support of various immigrant groups, Labor Zionists succeeded in placing the Jewish national question on the congress's agenda. This initiative ensured that Zionist claims regarding Palestine were included in the Jewish case later presented to the postwar Paris Peace Conference.[3]

By staking a claim for the importance of Labor Zionism and the Yishuv in the American context, this book challenges many of the assumptions about Jewish and Zionist historiography that have prevailed for a full generation. It contests, for example, Arthur Hertzberg's assertion that American Zionism was "an emotion and not an ideology" that "existed to help the pioneers and to take pride in them."[4] Likewise, it refutes Howard Sachar's claim that American Jewry was "Zionized" in the wake of World War II. Sachar maintains that "a survivalist threshold had been reached in the Jewish condition, and it impelled the urgency of an unconventional solution."[5] Both approaches vastly oversimplify the American Jewish scene. They wrongly suggest that American Jews had a monolithic attitude toward Zionism and reduce the movement's American manifestation to a vicarious or, at most, an ephemeral phenomenon. They also neglect American Jewry's centuries-old fascination with the Holy Land and, at least implicitly, ignore Zionism's lasting impact on American Jews in the poststate period.

That Zionism failed to create a mass movement in the United States or to generate substantial American Jewish immigration to Palestine is not a new observation. To understand American Zionism, however, we must consider both the movement's unparalleled ability to galvanize American Jewish public opinion in times of crisis and its cultural vitality and political diversity.[6] That is, we must examine both Zionism in the context of interwar and wartime American Jewish politics and the broad spectrum of American Jewish society, including youth, educators, women's organizations, intellectuals, and various social and religious groups. In short, the interplay between Zionism and American Jews reveals a mélange of secularizing tendencies, language preferences, forms of religious observance, generational discord, ethnic divisions, socioeconomic distinctions, and disparate political ideologies. Such multiformity requires an integrated methodological perspective akin to the French Annales school's notion of "the history of mentalities."[7] In this way, it is possible to evaluate the nexus between American Jews and Zionism in quantifiable objective terms and also with respect to American Jewry's protean self-perception—a context in which Labor Zionism played a defining role.

The political transformation of American Zionism went hand in hand with the building of the Yishuv's socioeconomic infrastructure by the Labor Zionist movement. Viewed in historical perspective, this symbiotic process sheds light on a significant watershed in Zionist and Jewish history: by the interwar period, the balance of power in Jewish life was shifting away from the diaspora and toward the ascendant Zionist leadership in Palestine. During the interwar period, Labor Zionism became the hub of the world's Zionist social, cultural, and political activity, its authority radiating to the farthest reaches of the diaspora. By the 1940s, Labor Zionism's pragmatic wartime strategy became the basis of American Jewry's campaign for Jewish statehood. First at the Biltmore Conference of 1942 and then at the American Jewish Conference of 1943—both of which Labor Zionism championed, as it had the American Jewish Congress of 1918—the movement's twin objectives of rescue and sovereignty were affirmed. This view was articulated, among others, by American Zionism's wartime tribune Abba Hillel Silver, who declared there to be "but one solution for national homelessness." "That is a national home! . . . The reconstitution of the Jewish people as a nation in its homeland is not a playful political conceit of ours. . . . It is the cry of despair of a people driven to the wall, fighting for its very life."[8]

Zionism was originally imported to the United States by powerless east European Jewish immigrants. The swift acculturation and ascendance of the immigrants in the New World, however, coupled with the Yishuv's meteoric rise, set the stage for what the founder of Reconstructionism and Labor Zionist advocate Mordecai M. Kaplan deemed "a new American Zionism." Labor Zionism played a key role in defining the new Zionism of American Jews, a philosophy and program attuned to the changing reality of American Judaism and the needs of prestate Palestine. The movement served as a lens through which American Jews viewed nascent Palestinian and American society as many thought both ought to be: full of promise and opportunity, industrious and expansive, and, not least of all, capable of elevating the human condition. The dynamic tension inherent in such romantic preconceptions sparked American Jewry's idealization of the Yishuv and the growing preoccupation with Labor Palestine as the best hope for alleviating European Jewry's distress, a sentiment that gained widespread currency with the advent of Nazi Germany. In time, the historic encounter of American Jews, Labor Zionism, and the Yishuv gave rise to the American Zionist campaign for Jewish statehood. It also paved the way for Zionism's trajectory from the margins to the mainstream of the American Jewish experience.

1

The American Setting

On the eve of her departure for Palestine in January 1920, Henrietta Szold, the founder of Hadassah, wrote to her friend Alice L. Seligsberg: "It will take the gentleness of the dove and the wisdom of the serpent if the situation [in Palestine] is to be met in a constructive spirit."[1] Szold's statement prefigures American Zionism's transformation into an important political force. It also reveals a distinct American Zionist sensibility that stressed the need for consensus politics and practical schemes for the Palestine Jewish community's development. Szold recognized that the effectiveness of American Zionist leadership, on the one hand, depended on good relations with American Jewry's elite non-Zionist patriarchs, especially those of the American Jewish Committee, and the cooperation of the Jewish immigrant community, from traditionalists to members of the non-Zionist Jewish workers' movement. On the other hand, it required close collaboration with the leaders of the World Zionist Organization, the Yishuv, and, at a later date, the Jewish Agency for Palestine.

Such a multifaceted orientation contains the seeds of collaboration and the potential for cooperation. It is germane to both American Zionism and the American Jewish experience, which, by virtue of its distinctive postfeudal and postemancipationist origin, differs fundamentally from that of European Jewish society. American society's "sheer formlessness," it has been observed, allowed Jews to live side by side with other heterogeneous groups. This unique situation gave rise to the expectation that the pattern of "true American living [would be] worked out by immigrants and [native-born] Americans in a continuing process of give and take."[2]

European Jewry, however, was forcibly segregated from mainstream society until the eighteenth century when the movement for Jewish emancipation began. Not surprisingly, emancipation was especially strong in western and central Europe owing to the numerical insignificance of the Jews in these lands, their facility for social and economic modernization, and the relative speed of their legal amelioration.[3] In contrast, the Balkan and east

European Jewish communities were seemingly impenetrable to the forces of emancipation. Because of strong traditional values in these areas and the enforced separation of the Jews living under Russian and Romanian domination, a core of Jewish intellectuals emerged, arrayed against the camps of both Western assimilationism and Eastern religious orthodoxy. Neither the doctrine of emancipation nor the helpless torpor of Jewish life under the old regime offered them hope for the future.[4]

Nonetheless, in the early nineteenth century, some Jewish thinkers broke away from the traditional Jewish mainstream. These Zionist forerunners argued that the creation of Jewish settlements in the Land of Israel was a necessary prelude to the redemption of the Jewish people. In short, even before the Russian pogroms of 1881–1882 erupted following the assassination of Czar Alexander II, both Western emancipation and the east European status quo were under attack from a variety of nationalist positions.[5]

That the pogroms destroyed hopes for Jewish emancipation in Eastern Europe is well documented.[6] Particularly striking is the fact that the liberal leadership of Russian Jewry failed to meet the challenge of Jewish self-defense and relief. In the ensuing vacuum, the Pale of Settlement was wracked by widespread communal misery, in which the ideologies of Jewish socialism, territorialism, and nationalism rapidly took root and flourished. These new ideological camps were largely made up of young people and thus contained a strong element of generational conflict;[7] all shared a predilection for Russian populism. The Jewish intelligentsia followed the example of social revolutionaries like the Narodnik (People's Will) Party and sought to create a bond with the toiling masses by "returning" to the people.[8] Even after the pogroms, Russian Jewish radicals continued to uphold this notion as the guiding principle of their political and cultural work. The most obvious problem they faced was that of Jewish refugees. A rivalry immediately developed between the Amerikantsy, notably the Am Olam (Eternal People) movement that advocated Jewish resettlement in the United States, and the Palestintsy, represented by the socialist Zionist Bilu pioneers who favored Jewish colonization in Palestine.[9] Notwithstanding economic pressures, the debate among radical youth turned on the question of whether the United States or Palestine was more suitable for Jewish national renewal.

On the other side of the Atlantic, "Zion" and the "Land of Israel" always enjoyed pride of place in American consciousness. Since the days of America's Pilgrim fathers and the early settlement of New England, the notion of rebuilding Zion had been a persistent theme in American life and letters. The leaders of colonial New England—mostly divines and scriptural authorities—strongly influenced early American society in the seventeenth and eighteenth centuries. Their biblical perspective spawned the principle of "covenant theology" and gave rise to the democratic political tradition that distinguished early American life.[10] This bipolar existence always was subject to the practical exigencies of the New World. Gradually, though, a highly cosmopolitan American outlook emerged, one in which the eschatological concept of the "return to Zion" was central but that nevertheless sought ways of making—through both voluntary and persuasive means—the emergent American society into a fully Christian nation.[11]

From the outset, colonial America and later the United States provided fertile terrain for successive waves of incoming European immigrants, including the ideas and movements they transplanted to American soil. By the nineteenth century, the northeastern seaboard had become a center of liberal political and religious trends.[12] To this the Jewish immigrants brought their Old World mentality, a mélange of rational, spiritual, and cultural attributes.[13] In most urban centers, the admixture of different Jewish immigrant groups led to communal friction. For example, an extraordinary instance occurred in 1882 when Boston Jewish leaders shipped back 415 Russian Jewish refugees to New York, fearing that the new immigrants would become a financial burden.[14] On the whole, however, even though American Jewish life was punctuated by periods of ethnic rivalry and division between *yahudim* and *yidn*, American Jewish society generally proved to be a congenial atmosphere for newcomers from central and eastern Europe.[15] As the Boston communal leader Abraham P. Spitz remarked in 1892:

> We who live in this great country, God's most favored land . . . can hardly realize the persecutions to which our coreligionists in Russia have been subjected. . . . We must and shall receive them with open arms. . . . We must teach them the manners and customs of an enlightened community . . . thus enabling them to become useful and desirable citizens."[16]

By the end of the nineteenth century, Jewish immigrants arriving in the United States were greeted by a relatively stable communal infrastructure, one that for the most part was prepared to care for them. They also found an environment that provided them with the scope and inducement to define their own communal needs and create mechanisms for self-support and mutual assistance.[17]

The rapid acculturation of Jewish immigrants in the United States led to the proliferation of local Zionist societies.[18] Like other immigrant associations, the Zionist clubs were not large, and their membership rosters were far from stable. But their presence was felt in the wider community. Viewed historically, the strength of American Zionism was never contingent on its size or, at a later stage, its fund-raising ability. Instead, American Zionists were most influential as leaders who helped inculcate in American Jews a sense of kinship and responsibility for the Yishuv and who helped build bridges between the two societies.

The earliest American Hibbat Zion (Lovers of Zion) groups were east European transplants that sprang up throughout New England beginning in the 1880s.[19] Initially, these groups, also known as Hovevei Zion, considered themselves part of the European mother organization, as is apparent in a "special notice" issued by the Lovers of Zion Society of East Boston in 1899:

Dear Member:

You are hereby given Notice that this Society will meet hereafter on every Sunday at 11 a.m., in Ohel Jacob Hall, Cor. Grove and Paris Sts., and no notices or Postal Cards will be send to this affect [sic] hereafter, except on Special Meetings.

You are also requested to be present at the meeting which will be held next Sunday, as there is very Important Business to be Transacted such, as to send the (Scheckel) 25c. for each *good standing Member* to the Central Federation of Zionists in Wiena (Austria.)

You are also notified that Mr. A. Fin has been dully [sic] selected as a Collector for this Society and is authorized to Collect Dues and other fees, until further notice.

With greeting for Zion,
Per order of LOUIS B. MAGID President
Nathan Bloch Sec'y[20]

Throughout America, a plethora of Hebrew-speaking clubs and fund-raising associations were organized for land purchases in Palestine, and by the turn of the century, the United States was home to scores of different Zionist groups with Americanized names such as the Uptown Zionist Club, Oir Zion Lodge, Dorshei Zion, Hebrew National Association, Zion Literary League, International Order of the Knights of Zion, Flowers of Zion, Bnai Zion, Bnoth Zion, Ladies' Zion League, Helpers of Zion, Maccabees

Zion Branch, American Daughters of Zion, and Philadelphia Zionist Society.[21] As these colorful names reveal, early American Zionists displayed a
variety of cultural, religious, and political interests. This pluralistic environment also encouraged the establishment of local branches of the Mizrahi
Party, a religious Zionist movement dedicated to the resettlement of the
Jewish people in Eretz Israel according to the precepts of the Torah, and
the Labor Zionist Poalei Zion Party, which interpreted the cause of Jewish
national liberation in Marxist terms. Most urban centers even included a
few Zionist synagogues with names like the Bialystocker Congregation
Adath Yeshurun, Adas Zion Anshe Kowno, Ahavath Achim Anshe Usda,
Poel Zedec Anshe Ilio, Tifereth Jerusholaim, and Chemdath Zion.[22] This
array of Zionist immigrant creations augmented the existing communal
infrastructure of native-born American Jews.

The pluralistic character of the New World differed dramatically from
the restrictive environment of Europe. Whereas American Zionism continued to identify with the European mother organization, American Zionists
were also inclined toward a synthesis of Zionism and American ideals. This
was especially true of native-born Jews sympathetic to Zionism, many of
whom sought to promote Jewish national sentiment as a facet of modern
American Jewish identity. In 1905, Josephine Lazarus, sister of the poet
Emma Lazarus, suggested that "Zionism, like Americanism, is an emancipation, a release from enforced limitation and legislation, from a narrow
petty, tribal polity of life, whether social or religious, and from old-world
prejudice and caste."[23]

A similar sensibility prevailed in the Jewish immigrant sphere. Jews of
east European extraction, however, also exhibited a marked degree of ambivalence about American society that reflected their distinct cultural orientation. As early as 1888, for example, the *maskil* (enlightened Jew) A. A.
Rogovin observed that although American Lovers of Zion operated in a
climate of unprecedented freedom, Jewish nationalism in the New World
was nonetheless constrained by its own problems.

> The members [of Hibbat Zion] live in the land of America, a land in which
> a large part of our brothers has forsaken our Torah and language and does
> not want to hear about the land of our fathers. For what do they lack here!
> The rich and powerful people who pay their rabbi twelve thousand dollars a
> year have already erased any mention even of Jerusalem from their prayer
> books. And also many of our less pretentious and younger brothers have
> already forgotten Zion even without erasing its mention from their books,

since they do not pray at all. They know neither our Torah nor language because they have not studied. Even those who brought their knowledge with them from Russia and Poland seek to discard it.[24]

Successive waves of east European Jewish immigrants underscored the debate about Jewish identity in the New World. East European Jewry's nationalist impulse, however, was not totally unprecedented in American Jewish life. An incipient form of devotion to Zion, as we have already seen, had existed in the United States since the colonial period.[25] This sentiment reached a climax in 1825 when Mordecai M. Noah, an eccentric diplomat, devised a grandiose scheme to create a Jewish state on an island in the Niagara River opposite Buffalo, New York.[26] In another curious episode, Warder Cresson, a convert to Judaism who briefly served as the American consul in Palestine, assumed the name Michael Boaz Israel and established an agricultural colony near Jerusalem in 1852.[27] Finally, the well-known poet Emma Lazarus advocated the restoration of a Jewish homeland in her *An Epistle to the Hebrews* (1882–1883).[28]

Lazarus was profoundly influenced by a monograph entitled *Autoemancipation: Ein Mahnruf an seine Stammesgenossen von einem russischen Juden* (Autoemancipation: an appeal to his people by a Russian Jew) (1882).[29] Published anonymously by Leon Pinsker in the aftermath of the Russian pogroms of 1881–1882, this proto-Zionist treatise became the manifesto of Hibbat Zion.[30] Reflecting on Pinsker's essay, Lazarus noted: "The incidents of current Jewish history, the swelling voice of Jewish patriotism, [and] the urgent necessity of escape from an untenable position among the nations, have combined to transform me into one of the most devoted adherents to the new dogma."[31]

Such nationalist views did not differ dramatically from those of Lazarus's contemporary Rabbi Bernhard Felsenthal who, despite his unfamiliarity with Pinsker and his loyalty to Reform Judaism, gradually came to consider Palestine "a practical solution to a philanthropic problem."[32] Felsenthal later developed a religious rationale for his Zionist proclivities, but at this early stage he, too, believed in American Jewish noblesse oblige.[33]

In the late nineteenth century, as Zionism steadily penetrated American Jewish life—a phenomenon buoyed by the waves of east European Jewish migrants—Hibbat Zion groups sprang up along the east coast. The movement also spread northward to Montreal, southward to Philadelphia, and as far west as Omaha. Nascent Hibbat Zion contained a sprinkling of Jews of central European descent, including Rosa Sonneschein, later the editor of *American Jewess*, a women's magazine published in Chicago and New York from April 1895 to March 1899,[34] and Adam Rosenberg, head of New York's Shavei Zion (Returners to Zion) society. Both persons typify the early movement's self-conscious striving to mix political activism with social respectability. Sonneschein, a pioneer of Jewish social service, viewed philanthropy as a religious and moral obligation.[35] Rosenberg, a lawyer and religious scholar, maintained American ties with the European-based movement and undertook a mission to establish settlements in Palestine for American immigrants.[36] Later, in 1897, both Sonneschein and Rosenberg attended the First Zionist Congress held in Basel, Switzerland.

The first American Zionists were mostly Russian and other east European Jews. Although intellectually compatible with figures like Sonneschein and Rosenberg, the east Europeans retained a distinct sociocultural sensibility and political self-awareness. When Rabbi Moses Weinberger, an orthodox Hungarian immigrant, characterized New York's Hovevei Zion as made up of "upstanding" Russians and Poles—"men of knowledge[,] . . . scholars, intellectuals, and excellent writers"[37]—he was describing a mentality forged on the anvil of czarist oppression. For these engagé east European Jewish intellectuals, the fledgling Zionist movement represented a hope reborn as well as a lifestyle. They were passionate nationalists who viewed Eretz Israel in personal and existential terms. In addition, they supported an ambitious network of nationalist periodicals, including Dr. Joseph Isaac Bluestone's Yiddish journal *Shulamit*, Wolf Schur's Hebrew weekly *Hapisgah* (The Mount), Ephraim Deinard's Hebrew literary publication *Haleumi* (The Nationalist), and Kasriel Hirsch Sarasohn's *Haivri* (The Hebrew), Deinard's competitor.[38] By 1890, the American Lovers of Zion had established a presence, including several women's groups, in virtually every major metropolitan center.[39]

Hibbat Zion also made significant inroads into different spheres of American Jewish leadership. In its first phase, the movement challenged the American Jewish establishment and won the support of prominent figures like the Yiddish publicists C. D. Birkahn, N. Chazan, and Jacob Fishman; New York attorneys Isadore D. Morrison and Jacob Siegel; and Rabbis Henry Pereira Mendes, Aaron Wise, Shepsel Schaffer, and Alexander Kohut. Even Rabbis Marcus Jastrow, Benjamin Szold, and Sabato Morais displayed some enthusiasm for Zionism.[40] The movement also aroused the sympathetic interest of the Yiddish, Hebrew, and Anglo-Jewish press which, though far from uniform in its attitude, showed increasing interest in the Zionist cause. Finally, the very presence of the nationalist camp (despite the relatively small size of its dues-paying membership) sharpened the atmosphere of ideological debate and, in key instances, compelled the leaders of Reform Judaism and Jewish labor to reevaluate their positions. An example is the 1885 declaration by the Central Conference of American Rabbis, the national association of Reform rabbis belonging to the Union of American Hebrew Congregations:

> We recognize in the Mosaic legislation a system of training the Jewish people for its mission during its national life in Palestine, and today we accept as binding only the moral laws . . . but reject all such as are not adapted to the views and habits of modern civilization. . . . We consider ourselves no longer a nation, but a religious community, and therefore expect neither a return to Palestine . . . nor the restoration of any of the laws concerning the Jewish state.[41]

Likewise, in 1890 a conference of organized Jewish labor defined itself in opposition to American proto-Zionism:

> There is no Jewish question in America. The only Jewish question which we recognize is the question, how to prevent the development of such "Jewish questions." Only because we alone, Yiddish-speaking citizens, can have an influence among the Jewish immigrants; only because we speak their language and are familiar with their lives—only because of this are we organizing this special Jewish body. The Yiddish language is our tool; one of our goals is to erase all divisions between Jew and non-Jew in the world of the workers.[42]

Modern Jewry's existential crisis, escalated by the persecution of east European Jewry in the late nineteenth century, served as a catalyst for the quasi-nationalism of mainstream American Jews. In the United States, this process was exacerbated by domestic antisemitism,* the collapse of the liberal paradigm to which American Jews were accustomed, and the fear that Judaism might disappear.[43] Against this backdrop, Hibbat Zion can be seen as a relatively accurate indicator of early Zionism's impact in the

---

*The German antisemite Wilhelm Marr (1818–1904) coined the term *antisemitism* in 1879 and subsequently introduced it into the political lexicon by founding the League of Antisemites, the first modern popular political movement based on anti-Jewish sentiment. I use the spelling "antisemitism" in this book to avoid the misconception that there is such an entity as "Semitism" opposed by Jew haters. That is, antisemites are opposed to Jews and Jewish civilization, not "Semites." For further analysis, see Ben Halpern, "What Is Antisemitism?" *Modern Judaism* 1 (1981): 251–262.

United States: in a negative sense because of the opposition that it aroused, and in a positive sense because it clarified and amplified latent possibilities in American Jewish life. The emergence of Hibbat Zion on American soil, enlivened by the full-blooded cultural nationalism of east European Jews, made Zionism more than a transitory phenomenon or a passing charitable interest. In fact, Hibbat Zion did the initial spadework that led to Zionism's subsequent success in the United States.

When Theodor Herzl burst on the scene in 1896 and galvanized modern political Zionism, the American movement's infrastructure was already in place. The proto-Zionist groups and societies in the New World, many of which had previously been affiliated with Hibbat Zion, were organized according to varying orientations. Some professed distinctive intellectual and cultural agendas. Others were primarily philanthropic or devoted to acquiring land in Palestine. There was also a scattering of activist political cells. The site of the first large-scale, well-organized response to Herzl's call was Chicago. Leon Zolotkoff, a well-known east European intellectual and later editor of New York's pro-Zionist *Yidishe tageblat* (Jewish Daily News), led a group of "Russians," including the merchant brothers Bernard Horwich and Harris Horwich, in establishing Chicago Zionist Organization Number One. This association provided the nucleus of the Order of the Knights of Zion, a midwestern, interstate, Zionist fraternal organization. The Chicago group's name change reflected the members' conscious "emulation of . . . the Knights of Labor and the Knights of Columbus . . . [including] their mysteries and rituals."[44]

In New York, a group of east European intellectuals swayed by Kasriel Hirsch Sarasohn, founder of the *Yidishe tageblat*, engineered the creation of the Federation of American Zionists (FAZ). On July 4, 1898, a date no doubt chosen for its symbolic importance, the group convened a "national assembly" of nearly one hundred Zionist societies, including a New York City delegation representing thirty-six groups with five thousand members, Chicago delegates representing one thousand members, Baltimore delegates representing five hundred members, a few delegates from outlying metropolitan centers, and even a contingent from Alliance, a Jewish agricultural colony located in southern New Jersey.

Although the FAZ absorbed many Hovevei Zion groups, like the Knights of Zion, it too shed any outward signs of Old World trappings and nomenclature. Adopting an explicitly New World approach, the FAZ approved an American-style constitution and elected a reluctant Richard J. H. Gottheil to be its first "president." Gottheil, a professor of Semitic languages at Columbia University, was "conspicuous by his absence" at the FAZ's first national meeting and was chosen over Chicago's Leon Zolotkoff because of his "better name." The professor was the son of Rabbi Gustav Gottheil, the well-known leader of Reform Judaism's flagship Temple Emanu-El in New York City, who was himself moderately disposed to Zionism in his last years. (In 1902, when Jacob De Haas arrived in the United States at the request of Theodor Herzl, Gottheil was reelected president but swiftly fled the Zionist scene.)[45] In addition, the FAZ's founding convention elected Shepsel Schaffer, Bernhard Felsenthal, Marcus Jastrow, Joseph Isaac Bluestone, and Zvi Hirsch Masliansky "vice presidents"; C. D. Birakhan "honorary treasurer"; and Stephen S. Wise "honorary secretary."[46]

Even though half the FAZ's elected officials were east Europeans, the new organization supplied American Zionism with a thoroughly Western gloss. It immediately attracted a number of prominent acculturated Jews, and despite the movement's professed allegiance to Herzlian Zionism, it continued to engage almost exclusively in local cultural work and philanthropic efforts aimed at supporting land acquisition and colonization in Palestine.[47] "While any violation of the fundamental principles of the Basel Platform [the political program of the Zionist Organization] is sternly rejected," explained Richard Gottheil, "there has been manifest a greater readiness to undertake work in Palestine upon a practical basis without first waiting for the final results of diplomatic and political action."[48] In this way, early American Zionism developed a program based on the striving of east Europeans for national renewal and the need of acculturated American Jews for a new mode of positive cultural self-expression.

If the FAZ signaled a political breakthrough for Zionism generally, it also served a latent social function for Jewish immigrants who sought to infuse American Jewish life with east European cultural-national values.

In this regard, the impact of east European Jewish immigrant intellectuals was substantial. For example, consider Zvi Hirsch Masliansky, a native of Slutsk, Belorussia, who immigrated to the United States in 1895 after more than a decade of intensive Zionist activity in eastern Europe.[49] Welcomed as a hero by America's Yiddish-speaking immigrants, Masliansky quickly adapted to the new conditions of American Jewish life.[50] He was widely admired and helped popularize Zionism through his regular Friday evening sermons at the Lower East Side's Educational Alliance. Masliansky's lectures were originally commissioned by New York's German Jewish elite. The affluent uptown leaders Jacob H. Schiff, Louis Marshall, and others hoped that Masliansky would "use his talents to inspire the aliens with a proper understanding of what America expected from them."[51] However, much to their chagrin, Masliansky proved to be a fiercely independent interpreter of both American Judaism and Zionism. "The origin of our national life over three thousand years ago," he declared,

> was a healthy one, and finely liberal; the foundation of our government in accordance with the principles of our Torah were republican. . . . But all this was in days long gone by. . . . We have lost the desire and the inclination for political life; we acquired the character of the wanderer. . . . The great American humorist Mark Twain . . . exhorts to Jews to shake off the dust of exile in this free land, and advises us to take a greater interest in politics. . . . And our own Midrash points out even more explicitly and correctly what we should do. . . . The Midrash says: "Shake yourself, O exiled people, from the dust of exile. . . . Woe unto thee if others shake thee. . . . Help thyself, give a body to the spirit, be not homeless, and other nations will not look upon thee as a ghost, and they will not fear thee. Then wilt thou lead a normal life."[52]

As this typical sermon illustrates, Masliansky used his pulpit as a weekly propaganda forum. His provocative and original views held the attention of popular audiences and scholars alike. Indeed, many younger American Zionist leaders, including Louis Lipsky, Stephen S. Wise, Abba Hillel Silver, and Judah L. Magnes credited Masliansky with playing a central role in their ideological development.[53]

East European Zionism also influenced American Jews from the bottom up. Henrietta Szold, for example, the founder of Hadassah and years later the director of the Jewish Agency's Youth Aliyah department, was, from a young age, sympathetic to the cause of Hibbat Zion. Szold was an admirer of Emma Lazarus and influenced by the proto-Zionism of her father Rabbi Benjamin Szold, who dissented from Reform Judaism and was one of the precursors of the Conservative movement.[54] While she was teaching English to Jewish immigrants in Baltimore's first evening school, Henrietta Szold's Zionism moved from the realm of abstraction to the practical sphere.[55] There she came into close contact with ardent Hibbat Zion members and developed her own understanding of Jewish nationalism. "I became converted to Zionism," she later recalled,

> the very moment I realized that it supplied my bruised, torn, and bloody nation, my distracted nation, with an ideal—an ideal that is balm to the self-

inflicted wounds and to the wounds inflicted by others—an ideal that can be embraced by all, no matter what their attitude may be to other Jewish questions.[56]

Even before Szold's Zionist "conversion," she was an important agent of east European Jewish nationalist and Zionist intellectual trends. In 1888 she was elected to the publication committee of the newly established Jewish Publication Society (JPS); Harry Friedenwald, an early advocate of Zionism, considered Szold's involvement in the JPS a political asset for the Jewish nationalist movement. His brother Aaron Friedenwald and other members of the JPS governing board, however, were generally perplexed if not shocked by Szold's strong will, independence, and formidable intellect. These men followed the wishes of the imperious philanthropist Jacob Schiff, who "wielded considerable behind-the-scenes power."[57] It took several years before Szold overcame the position of inferiority that this patriarchal setting imposed on her. But she gradually crossed over the professional barriers that lay before her, and in 1896, several months before the appearance of Herzl's *Der Judenstaat* (The Jews' State), she openly declared herself a Zionist—a sentiment, according to one American Jewish newspaper, "almost too profound for an American woman."[58]

The latter statement reveals the German Jewish perception of Zionism as a dangerous step toward the radicalization of American Jewish life. While west European Jews and their descendants wrestled with the dilemma of political and civic emancipation in the modern world, they generally feared the east European Jews' alleged revolutionary proclivities. Zionism, many west European Jews believed, was the linchpin for the populist forces that threatened to undermine the German Jews' sociocultural dominance.

Such a stance belied the commitment of American Jewry's elite to genuine social equality, and Henrietta Szold recognized the implications of this predicament for American Jewish women. Her keen insight was fully realized with the creation of Hadassah in 1912, a women's Zionist group that in time became the largest Zionist organization in the world and one of the most influential women's groups in the United States. In 1903, she commented that "girls once brought to the point of rebellion are more radical than boys, or they appear to be." "A woman's revolt affects the home, a man's the synagogue. There can be no doubt which is the more alarming and offensive. To the Jew, accustomed from time immemorial to regard Jewish women as symbols of loyalty, a daughter's insubordination is nothing short of catastrophe."[59]

During Szold's tenure in the leadership of the JPS, the society's hitherto ambivalent publication committee produced a string of nationalist and Zionist works, including several important items previously unavailable in English: Michael Davitt's *Within the Pale: The True Story of Anti-Semitic Persecutions in Russia* (1903), Simon Dubnow's *Jewish History: An Essay in the Philosophy of History* (1903), Nahum Slouschz's *The Renascence of Hebrew Literature* (1909), Ahad Haam's *Selected Essays* (1912), and Richard J. H. Gottheil's *Zionism* (1914).[60] In this way, Zionism circumvented the objections of American Jewry's elite leaders and tacitly won the JPS stamp of intellectual and philosophical approval. These volumes, which were intended for public consumption, even found their way into the homes and libraries of generally unsympathetic German Jews.[61]

Such incipient Jewish radicalism, in combination with the emergence of an increasingly organized and self-directed Jewish immigrant community, provided a serious challenge to American Jewry's so-called native leadership. The inability of elite Jews to reshape and streamline American Judaism in their own image, highlighted by the foregoing example, chipped away at the illusion of German Jewish omnipotence.

The watershed in this regard came in the wake of the Kishinev pogroms, the wave of violent Russian anti-Jewish riots that erupted in April 1903. The immigrant community reacted immediately and intensely to news of the pogroms that terrorized the Jewish populace living in and around the capital of Bessarabia. The Yiddish press, described by the sympathetic journalist Hutchins Hapgood as an "educative element of great value in the Ghetto," carried full reports and analyses of the Russian atrocities.[62] "An event of moment to the Jews, such as a riot in Russia," Hapgood noted "comes to New York in private letters, and is printed in the papers here often before the version 'prepared' by the Russian government appears in the Russian newspapers."[63] Serving as a vehicle for the outpouring of popular Jewish sympathy, the press announced protest meetings, the establishment of relief funds, and several mass street demonstrations. Meanwhile, the immigrant community wrongly perceived the response of German Jewish leaders to be slow, hesitant, and ambivalent.[64] Virtually overnight, immigrant radicalism came to the fore of American Jewish life. The east European leaders reacted swiftly and noisily, and much of their anger was directed against the Jewish establishment itself.[65]

The groundswell of immigrant activity, especially the radicals' claims to communal authority, alarmed Schiff, Marshall, and other patricians. Accelerated by the pace of Jewish immigration, events came to a head in October

1905 with the climax of the Kishinev pogroms. "Shall we wait until the Russians push us aside and speak for all American Jewry," asked Cyrus Adler, "or shall [we] lead the movement and give it a sane and conservative tone?"[66] In 1906, Schiff, Marshall, Adler, Mayer Sulzberger, and Oscar Straus, the most prominent members of the German Jewish elite, led a wealthy group of associates in establishing the American Jewish Committee, an organization that purported to speak and act on behalf of American Jewry.[67] Nonetheless, east European Jewish spokespersons like Chaim Zhitlowsky, Abe Cahan, and, later, Nahman Syrkin, as well as others with strong ties to the immigrant milieu such as Senior Abel, Abraham Goldberg, and Joseph Barondess effectively challenged the authority of the self-appointed American Jewish Committee leaders.[68]

Kishinev marked a turning point in American Jewish history.[69] Jews from every walk of American life, regardless of their religious leanings, ethnic backgrounds, and political attitudes, reacted with horror to the brutal treatment of the Jews in Russia and Poland. Many also looked to Palestine as a viable option for the resettlement of Jewish refugees.[70] The *American Hebrew* captured this unusual mixture of emotion, idealism, and pragmatism in a report on a public gathering held under Zionist auspices in July 1903:

> The theater was crowded from pit to dome. . . . Never before had I seen such an audience. . . . [It] was not made up entirely of Russian Jews. The most cultured specimens of the German Jews were there, the followers of all sorts of schools and fads sat side by side with the bearded Jew. What a triumph it was for the latter. Was it Zionism that wrought this miracle, or Kishinev? Chiefly the latter, I think.[71]

After the anti-Jewish rioting in eastern Europe subsided, as this statement correctly intimated, popular support for Zionism seemed to wane. In all outward appearances, interest in Zionism became cool and detached. American Jewry's collective attitude toward Zionism, a contemporary observer lamented, was "platonic." "The free Jews of America often keep up relations with [their Russian] brothers and parents who are still in captivity. They frequently send them aid. . . . Unable to bring them all to America, they pray for their deliverance in the future."[72]

In the wake of the pogroms, it became apparent that American Zionism's political fortunes were linked to the ebb and flow of public opinion in times of crisis. In the long term, Zionist leaders reasoned, the survival of Jewish nationalist sympathies required a substantive basis. To this end, a group of New York–based Jewish intellectuals gathered to form the Achavah Club in 1909. *Ahavah* is the biblical Hebrew word for "brotherhood, love, and friendship." The group's name consciously recalled a passage in the story of Joseph (Gen. 41:2) in which reference is made to a period of plenty "when people show themselves well disposed to one another" and "no one envies another person's property."[73] According to the Talmudic scholar Louis Ginzberg, one of the club's founders, the group intended "to clarify the profounder questions of Jewish life and, if possible, apply their views to the solution of those problems."[74] All the members were either active Zionists or sympathetic to Zionism. A brief survey of three pivotal members illustrates the influence of the east European Jewish immigrant milieu on Zionism in the United States.

Judah L. Magnes had already developed a close rapport with many Yiddish-speaking intellectuals when he invited a select group to found the Achavah Club.[75] Magnes himself was a Reform rabbi and a communal leader with close personal and professional ties to the German Jewish establishment. His interest in Zionism dated back to an earlier period when as a young rabbinical student at the Hebrew Union College in Cincinnati, he was deeply influenced by Ahad Haam's philosophy. Subsequently, Magnes's amalgam of Jewish, familial, and philosophical contacts made him uniquely equipped to serve as an interlocutor between the uptown and downtown Jewish communities. He was instrumental in creating the New York Kehillah, a comprehensive Jewish communal structure that existed from 1908 to 1922. The Kehillah was designed to unite the city's Jews and serve as a democratic model for American Jewry as a whole.[76] Paralleling these efforts, Magnes organized the Achavah Club to unite a group of persons steeped in Jewish scholarship, committed to the notion of *Gegenwartsarbeit* (Zionist work in the diaspora), and capable of serving as the New York Jewish community's intellectual and spiritual guides.

Chaim Zhitlowsky, a celebrated diaspora nationalist and socialist ideologue, was a friend of Magnes's and a founding member of the Achavah Club. Zhitlowsky, a colorful and important populist leader, played a role in almost every Jewish socialist and Zionist party that emerged on the Russian scene at the beginning of the twentieth century. After the Kishinev pogrom, Zhitlowsky settled in the United States in 1904. Despite frequent travels abroad, including a short stay in Europe when he was elected to the second Russian Duma, Zhitlowsky used the United States as his home base until his death. He was a widely admired lecturer in immigrant circles and often expounded on his synthetic view of voluntarist socialism, cultural nationalism, and Yiddishism. In his lifetime, Zhitlowsky swung between the antipodes of militant nationalism and utopian internationalism, yet he remained firmly committed to the notion of Jewish autonomism and a non-Marxist conception of Jewish socialism.[77]

Notwithstanding the public visibility of Magnes and Zhitlowsky, Israel Friedlaender was arguably the club's most original and creative Zionist thinker. Born in Wlodwa, Poland, and educated at Berlin University and the modern Orthodox Hildesheimer Rabbinical Seminary, Friedlaender's teaching experience in the West convinced him of the urgency of promoting Jewish national and cultural regeneration. He corresponded with both Ahad Haam and Simon Dubnow, a diaspora nationalist historian, and obtained their permission to translate into German some of their best-known essays. Friedlaender was later invited by Solomon Schechter, a world-renowned rabbinic scholar and leader of Conservative Judaism, to assume a position at the Jewish Theological Seminary of America.[78] In the United States, Friedlaender became the major translator and transmitter of Ahad Haam's ideas, although in many respects he actually advocated a Dubnow-ian position. " 'Zionism plus diaspora, Palestine plus America,' " one historian has asserted, "was Friedlaender's classic statement, and it led him and his colleagues to American-centered Jewish activities, rather than to the Palestine-centered endeavors of Ahad Haam."[79]

The Achavah Club provided fertile soil for the transplanting of Labor Zionist ideals and values to American Jewish society. Like the "Judaeans" in New York, the club was an early attempt to combine American Jewish intellectual, spiritual, and organizational leadership.[80] It also was a forum for the articulation and blending of seemingly irreconcilable ideological positions. Bringing together such disparate figures as Magnes, Zhitlowsky, Friedlaender; the philosophers Louis Ginzberg and Mordecai M. Kaplan; the Yiddish playwright David Pinsky; Zionist activists Bernard Richards, Louis Lipsky, and Mizrahi leader Gedaliah Bublick; and the innovative Jewish educator Samson Benderly, the Achavah Club promoted Zionism as a pluralistic ideological movement. The group restricted its membership, however, to "adherents of National Judaism."[81] In fact, a number of Achavah participants—notably Zhitlowsky, Pinsky, Leon Moiseiff, Abraham Lubarsky, Shmaryahu Levin, and Arnold Kretchmar—were closely associated with the American Poalei Zion Party.[82]

The topics debated by the group and the presentations of guest lecturers, all which were recorded in Friedlaender's detailed *Minute Book*, reflect a wide variety of Jewish concerns and ideas. Some examples are Magnes on "Practical Issues Presenting Themselves from the National Jewish Point of

View to a Rabbi of a Reform Congregation," Zhitlowsky on "The Rela-
tion of Jewish Religion to Jewish Nationalism," Friedlaender on "The
German and the Russian Jews," Louis Lipsky on "The Zionist Situation in
New York City," and Shmaryahu Levin, a Russian Zionist leader, on
"Jewish Problems in Palestine." David Pinsky, a noted Yiddish playwright,
read aloud from his *Der shtumer moshiah* (The silent messiah).[83]

The Achavah Club transcended linguistic, ethnic, cultural, and political
boundaries by including representatives from across the Jewish spectrum—
rabbis rebelling against classical Reform and secularists opposing Yiddish
separatism, Western Jews steeped in the east European milieu and Russian
Jews trained in western Europe, American patriots committed to Zionism
and immigrant devotees of *Yiddishkeit* in the United States, non-Marxist
socialists who espoused national regeneration and Zionists rallying to the
socialist ideal. In short, the group's special appeal and strength lay in its
capacity to unite thoughtful leaders with diverse backgrounds and differing
points of view. "Zhitlowsky . . . and the other socialist revolutionaries and
radicals," the historian Alexander Marx later recalled, "were people I had
never met before . . . [they] were the kind of individuals I did not meet
otherwise."[84]

A discussion of early American Zionism is, in many respects, mainly a story
of Jewish life in New York City. To be sure, New York's Jewish community in the late nineteenth and early twentieth centuries exerted a strong
intellectual influence on the rest of American Jewry through its newspapers,
organizations, literature, and leaders. However, Zionism in the United
States and the intense social and political conflict it created in different
American Jewish cities were far from uniform.[85]

A striking contrast to New York City's Achavah Club, for instance, may
be found in the halls of New England academe. In 1905, Zionist societies
sprang up at Boston University Law School, Tufts University, and Harvard
University.[86] In fact, Harvard Law School served as a point of entry and
later a center of gravity for many leading American Zionists, such as Louis
D. Brandeis, Felix Frankfurter, Robert Szold, Julian W. Mack, Alexander
Sachs, and Benjamin V. Cohen.[87] At Harvard, notes Ben Halpern, "a few
Jewish students, intent on absorbing America . . . defended their distinc-
tiveness in the citadel of Wasp culture. . . . They were encouraged by some
Judeophile Yankee professors who were not otherwise partial to Jews."[88]
The three most influential Harvard scholars who favored Jewish cultural
activity were Nathaniel S. Shaler, whose study of ethnicity and nations led

him to conclude that diversity was both unavoidable and a spur to human progress; the philosopher William James, who viewed American society as a composite of many ethnic groups; and the historian George Santayana, who posited that New England's cultural distinctiveness was rooted in its pluralistic tradition.[89]

Among the most promising young Jewish minds first attracted to Zionism at Harvard were Horace M. Kallen, Harry A. Wolfson, and Henry Hurwitz. (Hurwitz eventually left the Zionist fold.) Each provides an intriguing example of Zionism's impact on the twentieth century's first generation of highly educated, Americanized Jewish intellectuals of east European origin. In 1913, Kallen, Wolfson, and Hurwitz, disenchanted with the intransigence of elite German Jewish society and encouraged by the "new humanism" then being propounded in Cambridge, banded together to form the Intercollegiate Menorah Association (later known as the Menorah Society).[90] The Menorah Society, although a congenial gathering place for adherents of the Zionist ideal, was in actuality devoted to a wide range of Jewish cultural issues. Owing to its moderate Zionist orientation, however, the society did attract a group of Herzlian enthusiasts and even received a subsidy from the FAZ.

The Menorah Society's rapid growth was coextensive with the organization's increasingly universalist tone. After a few years, when it became clear that the society's interest in Jewish humanism would all but eclipse its original nationalist premise, an internal faction of political Zionists broke away to create the Intercollegiate Zionist Association of America (IZAA). The new organization's very name was intended to distinguish it from the Menorah Society. Like their European Zionist counterparts, the Menorah and IZAA sharpened their self-ascribed identities on the basis of competing cultural strategies and opposing political objectives.[91] We obtain an insider's view of this state of affairs from an essay in *Kadimah*, an IZAA volume named in honor of the first important Zionist students' society in western Europe:

> [The Menorah Society] did not die of old age, but, instead, committed suicide. It camouflaged its Zionism by reorganizing itself as a purely nonpartisan body so as to obtain a larger membership. It called itself the "menorah" . . . with a great deal of noise and a sprinkling of such decorative terms as "Jewish Culture" and "Hebraic Aroma."
>
> It is strange, but nevertheless true, that practically all the leaders and active workers in the Menorah organization are Zionists. They have accepted a compromise because they thought that they could reach groups whom a

Zionist society could not touch. Indeed, the thing of which the Menorah boasts now, when it talks to Zionists, is its little lists of prize conversions to Zionism. As a matter of fact, though, Zionism is quite as respectable as the Menorah brand of Jewish Culture—and perhaps a little more inspiring. . . . The Menorah, cautious about offending anyone by doing anything, often is about as interesting as a mid-Victorian debating society. If the Zionists had put their energies into Zionist societies, we should be better off. [This is not] to say that there is no virtue in the Menorah, but that what virtue there is [is] not of the Menorah.[92]

The Menorah Society's openness to American culture forced the political Zionists of the IZAA to evaluate their own attitude toward diaspora Jewish life and the Zionist program of Gegenwartsarbeit. Although this process of self-reflection did not originate with the Menorah-IZAA dispute, early Zionists like Harry Wolfson and Horace M. Kallen made their debut in American Jewish life as a direct result of such questioning. For example, Wolfson's poem "The Spirit of Hebraism," which he composed in Hebrew and recited at a gathering of the Menorah Society,[93] typifies the social idealism of many of his youthful contemporaries:

> Oh, my spirit awaits but my seeking
> To burst like a spring from the soil.
> And if once it be free from confinement
> It will vest in all fruit of my toil . . .
>
> It will speak from the lips of new Prophets.
> And their truth from the heights will be hurled,
> From a model city of Justice
> Where its flag will blazon unfurled.[94]

Although Wolfson was alluding to the reawakening of Jewish ethnic pride and even a cultural-national revival, he clearly stopped short of committing himself to the full-bodied nationalism of the Jewish immigrant milieu.

At this ideational juncture, Kallen diverged from Wolfson, thereby forging a new combination of political progressivism, cultural humanism, and the notion of Jewish autoemancipation. In 1913, Kallen created an exclusive fellowship called the Perushim (Pharisees or "separate"). The Perushim was a short-lived society whose function was similar to that of Bnei Moshe (Sons of Moses), Ahad Haam's Zionist order devoted to Jewish educational efforts and national revival.[95] The ranks of the Perushim included promising young American Zionists like Harvard alumni Israel Thurman, Henry Hurwitz, Alexander Sachs, and Benjamin V. Cohen; the educator Alexander

Dushkin; and women's leader Henrietta Szold. The members regularly reported to Kallen and were totally dedicated to the Zionist cause.[96]

When the Perushim disbanded, the members looked for new ways to extend their influence. Kallen himself joined Isaac B. Berkson, Hayim Fineman, Solomon Schiller, Israel Goldberg, and Emanuel Neumann to found Zeirei Zion Hitahdut, an offshoot of the non–Marxist Labor Zionist Party popular in educated Western circles.[97] Nahman Syrkin, Zeirei Zion's ideological mentor, was then living in the United States. A charismatic, albeit somewhat aloof, figure, Syrkin was a Zionist scholar-intellectual of international repute and, since his immigration to the United States in 1907, an active leader in American Jewish affairs. He exerted a strong influence over the younger generation of east European Jewish intellectuals, including those in the United States.[98] Unlike his contemporaries Chaim Zhitlowsky and Ber Borochov, the premier Marxist Zionist theoretician of his day, Syrkin was critical of the varieties of Dubnowian autonomism and historical determinism that were standard fare for Jewish radicals in the late nineteenth and early twentieth centuries. Although informed by such notions, Syrkin's outlook was consciously voluntarist, populist, and even prophetic in nature.[99] For him, it was simply inconceivable that a new Jewish society would be created on a basis of social inequality or political insecurity. "A classless society and national sovereignty," he wrote, "are the only means of solving the Jewish problem completely."[100]

Kallen was among the young Zeirei Zion intellectuals who absorbed elements of Syrkin's philosophy. Kallen was especially enthusiastic about Jewish colonization efforts in Palestine and believed that the *haluzim* (pioneers) represented the highest level of Zionist achievement.[101] To Kallen, the socialist Zionist pioneers exemplified the fusion of Jewish idealism and American progressivism.[102] These young men and women demonstrated the compatibility of a specifically Jewish mentality and a secular humanist philosophy under the rubric of national liberation. Such a combination, Kallen believed, modernized Judaism and opened the door for Jewish participation in the community of nations.

Less dogmatically inclined than Syrkin's, Kallen's philosophy was both rooted in the east European milieu and tempered by American Jewish existential reality. His new Zionist philosophy, which included a sizable quotient of Ahad Haamism, affirmed the contributions of diaspora Jews to their lands of residence and the importance of Eretz Israel in Jewish life. At the same time, he integrated this commitment into the political struggle for a viable and socially just national home in Palestine. A few years later,

Kallen transferred these concepts to the Pittsburgh Program, which became the official platform of American Zionism under Louis D. Brandeis.[103] The program affirmed Brandeis's insistence that constructive Zionist work depended on the consolidation of American Jewish communal support, contributions of major donors to the Zionist cause, the instrumentality of groups like the Palestine Development Council which granted loans to cooperative settlements and agricultural projects at low interest, the Palestine Economic Corporation which aided Palestinian enterprises on a strictly business basis, and the Palestine Endowment Fund which distributed funds to projects like the Hebrew University, the Palestine Potash Company, and several Histadrut-related ventures.[104] Kallen's formulation of these objectives gave Jewish nationalism a uniquely American cast, and in the early decades of the twentieth century, he emerged as American Zionism's premier philosopher.[105]

Kallen's significance notwithstanding, it was Louis D. Brandeis who put the stamp of American approval on the Labor philosophy of Zionism. Brandeis, the first Jew to be appointed to the U.S. Supreme Court, legitimized the emergent American Zionist platform. He demonstrated that the values of Jewish pioneering, social justice, and democracy could not only be amalgamated but also translated into popular parlance and an effective program.

The literature concerning Louis D. Brandeis's relationship to Zionism is vast.[106] In large measure, he was inducted into American Zionism as a result of his personal association with idealists like Kallen.[107] His nationalist sentiments were further strengthened by a sense of kinship with and admiration for the east European Jewish immigrant masses. Brandeis first came into sustained contact with the immigrant community when he mediated the New York City garment workers' strike at the behest of Louis E. Kirstein, an influential Boston Jewish philanthropist and vice president of Filene's department store. Captivated by the seemingly authentic Jewishness of the Lower East Side, Brandeis emerged from this experience a profoundly changed man.[108] Although he himself had never rejected his Jewish identity, neither had he previously given it much stock. Brandeis's newfound "deep solicitude for the spiritual and moral welfare of the Jews"[109] parallels the German Zionist fascination with the so-called Ostjuden.[110]

Even though the precise combination of factors that led to Brandeis's "Zionist conversion" remains a matter of scholarly debate, it is clear that the liberal Boston environment played a substantial role in his philosophical development. To be sure, Boston was a seminal—if not the preeminent—intellectual center of progressive American politics in the turbulent decades that bridged the nineteenth and twentieth centuries. In addition, the solidarity of Boston's local ethnic groups, particularly the Irish, did much to enhance the cosmopolitan character of New England's flagship community. In those years, the Boston Irish, including no less a figure than the city's mayor Patrick Collins, were outspoken in their devotion to Eire and the campaign for the Irish Free State. Similarly, explained Jacob De Haas, editor of Boston's *Jewish Advocate* and a close adviser to Brandeis, Boston Jews sought a haven for their oppressed coreligionists overseas. For the Irish and the Jews alike, De Haas posited, working for such a cause was neither a source of conflict nor an act of disloyalty.[111]

Brandeis himself, although highly sympathetic to the plight of east European Jewry, moved beyond the notion of Palestine as a refuge. His first public expression of support for constructive Zionist efforts in Palestine, in which he stressed that Zionism was the most effective Jewish program for improving society as a whole, took place at a meeting of Chelsea's Young Men's Hebrew Association in May 1913.[112] Zionism was not strictly a matter of noblesse oblige, he pointed out, but, rather, a prerequisite for the social and moral mission of American Jews. Brandeis fully articulated this view in a June 1915 address to the Eastern Council of Reform Rabbis:

> Multiple loyalties are objectionable only if they are inconsistent. A man is a better citizen of the United States for being also a loyal citizen of his state, and of his city; for being loyal to his family, and to his profession or trade; for being loyal to his college or lodge. . . . Every American Jew who aids in advancing the Jewish settlement in Palestine, though he feels that neither he nor his descendants will ever live there, will be a better man and a better American for doing so.[113]

Brandeis's message especially resonated with Zionists on the popular level, as illustrated by a leaflet advertising "Zion Flag Week," a Boston campaign organized by the Jewish National Fund during the week of Hanukah in December 1915. In true Brandeisian fashion, the leaflet urged that the goal of the campaign was to "provide work for laborers" in the Jewish National Fund's Palestine colonies. "When you help the National Fund, you help thereby to ameliorate Jewish need in a noble and practical way," it declared. "At the same time you help also to build the Jewish future. Buy this flag of Zion, and wear this emblem of Jewish nationality on the holiday of the Hasmoneans, giving generously at the same time to uphold the great Cause the Flag represents."[114]

When Brandeis assumed the mantle of Zionist leadership in 1914, he was fifty-eight years old. An accomplished lawyer, respected national figure, and, after 1916, an associate justice of the U.S. Supreme Court, Brandeis gave American Zionism a newfound prestige and legitimacy. Indeed, De Haas saw in Brandeis a successor to Herzl; student activists like the members of the Menorah Society and IZAA regarded him as a role model; Jewish immigrants venerated him as a champion of the working class; and Presidents Woodrow Wilson and Franklin D. Roosevelt (who referred to Brandeis as "Isaiah") considered him an important confidant.[115]

Brandeis's signal Zionist accomplishment was his capacity to energize a highly influential and politically effective group of leaders, especially the cadre of Harvard Law School alumni noted earlier. With Brandeis, Mack, and Frankfurter at its center, this innovative and powerful group provided American Zionism with a network of contacts and resources that, when marshaled, transformed the movement from a fledgling operation to a formidable political-economic enterprise.

With the onset of World War I, Europe's wartime political division, and the World Zionist Organization's ensuing predicament, American Zionists— and above all, Louis D. Brandeis—assumed a preeminent role in international Zionist affairs. As the only neutral base from which to freely operate, the so-called Brandeis group, an elite coterie of Wilsonian liberals that included some of Kallen's Perushim, carried out the Zionist organization's international assignments and was elevated to the status of titular leaders and spokesmen for the world movement.[116] On the domestic front, too, the Brandeis group's formulation of American Zionist interests proved fundamental, and here the Perushim played a critical role. Their influence, for example, is detected in the American Zionist organization's adoption of Kallen's progressive Pittsburgh Program. The program was attuned to the Yishuv's Labor Zionist ethos and included provisions for political and civil equality, national ownership of land and natural resources, a system of universal public education, and the use of the "cooperative principle" in all agricultural, industrial, commercial, and financial enterprises.[117]

In this period, Labor Zionism also became a significant mediatory force in American Jewish life. The 1914–1918 campaign to elect the American Jewish Congress, a democratic assembly representing all of American Jewry, was spearheaded by Poalei Zion's articulate spokesmen Nahman Syrkin, Ber Borochov, and Chaim Zhitlowsky and was opposed by the powerful

American Jewish Committee. The deliberations and electoral process leading up to the congress brought the Brandeis group into close association with the Jewish immigrant community.[118] Consequently, a strong bond developed between the Brandeis circle and the Zionist rank and file. Against the backdrop of the Balfour Declaration, this political realignment played a crucial role in persuading Woodrow Wilson's administration and the Allies, especially the British, of the Zionists' dominant importance in American Jewish affairs.[119]

After the war, the Brandeis group was ousted from its position of leadership by the Weizmann-backed Louis Lipsky faction, which charged that Brandeis, Julian W. Mack, and Felix Frankfurter lacked true Jewish nationalist convictions and were solely concerned with managing the Yishuv's financial interests. Although this line of attack distorted and even maligned the Brandeis group's intentions, it did touch on a raw nerve.[120] For Weizmann, the east European Jew, differed from Brandeis, the American Jew, in much the same way that the Intercollegiate Zionist Association differed from the Menorah Society, or Poalei Zion differed from the other Zionist supporters of the American Jewish Congress. And they all differed from the trickle of American haluzim—dating back to the days of Eliezer Jaffe and the original Hehalvz organization in Woodbine, New Jersey—who continued to emigrate to Palestine after the war.[121] The core imperative of east European Zionism—an unwavering commitment to Eretz Israel as the authentic home of the Jewish people—was also a litmus test that distinguished American variants of Zionism.

Although American Zionism's ideological quotient of "exile" survived from one generation to the next among the tenacious religious and socialist Zionist parties, it was the Brandeis "brain trust" that quietly implemented elements of Horace M. Kallen's Labor-oriented Pittsburgh Program through a range of capital investment schemes such as the Palestine Economic Corporation, American Zion Commonwealth, and Palestine Land Development Company. In this way, the Brandeis group circumvented official American and world Zionist policy by raising funds crucial to the operation of concessions like the Palestine Potash Company (later known as the Dead Sea Works) and hotels in Jerusalem and Tiberias, or, as in the case of a special project sponsored by philanthropist Benjamin Rabalsky, to create a Jewish settlement in the Afula region.[122]

The formative stage of the relationship among American Jews, Zionism, and the Yishuv was complex and, in many respects, indirect. The proliferation of proto-Zionist groups between the late nineteenth and early twentieth centuries—philanthropic groups, literary societies, intellectual cadres, women's clubs, and the like—gave rise to multiple perspectives on Jewish nationalism reflecting different localities, social circumstances, and cultural attitudes. In this period, American Zionism's various constituencies were gradually integrated, and the movement's orientation was elaborated. Neither a complete rejection of the Old World inheritance nor an unqualified acceptance of New World surroundings, American Zionism was unified by a philosophical rhythm attuned to changes in American Jewish life and the Yishuv. What emerged over time was a loosely bound political framework with a worldview that transcended immediate social and historical conditions and that was nevertheless capable of responding to contemporary needs and crises.

After World War I, Labor Zionism became an important force in the Yishuv and the World Zionist Organization. American Zionism increasingly responded to the romantic proclivities and political priorities of the Palestine-based movement. American Zionists placed a premium on Palestine as a progressive Jewish society-in-the-making, rather than as an object of pious devotion or American Jewish largesse. They were especially entranced with the Yishuv's pioneers, cooperative spirit, and renascent Hebrew language. Their adulation was, in part, the product of disenchantment with the American *goldene medine* (golden land) and horror at the rise of antisemitism at home and abroad.

Labor Zionist intellectuals played a significant role in this process, coalescing around small but effective groups such as the Achavah Club, the Perushim, and Zeirei Zion. In some instances, as in the campaign for the American Jewish Congress, they were particularly effective. In time, Labor Zionism became *the* Zionism of mainstream American Jewry—even though most American Jews themselves were unaware of this ideological development. In the broadest sense of the term, Labor Zionism validated the predominantly moderate spiritual and liberal political character of American Jewry. The movement also served a latent function by mediating and channeling American Jewish support for Palestine. The uniquely American brand of Zionism, with roots in the Jewish people's ancient past and the Old World, emerged from a complex process of intense and sustained exploration by American Jews of the meaning of their identity in the New World as well as the uplifted one symbolized by the Yishuv.

2

From Immigrant Party to American Movement

The Poalei Zion Party, the nucleus of Labor Zionism in the United States, was formally established in New York City in 1905.[1] Never more than several hundred members strong in its early years, the party was originally a cross between an association of left-wing Zionist political cells and a Jewish immigrant mutual aid society.[2] Unlike the two largest indigenous American Zionist groups, the Zionist Organization of America and Hadassah, founded in 1918 and 1925, respectively, Poalei Zion was an offshoot of the radical socialist Zionist party in Russia and Poland. The east European mother organization, which swiftly spread to towns and cities throughout the Pale of Settlement in the late nineteenth century, was self-consciously proletarian and promoted a militant blend of Zionism and socialism.[3]

American Poalei Zion quickly adjusted its operative principles and philosophical outlook to fit the practical exigencies of Jewish life in the New World. The movement gradually transcended the confines of party dogma and evolved as a multifaceted grassroots organization: a political bulwark, an immigrant self-help society, a forum of Jewish intellectual debate, a fund-raising vehicle, an educational alternative, and a social club. In this way, Labor Zionism provided a "home" for the many different American Jews who sympathized with the cause of Labor Palestine. In time, the movement also opened new channels of communication between the Yishuv and American Jewish society as a whole. New frameworks arose, such as the Geverkshaftn campaign, Pioneer Women, and *Jewish Frontier*. Meanwhile, extramovement activity assumed the form of communitywide ventures like the League for Labor Palestine and the National Labor Committee for Palestine. In sum, Labor Zionism's reformulation in the American setting impelled the transformation of a small immigrant party into a large-scale American Jewish movement.

★

American Poalei Zion's ranks were initially composed of workers who matured in the Jewish radical and secular milieu of the late nineteenth and early twentieth centuries. Many had previously belonged to the socialist Zionist party in eastern Europe. Their shared background formed a strong cultural and political bond and served as the basis for their association in the United States. Rallying to "the banner and torch of the Poalei Zion Party" in the New World, immigrant party loyalists hoped to influence American Zionism and organized Jewish labor.[4] In their opinion, the Zionist proposal for Jewish social and political emancipation was inextricably linked to nationalist and socialist principles; that is, in any Jewish state, the workers must possess the land and the means of production. "It is inconceivable that people will agree to the creation of an autonomous [Jewish] state based on social inequality," declared Nahman Syrkin, an important Russian theoretician of Labor Zionism who settled in the United States in 1908.[5]

> No new social contract will ever come to be unless its foundation is freedom. . . . The moment that all doors are opened to a system of laissez faire, the economic process will put its indelible stamp on social life. . . . For a Jewish state to come to be, it must, from the very beginning, avoid all the ills of modern life. . . . Its guidelines must be justice, rational planning and social solidarity. . . . The Jewish state can come about only if it is socialist; only by fusing with socialism can Zionism become the ideal of the whole Jewish people—of the proletariat, the middle class and the intelligentsia.[6]

This stance engendered the hostility of many middle- and upper-class American Jews. Acculturated American Jews, especially the German Jewish elite, were fearful of accusations of dual loyalty and alien degeneracy,[7] and they also worried that the Jewish immigrant community would be subverted by Yiddish-speaking radicals preaching separatist and class-conscious doctrines. The latter perception was not far from the truth, for Poalei Zion conspicuously promoted itself as an east European transplant opposed to the dominant forces of American Jewish life.[8] The party sustained, for example, the east European tradition of radicalism and antipathy toward religious observance. Poalei Zion challenged the American rabbinate's stronghold on Jewish communal life by creating Labor Zionist institutions to complement symbols of religious authority.[9] One such case was the party's local *hevrah kadisha* (burial society), an unusual combination of traditionalism and secularism. In addition to ritual preparation of the body for burial, the hevrah kadisha was responsible for draping the deceased member's coffin in "the blue-white flag of Zion or the red banner of Poalei Zion."[10] At the conclusion of the burial ceremony, members of the hevrah kadisha would lead the mourners in singing Poalei Zion's Shvuah (Oath), the Labor Zionist anthem.[11]

American Labor Zionism also replicated the trappings of clandestine party life in eastern Europe. This included an organizational chain of command: a secretary general, a central committee, subcommittees, and leaders and members of local party cells (later renamed branches and chapters). All these roles and functions were sanctioned by the party's constitution and reaffirmed at successive conventions. In this way, Poalei Zion established a political framework for its members that was frequently mobilized to tackle a variety of concerns, ranging from the formation of cooperative Labor Zionist groceries, bakeries, and butcher shops to fund-raising campaigns on behalf of the *haluzim* (pioneers) in Palestine.[12]

In some instances, the national party played a decisive role in American Jewish affairs. The most notable case was the American Jewish Congress of 1918 which, as Jonathan Frankel has demonstrated, proved to be a political coup for Poalei Zion's wartime leadership. Although it was dominated by an alliance of elite American Jewish leaders, the congress rank and file displayed an overwhelming sympathy for the Labor enterprise in Palestine. Poalei Zion's leaders—Nahman Syrkin, Ber Borochov, and Chaim Zhitlowsky—skillfully engineered through the congress the passage of a resolution calling for the British trusteeship of Palestine and the establishment of a Jewish national home.[13]

Poalei Zion's members, most of them Yiddish-speaking immigrants, possessed an exceptional esprit de corps. With the support of Russian Poalei Zion, party activists in the United States—despite their limited numbers—inserted themselves into the heart of the Jewish immigrant community's social, religious, and political battles. In one typical instance, the Russian Central Committee for Foreign Lands instructed the American party leaders as follows:

> We, as a party, which proclaims the worldliness of the Jewish workers' movement cannot contradict ourselves and declare that the social duties of the Jewish proletariat end in [eastern Europe]. Sincere Poalei Zion members have important tasks in America as well. First of all, you must educate and change the hundreds of thousands of Jewish workers in the "dollar land." In order to have . . . success in this respect, you must unite our activities with the activities of the American brother [read: socialist] party. . . . Bring in the healthy social spirit that you received in the Russian [Poalei Zion] Party. . . .

This is more logical than staying on the sidelines and concerning yourself only with criticism.[14]

In the fluid American setting, Poalei Zion activists readily adopted such a strategy. Indeed, many party members played leading roles in the immigrant and labor frameworks, which included fraternal orders, educational institutions, Yiddish libraries, political committees, fund-raising associations, cultural societies, and Yiddish journals.[15] In part, these efforts reflected Poalei Zion's elevation of Yiddishism to the position of a hallowed ideal. In this cosmology, Yiddish itself served a dual purpose as both a tool for reaching the Jewish masses and the touchstone of Jewish life in the diaspora. As one member explained:

> The strength of Poal-Zionism [*sic*] lies in this: that it builds the future upon the present, and for that reason its relation to Yiddish, to Jewish life in the Golus [exile], to the "*Golus* values," is more respectful than that of either Zionists or workmen. It is a party not for Palestine alone, but also for the *Golus* and its interests.[16]

In fact, Labor Zionists were for the most part "welcome in . . . the existing [labor] organizations," and the differences between the two camps "did not present a controversy based on immediate practical perspectives."[17] As in Europe before 1914, however, the two groups were separated organizationally by an ideological "chasm."[18] The leaders of the non-Zionist socialist camp, especially the Arbeter Ring (Workmen's Circle), were staunch internationalists and strenuously objected to all forms of Jewish nationalism.[19] They considered Yiddish a "temporary expedient" for Jewish workers who had yet to master English and find their place in the American labor movement.[20]

Poalei Zion's influence also extended to the world of Yiddish journalism. Beginning in 1906, the party launched *Der yidisher kemfer* (The Jewish Fighter), a combination house organ, literary forum, and propaganda tool.[21] The journal's success is best understood in the context of the Yiddish dailies, whose mass circulation rose from 66,000 in 1900 to 120,000 in 1904 and eventually to 500,000 in 1914.[22] The *Kemfer*, whose circulation never exceeded more than approximately 6,000 before World War II, was recognized for its high intellectual standards.[23] Initially edited by the distinguished figures Kalman Marmor and David Pinsky, the *Kemfer* grew to attract a devoted extramovement following under Hayim Greenberg, a member of Zeirei Zion (Youth of Zion) who later emerged as a prominent American Zionist leader. In the early decades of the twentieth century, the journal's frequent contributors also included the ideologues Ber Borochov, Nahman Syrkin, and Chaim Zhitlowsky; the political activists Manya Shohat, Joel Entin, and Berl Locker; and the writers Yehoash (Shlomo Bloomgarden), Shmuel Niger, Mani Leib, Shmuel Bonchek, Abraham (Walt) Liesin, and Haim Leivick.[24]

Poalei Zion made a successful incursion into American Jewish cultural life through the practical enterprise of the Yidishe Nazional Radikale Shuln (Jewish National Radical Schools), also known as the Folkshuln (folk schools).[25] Whereas traditional Jewish education emphasized religious training, the goal of the Folkshuln was to educate Jewish youth in the "Jewish national spirit."[26] When the Folkshuln first appeared in 1910, American Jewry's elite leadership considered them a serious threat. An early survey of Jewish education echoed this sentiment:

> A new agency, the most recently developed, is the National Radical School, established within the past few years in several of the large cities. These schools do not claim to be religious institutions; in some of them anti-religious teachings are inculcated. They are Jewish only insofar as they are conducted by Jews for Jewish children, and make Yiddish the language of instruction. Since their tendencies are opposed to the strivings of the great majority of Jews, they have no place in this inquiry.[27]

The Folkshuln offered an alternative educational curriculum that combined Jewish traditional and secular subjects. Both Hebrew and Yiddish were taught as living languages, and modern Hebrew and Yiddish literature was emphasized. Ancient Jewish history was taught alongside contemporary Jewish events. Classes in Jewish folklore and ethnology were accompanied by others in Jewish music and dramatics. Even courses in labor history and socialist economic theory were part of the regular program. What began as a secular version of Jewish Sunday schools rapidly became a full-fledged network of four- and five-day afternoon schools in several major urban centers. In addition, evening classes for working adults, lectures, and movement meetings all became regular features of the Folkshuln.

In many cities, the Folkshuln became principal sites of Zionist cultural and political activity, even attracting large numbers of secular Jews from outside the ranks of the Poalei Zion Party. The visible success of the Folkshuln in New York, Chicago, Philadelphia, and Baltimore prompted Labor Zionists to establish similar schools in urban centers across the country. Much to the consternation of the American Jewish establishment, these new institutions served as rallying points for Yiddish radical and secular-nationalist immigrant activity.[28]

The appropriation of Poalei Zion's weltanschauung and its subsequent reformulation by younger immigrant generations were essential to the movement's continued existence in the United States. This phenomenon stemmed from the steady acculturation of the membership and its changing social composition, and it also clearly delineated the boundaries of the movement's actual and potential constituencies. On the one hand, some party members continued to view their lives as inextricably linked to the world party and the "upbuilding" of a Jewish socialist state in Eretz Israel. On the other hand, the movement gradually adjusted to the rhythms of American Jewish life and developed frameworks for including people from outside the Labor Zionist fold. The movement's superstructure provided a meeting ground for these seemingly contradictory aspirations. Here different spheres of Jewish immigrant life intersected in such a way so as to complement the spiritual and philosophical needs of many socialists and nationalists. On the cultural level, too, American Labor Zionism created a broad network of social institutions and organizational frameworks that shaped various aspects of movement activity.

The numerically small Labor Zionist movement utilized its extensive contact with the immigrant community to influence developments in American Jewish life. "In the manner of David," recalled Abraham Goldberg, a former Poalei Zion organizer and subsequently a leader of the Zionist Organization of America (ZOA), "the little movement challenged the established giants to public debate."[29] Seasoned by the campaign for the American Jewish Congress and attentive to the cry for democracy in American Jewish communal politics, the party leadership assumed the role of vanguard and defender of the immigrant community's national interests. On the Zionist front, Poalei Zion defiantly challenged the ZOA's authoritarian leadership, particularly attempts by the Brandeis group to dominate the American Zionist agenda and conduct movement affairs along hierarchical, class-based lines. With each step in this direction, Nahman Syrkin claimed, the Brandeis-led Provisional Executive Committee for General Zionist Affairs relinquished the moral high ground for which it had fought so hard during the American Jewish Congress.[30]

In a telling instance, Poalei Zion accused the Provisional Executive Committee of attempting to avoid meeting the east European Zionists' "principle-claim" of proportional representation and scoffed at the Brandeis group's elitist pretensions. The Provisional Executive Committee, the Labor Zionists announced, intended to "establish for themselves a monopoly in all the Zionist affairs at this critical time. They want to remain in their own company."[31]

At a June 1917 American Zionist conference held in Baltimore, both the Labor Zionists and Mizrahi requested proportional representation on the Provisional Executive Committee's administrative and political bodies. To avert the east European Zionists' bid for power, the Brandeis group invited select religious and socialist Zionist leaders to join the Provisional Executive Committee as ad hoc members. This conciliatory move satisfied the Mizrahi leadership, which consequently withdrew its request for proportional representation in December 1917. Poalei Zion, on the other hand, refused to accept "concessions" from Louis D. Brandeis and his associates. On the basis of a separate agreement between the World Union of Poalei Zion and the Zionist Actions Committee, they argued, American Labor Zionists deserved to be represented on the Provisional Executive Committee as an independent entity.[32] At issue, the Poalei Zion leaders publicly explained, was a principle of the highest import: "The [Labor Zionists] are carrying on a bitter struggle with the [Provisional Executive Committee], whose undemocratic conduct they refuse to sanction. They withdrew from the [Provisional Executive Committee] because of the autocracy of the committee, and they refused to take part in the conference of the committee recently held in Baltimore."[33]

It is clear that the Brandeis group and Poalei Zion maintained divergent views concerning questions of Zionist political strategy and democracy in American Jewish life. In contrast to the east European notion of proportional representation, the Brandeisan Zionists favored the American system of simple majoritarianism. The concept of "winner-take-all," in which the victor represents all constituents and not merely his own supporters, ran counter to the maverick spirit and culture of Labor Zionism. Poalei Zion categorically refused to submit to the majority rule of the Brandeis group.

Mizrahi, on the other hand, led by Rabbi Meir Berlin (later Bar-Ilan), an important religious Zionist spokesman who lived in the United States between 1915 and 1926, sought a modus vivendi with the American Zionist leaders. Under Berlin's pragmatic and forceful leadership, Mizrahi waged a persistent campaign to exploit the pro-Zionist Orthodox sentiment that "mushroomed among the ever increasing settlement of East European immigrants."[34] "The land of Israel for the people of Israel according to the

Torah of Israel," Berlin had declared four years earlier during his tenure as secretary of the world movement.[35] Now he sought to translate this slogan into an effective American program.

By joining the Provisional Executive Committee, Mizrahi leaders hoped to increase their organizational visibility and clout. Poalei Zion, however, sustained the east European separatist tendency to which it and Mizrahi generally adhered in the early decades of the twentieth century. The Labor Zionists not only undermined the Brandeis group's efforts to centralize American Zionist activity but also legitimately accused Brandeis, Mack, and others of undemocratic tendencies.[36] In the long run, Poalei Zion's outspoken criticism of the American Zionist establishment indirectly supported the Louis Lipsky–led "opposition" in the Zionist Organization of America, an east European faction that eventually brought about the downfall of the Brandeis group.[37]

Labor Zionism also dramatically affected organized American Jewish labor's vision of Palestine and the Zionist enterprise. Years before they succeeded in winning the latter's support, however, Labor Zionists received encouragement from general American labor circles. As early as November 1917, the American Federation of Labor publicly endorsed the Balfour Declaration at a national convention of the American Alliance for Labor and Democracy, a short-lived organization cosponsored by antipacifist labor groups. The American Federation of Labor was the convention's backbone, and the federation's president, Samuel Gompers, a strong supporter of President Woodrow Wilson's policies, played a central role in winning the support of the rank and file for the Zionist cause.

Simultaneously, a group of prowar Jewish socialist leaders, including Nahman Syrkin, established the Jewish Socialist League of America. The American Alliance for Labor and Democracy and the Jewish Socialist League of America collaborated closely to mobilize Jewish labor groups to support the Allied war effort.[38] Syrkin, who was driven from the Poalei Zion's central committee in 1917 because of his pro-Allies stance, used the Jewish Socialist League as a vehicle to articulate and promote his wartime views. He quickly won the support of dissident members of his own party, Hehaluz (The Pioneer); leaders David Ben-Gurion and Yizhak Ben-Zvi, who spent most of World War I in the United States; and a large Jewish immigrant following that read about his views in the Yiddish press.[39] Syrkin also persuaded a group of prominent Jewish socialists, including the antipacifist theoretician Henry L. Slobodin, the editor of the *New York Call* Herman Simpson, the journalist Maurice (Katz) Kass, and the editor of *Der tog* (The Day) William Edlin. In September 1917, this cohort, which comprised the leadership of the Jewish Socialist League of America, issued a statement supporting the Allies and the Zionist cause:

> One of the principal reasons why the more thoughtful Jews are heart and soul with the Allies is because they recognize that the future of the Jewish race lies in the keeping of three great countries, the United States, Russia and England. These are the countries the most progressive elements of which have promised support to the movement for an autonomous Jewish Homeland in Palestine. . . . The Jewish Socialist League of America . . . stands for self-determination for all nationalities. It stands for a Jewish Homeland in Palestine.[40]

Labor Zionism's growing influence on the popular level can also be discerned from the brief history of the Thirty-ninth and Fortieth Battalions of Royal Fusiliers, the American regiments of the British-sponsored Jewish Legion. The Hehaluz organization, led by David Ben-Gurion, Yizhak Ben-Zvi, and Pinhas Rutenberg—all three of whom were expelled from Palestine by the Turkish authorities—formed the idealistic core of the legion's American recruits. The Hehaluz group, according to one member, was motivated by "the strong desire to participate in the liberation of the land of our forefathers and, if spared, to remain among its builders."[41] A large majority of the five thousand legionnaires, however, were neither Hehaluz nor Poalei Zion members. As a report to the Poalei Zion convention of 1918 explains, the volunteers came from diverse social and economic backgrounds. Most were workers, clerks, students, and persons from white-collar professions. More specifically, a study of 893 legionnaires revealed that only 342 were members of Poalei Zion. Meanwhile, 354 of the recruits were unaffiliated at the time of their enlistment; 105 were General Zionists; 58 identified themselves as socialists; 20 were trade union members; 12 were Mizrahi members; 1 was an anarchist; and 1 labeled himself an industrialist![42] The legion's variegated social, psychological, and economic structure reflects the success of the Labor Zionist movement's inclusive strategy. It also illustrates the allure that the notion of liberating the Jewish national home held for many American Jews.

Public displays of support for the legionnaires were common. For example, as hundreds of young recruits traveled along the eastern seaboard en route to the legion's British military training camp in Windsor, Ontario, they received an enthusiastic response from the region's Jewish communities. One sympathetic witness observed:

At every town in New England where the train stops on the way to Canada, crowds come out to wish Godspeed to the men who are going to fight for the Jewish people, for them . . . Hatikvah [The Hope] takes on a new sound and a new meaning in gatherings such as [these]. It is not the wail of a people which protests that its hope is not yet dead. It is the triumphant battle cry of a people whose hope is to be realized.[43]

Of the American recruits, only 2,500 legionnaires, from the Thirty-ninth Battalion, actually fought during World War I.[44] Both it and the British Thirty-eighth "Judean" Battalion were stationed in Palestine near Jericho. On September 22, 1918, they routed the Turks from a strategic ford of the Jordan River, north of the lake of Galilee, and opened the way to Damascus for the Australian and New Zealand cavalry.[45] After the war's conclusion, a group of 280 American legionnaires provided the nucleus for the establishment of Avihayil, a *moshav ovdim* near the oceanside town of Natanya.[46] Although relatively few in number, the former legionnaires comprised a significant segment of the six hundred American Jews who settled in Palestine during the 1919–1923 postwar wave of Zionist immigration.[47]

The Jewish Legion's contribution to the Allied war effort may have been minimal, but the unit had great symbolic value for American Jews. In addition to the political capital that American Jewish leaders derived from the legion, the voluntary enlistment of several thousand Jewish men in a specifically Jewish regiment unleashed a wave of American Jewish patriotism and pro-Zionist fervor. American Jews relished the image of a Jewish military force that would combat the stereotype of immigrant Jews as rootless, cowardly, and defenseless.[48] The Jewish Legion thus assumed an importance in American Jewish life disproportionate to its actual wartime role. The legionnaires themselves sustained this myth, as they were credited with and took credit for successes in which they played only a part.

The Jewish Legion's task was defined in Wilsonian terms as making the world safe for democracy and in Zionist terms as establishing a Jewish foothold in Eretz Israel. "The voluntary enlistment of Jewish boys," the chronicler Hyman L. Meites wrote, "impressed the world in striking fashion that the Jews not only wanted to regain Palestine but were willing to give their lives for it."[49] Meites's assessment and the preceding quotation, despite their exaggerated and self-congratulatory nature, reflect Labor Zionism's steady penetration of American Jewish life. Beginning with the Balfour Declaration in 1917, but especially after the war, the demise of the European empires and the rise of new nation-states engendered hope that Jewish independence would soon follow.

Poalei Zion's wartime activities demonstrated that the Labor Zionist message, previously the purview of small select groups, could attract broad American Jewish interest and support. Poalei Zion continued to exploit this favorable climate, and in doing so, it began to worry the American Jewish establishment. For example, on the eve of a party-sponsored workers' rally in 1918, the *Maccabaean*, the journal of the Zionist Organization of America, took the Labor Zionists to task: "If the [Poalei Zion] were not pursuing a misguided and mischievous policy, on the outskirts of the [Zionist] movement, there would be every reason to welcome the convention, which it has called for this month, of Jewish workmen sympathetic to Zionism."[50]

The editorial derided the Labor Zionists for advocating "class-struggle, class-interests and class-hatreds." Proclaiming such a course at variance with mainstream American Jewish and General Zionist sensibilities, the *Maccabaean* accused Poalei Zion of employing "Bolshevik tactics" and toeing the party line of its alleged Soviet mother organization. The *Maccabaean*, however, notwithstanding deep reservations about Poalei Zion's militant socialist leanings, held out the hope that the Labor Zionists would yet "recover their Zionist equilibrium." Should the Jewish workers and their leaders be won over by Zionism, the journal concluded, "it will be because they see a prospect of establishing a Jewish state, which will release Jewish national ambitions and national hopes."[51]

The *Maccabaean* editorial illustrates the ZOA leadership's concern that the Labor Zionists and their potential allies—the increasingly pro-Palestine Jewish working class—would threaten the interests of American Zionism's political establishment. It also reveals the shock waves and cultural clashes that permeated American Jewish life in the aftermath of the Russian Revolution. We obtain a glimpse of this situation in an unusually frank letter from Benjamin Rabalsky, head of the Zionist organization's regional branch in Boston, to Jacob De Haas, then secretary of the Provisional Executive Committee:

> There are candidates and prospects [in Boston] that would be made good Zionists but cannot afford to pay [dues] in advance. . . . There are others who would like to become organized Zionists but prefer to belong to a Jewish [read: Yiddish] speaking Zionist society. . . . I will repeat again that it is my opinion that Dorchester, Mattapan, Roxbury, Brighton, Newton, Watertown, Waltham, Lawrence, Fall River and other places near Boston should have strong organized societies. . . . Unless the [Zionist organization]

... take[s] such steps as is necessary to organize the masses, the Poalei Zion will do it.[52]

American Zionist leaders were wary of Labor Zionism because like the ZOA, Hadassah, and Mizrahi, Labor Zionism grew exponentially during the war. Before World War I, the Labor Zionist movement—the Poalei Zion and Zeirei Zion parties, the fraternal order Yidish Nazionaler Arbeter Farband,[53] and the variously named socialist Zionist youth groups—registered a mere 2,630 members in eighty-two locations.[54] By 1918, however, the Labor Zionist movement had increased to 200 active clubs with a combined membership of 7,000.[55] The clubs were located mostly in New England, the Middle West, and Canada. Although numerically insignificant compared with the Zionist Organization of America's 149,235 members (including Hadassah) and smaller than Mizrahi's 18,000 members, the Labor Zionists were in a position to act as a pressure group within American Zionism.[56]

Due to its small size, Labor Zionism's credibility and clout depended on political leverage rather than organizational size and fund-raising capabilities. The movement's strength as a link to the east European Jewish community, the party leadership confidently declared, derived from the fact that "neither the [Provisional Executive Committee] nor the Zionist Federation which backs it are able to fully avail themselves of the Zionist feelings which increasingly take hold of the large masses of . . . American Jewry. They have no access to the labor and democratic masses of the Jewish population."[57] But, the Labor Zionists averred,

> the masses do not find answers to all their questions either in Zionism, which lives almost exclusively with the thought of Palestine, nor in the labor movement, which is absorbed exclusively with labor interests. . . . [The Labor Zionist movement is] carrying on a life-and-death struggle with the official labor leadership, which is centered in the *Forward*, because of its indifference to the Jewish interests of the workmen, to the historical interests of the Jewish people.[58]

During World War I, Labor Zionism emerged as a force to be reckoned with in American Jewish life. The rank and file of Jewish labor gradually warmed to the cause of Labor Palestine, and the Labor Zionist movement used its newfound leverage to lobby American Jewish leaders. Although the Yishuv steadily garnered new support in this period, fundamental cultural and philosophical differences continued to divide American Zionism.

On one end of the spectrum stood Zionists sympathetic to the Herzlian program because it resolved a personal philosophical dilemma and provided a positive form of American Jewish self-identification. At the other were Zionist adherents for whom Jewish nationalist convictions were not only central to their self-conception but who also tried to actualize such beliefs in their own lives and who felt estranged, in varying degrees, from American society.

Thus Louis D. Brandeis, a revered—albeit aloof—Zionist leader of German descent, differed dramatically from Louis Lipsky, a journalist and Zionist functionary with close personal ties to the immigrant milieu. At another level, Abraham Goldberg, a talented Yiddish writer and speaker and a founder of Poalei Zion, diverged from David Pinsky, a Yiddish playwright and the editor of *Der yidisher kemfer*. Goldberg transferred his allegiance to the General Zionists; Pinsky used his influence to familiarize American Jews with the strains of immigrant Zionism. Collectively, Brandeis, Lipsky, Goldberg, and Pinsky offered a stark contrast to the legionnaires of the Thirty-ninth Battalion and certainly to Hehaluz and the group of American haluzim who established Moshav Avihayil. In short, the notions of exile and *hagshamah azmit* (self-fulfillment) divided American Zionism into distinct ideological categories. The many Zionist perspectives existed in a symbiosis of dynamic tension: the Americanized variants of Zionism provided a reservoir of support for groups steeped in the immigrant milieu, with the latter challenging and stimulating the Jewish commitment and content of the former.

Despite its own factions and divisions, Labor Zionism played a key role in this configuration. Together with other immigrant groups, particularly Mizrahi, it sustained from one generation to the next the wider American movement's ideological quotient of "exile." Unlike religious Zionism, however, Labor also provided a direct channel to the Yishuv's growing and increasingly important workers' movement. Poalei Zion and Zeirei Zion were living links to the Jewish community in Palestine and its everyday affairs. *Der yidisher kemfer* supplied American Jews with translated excerpts from the Hebrew press in Palestine. The party's central committee assumed responsibility for promoting Labor Palestine's economic and political interests in the United States. Accordingly, local and national party activists often served as the first point of contact for movement *shlihim* (emissaries), including individuals like David Ben-Gurion, Yizhak Ben-Zvi, Berl Katznelson, Manya Shohat, and Rahel Yanait, who later became the Yishuv's preeminent political leaders. Thus the American movement proved to be the bedrock of Labor Palestine's support in the "dollar land."

Following World War I, American Zionism generally and Labor Zionism particularly "achieved a new degree of recognition and legitimacy,"[59] a new status that changed the nature of American Jewish politics. In the aftermath of the Balfour Declaration of 1917 and the Paris Peace Conference of 1919, the German Jewish elite—notably Jacob Schiff, Felix Warburg, Louis Marshall, and others grouped around the American Jewish Committee—offered limited support to Palestine as an extension of American-sponsored relief efforts and a haven for Jewish refugees.[60] Similarly, the Jewish religious establishment and organized Jewish labor, though officially opposed to political Zionism, faced internal pressure from constituencies that viewed the Zionist enterprise in Palestine with growing interest and, in many instances, enthusiasm. The democratization of American Jewish life marked the end of German Jewish hegemony and a major shift in the orientation of the Jewish labor movement. In the postwar years, both camps were forced to redefine their political identities in relation to the Zionist idea and to yield control of Jewish communal life to a new generation of Americanized immigrants.[61]

Paradoxically, the postwar environment did not stimulate the Zionist movement's continued expansion in the United States. As American Jews entered a period of economic and geographic stability, the community as a whole became less polarized. The crusades that had divided Jewish communal life before the war receded into the past, and the organized Zionist movement—one of many groups seeking to impart a particular American Jewish agenda—was constrained to battle for its place in the sun. On the popular level, however, the boundaries between American Jewry's factions and ideologies blurred, and the Zionist idea of building the Jewish national home remained firmly planted in the American Jewish psyche. Most American Jews saw no conflict among supporting the Yishuv, joining immigrant societies and organizations, attending synagogue, sending their children to a religious school, and belonging to a trade union.[62]

In the era that John Higham has labeled the "Tribal Twenties," American Jewry's seemingly nonideological character was belied by communal responses to external threats.[63] U.S. immigration restrictions, university quotas aimed at Jews, and the antisemitic campaigns of the Ku Klux Klan and Henry Ford's *Dearborn Independent* threatened American Jewish security.[64] In response, American Jews rallied to communal efforts aimed at combating discrimination as well as strengthening and consolidating their place in American society. The Order of Bnai Brith, for example, grew in tandem with the Jewish immigrant community's swift Americanization and economic advancement. It emerged as American Jewry's leading membership group and reinvigorated the Anti-Defamation League.[65] In its avoidance of partisan and religious battles, Bnai Brith illustrated the American Jewish impulse toward communal and political consensus. Accordingly, antidefamation and cultural activities moved to the center of the Jewish public agenda while Jewish welfare abroad continued to rank as a paramount concern.

Against the background of the San Remo Conference in the spring of 1920, which established the framework for implementing the British Mandate in Palestine, and the ascendance of the east European Jewish immigrant community in the United States, American Zionist leaders and public opinion shapers, including key elements of the Yiddish press, exhibited tremendous confidence in the Zionist movement and the Yishuv.[66] They portrayed Palestine as a haven for beleaguered east European Jewry, a model of Jewish industry, and a new Jewish frontier. The image of "New Palestine"—"land of the new hope, land of the present and the future, and land of the West"—resonated with Jewish ideals as well as the American myths of pioneering, progress, and self-reliance.[67] Many Jewish groups modified this theme according to their specific outlook. Young Judea, a centrist Zionist youth organization affiliated with Hadassah, proclaimed the *shomer* (watchman) to be "the most romantic person in Palestine today."[68] In 1920, an assembly of Jewish workers at Cooper Union declared: "We shall sacrifice our own lives for the only possible guarantee of our national existence, for the construction of a Jewish Palestine based upon work and liberty."[69] Gabriel Davidson, manager of the Jewish Agricultural and Industrial Aid Society, linked modernization in the United States and Palestine. "Our American colonization experiments teach us," Davidson asserted, that social progress is "transcendentally a human problem. . . . The reestablishment of Palestine as the Jewish Homeland is an intensely practical proposition. . . . Only those should be allowed to enter who can contribute to building it up."[70]

As such popular conceptions illustrate, support for Zionism in the American Jewish community was much broader than the membership of any one Zionist group. To the dismay of Zionist organizers, however, this widespread pro-Zionist sentiment did not necessarily translate into substantive or quantitative movement gains during the 1920s and early 1930s. In fact, after World War I, membership in the American Zionist movement rapidly dwindled, and the number of shekels (membership dues) purchased by American Jews before the Zionist Congresses did not rise significantly.[71]

Nonetheless, the decade following World War I was a time of consolidation for American Zionism. American Jewry's relationship with the Zionist movement was strengthened by Palestinian and European figures like David Ben-Gurion, Yizhak Ben-Zvi, and Pinhas Rutenberg, each of whom was instrumental in creating the Jewish Legion's American units during World War I. Likewise, Aaron Aaronsohn, a leader of the nonsocialist Palestinian pioneers and darling of the American Jewish elite, and Vladimir Jabotinsky, the founder of Revisionist Zionism and chief architect of the Jewish Legion, stimulated the interest of the Jewish community's nonimmigrant and nonlabor segments.

A significant breakthrough was made between 1921 and 1922 when a talented Histadrut delegation composed of Manya Shohat, Berl Katznelson, and Yosef Baratz visited the United States. Although only moderately successful in their fund-raising efforts on behalf of the newly established Bank Hapoalim (Workers' Bank) and Jewish self-defense efforts, the delegation did establish an important foothold for Labor Zionism in the United States. Shohat, in particular, successfully cultivated close relations with several important Jewish leaders, such as Louis D. Brandeis, Henrietta Szold, Julian Mack, Joseph Schlossberg, Max Pine, Judah L. Magnes, Stephen S. Wise, Louis Lipsky, and Abraham Liesin.[72] These contacts proved to be crucial in the decades that followed.

Labor Palestine's success in the United States also stemmed from the philosophical predisposition of the Brandeis group. Faithful to the ideals of the Progressive Era, the group's members favored moderate social democratic schemes for building the Jewish national home. Although they were primarily concerned with developing the Yishuv's economic infrastructure, Brandeis, Mack, Frankfurter, and others were especially sympathetic to the objectives of the Labor movement in Palestine. Their support of the Histadrut, rural colonies, and other cooperative ventures was untarnished by the group's checkered relationship with American Poalei Zion. In any case, the Brandeis group helped legitimize Labor Palestine in the eyes of mainstream American Jews and alleviate fears of the Labor Zionists' militant propensities.[73]

The Brandeisian outlook continued to color American Jewish perspectives on Zionism and the Yishuv even after Brandeis himself lost a 1921 leadership contest to Louis Lipsky, the point man for Chaim Weizmann's allies in the United States. In fact, the Weizmann-Lipsky coalition's subsequent political and propaganda efforts derived from Brandeis's Zionist strategy, whose ideological underpinnings were elaborated in the Pittsburgh Program which, as noted earlier, was drafted by the former Zeirei Zion activist Horace M. Kallen.

Despite popular support, including some Labor Zionists, for the Lipsky forces, the new ZOA administration viewed the Poalei Zion and Zeirei Zion parties with suspicion. This was due, in large measure, to the collective psychology of the Lipsky faction which resented and feared the Brandeis group. It was also due to the Lipsky faction's relative insecurity vis-à-vis the new leaders of Labor Palestine, who continued to make important inroads among the ascendant east European immigrants in American Jewish society. The Lipsky administration viewed as especially threatening the combination of the ousted Brandeis group and the increasingly powerful Labor Zionists. As a result, the Labor Zionist parties were kept at bay and compelled to function outside the American movement's organizational mainstream.

The case of Hayim Greenberg, a noted Labor Zionist publicist and orator, is illustrative in this regard. Greenberg, whose first years in the United States coincided with the rise of the Lipsky faction, was (despite his close relationship with Chaim Weizmann) virtually shunned by the ZOA and United Palestine Appeal leadership. The respected Zionist intellectual and political leader Chaim Arlosoroff—who at Weizmann's behest spent extended time in the United States as a *shaliah* (emissary) between 1926 and 1929—witnessed this situation. He described the operative administrative policies of American Zionist leaders as "keeping the stranger out."

> A stranger in the sense of this program is everybody who does not belong (to the particular set of people in office . . .). Keeping out, in the sense of this program, means preventing anything that might lead to a regular cooperation and, in consequence, perhaps to share in the publicity which such cooperation entails. . . . [A] striking case is Mr. Hayim Greenberg. . . . Mr. Greenberg, though a [Zeirei Zion] Hitahdut member, is not only a man of rare gifts and character, but he has also come to enjoy, in the Yiddish speaking quarters of American Jewry, a high reputation as one of the most excellent speakers, writers, and lecturers in the country. He repeatedly offered his volunteer services both to the UPA and the ZOA, in the beginning of several successive seasons. The result of it all, to make a long story short, was that he has not, so far, been called upon *even once* to do the slightest thing for the

UPA [headquarters]. In much the same way, not one of the Zionist periodicals has taken cognizance of the remarkable editorials which, for years, he has contributed bi-weekly to [Zeirei Zion's] *Farn folk* [For the People]. No other consideration can have brought about this but the fear lest a different attitude would give credit and publicity both to Mr. Greenberg and to *Farn folk*, whereas publicity should be used as a political weapon to the exclusive benefit of those who "belong."[74]

Notwithstanding the hostility of the ZOA and UPA leaders, Labor Zionists performed a sizable share of organizational and political work in the United States. It did not take long before the services of Greenberg and other highly effective speakers were eagerly sought by local Hebraist and Zionist groups from across the political spectrum.[75]

The second-class status of Poalei Zion and Zeirei Zion prompted party leaders to consider new models for cultural and political organization. Greenberg and Arlosoroff played central roles in this regard. Ironically, the Brandeis group proved exemplary, as the displaced former leaders demonstrated the efficacy of coalition building and the numerous possibilities for circumventing official American Zionist policy. But American Labor Zionism's antiestablishment posture did not change immediately, and the switch from narrow partisan activity to extraorganizational strategy was gradual and costly.

A case in point is *Die zeit* (The Times), the short-lived Yiddish daily launched by Poalei Zion at the initiative of Nahman Syrkin and a handful of party stalwarts. Edited by the playwright David Pinsky, *Die zeit* attracted talented writers but could not compete with larger, better-established Yiddish newspapers.[76] Moreover, the paper's very existence sharpened internal disputes instead of unifying the party's factions. During her tenure as a member of the Histadrut delegation, Manya Shohat complained that American Poalei Zion was a "tempest in a teacup."

> The entire movement here is worthless. They are fed up with the way they have worked thus far, and *Die zeit* . . . is folding. . . . And all this is not because . . . there is no place for a newspaper such as this, on the contrary it is needed and very important. It is because the administration of the newspaper is totally ineffective.[77]

The major shift in party strategy was engineered by Shohat, Katznelson, and other Palestinian shlihim familiar with the American Jewish scene. Following the creation of the Histadrut, the Palestine-based movement tried to outflank the Weizmann-Lipsky forces and targeted American Jewish immigrants—particularly labor circles beyond the reach of the WZO's newly established Keren Hayesod (Palestine Foundation Fund)—in order to garner fresh support for the Yishuv. For example, in 1923, the Histadrut leaders, many of whom were familiar figures to the American Jewish immigrant world, appealed directly to the Fareinigte Yidishe Geverkshaftn (United Hebrew Trades, UHT). The UHT was socialist rather than strictly trade unionist in orientation.[78] Its declared aims were mutual aid and cooperation among Jewish trade unions as well as the development of new unions and the propagation of socialism among Jewish workers. This agenda was largely compatible with that of the Histadrut. Therefore, the UHT and the Labor Zionists reached common ground by focusing on support of the workers in Palestine rather than quarreling over the ideological principles of Jewish nationalism. Their alliance effectively ended the organized labor movement's monolithic opposition to the Yishuv. At a 1924 mass meeting in Cooper Union, the UHT leader Max Pine inaugurated the "Geverkshaftn campaign" and proclaimed: "This is the first time that Jewish workers in America meet to destroy a dogma and throw off the shackles that kept in chains thousands of our sisters and brothers whom destiny has brought to Palestine."[79]

The Geverkshaftn campaign raised more than $50,000 in 1924 but fell short of its $150,000 goal. Given the stiff resistance of the *Forward* (Der forverts), the country's largest and most influential Yiddish socialist paper, the 1924 campaign was nonetheless a small triumph. Consequently, when the *Forward*'s powerful editor, Abe Cahan, visited in Palestine in 1925, the Labor Zionists made a concerted effort to convert him. After touring Jewish settlements in different parts of the Yishuv, Cahan returned to the United States via Poland, where he witnessed firsthand the suffering of Polish Jews. These experiences had a profound impact on him, and Cahan subsequently adopted a pro-Labor Zionist position.

When the *Forward*'s attitude toward Labor Palestine softened, the floodgates of organized Jewish labor opened, and the Geverkshaftn campaign's fortunes rose dramatically. Many trade unions previously antipathetic to Poalei Zion now warmly welcomed the Geverkshaftn. Even the fervent socialist leader Baruch Charney Vladeck conceded that Labor Zionism deserved limited support. The situation of east European Jewry, Vladeck asserted in 1926, "is so distressing that nothing that has any bearing on Jewish life can be ignored by the labor movement. Palestine is connected with the situation of the Jews."[80] Although strong socialist opposition to Palestine and Zionism continued, Labor Zionist advances eventually gained the upper hand. To be sure, the Geverkshaftn sums were small compared with other American Jewish philanthropies, but the campaign did raise more than $100,000 in 1926 and $136,000 in 1927. After 1928, when Labor Palestine received the official endorsement of the International Ladies Garment Workers Union, the largest and most powerful American Jewish labor group, the campaign total rose to $170,000 in 1929 and $175,000 in 1930.[81]

The Geverkshaftn's success cannot be measured in dollars alone, however. Of particular interest is the changing context in which the Histadrut funds were raised. Unlike the Joint Distribution Committee, the Keren Hayesod, and the Brandeis group, which channeled large contributions from wealthy Jewish philanthropists, the Geverkshaftn was almost wholly dependent on numerous community groups, workers' associations, youth clubs, *landsmanshaftn* (mutual aid societies), Hebrew societies, and other regional supporters. From the vantage point of social history, therefore, the campaign's success exemplifies Labor Zionism's growing attraction for a cross section of the American Jewish community. Moreover, when viewing American Jewish economic aid to the Yishuv as a totality, this trend represented an increasingly important avenue of support. In the decades leading up to the establishment of the Jewish state, a disproportionate share of American Jewish funds were directed to projects that boosted and strengthened Labor Palestine.[82]

Relations between American Jews and the Yishuv also benefited from advances and innovations in the world of Jewish education.[83] In the United States, a loose partnership of Palestinian educators, Hebraist intellectuals, and Zionist activists was in large measure responsible for the expansion and, in some instances, creation of Hebrew teachers' colleges and modern Jewish schools in most metropolitan centers.

The Hebrew Teachers' College of Boston (1921), for example, was one of the country's earliest *ivrit beivrit* (Hebrew in Hebrew) centers. Supervised by Nissan Touroff, former director of the Yishuv's nascent school system, instruction at the college was conducted entirely in Hebrew. The United Hebrew Schools of Detroit (1919) and New York's Herzliah Hebrew Academy (1923), by contrast, focused on the so-called natural method, which stressed the cultivation of Hebrew as a living language intimately tied to Jewish life in Palestine.

The driving intellectual force behind these efforts was Samson Benderly, a noted Palestinian pedagogue and architect of the New York Kehillah's Bureau Jewish of Education (BJE). Under Benderly's watchful eye, the BJE instituted progressive educational methods and created the prototype for communal coordinating agencies for Jewish education. Perhaps Benderly's most important achievement, however, was winning over a talented cadre of young men and women committed to progressive Jewish education. Alexander Dushkin, a Zeirei Zion activist, was one of Benderly's most gifted students. In 1924, he was appointed head of Chicago's newly established College of Jewish Studies, which became "the hub of Jewish intellectual activity for the entire community."[84] From this base, Dushkin—like A. H. Friedland, Jacob Golub, Ben Edidin, Samuel Dinin, and Emanuel Gamoran—exerted enormous influence over a substantial Jewish constituency. With the end of large-scale Jewish immigration to the United States in 1921 and the rise of a new, native-born American generation, it became clear to Dushkin and his contemporaries that "we can no longer rely on the psychology of *galut* as motivation for our educational effort."[85] Instead, they collectively reasoned, American Jewish life required innovative educational curricula that stressed "survival values" pertinent to Jewish life in Palestine and the diaspora.[86]

In contrast, Dushkin's contemporary Isaac B. Berkson, who was also a Zeirei Zion activist, joined the Zionist Executive in Palestine where he worked closely with Henrietta Szold and helped shape the Yishuv's educational system. In this position, Berkson also helped sustain the Benderly-Touroff tradition of linking American and Palestinian Jewish educators. This intricate relationship is revealed in Berkson's ambitious plans for reorganizing Jewish education in the Yishuv according to modern American methods. In a letter to Dushkin, Berkson proposed:

> The Department of Education of the Zionist Organization must assume full responsibility for providing an elementary education for all Jewish children. . . . My idea is that you should be asked to come here next year to make a careful survey of . . . supplementary education, kindergarten education, secondary education and especially vocational and industrial education. . . . Your task would include the preparation of a [report] which could then be used in the work of organizing the Keren Hahinukh [Educational Fund] in America.[87]

Dushkin replied favorably to Berkson, noting: "If Miss Szold and you think that a survey of non-elementary educational work in Palestine is worth while and needs to be undertaken, I should be glad to consider it . . . it may be that uniting of these educational efforts would call forth energies hitherto untouched."[88] This brief exchange highlights the multifaceted relationship that developed between Palestine and American Jewish educators in the interwar years. Berkson's proposal—that the Zionist organization assume responsibility for Jewish education, that American methods be employed in educational work, and that Jewish education be sponsored on a transpartisan basis—identified the dominant features of the working relationship between Jewish and Zionist educational activists in the prestate period. If they themselves had not passed through the Labor Zionist ranks, the leaders of this effort at least subscribed to a view of modern Jewish life that valued the energies and achievements of the Labor enterprise in Palestine. One need only peruse the curricular materials of this period as well as the professional journal *Jewish Education*, which began publishing in 1929, to find confirmation of the importance of modern Hebrew, the Yishuv, and cooperative Zionist ideals in the growing network of Hebrew teachers' institutes, Jewish community colleges, principals' organizations, and teachers' associations.[89]

In this climate, informal Zionist education and Jewish summer camps also found the scope and inducement to grow. Many of these groups and institutions emphasized Hebrew, scouting, and *haluziut* (pioneering) and came under the direct influence of Palestinian shlihim.[90] In most cases, the shlihim were sponsored by the Histadrut and chosen from the ranks of the Yishuv's most dynamic leaders and best youth educators. Some, like Chaim Arlosoroff and Enzo Sereni, were particularly well suited to Labor Zionism's strategy of capturing the minds and hearts of American Jewish youth.[91] In the United States, they cast a wide net over the array of youth organizations and summer camps that mushroomed in this period. After the Zionist youth movements Hehaluz, Hashomer Hazair, Hashomer Hadati, Young Judea, and Betar provided the shlihim with a natural foothold, their influence quickly extended to college student groups like Avukah and the Hillel Foundation, as well as a range of Jewish educational camps. Tens of thousands of American Jews spent their formative years in these frameworks.[92] From this cohort emerged a sizable number of American Jewry's foremost communal leaders, rabbis, educators, and social workers—men and women who shaped American Jewish popular culture. By focusing on education, summer camps, and youth activity, Labor Zionism laid the groundwork for much of its later success.

By the late 1930s, the idea of Jewish communal responsibility for Jewish education had taken root all across the country.[93] From the Central Jewish Institute of New York to the Los Angeles Jewish Academy, the pioneering educational enterprises of the "Benderly boys" and others upheld Hebrew and the new Jewish life in Palestine as central values.[94] Against this back-drop, the ZOA Education Department, reestablished in 1937 after a hiatus of sixteen years, developed a program of its own for working with Jewish community schools. "The ideal would be," noted ZOA president Rabbi Solomon Goldman (subsequently the head of the League for Labor Palestine), "a chain of Zionist schools for children throughout the country."

> That is undoubtedly beyond us at present, but we should establish and main-tain contact with Hebrew schools, Talmud Torahs, Yeshivahs [*sic*], Folk-shuln, Sunday Schools, etc. . . . We can prepare teachers' guides on Palestine and Zionism. . . . It should be our business to provide biographies of Zionist personalities as well as books on Jewish history, Zionism, the Yishuv, Zionist history in America, the growth of Tel Aviv and Haifa and the colonies, old and young. . . . All this material . . . should discover and inspire with a Zi-onist content. . . . We must search out the ablest young Jewish minds in the country and nurse them for Jewish and Zionist leadership.[95]

In fact, Goldman's scheme for Zionist educational initiatives was never implemented by the ZOA. But his vision did accurately reflect the general orientation of Zionists and sympathetic non-Zionists, including Jewish community lay leaders, synagogue activists, rabbis, and members of the new Jewish teaching profession.

In 1941, data from twenty-six cities, comprising roughly 72 percent of the total American Jewish population, indicated that nearly 180,000 chil-dren were enrolled in Jewish elementary schools and 10,000 in Jewish high schools. When combined with the figures for children and youth enrolled in other educational institutions such as Talmud Torahs and Folkshuln, the total number was estimated to be considerably above 200,000. The study also concluded that the twenty-five Jewish education bureaus then in exis-tence were headed by educators and administrators, "all of whom, without exception, [were] Zionists and Hebraists." The same could be said "with even greater certainty," the study asserted, of the principals and teachers associated with the Hebrew teaching profession in the United States.[96]

On the whole, the non-Zionist members of the local Jewish agencies and boards that supervised the Jewish education bureaus ranged from sym-pathetic to indifferent to Zionism and Palestine. In rare instances, some non-Zionist lay leaders forbade singing the Zionist anthem "Hatikvah" (The Hope) and displaying the Zionist flag at children's gatherings. How-ever, there was generally very little interference in the curriculum of the Jewish schools by lay leaders. Indeed, most teachers and administrators viewed the Zionist enterprise favorably and tried to influence students by correlating Palestine with the teaching of Hebrew.[97] For this purpose, specialized syllabi and textbooks were developed by the Zionist educators A. H. Friedland, Zvi Scharfstein, Ben Edidin, and others.[98]

Perhaps the best example of the incursion of Zionist influence into a traditionally non-Zionist (and formerly anti-Zionist) sphere is Emanuel Gamoran's relationship with the Reform movement. Gamoran's Zionist proclivities, nurtured by Samson Benderly and honed as a result of his association with Zeirei Zion, especially his close contact with student activists at Stephen S. Wise's Jewish Institute of Religion, first became public in 1924 when he published *Changing Conceptions in Jewish Education.* "Palestine is a survival value," he wrote. "We should clearly face the fact that the free development of a people . . . cannot take place in a land where this people is a minority, however welcome. . . . The influence of the Jewish center in Palestine will make the cultural contributions of the Jews in America richer."[99]

Gamoran's pedagogy was acceptable to the Reform camp because unlike many other Zionist educators, particularly those adhering to Labor Zionism, he was not a secularist. In the 1920s, he joined the staff of the Union of American Hebrew Congregations where, in time, his tireless efforts resulted in the gradual infusion of Zionist motifs into the movement's educational literature. His curricula made Hebrew a regular part of course instruction, and he developed textbooks and primers that contained special units dealing with Zionism and Palestine. During the interwar period, the Union of American Hebrew Congregations was the only national Jewish organization to publish such materials, and in the 1930s and 1940s, many of Gamoran's texts were adopted by Conservative and Orthodox schools.[100]

Labor Zionism and the Yishuv also had a profound impact on Zionist women's activities. Much of the work in this regard was done by Poalei Zion's female members, who eventually broke away from the American party to form a separate Labor Zionist women's organization. The impetus for such a women's group came from the Histadrut emissary Manya Shohat. During her 1921/1922 trip to the United States, Shohat quickly discovered that the Histadrut delegates' fund-raising inadvertently competed with the American movement's existing drive to send tools and farm machinery to the Palestinian *kvuzot* (communes) as well as the World Zionist Organization's ongoing Keren Hayesod (Palestine Foundation) campaign.[101]

To avoid overtaxing American Poalei Zion's scarce resources, Shohat created an ad hoc committee of female members to raise $10,000 worth of kitchen and laundry equipment for the struggling kvuzot in Palestine.[102] The women's committee elicited the interest of a cadre of Zionist women activists, who worked hard to achieve their fund-raising goal. Neither the campaign nor the committee, however, was a top priority for Shohat. Instead, she devoted most of her energy to clandestine efforts to procure weapons for Hashomer (The Watchman), the Jewish self-defense organization of the Palestine labor movement. Nonetheless, her efforts did lay the foundation for the Pioneer Women organization, created three years later.

In 1924 when the Zionist leader Rahel Yanait (later Ben-Zvi) sought American Jewish financial support, she turned to the women who had previously participated in the ad hoc committee organized by Manya Shohat. Yanait was director of a girls' agricultural school and tree nursery near the Ratisbonne monastery in Jerusalem, the nursery being one of several such projects organized by the Palestine labor movement. Yanait requested financial assistance for the construction of a well that would end the school's dependence on the British Mandatory. (The Mandate administration, which implemented Britain's irregular policies in Palestine,[103] severely curtailed the water supply available to the nursery.)

Yanait drew up plans for a well with the assistance of the Jewish National Fund, the Zionist agency responsible for land acquisition and development in the Yishuv. Next she enlisted the support of Sophie Udin and six other Poalei Zion activists: Eva Berg, Leah Brown, Haya Ehrenreich, Luba Hurwitz, Rahel Segal, and Nina Zuckerman. The women recognized such an undertaking's possible political value for the Palestine labor movement. They also sought to exploit Yanait's call for help in order to assert their own agenda within the male-dominated Poalei Zion Party. Like many of their contemporaries who experienced the swift social, economic, and political transformation of American women in the 1920s, the cohort grouped around Udin reasoned that their objectives would be best advanced through an autonomous Labor Zionist women's organization. To this end, in March 1924 they published a carefully crafted letter written by Yanait in *Der tog* (The Day). In the letter, Yanait observed that "our tree nursery cannot exist without a well" and that during the previous two years, "more than 130,000 saplings from our *kvuzah* [commune] have been planted in 17 points in Galilee and Judaea."[104] The letter proved highly effective. The image of Jewish female pioneers tending "saplings" and reclaiming the wilderness of the Yishuv struck a responsive chord among working-class Jewish immigrant women. Udin and her followers succeeded not only in raising an initial $500;[105] they also exploited the enthusiastic communal response to Yanait's letter to buttress their campaign for an independent Labor Zionist women's organization.

The Poalei Zion Party's male leadership was generally opposed to creating a separate women's organization, as they feared that such a structure would undermine the party's credibility in the eyes of the immigrant community. Having long since "emancipated" Poalei Zion's female members and given them equal rights, they argued, there was no need to sponsor a new women's organization. However, such specious reasoning did not deter Udin, Berg, Ehrenreich, Hurwitz, Siegel, and Zuckerman. They asserted that the minuscule number of women in Poalei Zion—and their subservient roles as caretakers and child care providers within the party framework[106]—actually inhibited women from joining the movement. Only an autonomous Labor Zionist women's organization, they believed, would enable them to assume greater responsibility for the movement and realize their full potential.

Finally, in 1925 Udin appealed to the fifteenth annual Poalei Zion convention to approve the formation of a separate women's organization. "I explained, in the name of a small group of members," she later recalled in modest but revealing terms, "our desire to be a part of the party, an organic part, but *independent*."[107] With the support of Manya Shohat, Rahel Yanait, Goldie Meyerson (later Golda Meir), and other key figures in Moezet Hapoalot (Working Women's Council of the Histadrut), the American women's group officially seceded from Poalei Zion.

During the interwar period, an increasing number of American Jewish women became active in the Zionist movement. In fact, between the end of World War I and the establishment of the State of Israel in 1948, the number of women enrolled in the American Zionist movement grew tenfold, from approximately 30,000 to more than 300,000. During this period, Hadassah became the largest Zionist group in the United States, with 250,000 members. Meanwhile, Pioneer Women grew from 3,000 to 28,000 members.[108]

In 1926, the first convention of the newly established Women's Organization for the Pioneer Women of Palestine was held in New York City, and Leah Biskin was elected the group's national president. The convention declared the new women's organization to be completely autonomous in its political and educational work. It adopted a socialist Zionist platform and affiliated with the World Union of Poalei Zion, the Socialist International, and the World Zionist Organization. The group stressed the importance of ideological and political tasks over philanthropic activities. The 1926 convention articulated the following goals:

1. To help create a homeland in Palestine based on cooperation and social justice.
2. To give moral and material support to the Moezet Hapoalot.
3. To strive through systematic cultural and propaganda work to educate the American Jewish woman to undertake a more conscious role as coworker in the establishment of a better and more just society in America and throughout the world.[109]

In just a few years, Pioneer Women—the organization was officially renamed in 1939—mobilized more than forty clubs, with approximately three thousand members.[110] These idealistic, committed, and liberal young working women made time for political and fund-raising activities for girls' agricultural training schools in Petah Tikvah, Nahalat Yehuda, and Hadera, places most of them never expected to see themselves.[111]

In contrast to other American Jewish women's organizations, Pioneer Women stressed a philosophical orientation attuned to the Jewish immigrant milieu, holding as its central values the notions of Yiddishkeit (Jewishness), class consciousness, and feminism. In addition, Pioneer Women's members, proud of their cultural identity, shunned what they perceived to be the bourgeois trappings of Americanized groups like Hadassah and the National Council of Jewish Women. Pioneer Women "is not just one more organization of women," the movement leaders proclaimed. "It is an organization of women with the distinct task of advancing economic emancipation and the national rehabilitation of the Jewish masses."[112] Golda Meir, who was sent by Moezet Hapoalot as an emissary to Pioneer Women in 1928–1929 and 1932–1934, later recalled:

> Almost all these women were European born. They spoke Yiddish at home, and to people who didn't know them, I suppose they appeared very much like their own mothers, like typical working class *yidishe mamas* whose main concern was feeding the family and maintaining the home. But of course, they were much different. These were idealistic, politically committed, liberal young women to whom what was happening in Palestine really mattered.[113]

Golda Meir and other leaders of the women workers' movement in Palestine, including Beba Idelson, Hana Hisik, Rahel Katznelson Rubashov (later Shazar), Elisheva Kaplan, and Ada Maimon, played a conspicuous role in the life of the organization in the 1930s. They spent extended time in the United States as emissaries of Moezet Hapoalot and regularly toured Pioneer Women clubs in cities around the country, where they also promoted the Histadrut and the Zionist cause to general Jewish audiences. "They were really the soul of the organization," recalled Dvorah Rothbard, the head of Pioneer Women from 1942 to 1945. "Around them there was such a holy feeling! They were the ones who gave [Pioneer Women] content, who gave it wings, who gave it imagination."[114]

The interwar period witnessed Pioneer Women's gradual transformation from a women's auxiliary of the Poalei Zion Party to an independent American women's movement. As Pioneer Women's membership became increasingly Americanized and acculturated, the organization became less doctrinaire, and the use of English became widespread. The movement also steadily grew in this period, and the proceeds of its fund-raising campaign on behalf of Moezet Hapoalot rose sharply. In its first decade, Pioneer Women transmitted nearly $383,000 to Histadrut-related projects in Palestine. By 1939 it had 170 chapters in 70 cities and approximately 7,000 members. Of the 170 clubs, 85 were categorized as Yiddish-speaking and contained 4,500 members. It was nevertheless clear that the English-speaking clubs provided the point of entry for new and younger members between the ages of thirty and thirty-five, including a preponderance of recruits from outside the movement's ranks.[115]

Pioneer Women entered the decade of the 1940s with 250 clubs and a total membership of 10,000.[116] In addition to its traditional Zionist orientation and support for the Palestine labor movement, the organization now concentrated on bringing in "women from all walks of life" and imitating the social norms of other American Jewish women's organizations. The group's changing orientation in no way signaled a diminution of its emphasis on social activism, however, and in the years immediately preceding the establishment of the State of Israel, Pioneer Women sent nearly $1 million to specific projects and enterprises in the Yishuv.[117]

In sum, Pioneer Women emphasized the political importance of women in the American Zionist enterprise and provided a forum for working-class Jewish immigrant women who sympathized with the aims and ideals of Labor Palestine. In time, the organization opened new channels of communication between the Yishuv and the Jewish community in America.

In the 1920s and 1930s, philanthropy, labor, education, and Zionist women's organizations were crucial arenas in which Labor Zionism battled for the hearts and minds of American Jews. Even after the Labor bloc won control of the World Zionist Organization and the Jewish Agency in 1933, the membership of the American Labor Zionist movement remained numerically small. However, as the foregoing examples show, the Labor Zionist vision did gain currency as different streams of Jewish and Zionist life converged, gathered momentum, and grew to include groups and individuals from outside the ranks of the Labor Zionist movement. Like the Reconstructionist movement, which arose during the interwar years when many American Jews were fleeing from Judaism and organized Jewish life, Labor Zionism provided an increasingly secular and upwardly mobile American Jewish public with meaningful alternatives for social and political activity.[118] Nurtured by the belief that the Yishuv was the wellspring of modern Jewish culture, American Jews warmed to the vision of the Labor enterprise in Palestine. Labor Zionism's pragmatic approach to establishing a Jewish national home appealed to vast segments of American Jews, most of whom never joined the American Zionist movement.[119]

When the Great Depression reached its peak in the 1930s, the Jewish population of the United States was estimated at approximately 4.228 million.[120] Of this number, the entire American Zionist movement comprised 63,850 individuals, or a little more than 1.5 percent of the total U.S. Jewish population.[121] Economic hardship was the primary reason for the movement's small size; most American Jews simply could not afford to pay dues to a membership organization. Indeed, in 1929 the Brookings Institution estimated that an average American family required $2,000 a year just to survive. At the time, the economists further calculated, nearly 60 percent of Americans earned less than this amount. By 1932, when the Depression hit bottom, the average American family's income had plummeted to $1,348 or "barely enough to survive."[122] Between 1929 and 1933, the ZOA sustained a concomitant drop in membership of more than 50 percent, continuing the steady decline from 18,031 to 8,927 members.[123] Hadassah deviated only slightly from this trend and by 1930 had increased its original membership of 27,475 to 34,483. Then its numbers fell, and in 1933 Hadassah reached a low of 23,764 members.[124] Only Mizrahi, which claimed to have 20,000 members, seems to have maintained its strength throughout this period. Mizrahi's claims are probably accurate, reflecting the homogeneity and stringent political orientation of the Orthodox community. It is instructive to note, however, that "members of the multi-party ZOA affiliated with Orthodox congregations far outnumbered their Mizrahi . . . counterparts."[125] Finally, Poalei Zion ranked fourth in line after Hadassah,

Mizrahi, and the ZOA, numbering approximately 5,000 members. Pioneer Women claimed another 3,000 members.[126]

The situation of American Zionism mirrored that of other American Jewish organizations in the wake of the Depression. The membership of the powerful International Ladies Garment Workers Union, for example, was reduced from 70,000 in 1928 to 14,000 in the years immediately following the stock market crash.[127] Likewise, during this period, membership in the Order of Bnai Brith fell from a high of nearly 100,000 to 30,000.[128] Even the affluent Union of American Hebrew Congregations descended from more than 61,000 dues-paying families and individuals in 1930 to roughly 52,000 in 1934. Were it not for the Union of American Hebrew Congregation's policy of retaining families and synagogues unable to pay membership dues, these figures would surely have been lower.[129] In general, the desperate economic situation of the early 1930s helps explain the frugal economic behavior and low membership levels of American Jews. This pattern corresponds to scholars' findings that despite their relatively high levels of education and white-collar occupations, Jews suffered financial devastation no less than other American ethnic groups did.[130]

American Zionism's weakened condition in the United States compelled the constituent Labor Zionist groups to reassess their own political future. Meanwhile, after a lengthy public debate and protracted negotiations, Palestinian Poalei Zion and Hapoel Hazair (The Young Worker) united to form Mifleget Poalei Eretz Israel (Workers' Party of Eretz Israel, Mapai) in January 1930. Hapoel Hazair, a moderate socialist Zionist party established by graduates of the east European Zeirei Zion, was the first indigenous Jewish nationalist party in Palestine. The name reflected the party's conscious efforts to differentiate itself from Poalei Zion. Hapoel Hazair rejected Poalei Zion's theories of international class struggle as being incongruous with Palestinian reality. Nevertheless, Hapoel Hazair fully cooperated with Poalei Zion in all spheres of practical activity.[131] American Zeirei Zion, established in 1920, was a small organization based on Hapoel Hazair's Hebraist, non-Marxist orientation.

Mapai's formation in Palestine accelerated the pace of Poalei Zion's and Zeirei Zion's impending merger in the United States. On one level, the American movement's decision in 1931 to form the United Jewish Socialist Labor Party Poalei Zion–Zeirei Zion (PZ–ZZ) grew out of distinctive regional conditions: the steady acculturation of Jewish immigrants, Labor Palestine's growing popular appeal, and the economic reality of American society were three key factors that propelled the Labor Zionist movement to consolidate its forces. On another level, the union reveals the American movement's Palestinocentric orientation. In concert with Mapai (and unlike Labor Zionist groups in other parts of the diaspora), the American movement abandoned its formerly Yiddishist character. Although the organization was still several steps away from adopting a pro-Hebraist position, its doors were now open to American Jews beyond the immigrant sphere.

The first PZ–ZZ convention, which met in Baltimore in 1932, exemplified these and other changes in the movement's ideology and structure. Expanding the movement's ranks was the paramount issue of the convention. Among the various topics on the agenda, the role of several new English-speaking branches was one focus of attention. In a sense, however, all questions concerning the importance of English were resolved even before the convention took place. This is illustrated by the design for the convention's souvenir booklet, which was written half in Yiddish and half in English.

It is also instructive to consider the booklet's cover illustration (see figure 1), originally designed for the United Palestine Appeal's 1926 fundraising campaign. Two young adults, appearing confident and self-assured, gaze at the valley behind them. That they occupy the high ground provides not only artistic perspective but also a hint of their elevated spiritual status. This message is further sharpened by the fact that the man and woman hold similar tools—a sign of their equal roles. The cultivated landscape symbolizes the notion that theirs is not a utopian scheme; rather, it is a plan and (literally) a common vision that is being successfully implemented. By contrast, the characters' own biological potential has yet to be consummated. In biblical terms, their next task in building the Jewish nation is to be fruitful and multiply.

And yet, were it not for the small star of David, there would be nothing distinctively Zionist or even Jewish about the illustration. Thus, in the upper left-hand corner, the artist has inserted the Hebrew word *Zion* in the star as a means of definitively locating the entire image in the Land of Israel. Finally, conspicuously absent from the picture is the Poalei Zion emblem (a circle containing a torch, rising sun, hammer, scythe, and Hebrew lettering) or any other indication of the party's militant Russian socialist inheritance.

At a minimum, this romantic portrayal of hearty pioneers suggests a turning point in the members' self-perception. In place of Poalei Zion's

1. Souvenir Book of the United Jewish Socialist Labor Party Poalei Zion–Zeirei Zion (September 1932). Courtesy of the American Jewish Historical Society.

customary militant iconography, the souvenir booklet substitutes a softer, even ambiguous, image. The illustration fits the popular American stereotype of building up Palestine in the interwar period, and at the same time, it echoes the pioneering myth of the American frontier. The convergence of these romantic images suggests several common themes and issues: independence, adventure, industry, physical strength, youthful optimism, surety of purpose, and expansion.[132] Finally, the illustration reflects generally the growing enthusiasm of American Zionists for pioneers in Palestine.

Motivated by the desire to "break in to the general Jewish community," the PZ–ZZ delegates resolved to initiate a new campaign for English-speaking members.[133] As part of this effort, the convention decided to publish an English journal called the *Labor Zionist*. The first issue appeared just weeks after the convention and surveyed a broad range of political and ideological concerns. Shortly thereafter, in the hope of attracting a broader Zionist audience, the name of the publication was changed to *Labor Palestine*. The readership of *Labor Palestine*, however, consisted primarily of movement members. The journal appeared infrequently for approximately a year and a half, but measured against the high expectations of the Baltimore convention, it was a dismal failure.

The boost needed to expand PZ–ZZ's ranks came from another source, namely, the party's sister movement in Palestine. The achievements of the haluzim—that is, the creation of the kibbutz movement, the establishment of the Haganah self-defense organization, and especially the formation of the Histadrut—culminated in the consolidation of Labor Zionism's position in the Yishuv and the World Zionist Organization. These practical accomplishments had both important moral and political value. For the first time, at the Eighteenth Zionist Congress, the Labor Zionists became the largest voting bloc. The 318 delegates to the congress consisted of Labor, 138; General Zionists, 74; Revisionists, 45; Mizrahi, 30; Radicals, 15; and Jewish State Party, 8.[134] The Labor Zionists' increased worldwide political clout gave American PZ–ZZ an inflated status, one that was certainly disproportionate to the size of its national membership.

PZ–ZZ exploited its political windfall by organizing an extramovement association in support of the Histadrut. In 1933, it created the League for Labor Palestine and actively solicited the membership of pro-Labor scholars, intellectuals, communal leaders, and rabbis from all walks of American Jewish life. The League proposed "to enlighten its members about Palestinian labor and the activities of the Histadrut; to create around the work of Palestinian labor an atmosphere of friendship and encouragement; to raise funds for activities of the Histadrut by contributions from the League membership and nation-wide campaigns."[135]

The League grew to three thousand members in sixty locations in the first year and won support from a cadre of prominent Jewish figures and other well-known personages.[136] The League's leadership discussed the feasibility of issuing a new, high-profile Labor Zionist publication, and they solicited the advice of several Jewish communal leaders to gauge potential interest in such a journal. The reply of Emanuel Gamoran, who was a disciple of Samson Benderly and a pro–Labor Reform Jewish educator, summarized the skeptical mood of many respondents:

> I am very much interested in the work of the Labor Group in Palestine, as well as in their general outlook. There also can be no doubt that it would be a fine thing to convey to the Jewish world what the Histadrut is doing. I wonder, however, to be perfectly frank with you, whether there is any point to the starting of another magazine at the present time, when so many of those that are already in existence, are struggling and find it difficult to survive. Would it not be possible to obtain sufficient space in magazines now available for the type of information which we wish to convey, and even if it were not possible to do that, would you be inclined to believe that this is the time to undertake such a new venture? . . . One of the difficulties is, I think, that we have not yet found a way of reaching those people who ought to be reached by this literature.[137]

In October 1934, PZ–ZZ and the League jointly decided to discontinue *Labor Palestine* and publish a new journal in its place. Marie Syrkin and Hayim Fineman chaired a committee to discuss final plans for the new publication. The committee recommended an editorial board led by Hayim Greenberg, and it offered suggestions for the journal's various departments: editorials; articles; short stories and poems; reviews of English, Yiddish, and Hebrew books; regular correspondence from Palestine, London, Paris, and Warsaw; monthly surveys of labor and Palestinian news; and an organizational section of the League, PZ–ZZ, Pioneer Women, Hehaluz, and the Labor Zionist youth movement. It was estimated that the journal would operate at an initial loss of $2,000 per year, a significant sum for the financially struggling movement. "But that was to be expected," according to the minutes, because "no [monthly] in the United States can pay unless it has a circulation of about 20,000."[138] Such a readership, though ambitious, did not seem insurmountable, and the committee members approved the general plan.

Next, the committee members expressed the following sentiments concerning the journal's name:

> First preference: "New Commonwealth." Second: "Frontier."
>
> [One individual] is in favor of "New Commonwealth" because it expresses the aims and ideals of the League, and because it is well-sounding.
>
> [Another] feels that the word, "Commonwealth," sounds archaic—19th century.
>
> [A third] thinks that the word "Jewish" should be part of the name—either "Jewish Commonwealth" or "Jewish Frontier," to make the name specific and exact.
>
> [A fourth] feels that the word "Frontier" is more lively and revolutionary a name than "Commonwealth" which is too heavy and bombastic; but the word, "Jewish," should be prefixed so that the name should read "Jewish Frontier." Whereas "New Commonwealth" gives no hint of our aims and ideals in America, "Jewish Frontier" does.
>
> [A fifth] thinks that "New Commonwealth" may be confused with the Catholic publication, *Common Weal.* And "Frontier" connotes too much America—it brings to mind the Western pioneers.
>
> Decision . . . 7 in favor of "Jewish Frontier" and 5 in favor of "New Commonwealth." Unless there is another publication called "Jewish Frontier," the magazine will bear that name.[139]

Both the process of reversing the committee's original preference for the new journal's name and the extent to which the participants in the discussion consciously sought to incorporate the "aims and ideals of America" are revealing. In regard to the term *commonwealth*, more was at risk than being mistaken for the Catholic journal *Common Weal.* Nor was it simply a matter of linguistic aesthetics. The term *commonwealth* overtly suggested the legacy of the Davidic kingdom and posited the creation of an independent Jewish polity in Palestine. The appeal of such a message—though faithful to PZ–ZZ's ideological doctrine—would once again be limited to Zionist adherents. Indeed, General Zionists like Louis D. Brandeis also employed such terminology. To strike a balance between the images of revolutionary and patriotic Jews, the committee adopted the synthesis *Jewish Frontier*, by which it hoped to distinguish the new journal and open a new channel of communication with mainstream American Jews.

The Labor Zionists incorporated two important lessons learned from the success of the mass Yiddish dailies, especially the *Forward.* First, ideological purity and political effectiveness were not necessarily compatible strategies. Second, in the interest of widespread appeal and journalistic breadth, narrowly defined party agendas must be sacrificed. As Abe Cahan himself maintained, "The *Forverts* is not only an organ for socialists; it is a socialist daily for Yiddish-speaking readers."[140] Similarly, the League for Labor Palestine sought to nurture specifically Jewish interests among American Jewish readers. By appealing to the acculturated sensibilities of American Jews, Labor Zionists hoped to market a palatable version of Jewish socialist and nationalist aspirations.

Jewish Frontier's appearance in December 1934 signaled an important watershed in extending the reach of the American Labor Zionism. It reflected the movement's commitment to a wider Jewish public as well as the realization that its potential audience was becoming increasingly Americanized in speech and temperament. The new journal achieved a remarkable level of prestige as a result of Hayim Greenberg's editorial efforts. It simultaneously published lively critical and literary pieces and attempted to bridge the gap between movement veterans and the vast English-speaking world of American society. For the first time, the message of Labor Zionism reached previously removed spheres of American Jewry. The movement's agenda was clearly enunciated in the *Frontier*'s premier issue:

> We consider the creation of a Jewish labor society in Palestine as the chief task of our generation. This does not mean, however, that we will disregard the tormenting problems of Jews in the diaspora countries. We consider it our function to mirror the Jewish struggle for existence in the difficult transition period which whole countries and continents are now experiencing. Because we are "Palestinocentric," we cannot ignore the diaspora. We cannot be indifferent to the problems of world Jewry in general or American Jewry in particular because the diaspora is the reservoir from which the Jewish homeland must be fed, and because we feel that the anguished problems of Jews the world over must be examined in the light of our analysis. Heartened by the social and cultural rejuvenation of the Jewish worker in Palestine, we will conscientiously seek means of reconstructing our American Jewish life on the basis of productive labor and of cultural expression.
>
> We believe that the new values created in Palestine—the rapture of pioneering, the ennobling of human labor, the heroic attempt to elevate social relationships—are beginning to stimulate Jewish life everywhere. We seek to strengthen the dynamic influence of Palestine Labor on Jewish life in America by means of an informed alert, public opinion. Particularly today, when reaction and suicidal cupidity threaten to invalidate all that has been achieved in Palestine, we feel that there must be a publication which will interpret contemporary events in Palestine and take its stand on the frontiers of Jewish life throughout the world. We represent that synthesis in Jewish

thought, which is nationalist without being chauvinist, and which stands for fundamental economic reconstruction without being communist. Only such a synthesis can answer the need of the disorientated modern Jew.[141]

The development of a new literary approach went hand in hand with an internal reevaluation of the American movement's fundamental stance. The stringent political platform of previous years, that is, the Borochovian canon—"Our ultimate aim, our maximum program is socialism. . . . Our immediate aim, our minimum program is Zionism"—was dramatically reversed.[142] Adjusting to the problems and possibilities of Jewish life in America, the Labor Zionists effected a subtle but nonetheless considerable shift in movement policy. Palestine was transformed from a personal imperative into a "preference . . . as a potential Jewish territory" and the "chief channel for the flow of Jewish energy."[143]

In the 1930s, against the backdrop of changes in American Jewish life generally and Labor Zionism particularly, many rabbis found the scope and inducement to support Labor Palestine. In 1935, several hundred Reform and Conservative rabbis issued a joint statement entitled "The Rabbis of America to Labor Palestine." Stephen S. Wise, the group's spokesman, characterized the declaration as an affirmation of the rabbis' "basic agreement with the policies and practices of the Histadrut [and] Labor Palestine."[144] He further described Labor Palestine's efforts to build a cooperative society in Eretz Israel as the "summum bonum" (chief good) of Jewish life. He was joined by 240 other Reform rabbis, who summarized the Labor Zionist cause as follows:

> Its aim is to avoid erecting another social structure resting upon the sands of injustice and inequality. Its purpose is to appraise economic endeavor by the rule of service to the community rather than private profit. It seeks to secure a decent living standard for all workers. It underlines the importance of the welfare of the many rather than the luxury of the few. It stands upon the principle of the right of labor to bargain collectively. . . . It is engaged in the effort to . . . rehabilitate the middle class and direct it toward fundamentally productive channels of work. . . . This program of the Histadrut in Palestine, and the League for Labor Palestine in America, seems to us to be at one with the essential principles of prophetic idealism.[145]

Likewise, the Rabbinical Assembly of America, that is, the Conservative movement, officially declared:

We share with the Histadrut those religious ideas and ideals which recognize the sanctity and dignity of human life and which strive for the establishment of a society in which these ideals will be realized. We agree with the Histadrut that only through a cooperative commonwealth can such a society be established and these religious ideals be achieved.

We see in the Labor movement in Palestine the only instrument for obviating in that land the economic sins which have beset the modern world. As religious men we must give our whole-hearted support to the idealistic aspirations of the labor movement in the upbuilding of our homeland.[146]

The rabbis' statements are noteworthy for several reasons. First, they signaled an unprecedented endorsement by an important segment of American Jewish leaders for a particular Zionist agenda. This is all the more remarkable when considered in light of mainstream American Jewry's ambivalence toward Zionism and the Yishuv before World War II. The statement also contrasts sharply with the previous stance of the American Jewish religious establishment, which in its most extreme guise adhered to the unequivocal formula that "America is our Zion."[147] Second, it demonstrates a strong American Jewish disposition toward Labor Zionism as the most viable program to build the Yishuv. In a manner similar to Brandeis's dictum that "Zionism equals Americanism," the rabbis virtually endorsed the conception that Palestinocentrism equals Labor Zionism.[148] In part, this explains why the League for Labor Palestine and the *Frontier* made new inroads into American Jewry. In fact, the American Labor Zionist movement nearly doubled in size from 11,000 members to approximately 22,000 members between 1935 and 1937.[149] Third, the endorsement indirectly indicates the rabbis' negative view of Revisionist Zionist attempts to establish an American base in the latter 1930s.[150] In pointed reference to Revisionist claims, the Rabbinical Assembly of America—many of whose members were moderately supportive of socialism—publicly refuted the charge that Labor Zionists provoked class strife. Instead, the rabbis deemed such accusations "a cloak behind which reactionaries have taken refuge to attack those who strive to defend the rights of the oppressed."[151]

The creation of *Jewish Frontier* and the rabbis' endorsement of Labor Palestine highlight the intersection of Labor Zionism and American Jewish life in the middle 1930s. Such developments were not merely manifestations of accommodationist strategies. Instead, they reflect a thoughtful and collaborative reassessment of American Jewry's evolving character during the interwar years. To be sure, American Labor Zionism was idiosyncratic in its philosophical orientation. Party discipline often yielded to the exigencies of American Jewish life. Despite the movement's fractious and frequently disorganized character, on the whole it responded positively to opportunities for collaboration with other groups.

In the decades that bridged the world wars, American Labor Zionism consolidated its support network on the regional and national levels. It did so while preserving its unique character, affirming the centrality of Eretz Israel in Jewish life, and raising the profile of the haluzim in Palestine. Yet like other American Zionists, Labor Zionists counted themselves among the fortunate Jews of the Western diaspora and felt a special sense of kinship with their American brethren. Consequently, except for a self-selecting group of socialist Zionist youth, the American Labor Zionist movement ceased to promote *shlilat hagolah* (negation of the exile) and *kibbutz galuyot* (ingathering of the exiles) as the crux of its philosophy. Instead, Palestine was billed as "a home for millions of Jews who feel themselves economically, politically or spiritually homeless in various countries of the world."[152] To be sure, this characterization did aptly describe the predicament of European Jews after 1933, but it was not a category in which American Zionists placed themselves. In many ways, Labor Zionists remained distinct from their coreligionists, but on one score they were in complete agreement: the American diaspora was different.

3

The Zionist Pioneer in the Mind of American Jews

Between 1881 and 1924, the American Jewish community absorbed approximately two million Jewish immigrants from eastern Europe. In the wake of this historic encounter, American Jewry became preoccupied, at every level, with the quest for a new and meaningful social and cultural synthesis. With the onset of World War I, the interests of American Jews and the Zionist movement intersected. During this period, Zionist propaganda fired the American Jewish imagination and became integral to the relationship between American Jews and the Yishuv. An examination of this phenomenon yields two conclusions. First, on the whole, American Jewish attitudes toward Zionism and the Yishuv were disproportionately influenced by perceptions of the pioneering enterprise in Palestine. This pattern crystallized during the interwar period and reinforced American Jewry's growing attraction to the Jewish state-in-the-making. Second, the Labor Zionist movement itself nurtured this development by promoting a distinct image of the *haluzim* (pioneers). No official decision was ever made in this regard, but in time, Labor's relentless propaganda campaign penetrated the divergent and disparate spheres of American Jewish life.

Emma Lazarus was one of the first American Jewish writers to use literary images and motifs that anticipated American Zionist mythology. For example, in "The Banner of the Jew" (1882), she glorified the nationalist heroism of ancient Jewish warriors:

> Wake, Israel, wake! Recall today
> The glorious Maccabean rage,
> The sire heroic, hoary-gray,
> His five-fold lion-lineage:
> The Wise, the Elect, the Hep-of-God,
> The Burst-of-Spring, the Avenging Rod . . .

O deem not the dead that martial fire,
Say not the mystic flame is spent!
With Moses' law and David's lyre,
Your ancient strength remains unbent.
Let but an Ezra rise anew,
To lift the banner of the Jew![1]

Lazarus's poem, composed in the aftermath of the Russian pogroms of 1881–1882, rejects the status quo of Jewish life in the diaspora. In contrast to the defenseless Jewish population of eastern Europe, Lazarus depicts Jewish standard-bearers who wage battle against a world of oppressive gentile forces. Her heroes are transcendent Jews who possess extraordinary powers and are poised to overcome all obstacles. Referring to Ezra the biblical scribe, she implies that those who zealously defend Jewish life will bring "the springtime in the national history of Judaism."[2]

Lazarus also publicly decried the political neglect of the Jews by Western civilization. She held that the unimpeded abuse of "a handful of wretched Jews" in the East disgraced all of humanity. "The Jewish problem is as old as history, and assumes in each age a new form. The life or death of millions of human beings hangs upon its solution; its agitation revives the fiercest passions for good and evil that inflame the human breast."[3]

Lazarus was not an original Jewish thinker like Leon Pinsker, whose anonymously published *Autoemancipation: Ein Mahnruf an seine Stammesgenossen von einem russischen Juden* (Autoemancipation: an appeal to his people by a Russian Jew) (1882) she greatly admired.[4] Yet her outspoken efforts on behalf of east European Jews did attract the attention of many acculturated "German" Jews. Furthermore, her proto-Zionism, which fused a romantic conception of the Jewish past with a passionate concern for current Jewish affairs, struck a responsive chord among traditional and Reform Jews as well as the early generation of Lovers of Zion in the United States.[5]

A decade later, the Vienna-based journalist Theodor Herzl, the founder of political Zionism, employed similar themes in "A Solution of the Jewish Question." Herzl's article first appeared in London's *Jewish Chronicle* in January 1896 and preceded the publication of his treatise *Der Judenstaat* (The Jews' state) by a month. In the article, Herzl contemplated the social and political climate of Europe as well as the "human resources" required by the Zionist enterprise:

It is remarkable that we Jews should have dreamt this kingly dream all through the long night of our history. Now day is dawning. We need only rub the sleep out of our eyes, stretch our limbs, and convert the dream into a reality. . . . We who are the first to inaugurate this glorious moment, will scarcely live to see its glorious close. . . . Our lives represent but a moment in the permanent duration of our people. This moment has its duties. . . . And what glory awaits those who fight unselfishly for the cause! A wondrous generation of Jews will spring into existence. The Maccabeans will rise again.[6]

That Herzl, like Lazarus, chose the Maccabees to symbolize his plans for Jewish renaissance is not surprising. He glorified the leaders of the Hasmonean revolt as exemplars of Davidic bravery capable of inspiring contemporary Jews. In his view, the fusion of prophecy and politics held the key to transforming Jewish reality, and he intentionally espoused a Zionist mythology of transcendent and metahistorical proportions.[7] Echoing Western imperialist sentiment typical of the fin de siècle, Herzl maintained that political Zionism would redound to the betterment of all humanity: "The world will be freed by our liberty, enriched by our wealth, magnified by our greatness."[8]

Lazarus's and Herzl's Jewish nationalist mythology can be located in the context of Oriental and Occidental symbolic tradition.[9] Their "glorious" and "wondrous" Maccabean prototypes differ in significant ways, however, from archetypal Eastern and Western heroes. The "standard path" of the hero, Joseph Campbell tells us, is to "venture forth from the world of common day into a region of supernatural wonder."[10] The Jewish hero, on the other hand, is confronted by situations for which he does not necessarily volunteer. Rather, he is compelled by external forces to act. Indeed, Jewish mythology abounds with ordinary people who reluctantly become heroes as a result of extraordinary circumstances.

Another factor that sets apart Jewish hero mythology is the singular context of the Jewish diaspora, a framework rooted in the concepts of "exile" and "chosenness." Lazarus's and Herzl's themes are meant to dramatize the predicament of Jewish life in the late nineteenth century. The proto-Zionist and Herzlian heroes break with their past and contemporary society in radical ways, and they subsequently undergo a process of this-worldly self-transformation. Their tasks, fraught with hardship and danger, are intended to demonstrate selfless devotion to the cause of rebuilding Zion. In sum, they embody the concept of *shivat Zion* (the return to Zion) and the fulfillment of Jewish prophecy, *kibbutz galuyot* (the ingathering of the exiles).' Even the restoration of the Jewish polity is viewed in quasi-religious terms, as it advances the interests of the Jewish people and humanity.[11]

Such heroic icons and motifs also fueled the discontent of Jewish youth in eastern Europe. Herzl's insight into the power that lay behind such symbolism, especially in an era of rising antisemitism and pogroms, was crucial to the success of early Zionist propaganda.[12] The vision of Maccabean resurgence lent weight to Herzl's credibility and captured the minds and hearts of the younger generation, particularly in the Pale of Settlement. There the Russian revolutionary climate produced a cohort of Zionist youth who were also inspired by the message of radical socialism. A movement of Zionist pioneers emerged from this element, and they proclaimed themselves the advance guard of the Jewish people. They called themselves haluzim, a term derived from the biblical story in which Moses commanded the tribes of Gad and Reuben to take part in the invasion of Canaan: "We ourselves will cross over as haluzim, at the instance of the Lord, into the land of Canaan; and we shall keep our hereditary holding across the Jordan."[13] The term haluz also appears in the book of Joshua: "And [Joshua] said unto the people: 'Pass on, encompass the city, and let the haluz pass on before the ark of the Lord . . . ' and the haluz went before the priests that blew the horns."[14]

Most east European haluzim hailed from traditional households and purposely chose to identify with their biblical namesakes. In this way, they co-opted the primacy of the haluz in biblical space and time as well as the sense of divine mission symbolized by the haluz. Generational discord also played a key role in the formation of their identity.[15] The gradual disintegration of traditional communal authority and the bleak prospects for the future of east European Jewish life reinforced the younger generation's sense of despair. Secular educated Jewish youth found further justification for their grievances in the Russian radical milieu where some of the most influential literati and theorists celebrated epic battles between fathers and sons.[16] In the wake of the pogroms and the expulsion of the Jews from Moscow, many disillusioned Jewish radicals, including some who previously forswore their identity as Jews, embraced Herzl's modern national mission.[17]

The concept of Jewish nationalism gradually permeated east European Jewish popular culture. Zionist hero mythology stimulated broad segments of Russian and Polish Jewish society, and Herzl himself was rapidly integrated into the Zionist hero legend.[18] Likewise, groups of socialist Zionist youth romanticized the Biluim, the pioneer forerunners of the Second Aliyah whose name derived from the biblical phrase "O house of Jacob, come, let us walk" (Isa. 2:5).[19] Joseph Vitkin's "Call to the Jewish Youth"

(1904) is an excellent example of this. Vitkin made explicit the connection among the glory of ancient Israel, the Biluim, and the members of diaspora haluz groups: "Hasten and come, O heroes of Israel! Revive the days of the Biluim with increased strength and valor."[20] Following the precedent established by Herzl and others who mixed biblical and modern themes, Vitkin exploited the younger generation's messianic sensibility by placing responsibility for the Zionist "hero task" squarely on the shoulders of Jewish youth.[21]

The late nineteenth and early twentieth centuries witnessed several competing east European attitudes toward Jewish life in the New World. Socialism, Zionism, anarchism, Communism, and traditional Judaism all existed in a state of dynamic tension. East European Jewish immigrants responded in part to their environment on the basis of these differing cultural and philosophical viewpoints. Then in 1903, this fragile and chaotic immigrant milieu was completely torn asunder when the tide of Jewish migration surged in the aftermath of the Kishinev pogroms.[22] Continued waves of anti-Jewish rioting in eastern Europe and the failed Russian revolution of 1905 exacerbated these trends.[23]

Jewish immigrants arriving in the United States after the turning point of 1903–1905 swelled the ranks of local Jewish mutual aid societies, landsmanshaftn, trade union groups, settlement houses, and Zionist associations.[24] The new wave of immigrants came face to face with an earlier generation of Russian, Polish, and Romanian Jewish ex-patriots, large numbers of whom were already becoming integrated into American society. The latter group, unlike the central European Jews who preceded them, neither were assimilationists nor were inclined toward Reform conceptions of American Judaism. Instead, the early waves of east European Jewish immigrants formulated their own New World identity.

Against this backdrop, we can gain insight into the emergent haluz image by examining the different responses to the program of cultural nationalism. One approach is well illustrated by the case of Abraham Isaac Saklad, a native of Slonim, Russia, who emigrated to Boston in the early 1880s. Saklad, a staunch Hebraist, founded a school whose language of instruction was Hebrew. His ethical will, which he composed during a 1906 visit to Turkish-ruled Palestine, admonished his family to

> be good Jews, and let all that is Jewish be close to your hearts. For the Jew
> is distinct among the nations wherever he may dwell upon this globe. . . .

Should you, by chance, be employed in menial work, it matters not, for as long as the work is honest your soul will be clean and at peace. Do not forever strive to be a doctor or a lawyer, for therein is trouble and travail everywhere. . . . Love the land of your forefathers, and come, like myself, to visit the Wailing Wall. Dear Children, pay heed to these words. Keep them impressed in your hearts. Children, you are building a better world.[25]

Saklad's will bears the unmistakable imprint of the east European Jewish immigrant milieu. Devoted to diaspora Jewish life and the notion of Jewish cultural autonomy, Saklad was a passionate nationalist who viewed Eretz Israel in both personal and existential terms. His wariness of bourgeois professions and glorification of physical toil also reflects, at least implicitly, the radical proclivity of his generation. Such tendencies were manifest in concrete form by the Am Olam (Eternal People) movement in America and the haluzim in Palestine.[26] In short, the weltanschauung of Saklad's generation, which opposed the prevailing American Jewish veneration of "the learned professions" (law and medicine), was rebellious and, in many instances, revolutionary.[27]

Saklad's statement is also an excellent example of American Jewry's budding attraction to the concept of "upbuilding" the Yishuv. For enthusiasts like Saklad, "menial" and "honest" labor symbolized the transformation of Jewish life in toto, in both its traditional and modern forms.[28] It offered a blueprint for the physical and spiritual regeneration of the Jewish people. Saklad, aware that the American reality propelled Jews in professional and industrial directions, emphasized the centrality of Eretz Israel in the Jewish spiritual and temporal worlds.[29]

By contrast, Eliezer Jaffe, a Russian immigrant youth, viewed Zionist pioneering as a personal imperative. In 1904, Jaffe immigrated to the United States to conduct Zionist propaganda work among east European Jewish immigrants. His persistent efforts led to the unification of several small groups of would-be haluzim in New York City.[30] In 1905, just a few years before Russian Hehaluz was formally established, Jaffe helped create the Hehaluz-Zion Circle, the first pioneering Zionist youth movement in the United States. The members proclaimed themselves the "avant garde of the battle to liberate [the Jewish] nation," and they advocated a radical program based on the territorial concentration of the Jewish people in Eretz Israel. They viewed themselves as heirs to the tradition of the Biluim and believed that only a revolution in their personal lives would lead to the creation of a Jewish state.[31]

Despite Jaffe's success in uniting several socialist Zionist groups on the eastern seaboard, including some affiliates of the Poalei Zion Party, American Hehaluz remained a small and exclusive organization. After a brief agricultural training period in Woodbine, New Jersey, the group decided to reorganize and form a new society, hoping to appeal to a broader constituency and attract newcomers from nonimmigrant Jewish circles. Thus in 1908, Hehaluz was reconstituted as Haikar Hazair (The Young Farmer). While retaining most of the original Hehaluz platform, Haikar Hazair relinquished the claim of complete organizational autonomy and affiliated with the Federation of American Zionists, the official wing of the world Zionist organization in the United States. This arrangement was a marriage of convenience. The FAZ, embroiled in a protracted struggle over the leadership of the American Zionist movement, sought allies and means of increasing its numbers in order to combat the antiestablishment claims of its chief rival, the Order of the Knights of Zion in Chicago.[32] For its part, Haikar Hazair exploited the FAZ's support and adopted the dual strategy of reaching potential recruits beyond the socialist immigrant sphere and directly contacting American-born Jewish youth. Haikar Hazair's efforts were unsuccessful, however, and the group disbanded in 1912 when its core members, including Jaffe himself, emigrated to Palestine and joined the Kinneret settlement in the Jordan Valley.[33]

The cases of Hehaluz and Haikar Hazair reveal the web of forces that shaped American Jewish attitudes toward the haluz archetype before World War I. Unlike east European Hehaluz, which emerged in the final years of Imperial Russia's repressive czarist regime, the American haluz movement arose in an atmosphere of unprecedented religious and political freedom.[34] As revealed in the Hehaluz constitution and a 1908 photograph of the group, the members of the Hehaluz-Zion Circle were aware of their unique position. The photograph, taken in the Woodbine agricultural colony, shows a group of nineteen young men in front of Zionist and American flags (figure 2). A portrait of Herzl hangs below the Zionist flag; a portrait of U.S. president Theodore Roosevelt is beneath the American flag. The men are neatly groomed and dressed in military uniforms and hold a banner shaped like a star of David bearing the words "Hehaluz-Zion Circle" (*sic*).[35] Although the group proudly displays its Jewish and American affinities, the photograph betrays a lack of syncretism. On the one hand, the members of the Hehaluz-Zion Circle subscribed to Herzl's nationalist program and an east European view of organic Jewish nationhood. On the other, they acknowledged their debt to America's pluralist tradition and responded enthusiastically to the call of Western liberalism. This paradox,

2. Photograph of Hehaluz–Zion Circle, Woodbine Colony, New Jersey (1908).
Courtesy of the Lavon Institute for Labor Movement Research, Tel Aviv.

Anita Shapira asserts, was characteristic of early socialist Zionism, especially in the West.[36]

The doctrine of *hagshamah azmit* (self-realization), the act of immigration to Eretz Israel embodied by the haluz, linked Hehaluz and its successor Haikar Hazair. This idealistic goal was a logical extension of the classic Zionist position known as *shlilat hagolah* (negation of the exile). Regarded by both groups as a sine qua non, the concept of hagshamah azmit separated the haluzim from mainstream American Zionist activity. It also served a variety of less apparent purposes. First, it answered the psychological need of Zionist youth who wanted to distinguish themselves from their elders and provided a constructive framework for channeling the young pioneers' rebellious and revolutionary passions. Second, it invested the haluz movement, an avowedly secular framework, with a sense of sacred purpose. Living in Eretz Israel, the haluzim claimed, fulfilled one of Judaism's central tenets. In fact, a generation earlier, no less a figure than Rabbi Samuel Mohilever, the leader of east European Hibbat Zion, defended the special role of secular pioneer youth in rebuilding the Jewish homeland.[37]

It was in this context that American haluzim identified themselves as the modern inheritors of the Jewish people's religious-historical legacy. Jaffe was among the first to articulate this view in the United States, advocating the emigration of groups of haluzim to Palestine and their settlement on the land. These youth, he asserted, would fulfill Herzl's vision and spur the political and economic regeneration of the Jewish people. In fact, he went further, insisting that haluzim who returned to the diaspora should be expelled from the Zionist movement and shunned: "We have no use in our ranks for weak individuals not prepared to sacrifice themselves in the ongoing life struggle for the advancement of our nation."[38] Jaffe believed that the power of the Zionist hero myth depended as much on winning a decisive moral victory as it did on entering the fray,[39] and he contended that haluzim who returned from Palestine tainted and jeopardized Zionist idealism.

No doubt Jaffe also had in mind the lackluster performance of the FAZ, the Knights of Zion, and the scattered Lovers of Zion groups when he decried the alleged failure of haluzim who returned to the United States. From his east European perspective, these groups—which in 1918 merged to form the Zionist Organization of America—were exploiting Jewish nationalist sympathies solely for utilitarian organizational needs. Jaffe was correct in at least one respect: American Zionists were ambivalent about the doctrines of hagshamah azmit and *haluziut* (pioneering).[40]

Before World War I, most affiliated Zionists viewed Eretz Israel in "Ahad Haamist" terms, that is, as a spiritual center that would uplift the Jewish diaspora.[41] The rabbinical scholars Israel Friedlaender, Judah L. Magnes, and Solomon Schechter were among the leading proponents of this conception. As Schechter himself explained in 1906,

> The activity of Zionism must not be judged by what it has accomplished in Zion and Jerusalem—where it has to deal with political problems as yet not ripe for solution—but by what it has thus far achieved *for* Zion and Jerusalem, through the awakening of the national Jewish consciousness.[42]

According to this outlook, even secular haluzim fulfilled a special quasi-spiritual role for American Zionists, functioning as proxies for American Jews who were unable and unwilling to assume direct personal responsibility for building the Yishuv. Despite their relatively small numbers, the haluzim in Palestine served as a living link to the Jewish national home. This relationship was not unlike the traditional one that had existed for centuries between diaspora Jews and the Holy Land. Only now, American Jews considered the haluzim to be the modern agents of national redemption, and they regarded the haluz movement literally and figuratively as the cornerstone of the "House of Israel."

The philosophical approach of Young Judea, the ZOA's centrist youth organization, exemplifies this trend. Young Judea sustained a vicarious and distinctly American fascination with the Zionist pioneering enterprise. A 1912 issue of the *Young Judean*, for example, contains the following story and commentary entitled "Jewish Minute Men":

> "Father, buy me the weapons of a *shomer* [Hebrew watchman]," said a little Palestinian Jew when asked to choose a [Passover] gift for himself. "And what will you do with the weapons?" inquired the father smiling. "Fight off the robbers!" came the prompt reply.
>
> This little story illustrates the development of a new type of Jewish heroes—the *shomrim*, or Jewish watchmen of Palestine. Formerly the Jewish settlers would hire Arab watchmen to protect their lives and property from the half-savage Bedouins and lawless Arabs, who cannot distinguish between "mine" and "thine." Curiously enough the colonists had no faith in the bravery of Jewish watchmen but considered them incapable of fighting off robbers and enemies. Gradually, however, they learned that their so-called watchmen were helping their Arabian countrymen to rob the Jews of the fruit of their toil. At the same time, the shomrim by fearlessness, by undying devotion and loyalty to duty, finally won the admiration of everyone. Now all the colonies are replacing their Arab watchmen with Jewish men and the results are startling. Thefts and robberies have stopped as if by magic, and general order has been established.
>
> But this great change could not come about without precious sacrifices. Thirteen young, heroic, patriotic Jews have fallen in encounters with the enraged and jealous Arabs. The thirteenth, Sacharoff, was recently shot by cowardly enemies in Rishon le-Zion and died a martyr to his Zionist convictions. Peace be unto his memory![43]

"Jewish Minute Men" entwines a diverse array of symbols and Americanizes the image of the shomer, the functional equivalent of the haluz. Set against the backdrop of Passover, the holiday celebrating Jewish liberation from Egyptian bondage, the tale proudly depicts shomrim guarding local colonists and their property. Like the patriots of the American Revolution

3. Illustration from *Young Judean*, October 1912. The caption reads "Yigael fired, one Arab was wounded, the horse of the second killed." Courtesy of the American Jewish Historical Society.

and the cowboys of the Wild West, the shomrim ride horses, protect the frontier, and defy the "half-savage" and "lawless" indigenous inhabitants (figure 3). Acting as a self-regulated police force, the shomrim are loyal and dutiful, end thefts and robberies "as if by magic," and restore public order. In this formative period, such stereotypes became prevalent in American Zionist thinking. Zionist leaders, too, fostered blatantly romantic portrayals of the Yishuv. In 1915, for instance, Louis D. Brandeis declared:

> In the Jewish colonies of Palestine there are no Jewish criminals; because everyone old and young alike, is led to feel the glory of his people and his obligation to carry forward its ideals. The new Palestinian Jewry produces

instead of criminals, scientists like Aaron Aaronsohn, the discoverer of wild wheat; pedagogues like David Yellin; craftsmen like Boris Schatz, the founder of the Bezalel [School for Industrial Arts]; intrepid *shomrim*, the Jewish guards of peace, who watch in the night against the marauders and doers of violent deeds.[44]

Israel Friedlaender, a communal leader and rabbinical scholar, was another eminent agent of nationalist optimism. In 1917, he supplemented his classic formulation "Zionism plus diaspora, Palestine plus America"[45] with the following hopeful assessment which he published in the *American Hebrew:* "In one generation [the Jews of Palestine] . . . have evolved a new form of Jewish self-government, a self-government without an army, without a police, without jails and without coercion—and without a single theft and without a single murder."[46] Friedlaender himself was murdered in 1920 while on a Joint Distribution Committee relief mission in Ukraine.

The shomer/haluz composite implicit in Friedlaender's idealized pioneering community and explicit in "Jewish Minute Men" and Brandeis's remarks, highlights the mentality of American Jews who yearned for the creation of a model Jewish society in Palestine. The shomer/haluz is portrayed in heroic and very American terms, in a context of good versus evil; the non-Jewish villains are vanquished, and the Jewish heroes either are victorious or die as martyrs to the Zionist cause. Why did organizations like Young Judea and individuals like Brandeis and Friedlaender—all of whom surely had access to more realistic information—portray the haluzim and the Yishuv in this manner? The answer is, perhaps, revealed in a 1914 issue of the *High School Zionist:*

> Shall I tell you that Palestine is a land of sickness, that the Arab there annoys the [Jewish] colonists, that poverty reigns there, that the hardships are innumerable? But the soul of me forbids it. It loves to picture the beautiful side.
> . . . It bids me to say unto you, who have never seen Palestine but in your dreams, that there—there in the mountains of Asher and Naphtali and Mount Hermon—upon the verderous country, upon the rushing rivers, upon its heavens of the East whither you turn in silent prayer lies a land, not inhabited by the hyena and the jackal and traversed only by the Bedouin, but adorned with the fig tree, under which the men of Israel sit. The soul of me bids me try—I may be able to help fan up the breath that will wake up these dead bones. Palestine, I shall not forget thee, and I shall sing thy praises from the housetops, for it is not I but you in all your might and renewed majesty who sing through me.[47]

This text demonstrates the willingness of most Jews to ignore the hardships of Jewish life in Palestine, instead viewing the haluzim and the Yishuv through the prism of their Americanized identity. Like members of other ethnic groups, the *High School Zionist* alleged, Zionists were "broad-minded enough to disclaim the accident of birth and to ally themselves to Italians and Irishmen and Germans." They wanted to face non-Jews as equals and establish a foothold in American society without succumbing to assimilationist pressures. Thus they exploited the image of an unspoiled Jewish Palestine to assert their communal power and adventurous spirit. Their message echoed the New World myth of abundance and opportunity, and they deliberately linked their romantic conceptions of the American and Zionist frontiers.

Another type of Zionist hero depicted in the *Young Judean* is the haluz as farmer. In the article "Jewish Arbor Day" (an Americanized construct of the Jewish holiday Tu Bishvat, the festival of the new year of trees), a haluz is shown planting olive trees while instructing another young pioneer and a boy in the sacred national task of "afforestation" (figure 4). A woman carrying a basket approaches, and behind her, nestled at the bottom of a valley, is a small Jewish colony surrounded by olive groves. Describing this idyllic scene, the writer notes:

> Long, long ages ago, our forefathers living each under his own vine and fig tree in the Land of Israel celebrated Arbor Day. . . . Just how the custom began, nobody knows now. . . . From a tradition of the Jewish past, it has been transformed into a symbol of the Jewish future. All of the Young Judeans know how Jewish pioneers have settled in the old land as colonists and made the desolate, arid wastes to bloom, as of old.[48]

The purpose of the article "Jewish Arbor Day" is threefold. First, the writer depicts the haluzim in romantic agrarian terms. In this way, she neutralizes the image of Palestine as a harsh and inhospitable land, and the haluz assumes the exalted position of caretaker and guardian. Second, the haluz is glorified as a transcendent figure, a living link between the Jewish past and future, a proxy whose selfless devotion revives the Palestinian landscape and the Zionist claim to the land's "blessed soil."[49] Third, the piece is essentially propagandistic, explicitly appealing to the reader to support the Jewish National Fund's tree-planting efforts.

As both farmer and redeemer, the haluz was central to American Zionist mythology. Whether ancient or modern, imaginary or realistic, the haluz motif illustrated a productive and metaphysical relationship between the

4. Illustration from *Young Judean*, January 1912. The caption reads "Planting the Olive Tree." Courtesy of the American Jewish Historical Society.

Jew and the Land of Israel (figures 5 and 6), which helps explain why Aaron Aaronsohn, the charismatic Palestinian agronomist mentioned earlier, was so popular with American Zionists. Even non-Zionist American Jews, including elite "German" Jews opposed to Zionism, were enraptured by Aaronsohn. He symbolized the promise of the new generation, specifically "young Palestinian Jews," and was considered a premier representative of the Yishuv's industrious Jewish colonies.[50] "Are you not proud," the *Young Judean* asked rhetorically, "that [wild wheat] was discovered in Palestine—your land and by the efforts of one of your people—a Jew?"[51]

During World War I, the emerging American Jewish fascination with the haluz was exploited by Labor Zionist propagandists. In this period, David

5. "Agriculture in Old Palestine." The original caption read, "The agricultural implements used by the natives of Palestine are the same as were used by the Romans in the first and second centuries. It does not require an agricultural expert to recognize how primitive this team and driver are."

(כיאנראפישע נאטיץ)

דער ליעבלינג פון זיינע חברים וועכטער און איינער פון די בעסטע איבערגעגעבענסטע ארבייטער און מעהינסטע רייטער און שיסער אין ארץ ישראל — איז
געווען דער פריהצייטיג געפאלענער מאיר חאזאנאוויטש.

6. Title page of Meir Hazanovich biography in *Yizkor*, ed. A. Hashin and D. Ben-Gurion (New York: Poale Zion Palestine Komite, 1916).

Ben-Gurion, Yizhak Ben-Zvi, and Yaakov Zerubavel, three Russian political activists expelled from Palestine by the ruling Ottoman regime,[52]
made a concerted effort to revitalize the now-defunct American Hehaluz
movement. In 1916 they published an influential pamphlet entitled *Hehaluz: prinzipn un oifgebn* (Hehaluz: principles and aims). Among the articles,
Ben-Gurion's "Who Will Give Us the Land?" is a striking example of
Zionist hero mythology transplanted to the American scene. The article
had two major objectives. First, Ben-Gurion argued in favor of socialist
Zionism on pseudoreligious grounds. He did so by modeling his treatise
after Haim N. Bialik's famous poem "Shir haavodah vehamlakhah"[53]
(Song of work and labor), which was a secular Zionist alternative to "Birkat
hamazon,"[54] the traditional grace said after meals.

Like Bialik, whose poem refuted Jewish liturgy and sanctified the cultural-political values of the Labor Zionist movement in Eretz Israel, Ben-
Gurion employed traditional themes and terminology to give his manifesto
religious overtones. He pointed to the "darkness" enshrouding the Jewish
people (i.e., exile) and the "bolt of light" that would "redeem and liberate"
the nation (i.e., Zionism). The "catastrophe" of homelessness, he observed,
flowed from the defeat of the Bar-Kokhba revolt in 135 C.E. down to the
present. At last, the time had come for a new generation of Jewish warriors
to "sound the shofar [ram's horn] blast of the Messiah" and rouse the
Jewish people from its dormant state.[55]

Ben-Gurion also tried to distinguish Labor Zionism from other schools
of Zionist thought. Obliquely referring to the world movement's Herzlian
philosophy and the FAZ's Brandesian leadership, he questioned the efficacy
of attempts to "conquer" Eretz Israel through "political and diplomatic
conjuring tricks." He also denigrated the militaristic brand of Zionism promoted by Vladimir Jabotinsky, the right-wing Zionist leader who espoused
the creation of a separate Jewish regiment to fight with the Allies in World
War I. Such a unit, Jabotinsky argued, should be stationed in the Middle
East to safeguard Western interests and provide a foothold for the Jews in
Palestine.[56] Ben-Gurion's initial view, however, was that neither legal ar-
rangements nor the "force of arms" would ensure Jewish freedom in Palestine. Only the ingathering of the Jewish people in its own land and the
creation of a Jewish workers' society in accordance with Ber Borochov's
determinist "stychic" (read: spontaneous) process would guarantee the successful establishment of the Jewish national home.[57] "Not by money, not
by recognition of our rights," Ben-Gurion declared, "and not from the
hands of the peace conference shall we receive our land. The Jewish worker

who will come to establish roots in the land, to be renewed, and to live there—he will give us the land. Eretz Israel shall be ours if we become her workers."[58]

Ben-Gurion's article displays an important facet of Labor Zionist propaganda in the United States. Employing biblical motifs and Marxist rhetoric, "Who Will Give Us the Land?" was an attempt to win Jewish immigrants to the Labor Zionist movement by appealing to their religious and philosophical sympathies. To a limited extent, Ben-Gurion, Ben-Zvi, and Zerubavel succeeded, at least insofar as the reorganization of American Hehaluz was concerned. With the escalation of the war, however, popular sentiment increasingly favored Jabotinsky's plan for a Jewish legion. In light of this trend, Ben-Gurion and Ben-Zvi adjusted their scheme to fit the changing Jewish political climate. They not only threw their support behind the idea of a Jewish military force but also assumed the leadership of the campaign in the United States.

Yizkor (Remember), a memorial book published in New York in 1916 by the Poalei Zion Party, also exemplifies Labor Zionist propaganda in the United States. Edited by Ben-Gurion and A. Hashin, the Yiddish volume pays homage to the fallen shomrim of the Yishuv. (*Yizkor* derives its title from the traditional Jewish memorial service.)[59] Paradoxically, even though *Yizkor* commemorates the martyrdom of several haluzim, it is essentially a secular propaganda vehicle. Its message is conveyed by icons and motifs that substitute Labor Zionist notions for traditional religious themes.[60] The book's cover is all black, embossed with gold lettering (figure 7). In the upper left-hand corner, a prominent design spells out the word *yizkor*. Drops fall from the intertwined letters which, according to Jewish tradition, represent different spiritual and mystical properties.[61] Accordingly, the book assumes a dualistic quality by symbolizing both the sacred and the profane tasks of the Zionist enterprise. Whether the drops represent blood, sweat, or tears is unclear. Perhaps, like the letters themselves, they are meant to indicate all three dimensions simultaneously.

The frontispiece of the volume also uses a black background (figure 8), although in this instance, it is a night sky broken by the stars, the moon, and the word *yizkor*. In the foreground, a shomer stands guard, mounted on a horse. Dressed in typical Palestinian garb, he wears a *kafiyah* (Arab headdress) and holds a rifle. Behind him, a body of moonlit water meets the shoreline, and the horizon rises to the walls of an ancient fortress situated atop a bluff. The scene is meant to be a dramatic and powerful evocation of Zionist hero mythology, echoing some of contemporary Hebrew

7. Gold-embossed lettering on the cover of *Yizkor*, ed. A. Hashin and D. Ben-Gurion (New York: Poale Zion Palestine Komite, 1916).

8. Frontispiece of *Yizkor*, ed. A. Hashin and D. Ben-Gurion (New York: Poale Zion Palestine Komite, 1916).

fiction's dominant themes.[62] The recurrence of the word *yizkor* is significant, too, as it offsets the book cover's melancholic emblem and underscores the importance of the shomer's courage, fortitude, and faith.

Among the volume's other revealing graphics is a toppled *menorah* (candelabrum). Despite its horizontal position, the menorah continues to burn as flames and smoke rise, scorching what appear to be draperies in the Holy Temple of Jerusalem (figure 9). Beside the menorah lies a book, and on its cover is written *yizkor*. Set in this context, the solitary dictum is reminiscent of the popular Zionist motto "In blood and fire did Judea fall; in blood and fire shall Judea rise."[63] As such, the menorah signifies more than the conquest of Palestine; it also represents a struggle between the Jewish people and *goyei haarazot* (the nations of the world), a battle of apocalyptical dimensions between good and evil.[64] The haluzim—like the Maccabees who entered the desecrated Temple—will act as divine agents and reestablish God's kingdom on earth.

Despite their tireless propaganda efforts, Ben-Gurion and Ben-Zvi failed to turn Hehaluz into a large organization. Both men traveled across the United States and Canada, establishing the seeds of haluz groups in several cities and towns[65] and hoping that their efforts would be aided by general and Jewish interest in Palestine as well as the wartime atmosphere.[66] Furthermore, they thought their unusual status as Palestinians—as was the case with Aaron Aaronsohn—would be helpful. Unlike Jaffe, who had little previous experience in Zionist politics and none whatsoever in Palestine, by the time Ben-Gurion and Ben-Zvi arrived in the United States, they were central players in the Palestinian labor movement. They therefore could speak with authority about actual conditions in the Yishuv and move easily within Jewish immigrant and Zionist circles. In 1918 they even published a Yiddish book entitled *Eretz yisroel* which described the geography and inhabitants of modern Palestine.[67] Such efforts, they believed, would resonate with the cultural values of the Jewish immigrant masses and attract a new cadre of American haluzim. The Zionist troika could not, however, overcome the indomitable trend of Jewish acculturation in the United States, and in their travels, they went almost unnoticed by the American Jewish press. Their "brethren," Ben-Zvi lamented, had been "seduced by the fleshpots of America, where "everything is done in a pragmatic, mercenary way."[68]

Nonetheless, the wartime atmosphere did spark new interest in Palestine. When Palestine was cut off from European markets and banks, the American Jewish community rallied to its defense. The American Jewish Joint Distribution Committee alone provided "nine hundred tons of food and

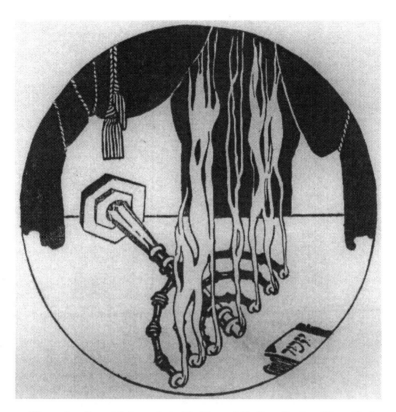

9. Illustration from *Yizkor*, ed. A. Hashin and D. Ben-Gurion (New York: Poale Zion Palestine Komite, 1916).

medicine" in 1915, and by 1918, it had transmitted a total of $2,257,300 to Palestine through the Zionist Relief Commission. Such support was crucial to the Jewish national home's security and stability.[69]

Kadimah, a book published by the Intercollegiate Zionist Association of America (IZAA) in 1918, is one barometer of wartime American Jewish attitudes toward Zionism and the haluzim. The title of the book, adapted from the name of a European Zionists students' society, is translated in the preface as follows: "It means 'Eastward,' it means 'Back to the days of old,' and it means 'Onward.' Today the word has an additional meaning. It is the Hebrew for 'Forward, march!' "[70] That the members redefined the organization's name to fit a contemporary outlook demonstrates their independent thinking and understanding that American Zionism was based

10. Cover of *Kadimah*, ed. David S. Blondheim (New
York: Federation of American Zionists, 1918).

on a reality different from that of its European counterpart. Arguing that
"the struggle of the nation has strengthened the bond of nationality, quick-
ened the memory of a common fatherland, [and] kindled love for Judaism
and Jewish life" among Jewish college-age youth, the IZAA saw itself as a
"self-sacrificing" coterie dedicated to constructive Zionist work.[71]

The IZAA especially admired the example of the Jewish Legion. On the
book's cover is a silhouette of soldiers marching past a mosque and date
palms (figure 10). The heroic pose is a reminder that the Jewish
legionnaires—despite the Star of David on their caps, the word *Judeans* in
their shoulder insignias, and the use of Hebrew in their military
commands—considered themselves indistinguishable from other members
of the Allied forces.[72] The medium of the silhouette reinforces this point.

Were it not for the Hebrew word *kadimah* below the picture, there would be no hint of the regiment's specifically Jewish character.

In a chapter of *Kadimah* entitled "Hagdud Haivri" (The Jewish Legion), the members of the roughly 1,300 American recruits are described as lawyers, teachers, and students. Their passion for Hebrew and "eternal youthfulness" is said to reflect the fact that the soul of Joshua, David, and Judah Maccabee "has not been dead, but dormant." Many of the soldiers come from European backgrounds, the writer apologetically concedes, but they "long to shed their blood for the Jewish people" and represent the best of American idealism.[73] As such, they are true not only to their biblical heritage but also to all of Western tradition: "Dulce et decorum est pro patria mori" (It is sweet and glorious to die for one's country). To substantiate this claim, the writer offers the following description of a Jewish immigrant recruit:

> A Jewish driver entered the recruiting office and asked in uncouth Yiddish, "Do you take soldiers here for Palestine? I want to go myself." "Your age?" "Thirty-one." "Are you an American citizen?" "No." "Are you out of work?" "I make thirty to thirty-five dollars a week." "Why do you want to go?" He burst out in a rage and came near hitting the recruiting officer. "Are you a Jew? When they are fighting for Palestine, will I stay here? I can kill twenty Turks for one breakfast."[74]

The notion that the war served as a catalyst in transfiguring the "trembling, cowering denizen of the Ghetto into a stalwart, self-respecting Jewish soldier" was crucial to the self-image of the IZAA. Like the silhouette described earlier, a photograph of "members of the Third American Contingent of the Jewish Legion" attempts to show that native-born and immigrant recruits are indistinguishable (figure 11). Dressed in proper military attire and posed in orderly rows in front of New England barracks, the Jewish Legion is the very picture of an American force. Finally, the chapter noted "the mild surprise and mild admiration" of gentiles who saw "Jews [wearing] a Jewish uniform."[75] Despite its self-satisfied tone, this apologia betrays the IZAA's ambivalence about the need for Jewish separateness. Although its members viewed themselves in the context of Zionist mythology, they resisted decisively linking their fate to creating the Jewish national home.

After World War I, the Jewish traffic between the United States and Palestine greatly increased, giving rise to a popular and, in time, standardized

11. Photograph from *Kadimah*, ed. David S. Blondheim (New York: Federation of American Zionists, 1918), 25.

image of the haluz. Two factors were significant in this process. Most important, in the immediate postwar years the abstract and Americanized haluz image, which was cultivated by centrist Zionists, swiftly penetrated mainstream American Jewish culture. This development is ironic, especially in light of the fact that the Third Aliyah, the postwar wave of 37,000 new Jewish immigrants to Palestine, was made up largely of militant socialist Zionist youth.[76] Indeed, only a select group of American Jewish youth, mostly socialist Zionists and Hebraists themselves, viewed the new haluzim as personal role models. Meanwhile, the majority of American Jews were drawn to Louis D. Brandeis's vision of the haluzim as "Jewish Pilgrim fathers." To be sure, in the prestate period, American Zionism dutifully reflected the Brandeisian vision of Palestine.[77]

Second, Jewish educators were particularly important as organizational leaders and activists—including rabbis, journalists, and other figures in positions of communal authority—who played a role in transmitting the Zionist message to American Jews. As noted earlier, a cadre of trained Jewish educators came to the fore of American Jewish life during the interwar period.[78] This talented and skilled cohort significantly enhanced the process by which upwardly mobile and increasingly secular American Jews were

introduced to Zionism and the haluzim. Their success stemmed partly from their ability to blur the ideological disjunction between Jewish life in the American diaspora and the Yishuv. Furthermore, as Jewish immigrant youth became socialized to American norms and values through public education, they became responsive to adults who could help negotiate their Americanization. Thus the authority of Jewish educators generally grew as it became commonplace for adults to advise and supervise Jewish adolescent activities, especially those supported by the Jewish community.

A case in point is that of Alexander Dushkin and Isaac B. Berkson, former Zeirei Zion members and disciples of the Palestinian Jewish educator Samson Benderly, who warmed to the cause of Zionist education partially as a result of their own Hebraist youth experiences. As adults, they showed a keen interest in the educational activities of Jewish communal institutions like the National Farm School, an agricultural training program located in Woodbine, New Jersey. In 1919, after spending part of the summer in this setting, Dushkin wrote to Berkson about efforts to "strengthen Zionist influence there."

> Our three week stay here has been quite profitable and very pleasant. You paved the way for a fine understanding with the boys. . . . We were able to continue the general spirit of Jewish good fellowship which you introduced. Everybody is highly pleased all around. We continued the Friday evening

singing and reading hours, and toward the end, not only the students and the faculty, but a good many of the neighbors also attended these gatherings. I gave them a series of talks on Jewish history, and Herbert continued assiduously at his self-imposed task of teaching Hebrew. . . . Besides, we had a rather imposing commemoration of *Tisha Beav* [Ninth of Av], with Hurwich chanting the *Eiha* [Book of Lamentations]; held a herring and pumpernickel party on our porch; went on a camping expedition at Shaminy Creek with roasted corn and Jewish stories and songs as the *pièce de résistance*; and last night the boys gave us a surprise party at our Farm House. . . . At present the National Farm School is the only school of its kind in the country. . . . It is very much worthwhile to . . . perpetuate these [efforts and] summer courses.[79]

Dushkin's letter reflects the impact of adult educators on the emergence of groups of American Zionist youth in the postwar period. With their enthusiastic faith in the revitalizing power of Hebrew, many of these teachers were central to the effort to modernize American Jewish education. They also became pioneers in the Jewish summer camp movement, in which youth experienced Jewish education in an informal yet intensive group setting. This environment eschewed traditional methods of instruction, relying instead on Hebrew as the language of daily communication and on educational themes related to Jewish nationalism and the Zionist enterprise.[80] A number of Zionist camps also were established by activists who recognized the appeal of summer recreation facilities as laboratories of movement living.[81]

By substituting adult instruction for peer leadership, most Jewish youth frameworks kept the Zionist notion of hagshamah azmit at bay. In the American Jewish setting, the Zionist activist Jessie E. Sampter observed, the youth leader "is needed chiefly as intellectual and moral guide, as umpire and critic."[82] In most situations, however, this role was assumed by adults and professionals whose Zionist viewpoint was notably undogmatic. Men like Dushkin and Berkson were supportive of would-be American haluzim, but they did not rate their success in terms of American Jewish immigration to Palestine. Against this backdrop, Sampter's statement shows the enormous gap between mainstream American Zionist activity and groups that subscribed to the doctrine of hagshamah azmit. It also helps explain why the haluz, previously symbolized by the youthful pioneer who immigrated to Palestine, increasingly came to be viewed as an abstract hero. Instead of a flesh-and-blood figure who lived and worked in Eretz Israel, the haluz was mythologized as the vicarious embodiment of "the hopes and aspirations of [the] whole people" and "the energy of the whole nation."[83]

The Hebrew journal *Shaharut* (Youth) illustrates this transformation. Created in 1915 by Zvi Scharfstein, a well-known Hebrew publisher, educator, and journalist, *Shaharut* was issued by the Bureau of Jewish Education in New York City. It was originally devoted to teaching Jewish subjects and the Hebrew language. However, after the Balfour Declaration in 1917, the journal shifted its focus to short stories and articles about Jewish life in Palestine. Some sketches even taught readers about early groups of Russian haluzim and their travails in the Yishuv. The journal extolled the Zionist heroism of the pioneer settlers, proudly observing that "Jews who choose to live in their own land will live according to their own laws. Everything will be Jewish [in character] . . . the very atmosphere will be Jewish."[84]

Shaharut's metamorphosis into a Zionist journal is not surprising. Scharfstein's illustrations and themes, however, are a revealing barometer of the changing mind-set of Hebraist activists and Jewish educators in this period. In 1918, for example, Scharfstein switched to a standard title page for *Shaharut* that he used for two years (figure 12). It depicts three youths in a small boat rowing toward the Palestinian shore. The youths, two boys and a girl, are healthy, strong, and dressed in modern attire. They are gazing at the coastal town, transfixed at the sight of the walled community's dome-shaped buildings and its numerous date palms and cypress trees. The girl is pointing in the direction of the town while one of the boys rows and the other stands at the boat's bow, holding a small Zionist flag and waving. The water is calm, the sky does not appear threatening, and above the scene rises the Hebrew word *shaharut*.

Compare the straightforward nationalist message of this title page with the journal's new masthead in 1920, which represents a return to more traditional forms of Zionist mythologization (figure 13). It employs biblical and quasi-messianic themes, juxtaposing Pharaoh and Moses. Pharaoh sits on his throne, menacingly brandishing a whip and scowling, and behind him rise the Egyptian pyramids. Below his feet is emblazoned the phrase *mishiabud* (from slavery). Moses, grasping the tablets of the Hebrew law, is standing directly opposite the Egyptian ruler, looking at him. Behind Moses, a winding path leads toward a Palestinian landscape and a radiant sun. Completing the thought expressed beneath Pharaoh, the Hebrew phrase under Moses reads *legeulah* (to redemption), and between the two figures rises the bold pronouncement *shaharut*.

12. Cover of *Shaharut*, April 1918, Brandeis University Libraries.

13. Masthead of *Shaharut*, March 1920, Brandeis University Libraries.

The title page used between 1918 and 1920 synthesizes the ideas of homecoming and a new beginning, and the masthead that replaced it symbolizes the ongoing struggle of the children of Israel for freedom and deliverance. On one level, the change in strategy implicitly reflects the impact of "Ahad Haamism" in the American context. Western Jews, according to Ahad Haam, faced the paradoxical situation of "slavery in freedom," needing to free themselves of assimilationist pressures and to take active steps to preserve their own cultural vitality.[85]

The illustrations also appear to be expressions of Zionist mythology increasingly attuned to the American psychology of *Shaharut*'s youthful audience. The title page and masthead reflect vastly different approaches to the concept of Zionist self-realization. On the title page, the children are themselves agents of national redemption. Their journey in the boat, which they are physically steering toward the Palestinian shoreline, symbolizes the act of hagshamah azmit. In the second illustration, the Hebrew journal serves as the mediator. It is suffused with abstract messages of Jewish mission and messianism and lays no claim to immediacy or primacy of action. In short, the masthead's simplicity and ambiguity open the door to all those sympathetic to Hebraism and Zionism.

Still other Jewish educators played a role in blending American and Zionist images of Zionism and haluziut. In 1919, for example, Rabbi Leon Spitz of New York's Jewish Welfare Board formulated policies and methods for "correlating American and Jewish patriotism." He advised Zionist youth leaders that "American and Jewish patriotism should be wedded so as to cultivate the complete and harmonious American Jewish nature and spirit and to have the boys and girls develop the consciousness that American and Jewish patriotism are one whole."[86]

Spitz also outlined a plan for observing American and Jewish holidays. He matched seemingly complementary holidays and argued that they should be celebrated in tandem. "Americanism," he emphasized, must be central to the celebration of Jewish festivals as well as youth clubs' regular activities.

> [George] Washington's expeditions and strategy are paralleled with the exploits of Judah the Maccabee on Hanukah. Liberty, an American and Jewish ideal, may be discussed on Pesah [Passover] or on Hanukah. On Hanukah an interesting discussion would center around the parallel of Tories and Patriots, and Hasidim and Hellenists in Washingtonian and Maccabean times. On Shavuot [Pentecost] discuss the influence of the Bible upon the American people, or upon the founders of the American colonies.[87]

Spitz also stressed the importance of aesthetic innovations. The club meeting house, he explained, should reflect the enmeshing of American, Jewish, and Zionist values.

> In its physical appearance, the club room should be representative of the harmonious blending of the American Jewish atmosphere. The American and Jewish flags may be crossed, decorations intertwined, symbolisms placed side by side, the library shelf should embrace literature suggestive of both American and Jewish cultures, the bulletin board should have clippings of American national interest as well as of Jewish interest, and pictures and portraits of American men and historical spots and should grace the walls side by side with those of Jewish significance. The result obtained should be such that any stranger as he enters the room for the first time, should at once and of his own accord recognize in it the meeting room of an American Zionist club.[88]

Spitz's intentional reformulation of Zionist values sharply contrasts with the Hehaluz vision described earlier. His approach is based on an ideological and practical innovation that gained currency in the 1920s. If the lack of syncretism among immigrant Zionists was challenged by Americanized Hebraists like Dushkin, Berkson, and Scharfstein, Spitz represents a return to the Brandeisian notion that Zionist activity is a noble extension of American values and ideals.

Certainly, Spitz's emphasis on American Jewish patriotism was also a response to the anti-immigrant, antiradical, and antisemitic trends of the 1920s. This was the period when Henry Ford's *Dearborn Independent* reprinted the age-old antisemitic forgery, *The Protocols of the Elders of Zion*. It was also a time when American nativism flourished and the U.S. Congress halted the waves of southern and east European immigration.[89] Communal agencies like New York's Jewish Welfare Board and Jewish leaders like Rabbi Leon Spitz were keenly aware and fearful of such sentiments and sought to mold and even neutralize Zionist activity by imposing educational guidelines and restricting financial support to groups that adopted their strategy.

Spitz's instructional critique presumed a degree of acculturation that was anathema to radical Zionists of the immigrant milieu. Among many native-born youth, on the other hand, such Americanized Zionism struck a responsive chord. This is exemplified by "The Conquest of the Soil," published by Sarah Kussy, a leader of the Conservative movement's National Women's League, in a 1925 issue of the *Young Judean*. "You have heard

much about the new colonies that are now springing up all over Palestine,"
Kussy exclaimed.

> How are they actually being built? Do our Jewish pioneers work as did the
> Pilgrim Fathers in Massachusetts in 1620? Do they, too, cut down trees, build
> log cabins, make paths through thick forests and hunt game?
>
> Well, they work at least as hard as did the early settlers of America,
> though not exactly in the same way. Our pioneers, too (*haluzim* they are
> called) must build their own homes, but, they do that not by felling trees,
> for the forests of Palestine were cut down long ago and never replaced. Their
> task is much harder. They build of stone instead of wood, of stone that is
> firmly imbedded in the soil from which it can be removed only with the
> greatest difficulty. These stones must be cut and shaped for building, which
> takes much longer than sawing logs. Nor can the settlers live by hunting,
> since game does not abound in Palestine. They must wrest food from the
> earth by the sweat of their brows, by ploughing the fields, and planting and
> reaping the harvest.[90]

Kussy's romantic depiction of the haluzim retains a traditional role for
women and girls. After describing the arduous physical labor of the male
workers, she notes that the haluzim break for lunch at one o'clock in the
afternoon:

> The men stopped their labor and with tools over their shoulders came along
> making their way to the common dining room of the settlement. Did they
> have to cook their own meals? No, that task was spared them, for *haluzot*,
> young women workers and settlers, were there to do that for them. These
> girls cook, wash house, mend for the men and help them in other ways as
> well . . .
>
> "Do you find your work hard?" I asked a girl. "Not very," she answered,
> then shrugging her shoulders added with a smile, "We are doing it for
> ourselves, for the Jewish people, not for strangers."[91]

Kussy's depiction of gender relations in Palestine reflects her own bias as
well as the place of women in the new Zionist culture. Her statement
displays what one historian deems "the complex social reality of a multi-
cultural milieu."[92] In other words, the dynamic immigrant setting simultaneously altered traditional gender roles even as it reinforced certain social
patterns. Thus the sexual division of Zionist labor paradoxically broke new
ground for Jewish women at the same time it replicated traditional female
roles.

Kussy's description also projects American attitudes onto the haluzim.

Many American Jewish youth viewed the haluzim as role models and reifications of American Jewish values and ideals. Hard work, thrift, self-sacrifice, and industriousness—all equally suggestive of the haluz and the American icon Horatio Alger—were merged into one integrated American Zionist sensibility. Although detached from the daily struggles of the haluzim, centrist Zionist youth viewed the nationalist experiment in Palestine as a reflection of their self-worth. In this vein, as Kussy explained,

> the colonies we have planted with such labor, love and devotion are succeeding. . . . We will always hear good news if we deserve it, if every Jewish man and woman, and every Jewish boy and girl, will do whatever he or she can to help in the rebuilding of Eretz Israel.[93]

Between the world wars, American Zionism was driven by conservative rather than expansionist tendencies. On both the elite and popular levels, emphasis shifted away from membership campaigns and toward the consolidation of Zionist gains. The accomplishments of the Labor Zionist movement in Palestine and the image of the haluz played a pivotal role in this process.

In 1919, for example, the Zionist leader Louis Lipsky called on American Jews to view themselves as full partners in the Zionist enterprise:

> I am writing to you from Jerusalem, the Holy City, which is now visibly becoming the New Jerusalem of a reinvigorated Jewish Nationality.
>
> I have just returned from a week's tour of the Valley of Esdraelon, *the Emek*, which was purchased by the [Jewish] National Fund, and which is now being settled, *with amazing energy*, by several thousand pioneers . . .
>
> I spent some time in Tiberias, Haifa and Jaffa (Tel Aviv). It may be said of all four cities that Jewish enterprise, zeal and forcefulness are transforming what were before backward, antiquated, dust covered unwholesome towns into bustling, expanding, aggressive modern cities . . .
>
> *All this is due to Jewish initiative.*
>
> The elements of our effort to make the Jewish National Home are land, labor and capital. The three may be summed up in the one word *Capital*.
>
> Bare hands cannot easily conquer a bare land neglected for centuries. There must be investment of labor. Labor must have reserves of strength, which is capital . . .
>
> To augment the powers of labor, to make the land serviceable for larger numbers, *national capital is needed to force the pace* of growth.
>
> *The Keren Hayesod is the National Capital of the Jewish people* . . .
>
> In all of Jewish Palestine, American Zionists are esteemed, not only be-

cause of their devotion to the cause, but because of the feeling of confidence they inspire.

It is felt that while American Zionists continue strong in faith and in work, the future is assured . . .

Let us who still live in the lands of dispersion not fail to do our duty to the fullest extent.

Hoping to greet you again upon American soil, I am, With Zion's hope, Cordially yours, Louis Lipsky[94]

Lipsky's letter highlights the elasticity of the haluz image as well as American Jewish ambivalence about the Zionist imperative of hagshamah azmit. His idealized portrait of the Yishuv is paradoxical, as he stresses the unique character of Palestine and the transformational nature of Zionist efforts on the land. At the same time, he argues that the Yishuv's stability depends on outside sources of funding. Philanthropic support of the Yishuv, he declares, is an extension of the self-realization of Zionist pioneers. In Lipsky's scheme, American Jewish charity is as important to the future of Palestine as is the labor of the Jewish settlers. His letter exudes optimism, confidence, and—not unlike the earlier depiction by Sarah Kussy—a vicarious sense of involvement in the life of the Yishuv. Writing from Jerusalem, the locus classicus of Jewish civilization, Lipsky's letter is styled to sound like a prophetic declaration, with his descriptions of the land, pioneers, urban centers, and rural settlements cast in metahistorical terms. Meanwhile, he uses a fashionable philosophical gloss and argues that capital is the glue that binds the land and its laborers.

Appealing to the reader's sense of philanthropic largesse, Lipsky lays responsibility for the Zionist dream at the doorstep of American Jews. European Jewry has offered up its sons and daughters, he contends implicitly, and it is American Jewry's duty to sustain the Zionist enterprise. Such a weighty financial burden requires dedication, innovation, and tireless commitment. Like the haluzim, American Jews face specific challenges, namely, "laying broad foundations for the national home" and "enabl[ing] Palestine as far as possible to become self-sufficient."[95] To this end, Lipsky claims, the Yishuv requires Jewish economic as well as physical strength. Lipsky even purports to speak on behalf of the Yishuv's populace. Linking their psychological well-being to continued American Jewish support, he offers an alternative form of modern haluziut by elevating American Zionist philanthropy to the position of a hallowed ideal.

Lipsky's philosophical orientation was broad enough to appeal to different constituencies and to encompass varying interpretations. In practice, the partnership that gradually emerged among the efficiency-oriented American Zionists, the coalition of gradualists led by Chaim Weizmann, and the Labor Zionist movement validated the facts on the ground in Palestine and enlarged the scope of Zionist political consensus. As the Zionist technocrat Arthur Ruppin perceptively remarked, whereas most land acquisition and settlement activity was carried out by the Labor enterprise, "both the *haluzim* and the *baalebatim* [bourgeoisie] have, with their respective mentalities, their place in our colonization work."[96] Ruppin was essentially a pragmatist and therefore sympathetic to the aims of the Labor movement.[97] In his view, the so-called baalebatim, especially American Jews, played an important role in developing the country's urban, rural, commercial, and industrial spheres.[98]

As Ruppin anticipated, the most successful economic ventures during the 1920s and 1930s were those initiated by baalebatim like the Brandeis group. Deposed from the leadership of the Zionist Organization of America in 1921, the New England–based Zionist brain trust quietly and effectively pursued its agenda through a range of capital investment schemes such as the Palestine Economic Corporation, the American Zion Commonwealth, and the Palestine Land Development Company. Such operations enabled Brandeis and his associates to sustain a carefully constructed agenda that implemented the group's progressive and Wilsonian assumptions about "rebuilding Palestine on approved social and economic lines."[99] In a 1925 memorandum to the Palestine Economic Corporation, one of Brandeis's so-called lieutenants, Bernard Flexner, noted:

> It may be expected that there will be a unanimity of opinion that the policy of the [Palestine Economic] Corporation in its initial stages of activity must necessarily be guided as stated in the prospectus so "that its shareholders, present and prospective, will expect its funds to be so employed as to stimulate a healthy growth of industry and commerce rather than to realize the largest or quickest financial returns."[100]

As this statement shows, the Brandeis group did not make financial reward its chief priority, although they were zealous in the cause of Zionist fiscal responsibility. Indeed, they raised significant start-up capital and investment funds crucial to operating public concessions, initiating private businesses, and "stimulating cooperative enterprises."[101] In this way, the group sought to place the Yishuv on a sound economic footing. The Brandeis group's projects included the hydroelectric power plant created by the engineer Pinhas Rutenberg; the Palestine Potash Company (later known as the Dead Sea Works); hotels in Jerusalem and Tiberias; Bank Hapoalim (Workers' Bank), the central bank of the Palestine Labor movement responsible for long-term agricultural and industrial credits; "an economically and socially sound housing policy" for new immigrants and workers in urban centers; and, as in the case of a special undertaking sponsored by the philanthropist Benjamin Rabalsky, the establishment of a Jewish communal presence in the Afula region.[102] As a whole, such projects allowed the Brandeis group to circumvent official American and world Zionist policy while bolstering a social democratic vision of Zionist development in the Yishuv.

In time, most Zionist leaders adopted a quasi-Brandeisian outlook in general and a laissez-faire policy with regard to specific forms of Jewish colonization in Palestine. Even Brandeis's opponents and detractors used this strategy. As a result, it became commonplace to rely on abstract perceptions of the haluzim when appealing to American Jewish liberal sympathies and raising funds for Zionist purposes. This orientation was reinforced by an evolving movement supraculture that cut across social, religious, and political lines. In fact, American Zionist activity during the interwar period was characterized by an unprecedented proliferation of meetings, conferences, fund-raising campaigns, and publicity drives.

More often than not, various groups employed the same terminology interchangeably, for example, "the Jewish upbuilding of Palestine," "Jewish national restoration," "rebuilding the Jewish national home" and "reclaiming the Land of Israel." Weizmann himself understood the efficacy of this phenomenon. "Palestine is intended to be mainly an agricultural country," he conceded during a visit to the United States in 1925.

> The Jewish community of Palestine, having as its basis the ideal of a national revival, must stand firmly on the land and embrace both an agricultural and cultural revival. . . . We are, naturally, in choosing the pioneers looking mainly for such a type as would be fit and willing to settle on the land. . . . Some have been engaged in speculative thoughts with regard to the agricultural experiments made by the *kvuzot* . . . which received support from the Zionist Organization. In the minds of some, these experiments arouse considerable discussion as to whether the cooperative or communistic form of settlement is appropriate. . . . At any rate, the solution must develop from within the ranks of the workers. The Zionist Organization, just as any other organization with the purpose of encouraging a pioneer settlement, must act as a father. While advising and supporting, it must not interfere directly. The solution must come from within.[103]

Brandeis's and Weizmann's orientations highlight the extent to which the major Zionist leaders anchored their gradualist approach to Jewish colonization and settlement in the pioneering efforts of the haluzim. "Palestine is a miniature California," Brandeis asserted. "The country will be built 'dunam by dunam,'" Weizmann declared. As Lipsky had done in 1919, the infusion of Zionist economic strategy with such pioneering themes implicitly placed monetary support for Zionism on the same footing as the self-actualization of the haluzim. Many American Jews identified emotionally with the Yishuv and felt that the pioneer settlers' success depended on their charitable largesse. This attitude, which in part stemmed from the fact that the Yishuv survived World War I because of American Jewish aid, was promoted by the leaders of the Zionist organization.

Zionist leaders also carried the battle for American public opinion into the popular arena, with Stephen S. Wise one of the movement's most effective spokespersons. In the mid-1920s, he participated in several high-profile public debates aimed at increasing the visibility of the Zionist cause. In October 1927, for example, Wise met Clarence Darrow at Chicago's prestigious Reform Sinai Temple to debate the topic "Is Zionism a Progressive Policy for Israel and America?" Wise tried to promote the Zionist claim by extolling the Jewish pioneers in Palestine who "translate the wilderness into a land of beauty and richness and nobleness."[104] This metamorphosis, he maintained, had "not only given the Jew security and peace in the face of oppression . . . [it also] ended the confession of the Jews that we are nothing more than a religion."[105] Like the return of Alsace Lorraine to the French and Belgium to the Belgians, Wise suggested that "the very essence of progressive policies and principles" is the return of Palestine to the Jews.[106]

Wise also pointed to the haluzim as the embodiment of Jewish national aspirations. He called particular attention to the Lower Galilee as a model of innovative farming techniques and the coastal plain for its abundance of citrus groves, asserting that Palestine's "hillside soil is the richest soil in the world."[107] To this, Darrow replied, "Now here comes a Jew and tells you that the side of a hill is richer than the valley. A dickens of a farmer, isn't he? Anybody whoever came within gun-shot of a farm knows that all the richness of a hill is washed down into the valley."[108]

Wise's faulty knowledge of agriculture notwithstanding, his comments indicate the special role that American Jewish leaders assigned to the Jewish pioneers. Zionist colonization, he argued, was the road to modernizing Jewish life and eradicating the misery caused by antisemitism. He also claimed that once aware of the conditions in Palestine, all Americans committed to progressive values and ideals would readily support this new Western frontier. Wise wanted to persuade his audience that Zionism enabled ordinary Jews to help themselves, even to do extraordinary things. He praised the regenerative possibilities represented by the haluzim. The haluz, according to Wise, adopted new surroundings, learned a new occupation, changed his or her language, and merged Jewish tradition with Western sensibilities.

In 1930, the Brandeis group returned to power after nearly a decade in the minority of the Zionist movement. But as indicated earlier, Brandeis and his followers were not idle during this period. In fact, Brandeis himself had carefully and systematically cultivated a range of contacts.[109] This network, the elite leaders felt, would enable them to reach mainstream American Jews. "The kind of influence we [exert] in the press, such as [Stephen S. Wise] now has," Brandeis explained to Julian W. Mack, a jurist and Zionist leader, "is more potent than any publicity man can exercise."[110]

Brandeis himself took a special interest in the activities of the haluzim, especially the Histadrut. Following the publication of the "Memo of the General Federation of Jewish Labor in Palestine" in the *Palestine and Near East Economic Magazine*, for example, he recommended that "an ample number of copies of this should be secured" and dispatched to "serious minded newspaper men."[111] During the interwar years, Brandeis's interest in the Labor movement, both as a measure of Palestine's progress and as a propaganda tool continued to grow. He frequently corresponded with people close to the Labor movement in Palestine, and they supplied him with raw data about Jewish workers, pioneer settlements, Arab-Jewish relations, and a host of related issues.[112] Such information, Brandeis suggested, could be effectively used in American Zionist propaganda work.

The pro-Palestine case is, to a degree not commonly recognized, infinitely stronger than it was . . . in 1920. And it is a case with such varied material for appeal—that a discriminating, penetrating speaker can reach the heart, the head and ultimately the pocket of almost every category of Jew who may be exposed—so numerous are the facets of the crystal. . . .

The condition of the Jews in the diaspora in 1930—as compared with 1920 and 1914—has worsened to such a degree, that the belief of thinking Jews that the Jewish problem would be solved by growing enlightenment in the diaspora must have been seriously shaken—if not shattered. . . .

An intimate knowledge of the trials and sufferings of the pioneers, both early and recent, will supply abundant material to all who love adventure and heroes, all who can be stirred by talks of men and women ready to risk and give all in the service of a great cause. The aspiration and striving of the [Labor Zionist movement] and the achievements should appeal mightily to our Progressives.

Thus the material is a rich storehouse of ammunition available for attack upon Jews of any class; upon the hard-headed or the soft-hearted; upon Orthodox or Reform; upon believer or those of religious unbelief; upon the practical man and the idealist. One has only to know the material and to select tactfully that adapted to particular audiences. . . .

Every opportunity to speak which offers, however modest or unpromising, should be availed of; and effort should be continuously and persistently made to create opportunities. Lodges, clubs, societies, gatherings social or serious—should be taught—whatever their character.[113]

In addition, Brandeis showed keen interest in news reported in the *Palestine and Near East Economic Magazine* and the Labor daily *Davar* (The Word). During this time, *Davar* issued a weekly English supplement,[114] and Brandeis passed much of this information on to his lieutenants, instructing them to use it in their extensive public relations efforts. In a typical instance, he told them: "When [Wise] takes up publicity with periodicals and the press, I think he will find no material more effective than [Moshe] Smilansky's article 'Jewish colonization and the Fellah' which fills the special . . . issue of the *Palestine and Near East Economic Magazine*."[115]

Brandeis also considered *Davar*'s English supplement to be a particularly useful propaganda tool, and he directed Robert Szold to launch a campaign to make both publications accessible to the general public. The guiding principles of such a drive were

(a) That in every city in which we have active Zionists they be instructed to request that the public library subscribe to *Davar English Weekly Supplement* . . . and for the *Palestine and Near East Economic Magazine*. . . .

(b) That a like request be made of the college library at every college in which there is an Avukah or Menorah Society.

(c) That a like request be made of the library committee of every Jewish Center.

(d) That the persons instructed to make the request be made to report to you on the results of their efforts.[116]

While elite leaders like Lipsky, Brandeis, Wise, and Mack enlightened American Jews about the Zionist pioneering enterprise on a grand scale, groups like the Pioneer Women's Organization performed much of the movement's spadework on the regional level. Pioneer Women—originally the women's auxiliary of Poalei Zion—served as a conduit to immigrant women who sympathized with the aims and ideals of the Labor Zionist movement. The masthead of the organization's journal *Die pionern froy* (The Pioneer Woman) conveys an unapologetic, egalitarian message (figure 14). A *haluzah* (female pioneer) carrying a basket and rake sets out to work in the fields. The image is framed by date palms, and in the background, the sun rises over the tents of a pioneer settlement. (The union bug beneath the illustration is also revealing!) The masthead articulates a simple and direct theme, namely, that working-class, Yiddish-speaking women are playing an important and central role in building the Yishuv.

The unpretentious quality of the illustration also provides a contrast to similar icons. Consider, for example, Zeirei Zion's earlier depiction of the haluz (figure 15). The Hebrew emblem of Zeirei Zion reflects the male-dominated composition of the small non-Marxist Labor Zionist group. Few American Jewish women at the time would have had the language skills necessary to join the group. Likewise, the use of English is a reminder of Zeirei Zion's American-born core. Finally, in the center of the illustration a haluz sows seeds by hand from a basket, and behind him rises a glorious sun. This fanciful depiction of agricultural work and the accompanying romantic Hebrew message appealed to only a handful of American Jews. For that matter, hardly any of the high-brow Zeirei Zion members actually envisioned themselves as future agriculturalists. By comparison, the image of the haluzah resonated with the values of hard work, physical toil, and sisterhood central to the self-perception of Jewish immigrant women and their Americanized daughters.[117]

The Pioneer Women's Organization tried to consolidate its ranks by tapping the vast reservoir of potential American Jewish female support for Labor Zionism. In many respects, the groundwork had already been laid by the International Ladies Garment Workers' Union and certain highly placed Hadassah members who publicly endorsed the Histadrut and the workers' settlements in Palestine. In 1930 Pioneer Women issued the following statement in English:

> The modern woman is taking her place in the front ranks of social life.
>
> Woman is playing a considerable role in the development of modern industry and production and strives side by side with man for the betterment of living and working conditions of toiling humanity and for a better social order.
>
> The Jewess, no less than the Jew, is now active in the various phases of our life, and the Jewish girl and mother aids powerfully in the upbuilding of Palestine in her own peculiar way—constructive, educational, and stimulat-

14. Masthead from *The Pioneer Woman*, December 1928. Courtesy of Naamat USA.

15. Emblem of Zeirei Zion of America (1922). Courtesy of the YIVO Institute for Jewish Research.

ing way. . . . The haluzah is right in the thick of the work of the rising Jewish commonwealth in Palestine. . . .

The Pioneer Women's Organization is not just one more organization of women, doing what others do. . . . It is an organization of women with a distinct task of furthering the economic emancipation and the national rehabilitation of the Jewish masses on the foundations of free labor and social justice. . . .

Through our affiliation with the labor wing of Zionism, we back the interests of the Palestine workers. . . .

Our own independent sphere of activity . . . is raising funds for the women pioneers in Palestine. . . .

The progressive Jewish woman, the worker or the helpmate of the worker, has found for herself in our organization an opening for her energy and spiritual craving that nothing else could satisfy in equal measure. We have learned to think and act independently. Our sense of responsibility of Socialism, the cause of the Jewish Homeland, has been heightened. The great liberating ideal and its modern and creative womanhood added to our self-esteem and enhanced the value of our contribution to humanity. Through association with so many comrades in our organization, we have grown in moral and mental stature and found a source of joy nothing else could give.

Deep enjoyment, unexcelled spiritual gain, and opportunity to learn— that is the triple benefit the Pioneer Women's Organization gives to its members.

Join our ranks! Share our ideal and our joy! Be a Pioneer![118]

Even though the "Aims and Objectives of the Pioneer Women's Organization" was published in English, the document's awkward syntax and inelegant grammar betrays Pioneer Women's inescapable immigrant origins. The text is also replete with references to self-improvement and education and reveals the group's latent Americanizing aspirations.

Although Pioneer Women did not want to be "just one more organization of women," its members did imitate the social and philanthropic behavior of mainstream American Jewish women's groups like Hadassah and the National Council of Jewish Women. The younger acculturated members, wrote Rose Kaufman (who later served as Pioneer Women's president), "like teas, attractive settings, flowers on the table, luncheons in a hotel—why not?"[119] Still, neither Hadassah nor the National Council for Jewish Women was automatically open to immigrant women. For many, therefore, joining Pioneer Women was tantamount to being not only a haluzah but also an American in the fullest sense.

It was also at this time that Pioneer Women undertook an educational campaign aimed at both Yiddish- and English-speaking American Jewish women. In 1931 the organization published *Vos arbeterns derzeyln* (The woman worker speaks), an anthology of personal reminiscences by *haluzot* (female pioneers) about their experiences in Palestine. The book included essays about the early years in several *kvuzot* (communes); life in Palestine during World War I; impressions of A. D. Gordon, Rahel Blaustein, and other notable figures in the Yishuv; Jewish family life in agricultural colonies; and several hitherto unpublished photographs of haluzim and Jewish colonies.

The book was well received, and in 1932 Pioneer Women published an English translation entitled *The Plough Woman*, which opened a window on Jewish life in Palestine to a largely uninformed English-reading audience. The well-known writer and Labor Zionist advocate Maurice Samuel translated the material and explained the volume's significance as follows:

> The new Jewish homeland has already produced a life with traditional forms. ... The word *shomer* can only be translated as "guard" or "watchman"; and yet the bald translation is quite as meaningless for the English reader, quite as void of the significance of the term as, let us say, a literal translation of the word *cowboy* into French or German. For the American cowboy of the past is not just a function; he is a tradition, a part of history, a heritage and a peculiarity. He is a unique type and institution. And the *shomer* of Palestine represents now in Jewish life a similar untranslatable phenomenon. ... He was a symbol of Jewish self-defense, of Jewish emergence from dependence, of Jewish pride. The thrill of the word must be understood not against the background of romantic adventurousness, but against a more significant background of national renaissance and a repudiation of an unhappy past.[120]

Samuel went on to explain the alleged profundity of the terms *kvuzah*, *kibbutz*, *haluz*, and *meshek hapoalot* (women's training farm). Such "word symbols," Samuel asserted, reveal the "extraordinary folk-depths of the [Zionist] movement, the deep and inexhaustible sources of a renaissance which, in effect, is only at its beginning."[121] As Samuel's comments imply, *The Plough Woman* was intended to be more than a straightforward translation of *Vos arbeterns derzeyln*. Appearing at the height of the Depression, a period that coincided with the Yishuv's rapid growth, the volume presented a poignant alternative to the misery and hardship of the Jewish working class in United States, pointing the way to individual fulfillment and collective redemption.

In a similar vein, right-wing American Zionist organizations adopted haluz imagery to praise Jewish redemptive possibilities in the Land of Israel. Betar, the youth wing of the Revisionist Zionist Party, which was established in the United States in 1931, exemplifies this trend. The organization derived its name from Bar Kokhba's last stronghold against the Romans in 135 C.E. and the acronym Brit Trumpledor (The Covenant of Trumpledor). The latter glorified Yosef Trumpledor, the fallen Zionist hero of Tel Hai fame who was, ironically enough, one of the founders of Russian Hehaluz before World War I.

An issue of the *Betar Monthly* from 1932 exemplifies the group's use of haluz imagery (figure 16). In the foreground, a soldier stands at attention outside a tent. His uniform is neat and smart, and his cap is decorated with a small menorah emblem. Another menorah rises above the opening of the tent. Behind the soldier are three different scenes: a plowman tending his field, an ancient town, and, immediately to the right, a Jewish pioneer planting a cypress tree. The scene depicts a Palestinian Jewish landscape in which the Betar haluz plays a central role. In it are temporary Jewish workers' settlements, like those of the Gdud Haavodah (Legion of Labor), as well as permanent villages and colonies. In the upper corner, a rising sun is emblazoned with the movement's name, Betar. The Betar haluz is clearly responsible for defending the Jewish national home.

In another instance, the *Betar Monthly* featured a portrait of its namesake Yosef Trumpledor gazing out from behind a menorah (figure 17). Over the menorah are inscribed the famous words that Trumpledor supposedly uttered in his last moments: "It is good to die for our nation." In both cases, militarism, physical preparedness, and sacrifice are portrayed as the movement's highest values, and selflessness and steadfast devotion are glorified as the litmus test of personal character.

These themes are also represented in *Hadar* (Honor), a Betar publication from the late 1930s (figure 18). The cover of *Hadar* stresses *hakhsharah haganatit* (military training), *hakhsharah ruhanit* (cultural training), and *plugot avodah* (labor battalions). Each of these concepts is adapted from similar, albeit less militaristic, Labor Zionist concepts. In the final analysis, although Revisionist Zionism did adopt the image of the haluz, it did not fundamentally alter the concept of haluziut. That historical legacy remained the exclusive possession of the Labor Zionist movement.[122]

In the early 1930s, the image of brawny, hardworking, and dedicated haluzim gradually entered the mainstream of American Jewish popular culture. Three factors influenced this development: the Depression, antisemi-

16. Cover of *Betar Monthly*, January 1932. Courtesy of the American Jewish Historical Society.

17. Cover of *Betar Monthly*, March 1932. Courtesy of the American Jewish Historical Society.

tism at home and abroad, and the Labor Zionist movement's political ascent in the Yishuv and the World Zionist Organization. Following the stock market crash and Hitler's rise to power, many Jews feared for the future of Western society. In the 1930s, American Jews experienced severe economic hardship, and they were also the victims of university quotas and virulent antisemitic attacks by the radio priest Father Charles Coughlin. The Yishuv, however, in inverse proportion to the fortunes of diaspora Jews, experienced a social and economic boom.[123] The Labor Zionist movement in Palestine, particularly the Histadrut, grew dramatically as a result of the influx of east European haluzim. In the process, Labor became less ideologically rigid and slowly transformed itself into a framework with mass appeal.

The changing role of Labor Zionism in the turbulent configuration of the 1920s and 1930s prompted a range of American Jewish responses. In 1931, for example, Meyer Levin published *Yehuda*, the first full-length American Jewish literary portrait of the Zionist pioneers in Palestine. The

18. Cover of *Hadar* 1 (1937). Courtesy of the
American Jewish Historical Society.

novel is set in a kvuzah in the Galilee, where a band of youthful, albeit
melancholy, haluzim are carving out a new life for themselves. The com-
mune is unexpectedly joined by an American Jewish businessman named
Mr. Paley. Mr. Paley's first name is never revealed; he is merely a stereotype
of the acculturated, middle-class American Jew. In every way, this character
offers a contrast to the simplicity and somber honesty of the young pioneers.

> In [Mr. Paley's] career as an insurance agent in the city of St. Louis, he had
> learned . . . the value of the psychological moment. Therefore he now pulled
> off his coat, his necktie, his collar, and standing before them in striped shirt
> with flapping throatband, announced to the whole room, no, to all Israel:
> "Comrades, I bring you the greeting of the West to East! . . . I have made a
> great journey through many hardships crossing half the world in order to see
> for myself if there was such a place where Jews were building themselves a
> homeland with the sweat of their muscles. And now I see the real article,

and my heart is full. Ah, you don't know how lucky you are! I would give half my life to be young again, to be one of you, to feel myself toiling every day among my comrades in the fields of Yisroael!" [*sic*].[124]

This ironic moment pits the romantic image of the haluz against the harsh reality of the Yishuv. As the novel progresses, there is something poignant, even endearing, about Mr. Paley's ability to come to terms with the trials of Palestinian Jewish life. He sheds the comfort of his American home for the physically challenging but spiritually uplifting experience of life in the kvuzah and ultimately proves to be a highly sympathetic character. No longer a pale reflection of his Palestinian counterparts, Mr. Paley symbolizes the American Jew's potential self-transformation into a devoted Zionist with a central and secure place in the pioneering enterprise.

American Jews were also introduced to Palestine and the haluzim through a combination of foreign-made films and newsreels. Early releases like *Dream of My People* and *Romance of New Palestine* attracted scant public attention. But with the maturity of the Jewish film industry in eastern Europe and America, several Zionist films did find their way into movie houses in major urban centers. In 1931, for example, the producer Joseph Seiden released the Polish film *Die shtime fun yisroel* (The voice of Israel). A hodgepodge of clips from other films, some of which antedate World War I, the American version of *Die shtime fun yisroel* has an English voice-over and includes travelogue shots of Palestinian Jewish colonies.[125] In 1934, Aleksander Ford's *Sabra* (later retitled *Haluzim* for its Tel Aviv screening) featured members of the Habima theater group and was shown to American audiences in Yiddish. The film depicts the life of a fictional group of haluzim in Palestine at the time of the Balfour Declaration. Their successful reclamation of a tract of arid land incites a band of nearby Arabs who attack the pioneers. Despite the group's small size, they successfully defend themselves and their new home. "This is just a little too much like our Wild West themes," wrote the critic for New York's *Daily News*, "when help always arrived at precisely the blackest moment before the dawn." But the critic agreed with the *New York Times* reviewer, who rated the film as being "equal to that of the best Soviet films."[126]

Similar to Ford's *Sabra*, Henry Stewart's *Die heilige shvue* (The holy oath) conveys a moralistic message about Jewish life in Palestine. Two frivolous immigrant youths living comfortably in the United States are begged by the girl's father to attend a Zionist meeting. The father attempts to persuade them by means of a sad recitation of Jewish history. The film subsequently alternates between fragmented sequences from Yiddish talkies and footage from Palestinian newsreels. The collage of Jewish history eventually gives way to scenes of orchards, agricultural colonies, cultural institutions, hospitals, modern Tel Aviv, and finally a parade of pioneer youth superimposed on the chastened immigrant couple.[127]

One of the most popular Zionist films of the period was *Land of Promise*. Released to the public in 1935, the English script of this hour-long German production was written by Maurice Samuel. It was distributed widely in the United States where approximately 1.5 million people paid to see it. Subsequently, the "March of Time" incorporated much of the footage in a newsreel that was seen by more than 40 million people in theaters around the country.[128] Unlike most films of Palestine, *Land of Promise* did not use any actors, although many of the scenes were undoubtedly staged. The cast of the film is listed as "The Jewish People Rebuilding Palestine." The strategy of using actual footage, asserted the *New York Times* reviewer, is proof "of the motion picture camera's ability to record history more vividly than any printed page."

> It is this device which permits the film to show Palestine as it was fifteen years ago without resorting to obvious fakery. The Arabs in their market places; the sad-faced old men flailing the wheat, rocking before the Wailing Wall—this was Palestine, says the camera, before the Jews flocked back to their homeland. And then, suddenly the lens is opened wide upon a dancing, singing group of young men and women on the foredeck of a liner [headed for Palestine], coming to give new life to the century-old city, coming to water its fields, run its factories, build its homes. The effect upon any audience is electric.[129]

American newspapers, too, showed keen interest in the Zionist enterprise and the haluzim. The tenth anniversary of the Keren Hayesod, for example, attracted the attention of three large New York newspapers. The *Herald Tribune* reported "only American Jewry can continue to carry the burden" of Palestinian development. "The most impressive results of Jewish devotion lie in the pioneer work in scientific agriculture and industry . . . [and] in the great Hebrew University . . . [which] has immense possibilities as a bridge between East and West."[130] The *New York American Editorial Page* stated: "Thanks to the help of the Palestine Foundation Fund, [American Jews] have built up schools for [the Jewish colonies in Palestine], stomped out trachoma and malaria and greatly improved the lot of 100,000 new colonists and as many Arabs; the project is no longer a dream but a reality."[131]

Finally, in regard to *The New Pioneers* the *New York World Telegram* observed:

> For [the Jews of Palestine], pioneering has meant not "Westward-HO!" but "Eastward-HO!" In the land of their biblical fathers they are reclaiming old ground to build them new homes. . . . Pioneers, the Palestinian Jews are digging a new life out of ancient soil. They are carving out a new homeland. The movement has won the imagination of this pioneering nation as well as the religious and racial loyalty of American Jews.[132]

A 1935 editorial published in Boston's *Jewish Advocate* demonstrates the prevalence of similar trends in American Jewish journalism. Entitled "Palestine—The Land of the Future," the statement occupies nearly an entire page of the newspaper and compares the haluzim with the American pioneers, especially their "intelligence and industry," "enthusiasm and hope," and "generous and neighborly spirit." Set against the background of Hitler's rise in Europe, the *Advocate* invokes images of the American Revolution and the Hasmonean revolt. It portrays the Yishuv as an outpost of Western and prophetic tradition, "nothing less than a miracle of miracles . . . a barren wilderness and forbidding mountainous region . . . so transformed by the genius, energy and persistence of the Jewish pioneers as to make this small land one of the most picturesque, productive and a bright spot in this darkened era."[133]

Such romantic treatment was often reinforced by illustrations and photographs of the haluzim. The artist Saul Raskin, for example, spent extended time in Palestine. His well-known paintings, sketches, and lithographs of Jewish life in the Yishuv were exhibited around the country, reprinted in the Anglo-Jewish press, and widely acclaimed by art critics (figures 19 and 20). In another instance, Rabbi Leo Shubow contributed a six-part series to the *Boston Traveler* that praised the revolutionary character of the Yishuv and emphasized the colonization efforts of the Jewish pioneers (figure 21).[134]

As popular depictions of haluzim became ubiquitous in American culture—making their appearance everywhere from literature to the news media to public galleries—a standard archetype of the haluz emerged. That the haluzim came to personify the entire Zionist enterprise in the mind of American Jews is evident from a few significant examples. For example, the

19. "The Hora, Dance of the Haluzim" (1935) by Saul Raskin. Courtesy of Eugene Raskin.

20. "The Way to a New Life" (1947) by Saul Raskin. Courtesy of Eugene Raskin.

21. "Palestine Today" (1938). Courtesy of the American Jewish Historical Society.

22. "Old and New Elements in Modern Palestine" (1935). Courtesy of *Jewish Frontier.*

three-panel mural in the lobby of the Society for the Advancement of Judaism, in New York City, shows artist Temima Nimtzowitz's sense of "Old and New Elements in Modern Palestine" (figure 22). The work, completed in 1935, contains a central panel, almost twenty feet long and five feet high, which is flanked on either side by two vertical panels measuring eight feet in height and five feet in width.

The panel on the left depicts the Old Yishuv. Near the ancient city of Tiberias, a group of ecstatic Hasidim dressed in nineteenth-century east European garb sing and dance with the Torah scroll. Meanwhile, traditional worshipers pray at the tomb of Rabbi Simeon bar Yohai in Meron, and two money changers frame the scene. These traditional images are juxtaposed with those in the vertical panel on the right, symbolizing the New Yishuv. In the new society, Palestinian Jewish life radiates outward from the center where a youthful builder carefully lays the building blocks of the Jewish state-to-be: advanced science, universal education (note that the young instructors, almost indistinguishable from their students, are guides and not pedants), modern technology, urban development and so forth. The builder's fellow workers, seemingly unfazed by their arduous labors, are building the foundation of the new society while pioneers pour forth from the city and countryside to unite in song.

The central panels contain romantic scenes of men and women pioneers working side by side and physically redeeming the land of the Jezreel Valley. The valley, a centerpiece of the Palestine labor movement's undertakings known popularly as "the Emek," achieved near-mythic proportions in contemporary literature and song. The scenes of lush green banana orchards, citrus groves, vineyards, and wheat fields, in which are sturdy haluzim dressed in blue shorts, loose shirts, and white sun hats, are set against the competing images of scorching yellow heat and a limitless blue sky. As such, the abundant and fertile Emek, famous for agricultural experimentation and innovative forms of social organization, represents the complete rejuvenation of Palestinian Jewish society.

Another notable depiction of the haluzim appears on the cover of the 1937 yearbook of the United Palestine Appeal (figure 23), the fund-raising instrument of American Zionism. The yearbook, published on the occasion of "Night of Stars," a performance commemorating the twentieth anniversary of the Balfour Declaration, included articles about Zionism and Jewish life in Palestine written by well-known American and world Zionist leaders.

The cover illustration glorifies the Yishuv in Jewish and Zionist terms.

23. Cover of the *United Palestine Appeal 1937 Yearbook on the Occasion of "Night of Stars"* (1937). Courtesy of the American Jewish Historical Society.

Dominated by two youthful haluzim, the illustration symbolizes the hopes and aspirations of the Zionist revolution and the Jewish people. Under the protective gaze of a biblical patriarch, the haluzim—self-confident, determined, and dressed in proletarian garb—are framed by a scythe and a basket of fruit. They are clearly endowed with Jacob's (read: Israel's) blessing. Above them is unfurled a scroll with the prophetic utterance "And Jacob shall return and none shall make him afraid." This phrase, adapted and slightly altered from Jeremiah 30:10 and 46:27, recalls the messianic and Zionist themes of the Jewish ingathering in the Land of Israel. But it is also, at least implicitly, a call to American Jewish arms. Against the backdrop of Arab riots in Palestine, the Nazi regime's persecution of central European Jewry, the Royal Peel Commission's investigation, and the plight of Jewish refugees, the biblical phrase assumes existential and transcendent meaning. Indeed, the biblical text, which itself refers to the destruction of other nations, is no doubt intended to evoke messianic associations:

> Fear not thou, O Jacob My servant, saith the Lord,
> For I am with thee;
> For I will make a full end of all the nations whither I have driven thee;
> But I will not make a full end of thee.[135]

Still more can be made of the illustration: The themes of ancient glory and modern Jewish renaissance are amplified by the juxtaposition of a mature scholar studying a text and a young boy tending a lamb. The boy represents a radical departure from traditional Jewish learning while at the same time invoking the biblical image of youthful David, the shepherd who inherited Saul's kingdom. Between the learned scholar and the young boy, a solitary haluz toils in a field. Although not as prominently featured as the pioneers in Temima Nimtzowitz's mural, this figure also anchors the entire scene, slowly but steadily reshaping the Palestinian landscape and enabling the fulfillment of the Zionist pledge to build the Jewish national home. Behind the haluz rise the buildings of Old and New Palestine. An exotic dome, akin to the mosques of Jerusalem's ancient city, stands in the foreground. In the background are two thoroughly modern institutions: the Hebrew University of Jerusalem and the Technikum (renamed the Technion in modern Hebrew), an engineering university built on the slopes of Mount Carmel in the port city of Haifa. Complementing this fusion of Western and Mediterranean motifs is a steamship in the upper left corner, a symbol of Jewish Palestine's advanced maritime development and strategic geographic location.

24. Cover of *Palestine Book* (1939). Courtesy of the American Jewish Historical Society.

25. "10 Years of Efforts and Achievements for Labor Palestine," National Labor Committee for Palestine (1933). Courtesy of the YIVO Institute for Jewish Research.

Such bold themes were frequently softened and even muted in an effort to appeal to the diverse spectrum of American Jewry, including many who might be totally unfamiliar with or philosophically indifferent to Labor Palestine. For example, the cover illustration of the *Palestine Book*, the official publication of the Jewish Pavilion at the 1939 New York World's Fair, portrays two youthful haluzim who face the future with dignity and optimism (figure 24).[136] However, in this instance, the Zionist pioneers are superimposed on a background of the ten tribes of ancient Israel. The result is a fusion of classical and modern imagery that de-emphasizes Labor Palestine even as it produces a seemingly neutral and apolitical portrait of pioneers in the Land of Israel. To be sure, there is no hint of any distinctive or particularistic national viewpoint here. The socialist-style iconography of toiling, brawny workers apparent in the previous two illustrations—both of which closely resemble the propaganda of groups like the National Labor Committee for Palestine (figure 25)—is here replaced by a portrayal devoid of identifiable partisan proclivities.

The *Palestine Book*, like the plethora of propaganda, literature, films, and newspapers examined in this chapter, demonstrates an important pathway by which pro-Zionist sympathy and support steadily penetrated American Jewish consciousness. In addition to reflecting the prevailing cultural attitudes, the *Palestine Book* also played an active and causative role in the development of American Jewish perceptions of Zionism and Labor Palestine. As a result of the cumulative effect of this and other media, the Yishuv—previously considered a distant backwater—was transformed into a new Western frontier and an outpost of American Jewry's communal interests.

The haluz was a unique Labor Zionist creation, but the image of the haluz was expropriated by many different groups. Thus it served a multiplicity of Jewish and national purposes: revolutionary, warrior, farmer, watchman, redeemer, builder, scientist, and even dashing young discoverer. The Labor Zionist movement vigorously exploited this phenomenon, as did other American Zionists who were eager to promote their own views. It is clear that intensive Labor Zionist and pro-Labor Palestine activity profoundly affected the nature of American Zionism. It is also true that most American Jews were won over by a quasi–Labor Zionist sensibility that spanned the social, religious, and political spectrum.[137] The veneration of the pioneers in Palestine cemented relations between disparate Zionist and Jewish camps, and it also elevated haluziut to the position of a hallowed American Jewish ideal.

4

Pioneers and Pacesetters

The Labor Zionist youth movement in the United States evolved from two organizations transplanted to American soil in 1903 and 1905, respectively: the Poalei Zion Party and Hehaluz (The Pioneer), a socialist Zionist pioneering group with roots in eastern Europe. In the early twentieth century, as noted previously, Poalei Zion was structurally and numerically weak. Its members were "animated by radical sentiments they knew not how to crystallize into a social program."[1] Hehaluz, meanwhile, had a rigorous social and political agenda but no solid organizational base. In 1912, the latter group disbanded when its members immigrated to Palestine.

The Labor Zionist movement's general lack of stability was an obstacle to substantive youth activity. After World War I, however, this situation changed dramatically. In the 1920s, a group of loosely affiliated youth cells coalesced around a semiautonomous national framework. This development led to the emergence of a unified Labor Zionist youth movement later in the decade. In the 1930s, the united movement played a leading role in training American haluzim, and it also became one of Zionism's chief frameworks for American *aliyah* (ascent, i.e., immigration to the Land of Israel). Finally, after World War II, many members of the Labor Zionist youth movement were centrally involved in the clandestine program of "illegal immigration to Palestine" known as Aliyah Bet.[2]

A series of case studies yield an instructive overview of Labor Zionism's impact on American Jewish youth in the prestate period and the emergence of the Labor Zionist youth movement before World War II. They also reveal the complexity of American Jewish attitudes toward the notions of *haluziut* (pioneering) and *hagshamah azmit* (self-fulfillment), ideals that resonated with both American and nascent Palestinian Jewish society.

Before 1914, no unified Labor Zionist youth organization existed. Rather, small groups of young Labor Zionists arose in different Jewish immigrant communities, primarily in New England and the Midwest. Then during World War I, David Ben-Gurion and Yizhak Ben-Zvi united roughly a hundred Poalei Zion *yugnt* (youth) and scores of like-minded young men under the aegis of a revitalized Hehaluz organization. This development led to the crystallization of two seemingly contradictory stands by Labor Zionist youth. On the one hand, the majority of Poalei Zion yugnt considered the party's political objectives in the United States—the democratization of American Jewish life, the creation of a class-conscious Jewish workers' movement, and the expansion of the Zionist movement—to be paramount. On the other hand, the haluzim viewed emigration to the Yishuv as the ultimate personal and ideological goal of Labor Zionism. The tension between these positions, *avodat hahoveh* (work in the present) and *avodat Eretz Israel* (work in the Land of Israel), was one of the salient characteristics of east European Zionism.[3]

The Balfour Declaration and the Jewish Legion generated tremendous interest in and support for the Zionist cause.[4] Consequently, scores of American haluzim emigrated to Palestine, including a group of American legionnaires who remained in Palestine following World War I and established the *moshav* Avihayil near Natanya and persons like Goldie Meyerson (later Golda Meir) and the members of Poalei Zion from Milwaukee.[5] The majority of Labor Zionist youth, however, remained in the United States. In August 1920, approximately three hundred Labor Zionist youth, most of whom lived in New England, united to create Poalei Zion Yugnt (Young Workers of Zion), the official youth wing of the American Poalei Zion Party. The new organization met in Pittsburgh and adopted the following platform:

> The aim of [Poalei Zion Yugnt] is to educate and prepare the Jewish youth for the struggle for the liberation of the Jewish nation, for the upbuilding of the National Homeland in Eretz Israel, for the emancipation of the Jewish working class together with the workers of all nations.
>
> The [Poalei Zion Yugnt] movement is a section of the Poalei Zion Party of America. The specific purpose of the youth movement is to prepare and to educate the American Jewish youth to aid and to become active partners in the struggle of the party.
>
> The [Poalei Zion Yugnt] movement dedicates itself to the fight against assimilation and to the education of Jewish youth in the spirit of progressive Jewish nationalism.
>
> The work of our members will consist of two parts: practical Poalei

Zionist and national Jewish activity, education and self-education along the
lines of secular and Jewish culture.

The language of the movement is Yiddish.

The youth movement is autonomous. The Central Committee will con-
sist of nine people, five from the ranks of the youth, and four senior *haverim*
[comrades]; one of the seniors will serve as secretary. . . . The four seniors
must be approved by the Central Committee. . . .

Decisions and actions opposed to Party policy can be vetoed by the Central Committee.[6]

The Poalei Zion Yugnt platform marked an important turning point in
the development of the Labor Zionist youth movement. It was Poalei Zion
Yugnt's first official policy statement, representing the first broad consensus
among Labor Zionist youth in America.[7] It also exhibited a distinct American orientation and ambivalent attitude toward the personal imperative of
aliyah. Indeed, although the platform emphasized the education of Jewish
youth for future membership in the senior party, it conspicuously omitted
any mention of Hebrew or the notion of *shivat Zion* (return to Zion).
Furthermore, the document can be measured against the platform of the
world Poalei Zion Party.[8] The platform, written by the leading Marxist
Zionist theoretician Ber Borochov—who himself was active in American
Poalei Zion between 1914 and 1917[9]—unequivocally states: "Our ultimate
aim, our maximum program, is socialism. . . . Our immediate aim, our
minimum program, is Zionism."[10] In contrast to this rigid east European
formula, it is apparent that the Poalei Zion Yugnt platform was fashioned
to suit the American group's particular needs. The paternalistic relationship
between the Poalei Zion Party and Poalei Zion Yugnt—despite the latter's
claim of autonomy—is amply illustrated by the senior comrades' influence
over the youth movement's central committee.

The platform also raises the significant issue of language. Like their
counterparts in the general Jewish labor movement, particularly the Bund,
Poalei Zion Yugnt viewed the Yiddish language as a tool for communicat-
ing with the Jewish immigrant masses.[11] But Yiddish also enabled them, as
one member put it, to follow "intimately the intellectual ferment in the
Jewish community where all currents of thought were represented and
collided."[12] In short, Poalei Zion Yugnt's uncompromising Yiddishist orientation was essentially pragmatic, and its conspicuous neglect of English
and Hebrew reflected a strong attachment to the Jewish immigrant milieu.
The platform's affirmation of Yiddish, in fact, belied the tension between

movement factions that favored the use of one language over the other. As Jewish immigrants increasingly became a part of the English-speaking world, a sea change in Jewish cultural life was taking place. To situate the dilemma roughly in the spirit of the times: Should the youth shed their parents' language in order to adapt to their American surroundings, and should they concentrate on learning the renascent language of the Yishuv? This was the central conflict of the Labor Zionist youth movement in the early 1920s. Neither English nor Hebrew offered an ideal solution, whereas Yiddish provided a palliative and held Poalei Zion Yugnt's identity crisis at bay.

During the interwar period, the city of Hartford, Connecticut, boasted a relatively affluent and well-organized community of twenty thousand Jews, including a diverse range of Zionist youth associations.[13] These favorable circumstances were also suited to the development of a local Labor Zionist group: the Junior Poalei Zion Club of Hartford.[14] The Hartford club never had more than fifteen to twenty members, mostly high school age adolescents and perhaps also a few young adults. The group was evenly divided between boys and girls, all of whom were immigrants or the children of immigrants.

Unlike most Labor Zionist youth groups in this period, the Hartford club kept a written account of its activities and meetings.[15] Although the record book itself was written in English, it is clear that the club conducted its business in a mixture of Yiddish and English. Moreover, a close analysis of the Hartford club reveals that despite the hegemony of Poalei Zion Yugnt's Yiddishist forces, the movement's English-speaking clubs represented an important countertrend. Indeed, so opposed were the Hartford members themselves to "restrict[ing] . . . club meeting[s] to any one, specific language" that they instructed a delegate to vote accordingly at a regional Poalei Zion Yugnt convention.[16]

The record book contains numerous references to Yiddish lectures and frequent recitations of articles from the *Daily News* (Dos yidishe tageblat) and the *Forward* (Der forverts). Was Yiddish simply a tool for them, a cultural identity to be shed once they were fully assimilated into American society?[17] Or was it a kind of secular spirituality, a quasi-religious alternative that linked them to Jews everywhere?[18] In actuality, the Hartford club provided fertile ground for both possibilities. Here the members found ample room for youthful experimentation with American society's social, cultural, and political opportunities. Viewed in this context, the interchangeability of Yiddish and English terms like *haverim* and "comrades," the *shvue* and "Our Oath," and Poale Zion Yugnt and "Junior Poale Zion" is significant. The free intermingling of words and phrases in the record book reflects an interim stage in the Americanization of the Hartford club members: a sense of belonging to both worlds.

Although the Hartford club conducted meetings in a mixture of languages, the members' desire to attract newcomers and participate in community events required the use of English.[19] Between 1919 and 1921, the club maintained a regular routine, meeting weekly almost without fail. Meetings began with group singing, followed by announcements and lectures or essays recited by club members. Occasionally, the club was addressed by representatives of the senior Poalei Zion Party or Zionist educators from the local Jewish community.[20] In such instances, the members usually prepared companion lectures and follow-up discussions. They also frequently conducted study sessions, choosing a theme or set of related issues that they examined during several consecutive meetings.

The Hartford club's social, philosophical, and ideological concerns reveal a group outlook. Applying their partisan vantage point to the world around them, the members assessed humanity's ills and fortunes from a moderate, non-Marxist, Labor Zionist perspective. To this end, they organized discussions and lectures on topics such as

1. "Moses Hess" (the early Marxist Zionist ideologist)
2. "Resolved that the Factory System has done more good to mankind than evil"
3. "Socialism"
4. "Resolved that Theodor Herzl did more than Karl Marx"
5. "Resolved that . . . Jewish capitalists must enter the fields of Palestine in order to make it compete with other countries"
6. "Resolved that the government should settle all disputes between capital and labor"
7. "Geverkshaftn Campaign" (the Palestine fund-raising campaign of American Poalei Zion)
8. "Resolved that strikes are a benefit for labor"
9. "Morris Hillquit" (a founder of the United Hebrew Trades and leader of the Socialist Party of America)[21]

Such forums demonstrate the club members' keen interest in issues related to their own identity as Jewish workers. They were also designed to attract new members and influence the tenor of debate among Zionist youth in Hartford. Furthermore, like the party as a whole, the Hartford club aspired to inculcate a pro-Palestine sentiment in the ranks of the local Jewish labor movement.[22]

The record book also documents the group's responses to current national and global political events. For example, a November 1920 meeting scheduled to debate "resolved that another world war is inevitable" was hastily canceled.[23] In its place, the club debated whether "immigration should be prohibited for two years."[24] This change reflects the group's alarm over a U.S. congressional debate that proposed severely restricting immigration. In fact, several months later, Congress did establish the principle of national-origin quotas, laying the groundwork for the Johnson-Reed Act of 1924. The club also expressed fear of the continuing military crisis in Europe and the catastrophic situation of Jews expelled from the eastern war zone.[25] Such incidents show their concern for the safety of relatives and friends in the Old World and highlight the group's immigrant identity.

On another level, the Hartford club exhibited a penchant for centralization, quasi-party trappings, and bureaucracy. The record book, with numerous references to club procedures, demonstrates a general preoccupation with enforcing club rules.[26] The journal also records the resignation of club officers and the withdrawal of individuals from club membership. On one such occasion, a split between the founding members caused a minority faction to secede and establish a Kemfer club.[27] The Kemfer clubs were part of an overall effort by Poalei Zion Yugnt's Yiddishist faction to create groups of Yiddish-speaking youth devoted to Old World party politics. In fact, the groups published and distributed the *Yunger yidisher kemfer* (Young Jewish Fighter), an imitation of the party's propaganda organ, the *Der yidisher kemfer* (The Jewish Fighter).[28] Like its namesake, the youth organ promoted the old guard's Borochovist agenda, a doctrinaire policy that increasingly came under fire from the steadily acculturating younger constituency.[29] With the establishment in 1920 of Zeirei Zion Hitahdut of America, the dispute came to a climax, and many disenchanted Poalei Zion members switched parties.[30] In 1931, these organizations, as noted in chapter 2, merged to form the United Jewish Socialist Labor Party Poalei Zion–Zeirei Zion.

A brief comparison of the Hartford club's progressivism and Poalei Zion's conservatism is revealing. The American party—like the world movement—was mostly male; even the party's youth branches and fraternal order, the Yidish Nazionaler Arbeter Farband, were largely composed of teenage boys. As a matter of fact, in 1925—five years after passage of the Nineteenth Amendment to the U.S. Constitution, guaranteeing universal suffrage—the party structure was still sufficiently exclusive to compel women to create their own separate organization, Pioneer Women.[31] In contrast, the full participation of the Hartford club's female members expanded the range of possibilities for the group's interaction with the local Jewish community. The meaningful involvement of girls also suggests that the Hartford club fulfilled certain social functions. Like other local youth groups, the club provided a place for girls and boys to participate equally. No less important, it was a venue for young Jewish immigrants of both sexes to meet. Last, it provided a framework for Yiddish-speaking youth to experiment with their American identities and adapt to their New World surroundings.[32]

The club's aim of integrating itself into Hartford's Jewish society is also evident in the decision to form a children's group. Since the early 1900s, Hartford's Jews had maintained a program of religious education for boys and girls as well as several Zionist clubs for both sexes.[33] A similarly designed Labor Zionist framework, the Hartford members reasoned, would answer the needs of Jewish immigrant children and perpetuate the Junior Poalei Zion club. In short, the members consciously adapted to American social and cultural norms and distanced themselves from the male-dominated and mostly adult-oriented Poalei Zion Party. The group's moderate philosophical approach and pragmatic emphasis both point to a sophisticated understanding of America's different social and economic conditions. The club was, as will become evident, prototypical of Poale Zion Yugnt's process of transformation.

The Detroit Kvutzah (*sic*) (collective) was an independent group of twelve haluzim attracted to the Labor Zionist youth movement by Ben Codor, the head of Poalei Zion Yugnt.[34] Organized in 1925 by a circle of friends and ideological companions, the kvuzah members attended the United Hebrew Schools of Detroit, and a few of them belonged to Poalei Zion Yugnt.[35] The kvuzah kept a Hebrew record of its regular meetings, which it also used as a diarylike journal for individual and group reflection. "Every useful idea, every piece of criticism, and anything else," one member explained, was to be included in the journal in order to compile "a true composite of the life of the kvuzah and the personalities and thoughts of each and every member."[36] The journal was a product of the kvuzah's intense self-awareness and preoccupation with intrapersonal relations. It was also an overt imitation of the haluzim in Palestine for whom the collective's notebook, usually called the *sefer hayim* (book of life) or *sefer zikaron* (book of memory), was a forum for conveying "inner feelings [that individuals] were unable to express in open discussions."[37] At the same time, the journal aided the kvuzah in its conversion to Hebrew, the Yishuv's principal language of discourse.

Most of the Detroit Kvuzah members were American born, and a few were east European immigrants who had come to America as young children. Many spoke three or four languages: Yiddish, English, Hebrew, and even Russian or Polish.[38] Given this typical background, how do we explain the members' romantic Palestinocentric proclivities? First, they came from working-class Jewish immigrant families, and many attended and participated in events at the local Yidishe Nazional Radikale Shuln, also known as the Folkshuln (folk schools), the Workmen's Circle School, and the Sholem Aleichem School—all of which emphasized Yiddish secularism and Jewish nationalism in varying degrees.[39] Second, the kvuzah members were influenced by their mentors and teachers associated with the United Hebrew Schools of Detroit, an institution known for its early pro-Zionist orientation.[40] Third, as illustrated by the 1922 Poalei Zion Yugnt platform and the Hartford club, language was an important tool for demarcating the youth movement's social, cultural, and ideological boundaries. In this respect, the Detroit Kvuzah went a step further, using language as a mechanism to create an integrated group identity. Explaining this objective, one member remarked, "Would that we had not to decide on that which should be an organic part of our lives, a full reflection of our innermost selves! We decided that the language [of the kvuzah] will be . . . Hebrew. This demands . . . that all the members know and relate to Hebrew as a *living* language."[41]

Actually, the kvuzah journal demonstrates that the members' lingua franca was Yiddish. To wit, the Hebrew texts are full of grammatical and spelling errors and awkward syntax and are interspersed with Yiddish poetry and prose. Nevertheless, the fact that the kvuzah conducted all its business and much of its cultural work in Hebrew demonstrates the special sense of mission it applied to the practical sphere.[42] It also parallels the findings of a 1926 Histadrut survey that found that less than half the Jewish working population in Palestine knew how to speak, read, and write Hebrew fluently before emigrating from the diaspora.[43]

The kvuzah also developed its own version of cultural Zionism. For example, in a ceremony to memorialize the Zionist thinker Ahad Haam, who died in 1927, the kvuzah members read excerpts from his essay "De-rekh hahayim" (The path of life),[44] selecting passages emphasizing the sig-nificance of Bnei Moshe (Sons of Moses, an elite society devoted to He-brew culture), Zionism, and Ahad Haam's teachings. The kvuzah's choice of reading affirmed its members' identification with Ahad Haam's dialecti-cal formula, that is, that Eretz Israel should serve as the Jewish people's spiritual center and nourish Jewish life in the diaspora. Despite the seeming contradiction between this view and the personal imperative of haluziut, the kvuzah members were attracted to the romantic image of Bnei Moshe. As one member explained,

> Ahad Haam understood that the majority of Jews would never settle in their tiny ancestral homeland, and therefore he viewed the new Eretz Israel solely as a strong spiritual center. . . . The influence of Ahad Haam became greater and wider from day to day, but his Torah of spiritual Zionism . . . fused over time with the Herzlian Torah of political Zionism. It is on the basis of this synthesis that the Zionist movement we know was created, the Torah of modern Zionism.[45]

This statement exemplifies the kvuzah's nuanced philosophical orienta-tion. On the one hand, it illustrates the impact of "Ahad Haamism" on the American context. The members themselves affirmed the positive value of Jewish life in the American diaspora.[46] On the other hand, it portrays pio-neering Zionism as an organic process of national rejuvenation. Like their east European contemporaries, notably the Third Aliyah (the Jewish im-migrant pioneers who settled in Palestine between 1919 and 1923), the Detroit Kvuzah viewed the task of nation building in evolutionary terms.[47] By combining these elements, the kvuzah members created an original synthesis that suited their special needs.

For the Detroit Kvuzah members, the scales were tipped by Yosef Ba-ratz, a Palestinian Labor leader and founder of Kibbutz Dagania who visited the United States in 1926. Upon his arrival, Baratz convinced another group of haluzim affiliated with Zeirei Zion Hitahdut of Philadelphia to organize the first American *hakhsharah* (training) farm in Petaluma, Califor-nia.[48] (The Petaluma experiment eventually folded.) Interested in this ven-ture, the Detroit Kvuzah consulted with Baratz and wholeheartedly adopted his proposal for hakhsharah. When the members completed high school in 1929, the Detroit Kvuzah enrolled in an intensive training course at the Michigan State Agricultural College. After four months of course work, they decided to invest $3,000 in a group fund and to pursue further practical training in southern New Jersey.[49] There they hoped to find employment at one of the region's many Jewish farms. Recalling the ensuing chain of events, one member wrote:

> We discovered a Jewish anarchist farmer, a non-Zionist, who nevertheless liked the idea of Jews who want to work in agriculture. He agreed to take us into partnership for one agricultural season. . . . The yield was good, but to our misfortune, it was also the year of the Depression. . . . There was no market for selling our produce . . . A year passed; we lost all our money; and meanwhile we received four [immigration] certificates. . . . Four couples married [and emigrated under] the fiction of married citizens, and the rest went as tourists.[50]

In December 1930, the Detroit Kvuzah became the first group of American haluzim to emigrate to Palestine since the end of World War I. Before leaving the United States, they convened a meeting of representatives from various socialist Zionist groups. Hoping to build on the excitement generated by their own impending departure, the kvuzah proposed the creation of a new group of American haluzim to follow in their footsteps.[51] These hopes, however, did not materialize, for the kvuzah's aliyah was not the result of a flash of inspiration. Rather, it was the act of a group of nonconformists who had gradually educated and trained themselves toward such an end. Unlike their contemporaries, the kvuzah members had extricated themselves from the powerful current of American Jewish acculturation. Others, attracted by the comfort and security of the Jewish economic position in the United States, saw no reason to embark on the unknown and potentially dangerous adventure in Palestine.

The acute social, economic, and political crises of the 1930s shocked many Labor Zionist young people. Like other socialists in this period, the crash of the stock market and the onset of the Great Depression convinced them that they were witnessing the end of one era and the dawn of another. They viewed the desperate economic plight of the United States as a telltale sign of international capitalism's imminent demise.[52]

Specifically, as socialist Zionists, they understood the situation in Borochovist terms; that is, the spectacular rise and collapse of industrial America represented the "rapid development of capitalism and the negations embedded in it."[53] Moreover, the Palestinian Arab riots of August 1929, in which hundreds of Jews were wounded and killed, greatly affected the Labor Zionist youth. The pretext for the riots was a clash over conflicting Arab and Jewish rights at the Western Wall. In fact, the tension between Palestinian Arabs and Jews had been steadily mounting since the previous wave of riots in 1921.[54] One member of Poalei Zion Yugnt later recalled,

> We had been under the emotional stress of two traumatic experiences in 1929. . . . Jewishly we were upset by the Palestine riots, during which the Arabs went on a rampage. . . . On the general scene we were profoundly shaken by the . . . stock-market crash and the subsequent depression. It is difficult to conceive what a sense of helplessness engulfed the country after the crash. Not only the headlines of tycoons turned paupers, news of millionaire suicides, confusing government statements, wild predictions and premonitions by economists, but gnawing doubts about the very foundation of our society upset every American. Those of us who were then in the Young Poalei Zion had the answers. We knew that Zionism would solve the Jewish problem; socialism the problem of society as a whole.[55]

The apparent fragility of America's socioeconomic order and the perceived assault on Jewish "national honor" by the Palestinian Arabs riots engendered a siege mentality among the ranks of committed Labor Zionist youth.[56] Feeling betrayed, many took stock of themselves and their ideology, finding in this youthful combination both psychological refuge and hope of an ultimate cure for humanity's ills. In this context, haluziut, "synonymous [in the minds of many] with self-defense," acquired newfound meaning as a vehicle for personal opportunity.[57] Although this was essentially a repackaged version of Ben-Gurion's and Ben-Zvi's earlier cry, "*lashuv el hakarka*" (return to the land),[58] the revolutionary conditions of the 1930s made the majority of Labor Zionist youth finally view *hagshamah azmit* (self-fulfillment) as relevant and realistic.

In 1931, Poalei Zion Yugnt officially merged with the Farband's youth wing to create the Young Poalei Zion Alliance (YPZA). Seeking to widen the scope of its educational and political activities, the YPZA established three new organizations. First, it created the Junior Young Poalei Zion Alliance, a section for children ages ten to sixteen, divided into the "Buds" and the "Intermediates." Second, it transformed the role of Unser Camp, the Farband family resort, and changed the institution's name to Camp Kvuzah. Next, following the lead of east European Hehaluz and the successful precedent established by the Detroit Kvuzah, the YPZA decided to sponsor several independent hakhsharah experiments in New Jersey and the midwestern states. These *hakhsharot* (training farms)—often no more than short-lived agricultural experiences—were devoid of any partisan character.

But they did include a core of YPZA members and shared the same objective: to prepare Jewish youth for agricultural life in Palestine.[59]

At the outset, only the YPZA showed any interest in officially sponsoring the hakhsharot. Gradually, however, other Zionist groups, including centrist and nonlabor groups,
The turning point came in 19
Hehaluz (Committee in Sup
screen applicants for emigrati
icates for the World Zionist
American haluzim by agricul

In 1933, with the backin
YPZA, the Vaad Lemaan H
America. In reality, the forn
of a few key YPZA leaders
Kibbutz Dagania Bet who
the United States.[62] Reacl
bearer), Young Judea, the I
Hazair (The Young Guar
constructed a diverse coalit
United States.

medicated
and
motivated

As the core of Hehaluz, the
over the new organization's agenda and goals. Meanwhile, the other constituent groups considered Hehaluz an expedient and productive arrangement for supporting their respective members' pioneering aspirations. An overtly political but officially "nonpartisan" organization, American Hehaluz affiliated with the world Hehaluz movement, and when its members immigrated to Palestine, they "automatically join[ed] the Histadrut."[63] By the end of 1933, Hehaluz boasted fourteen branches and 350 active members, three new hakhsharot (Parkeville, Maryland; Minneapolis, Minnesota; and Hightstown, New Jersey), and a regular publication, the *Hehaluz Bulletin*.[64]

Of the 350 Hehaluz members, only 20 percent were affiliated with the YPZA. Of the remainder, another 20 percent belonged to the Poalei Zion–Zeirei Zion; 12 percent were General Zionists; 10 percent were members of Hashomer Hazair; 2 percent were members of Gordonia; and more than 30 percent were nonpartisans known as *stam haluzim* (general pioneers). Moreover, it was estimated that 70 percent of the Hehaluz membership were American born and 80 percent were students.[65] These figures reveal an unprecedented group profile of Labor Zionist youth. Unlike their

predecessors, who were mostly blue-collar immigrants, the 1930s generation of haluzim was acculturated, highly educated, and predisposed to
white-collar work. But they were also committed Labor Zionists and emphasized the notions of Jewish "productivization" and a life of physical
labor in the Yishuv.[66] Their optimistic attitude appears all the more extraordinary in light of the fact that the world Hehaluz movement's share of
immigration certificates—including those for American haluzim—was significantly reduced during this period.[67]

The emergence and rapid development of Hehaluz raised questions
about the YPZA's function as the youth wing of the Poalei Zion–Zeirei
Zion. After 1933, the PZ–ZZ perceived its reservoir of potential membership to be in jeopardy. Indeed, the success of Hehaluz seemed to portend
the realignment of Labor Zionist youth with forces outside the traditional
PZ–ZZ ranks—a threat exacerbated by the active involvement of Histadrut shlihim. Baruch Zuckerman, an important American Labor Zionist
leader, described this intergenerational and intramovement conflict, noting
that PZ–ZZ "never formulated, nor has it ever been able to formulate,
wherein lies its independent political existence."[68] Focusing on the practical
implications of a strong American haluz movement, he asserted,

> Everyone will agree that there are masses of youth who will not enter a party
> youth organization but who will join a [haluz] movement. We must not
> estrange these elements. The party can eventually gain more members from
> a live *haluz* movement than it will from the sort of youth organization we
> have had until now. . . . If the party stubbornly insists only on the organiza-
> tion of party youth, then the youth will seek other ways for itself outside the
> party and often even outside the socialist Zionist ideology. On the other
> hand, if the party realizes that it must itself undergo certain radical changes
> and that only through a large organized *haluz* movement will the party itself
> begin to grow—then it will concentrate all its efforts on bringing Jewish
> youth into the ranks of Hehaluz and will not put obstacles in its path by
> demanding such things that can bode no good for the party itself.[69]

Zuckerman's analysis provides a useful backdrop against which to view
the changing social and political nature of American Labor Zionism. In
general, the interwar years witnessed the movement's structural and ideological transformation and Labor Palestine's increasing appeal on both practical and philosophical grounds for a broad range of American Jews. This
shift in political fortunes also influenced the movement's youth wing,

which gradually abandoned its militant party orientation and began to view the upbuilding of Palestine as a personal challenge. In this regard, Zuckerman perceptively depicted the Labor Zionist youth movement's spiritual and organizational ferment. Identifying the deleterious effects of the party's narrow framework, he predicted that a new and important ideological current was in the offing. No longer the sole purview of the PZ–ZZ, he asserted, Labor Zionism had to make room for fresh ideas and new recruits from outside traditional movement ranks.

But what particular needs did the Hehaluz organization fulfill that the YPZA did not? The answer lies in the Hehaluz agenda, which itself can be broken down into four components: physical training and fitness, Hebrew education, general cultural preparation (including practical living experience in a small cooperative framework), and aliyah. As such, the Hehaluz movement was truly unique. No other Zionist youth framework except Hashomer Hazair—which in the United States appealed to a very small group—instituted a systematic program to strengthen Jewish national identity and train haluzim.

The Hehaluz agenda, however, did have two serious flaws. First, though faithful to the concept of hagshamah azmit, the progress and success of Hehaluz necessarily threatened the movement's own existence, for the most energetic and committed members might emigrate to Palestine within two years. Second, the emphasis on individual development and experiential education, especially in the *kvuzot hakhsharah* (training groups), contradicted the movement's professed desire to become a mass youth organization with a unified ideology. These contradictions caused Jacob Katzman, a traditional, politically oriented youth leader from New England, to express concern that the highly atomized Hehaluz process would lead to the organization's implosion. Furthermore, he argued, because Hehaluz included the YPZA's most committed members, it would also cause the collapse of the Labor Zionist youth movement as a whole.[70]

Nevertheless, Hehaluz answered the real needs of its members in a way that the YPZA could not. It had an organizational vitality of its own. Moreover, the Hehaluz agenda was legitimized by the important Palestinian Labor leaders Yosef Baratz, Berl Katznelson, David Ben-Gurion, and Golda Meyerson, all of whom met with the Hehaluz leaders and visited the hakhsharot during their trips to the United States. Hehaluz also maintained direct contact with the Yishuv through Hanoar Haoved (Labor Youth), the Labor Zionist youth movement in Palestine, and the missions of influential Histadrut-sponsored shlihim.[71] Not least of all, the excitement generated by the emigration of seventy-four American haluzim between 1930 and 1931, including the Detroit Kvuzah, spurred the development of haluz factions in the YPZA.[72] In 1936, out of 1,030 dues-paying YPZA members, 92 were officially enrolled in Hehaluz, and only 26 were "transferred" to the party.[73] In sum, Zuckerman's prediction proved correct: the corresponding expansion of Hehaluz and decline of the YPZA reflected an important shift in the movement's ideological and structural emphasis.

The creation of Hehaluz caused the YPZA's leaders to examine their own cultural and educational emphases. Saadia Gelb, a leader of the Minneapolis YPZA, complained that most members had only "superficial knowledge" of Labor Zionism and that inordinate "attention [was paid] to political activity at the expense of . . . cultural work."[74] Speaking for the YPZA's haluz faction, Gelb asserted that the movement should try to introduce members to a wide array of cultural and intellectual stimuli. "Art, music[, and] literature," he explained, "are essential in the development of a creative socialist Zionist personality. Our educational work . . . must encompass our daily life."[75] A similar theme was emphasized by Ben Halpern, a member of the Boston YPZA. In contrast to Gelb, however, Halpern did not believe in a comprehensive approach to movement "cultural work." Instead, he regarded youth education as an organic process, one in which the individual was "not bound by any decision of the organization." "This is as it should be," Halpern declared, because it relieves the member of "feeling that if he . . . should fail to find his place in the [Labor Zionist youth movement] he would never be a worthwhile citizen of the world anywhere else."[76] Taken as a unit, Gelb and Halpern represent the bipolar tension that characterized the educational climate of the Labor Zionist youth movement at that time.

As a result of this debate, attention in the YPZA shifted to the development of the Junior YPZA, the children's section of the YPZA. Members of the Junior YPZA clubs—English-speaking boys and girls ages ten to sixteen—were educated in the "direction of haluziut," but they never received any "direct education for Hehaluz."[77] To attract the youngsters, the Junior YPZA clubs implemented an informal Jewish educational program based on holiday observance, scouting and camping, Palestinian folk songs and dances, conversational Hebrew, and games—a model that borrowed elements from the east European and German Zionist youth movement as well as the Boy Scouts of America.[78] The clubs were led by teams of young men and women, usually charismatic YPZA and Hehaluz leaders. The combination of talented youth leadership and ripe social conditions proved to be advantageous. Between 1930 and 1932, the Junior YPZA opened seventy clubs, mostly on the east coast and in the midwestern states, and the youth movement as a whole grew to approximately 1,600 members.[79]

The momentum of the early 1930s led Moshe Cohen, an innovative Minneapolis YPZA leader, to propose the creation of an independent Labor Zionist children's framework, a matter eventually considered by the 1935 YPZA national convention.[80] The convention generally supported Cohen's idea, with two distinct views emerging. One faction pleaded for complete autonomy. The other argued against "the danger of setting up a Frankenstein" and proposed an educational bureau of the YPZA to be known by the Hebrew name Habonim (The Builders). In the end, a compromise solution determined that Habonim would be "autonomous in educational matters, but subject to national executive committee decisions on all issues of politics . . . representation, and other major policy questions."[81] Moreover, the delegates unanimously favored a nondoctrinal educational agenda. "Haluziut," the convention declared, "shall be the central point, and a regard for Jewish and general socialist problems shall be vital portions of the program."[82] With this statement, the YPZA and Hehaluz positions were effectively synthesized, and a new hybrid arose: the Zionist Pioneer Youth Habonim.[83]

The Habonim organization grew quickly. Between 1930 and 1937, the number of Habonim (originally Junior YPZA) clubs grew from 65 to 101. In contrast, the number of YPZA clubs increased only from 37 to 38. We should clarify these figures, however, because in actuality, several older Habonim groups "graduated" to the YPZA while entire YPZA clubs occasionally "transferred" into the PZ–ZZ chapters of their respective cities. Nonetheless, the figures demonstrate that in seven years, the number of Habonim clubs increased twofold, and the YPZA's core constituency diminished. By 1937, the total number of Habonim, YPZA, and Hehaluz members climbed to roughly 2,800.[84]

How do we account for Habonim's rapid growth, and what does it tell us about the Labor Zionist youth movement after 1935? First, the new Habonim platform opened doors to the Jewish community that were previously closed to the party's youth wing. Although it continued to challenge American Jewry's status quo, Habonim's ideological position was moderate enough to mitigate fears that it might subvert the organized American Jewish community. Second, once Habonim's age limit was raised to eighteen, it provided a greater number of moderate Labor Zionist youth with a legitimate and supportive environment for their own development. In contrast to the YPZA, which continued to function as the youth wing of the PZ–ZZ Party, Habonim was self-consciously styled as "an organization in which [to] acquire a wide cultural background and array of desirable personal habits and social attitudes."[85] This approach was soon translated into a forceful and unambiguous new Labor Zionist youth identity: "We are young. . . . We are Jews. . . . We are Americans. . . . Now put all these words together and you have exactly what we are—young American Jews!"[86] Third, against a background of growing support for Zionism generally and Labor Zionism particularly, American Labor Zionism experienced a surge of support in most American cities, and these favorable conditions paved the way for the expansion of Habonim clubs.[87]

The Habonim clubs were also stimulated by frequent visits of national Habonim leaders and propaganda literature distributed by the Habonim central committee. In addition, the movement published *Haboneh* (The Builder), an attractive magazine designed to unify Habonim's educational agenda and foster a sense of belonging among members across the country. The growth of national Habonim was also nurtured by the creation of several regional Labor Zionist summer camps, a concept that can be traced to the opening of Camp Kvuzah in 1932. By 1936, Habonim operated six regional camps located near New York, Baltimore, Montreal, Detroit, Chicago, and Los Angeles. More than one thousand young people attended the Habonim camps, which were modeled after the *kibbutzim* (communal farms and settlements in Palestine) and directed by Labor Zionist youth leaders, including college students eager to apply the progressive educational theories of John Dewey, William Kirkpatrick, and E. T. Thorndike.[88] Ben-Zion Ilan, the first Poalei Zion Yugnt graduate to return to America as a Histadrut shaliah, foresaw the Habonim camps' success: "The most decisive months in our activity . . . will be the two summer months. . . . They may yet overweigh the rest of the year."[89]

Owing to the Labor Zionist movement's high profile, particularly after it gained control of the World Zionist Organization in 1933,[90] and the corresponding increase in American Labor Zionism's stature, Hehaluz and Habonim received considerable attention. In fact, they were given financial and political support by many prominent American Zionist leaders, including Louis D. Brandeis, Stephen S. Wise, Hayim Greenberg, Horace M. Kallen, and Mordecai M. Kaplan. They were also assisted by the Histadrut leaders Goldie Meyerson (later Golda Meir), Zalman Rubashov (later Sha-

zar), David Ben-Gurion, Berl Katznelson, Chaim Arlosoroff, David Re-
mez, and Eliahu Dobkin. These figures considered Labor Zionist youth
activity, especially the pioneering efforts of Hehaluz, uniquely important to
accelerating American Jewish support for the Zionist enterprise.[91]

It is ironic that despite the support for Labor Zionist youth activity in the
United States, Labor's dominant position in the World Zionist Organization and the Yishuv inadvertently created obstacles for American Hehaluz
and Habonim. In particular, as factional disputes and the dire circumstances
of east and central European Jewry increasingly preoccupied the attention
of Labor Zionism's major power brokers, youth affairs in the American
Jewish diaspora assumed less immediate significance. In 1934, for example,
after Lassya Galili completed a term as the Histadrut shaliah in the United
States, the Histadrut executive committee could not agree on his replace-
ment. Consequently, the already tense relations between Hehaluz and
Hashomer Hazair—which mirrored those of the Histadrut and the Kibbutz
Arzi (National Kibbutz) movement in Palestine—flared into an open con-
flict.[92]

Then, following the model of its east European counterpart, American
Hashomer Hazair demanded complete organizational autonomy, including
the right to conduct its own hakhsharah, supervise cultural and social activities independently, and propose a separate list of candidates for immigration to Palestine.[93] These conditions, all of which circumvented the authority of Hehaluz, were rejected by the American movement's national
executive. Eventually, David Ben-Gurion himself intervened to reach a
compromise solution.[94] In another instance, a world conference of Hashomer Hazair held in July 1935 debated the issue of relations between its
American branch and other haluz groups in the United States. The Palestine gathering concluded by strongly supporting the position of American
Hashomer Hazair. In response, the Labor leader Shmuel Yavnieli published
a rejoinder in the Palestinian daily *Davar* (The Word) that was critical of
Hashomer Hazair. He accused the world movement of excessive partisan-
ship and divisive tendencies,[95] an interchange that only exacerbated the
Hehaluz–Hashomer Hazair debate.[96]

As part of the Histadrut executive committee's attempt to calm the
situation, Enzo Sereni was sent to the United States in January 1936. His
tenure as a shaliah demonstrates the complexity of Zionist youth affairs in
this period. Sereni was a charismatic figure who had previously served as
the Histadrut shaliah in Germany, and his success with German Zionist

youth attracted the attention of the World Zionist Organization.[97] From the outset, as "shaliah and spokesman of the whole movement," Sereni opposed splitting Hehaluz along partisan or ideological lines. To appease the members of Hashomer Hazair, however, he agreed to sponsor a joint request that—if it was economically feasible—a second shaliah of the Histadrut (preferably a member of Hashomer Hazair in Palestine) be sent to the United States.[98] When the 1936 Arab riots delayed the processing of this request, Hashomer Hazair withdrew from active involvement in Hehaluz. In September, word finally arrived that a second shaliah would be sent, but only on the condition that Hehaluz assume full financial responsibility for both shlihim. This impractical suggestion embittered relations between Hehaluz and Hashomer Hazair. Subsequently, Hashomer Hazair refused to allow Sereni even to meet with its groups.

In contrast, Sereni was warmly received by the YPZA and Habonim. He participated in numerous meetings, seminars, and conventions and played an active role in designing and implementing Habonim's educational program, including its summer camps. He also introduced a new ideological concept to mainstream American Labor Zionist youth via Habonim: the synthesis of "intensification and expansion." Based on Sereni's previous experience in Germany, he believed that "we cannot become a mass movement. . . . We are a minority movement and we must be conscious of this when we consider expansion." The immediate task, he believed, was the qualitative development of the Labor Zionist youth membership. Once this was realized, the movement would be able to absorb newcomers and influence other Zionist groups. To this end, Sereni considered it essential to rid the movement of its "inferiority complex" and showed special interest in the development of relations with Avukah, Massada, and Gordonia.[99]

Despite the uncertainty caused by the Arab riots, the financial constraints of the Histadrut and Hehaluz, and the factional obstacles presented by Hashomer Hazair, Sereni promoted Labor Zionism among "English-speaking, assimilated Jewish youth." He traveled the country with Ben Halpern, then head of Hehaluz, organizing new Hehaluz groups of college-age youth and speaking on behalf of the Histadrut. Sereni was also the leading spirit behind several new movement undertakings, including the purchase of the movement's first permanent hakhsharah site in Creamridge, New Jersey; the publication in English translation of works by Yosef Haim Brenner, Ber Borochov, and A. D. Gordon; and the transformation of the *Hehaluz Bulletin* into a monthly publication.[100]

In addition, Sereni coedited the provocative book *Jews and Arabs in*

Palestine: Studies in a National and Colonial Problem (1936), the first comprehensive study in English of Arab-Jewish relations. A special advance edition of the volume was also published for the thirty-ninth annual convention of the Zionist Organization of America.[101] Widely praised, *Jews and Arabs in Palestine* contains a short history of the Arab-Jewish conflict, translations of seminal articles and addresses by leaders of the Yishuv, and Sereni's own controversial proposal, "Towards a New Orientation of Zionist Policy." In this essay, Sereni outlines a farsighted plan for reaching a peaceful settlement with the Palestinian Arabs, an approach that not only recognized the legitimacy of Arab territorial aspirations but also stressed the need for a fundamental revision of Zionist ideology:

> The progressive Zionist forces in the Yishuv have only one way out of [the] impasse [created by conservative Jewish political forces]—the creation of a state power that will reconcile the interests of both nations and guarantee to each nation complete autonomy over its own internal policies. . . . This means a renunciation of the ideology and practice of separate economies. This amounts to a conception of Palestinian problems that will be a revolutionary change since Zionism will necessarily have to renounce certain slogans that were of great importance as propaganda for the early development of Palestine.[102]

Paradoxically, Sereni's accommodationist stance—which challenged the "defensive ethos" of the Palestinian Labor movement[103]—was enthusiastically received by the members of Hehaluz and Habonim but did little to mend relations with the binationalist Hashomer Hazair. Not surprisingly, it also provoked consternation within the Histadrut executive committee.[104] In general, however, Sereni's nondoctrinal approach was well suited to the temperament of most American Labor Zionist youth in this period. Although he himself subscribed to a particular socialist Zionist agenda,[105] he opposed the notion of party discipline among diaspora youth and instead stressed the value of diversity:

> I am against one haluz prognosis for all countries and I doubt if the process that characterized Jewish life in Poland or Germany exists here. . . . Definitely, I shall not accept the explanation of the need [for] an exclusive aim in education. . . . From the time of Jabotinsky, I have objected to any explanations about a need of "Monism." . . . [106] [We] have to bring up a generation of youth whose outlook on life is to be *whole*. Zionist and Socialist *haluziut* ought to be desirable though not the single result of this education, it must take into account the American reality. . . . Naturally, in this expan-

sive country there is room for all sorts of approaches and movements. I hope that the Hehaluz here, as in Germany, will succeed in becoming the center of influence. . . . I therefore [emphasize] cultural work . . . [and] *hakhsharah* [as] the peak and symbol for the whole movement.[107]

In late 1936, the tension between Hehaluz and Hashomer Hazair reached a climax when the latter publicly accused Sereni of misrepresenting them in Histadrut affairs and sabotaging their organizational efforts. The allegations were reviewed by an independent committee and deemed to be false. Nevertheless, Hashomer Hazair reiterated its demand that a second Histadrut shaliah be sent from Palestine, causing Sereni to respond that under current circumstances, such a move would be tantamount to "recognition of the necessity for an equilibrium in the [Hehaluz] delegation . . . [a notion] contrary to the principles of unity upon which the Histadrut and Hehaluz are built." When the independent committee rejected Hashomer Hazair's stipulation, the organization's leadership declared its abandonment of "every responsibility for Hehaluz." Following this showdown, the Histadrut executive committee notified Sereni that in accordance with Hashomer Hazair's earlier request and because "the situation in Palestine demands that we keep the peace," a second shaliah would indeed be sent.[108] Even though its ostensible purpose was to maintain intraorganizational peace, the executive committee's action was also an effort to impose ideological discipline on its overseas ranks, and it reflected the Histadrut leadership's serious displeasure with Sereni's pro-Arab sympathies.[109] For his part, Sereni understood only too clearly the implications of such a move. Faced with what he considered to be an untenable political situation and despite the protests of the Hehaluz national executive, he resigned his mission.

Something much higher than a personal problem is involved in this case. . . . Should the Histadrut or the Hehaluz be conceived as a unity in which . . . [different organizations] are parts of the unity and subordinate to it? Or should they be conceived as a federation in which different people are *associated* in order to achieve certain interests[?] . . . Rather than have the child divided, I prefer to let the child be given over intact to the care of another *shaliah*.[110]

After urging the full cooperation of all sides, Sereni returned to Palestine in May 1937.

The Hehaluz national executive immediately turned to the task of restoring order and an atmosphere of mutual respect among its ranks. For its part, the YPZA leadership issued a statement aimed at burying the differences between Hehaluz and Hashomer Hazair:

> We regard the decision of the Histadrut [executive committee] . . . as another attempt to bring about the full cooperation of Hashomer Hazair in all matters of . . . Hehaluz. The implications of this decision are clear—Hashomer Hazair must now collaborate. . . . All their demands have been fulfilled and as proof of their sincerity must come their active participation in the Hehaluz and their acceptance of its sovereignty in specific Hehaluz functions.[111]

The statement was both a clarification of the YPZA's ideological position and a political tactic designed to push ahead with the Hehaluz agenda. In a larger sense, however, it reflected the extent to which pluralism, unity, and philosophical moderation had become operative concerns for American Labor Zionist youth. Having evolved from its yugnt origins into a distinctly American haluz framework, the Labor Zionist youth movement of the late 1930s rejected singular ideological doctrines and the weltanschauung of its east European and Palestinian counterparts. In 1937, Ben-Zion Ilan described the transformation of the movement in a letter to his friends at home:

> The Americans who came to [Kibbutz] Afikim in the early thirties would never recognize the movement today: scouting, Hebrew, work training, summer camps, handicrafts, choirs, dramatic groups, etc. We have freed ourselves to a great extent from the heritage of the party-oriented education bequeathed by the senior movement, and have really created a framework for the unimpeded expression of young people.[112]

In time, as the complementary agendas of the YPZA, Hehaluz, and Habonim became increasingly intertwined, the distinctions among the organizations blurred. In 1938, the YPZA, Habonim, and Gordonia officially merged, and in 1940, the YPZA's formal dissolution led to complete unification. As a consequence, Habonim was expanded to include young adults up to twenty-three years old.[113]

The Labor Zionist youth movement's vigorous activity and steady expansion reached a peak in 1939. Then, with the outbreak of World War II, Hehaluz begin to falter, and Habonim embarked on a new organizational phase. These related developments stemmed from a confluence of forces. First, the desperate plight of central European Jewry forced the World Zionist Organization to divert its limited immigration schedule and save as many Austrian and German Jewish youth as possible.[114] But the few immigration certificates allotted to American Hehaluz, compounded by the restrictions of the British Mandate, deprived the movement of its raison d'être.[115] Second, following the 1936 Arab riots, the return of approximately two hundred dispirited American haluzim proved to be a serious blow to the morale of the struggling Hehaluz organization.[116] Third, as the Hehaluz ranks were depleted, the YPZA and Habonim underwent a process of internal readjustment and turned to the expansion of Habonim camping in order to consolidate the movement's base. Thus ironically, while the numbers of American haluzim dropped, the regional Habonim camps experienced a surge in growth. By 1940, nine regional camps attracted a total of 1,500 campers.[117]

"The tendency most manifest in our movement these recent years," Ben-Zion Ilan wrote, "has been liberation . . . from the outlook and methodology [of] a party education whose roots were imbedded in foreign climes and artificially transplanted here."[118] Noting that only drastic revisions had freed the movement from outmoded and doctrinaire conceptions, Ilan posited that Habonim—because of its indigenous nature—provided the best opportunity to harmonize Labor Zionism's agenda and the liberal forces of American Jewish youth culture. One outcome of this process was the emigration of nearly a thousand American haluzim to Palestine between the world wars.[119] Another was the continuing involvement of young Labor Zionists in the social and political activities of the American movement.

In several important respects, the transformation of the Labor Zionist youth movement mirrored the process of Jewish acculturation in the United States. But it was the movement's internal resources—its capacity for ideological sensitivity and political realism—that enabled Poalei Zion Yugnt, the YPZA, Hehaluz, and Habonim to provide a wide array of American Jewish youth with a measure of control over their lives in the uncertain interwar period. Although American Zionist youth culture as a whole awaits a more comprehensive investigation, this chapter offers the following observation: A complex array of social, cultural, and political forces combined to produce the American Labor Zionist youth movement. On the one hand, the movement was aware of the Jewish immigrant milieu's inadequacy and the existential need for accommodation to the New World. On the other hand, the American haluz movement offered an alternative to the path of least resistance—total assimilation—by focusing the minds and hearts of Jewish youth on the task of building an ideal Jewry and an ideal society.

5

Harbingers of American Zionism

In the decades preceding the creation of the State of Israel, Horace M. Kallen (1882–1974), a philosopher of cultural pluralism, Mordecai M. Kaplan (1881–1983), the founder of Reconstructionism, Maurice Samuel (1895–1972), a writer and essayist, and Hayim Greenberg (1889–1953), a socialist Zionist ideologist, numbered among American Zionism's most prominent and eloquent spokesmen. In contrast to Louis D. Brandeis, Henrietta Szold, Stephen S. Wise, Louis Lipsky, and Abba Hillel Silver, they were not only important movement leaders but also original Jewish thinkers whose weltanschauung was rooted in the Zionist idea. Although far from unanimous in their social and political outlook, for much of the 1930s and 1940s they acted in concert under the aegis of the League for Labor Palestine. They appeared on the Jewish communal lecture circuit as representatives of Labor Zionism, and they promoted Labor Palestine in popular Anglo-Jewish publications like *Menorah Journal, Reconstructionist, Jewish Spectator, New Palestine,* and *Jewish Frontier.*

What unites Kallen, Kaplan, Samuel, and Greenberg historically, however, is not their participation in the Labor Zionist movement. Indeed, several other important Jewish intellectuals such as Ludwig Lewisohn, Marie Syrkin, Trude Weiss-Rosmarin, Charles Reznikoff, and, at a later stage, Max Lerner were also active supporters of Labor Zionism. Rather, they are distinguished by the pathbreaking quality of their Zionist activity on the American scene. Moreover, in a larger sense, their activities lead us to the core problematic of American Judaism: the nature of Jewish identity in the American setting. They represented new ideological and philosophical trends that ultimately transformed the way American Jews understood Jewish peoplehood and the Zionist cause.

In an era when American Jews and Zionists valued the notions of "belonging" and "normalizing Jewish life," Kallen, Kaplan, Samuel, and Greenberg were mavericks who challenged American Jews to reevaluate their uniqueness as well as their relationship to Zionism and Eretz Israel. In time, the orientation of most American Jews grew to resemble more closely their brand of Labor Zionism than any other Zionist variant. This was due in part to their unusual intellectual talents as well as their capacity to sustain a rich ideological and philosophical discourse with a wide spectrum of Jews and non-Jews. At the same time, the prevailing circumstances forced them to assume specific historic roles. Consequently, they provided American Jews with a sizable quotient of socially unifying leadership in the prestate era and emerged as the chief exponents of a new American Zionist outlook: a social and political vision attuned to the reality of American Jews and the needs of Labor Palestine. It was they who came closest to articulating the meaning of Zionism for most American Jews.

Of the four men examined in this chapter, Mordecai M. Kaplan, recognized as a "vital Jewish leader of the American community," was perhaps the one most celebrated during his lifetime.[1] He was born in Vilna, Lithuania. But when he was eight years old, his family came to the United States to join his father, who had immigrated a year earlier with Rabbi Jacob Joseph, an Orthodox rabbi brought over from Europe to unify New York's traditional Jewish community. Instantly immersed in the *goldene medine*'s (golden land's) diverse environment, Kaplan, despite his own father's standing as a learned rabbi, rapidly became alienated from Orthodoxy. In 1900 he earned a bachelor's degree from City College of New York, and in 1902 he was ordained a "minister" by the Jewish Theological Seminary of America (JTS). He was on the verge of abandoning the rabbinate when the Conservative movement leader Solomon Schechter asked him to take over the seminary's newly created Teachers Institute, an affiliation that marked the beginning of Kaplan's lifelong academic association with JTS.

Kaplan is best remembered by American Jewish historians as the philosopher of Reconstructionism and for his role in establishing the movement's base, the Society for the Advancement of Judaism (SAJ), in 1922. The most unusual aspect of Reconstructionism was Kaplan's emphasis on the centrality of Eretz Israel and the Yishuv in modern Jewish life. This conception presented a serious threat to the American Jewish establishment, which was mostly composed of affluent German Jews with classical Reform leanings. In the years following World War I, the tide of American Jewish life had turned, and the Reform movement in particular—which found it increasingly difficult to oppose the idea of Jewish statehood—was groping for a new conception of Jewishness.[2] By contrast, Kaplan presented a fresh and compelling alternative that was responsive to both Jewish tradition and American Jewry's changing character.[3]

Kaplan's attempt to place Zionism at the center of synagogal life—notwithstanding the originality of his Reconstructionist principles—is also what divided him from Conservative Judaism. For example, at the fifth annual convention of the United Synagogue of America, held just three months before Britain issued the Balfour Declaration in November 1917, Kaplan participated in a debate on whether the United Synagogue of America should "join with Zionists throughout the world in voicing the claim to a legally recognized and internationally secured homeland for the Jewish people in Palestine." The proposal, which was seriously opposed by Conservative movement leaders—including the influential American Jewish Committee officer Cyrus Adler—was eventually modified to reaffirm "the ancient Zionist hope in the early restoration of Palestine as the Jewish homeland as the means for the consummation of the religious ideals of Judaism."[4] In contrast to this depoliticized compromise, however, Kaplan advocated a decisive radical step: a declaration favoring Zionist political aspirations. He challenged the Conservative movement leadership to submit the resolution to a referendum of the United Synagogue's constituent bodies:

> I take the resolution with regard to Zionism as a very serious one, because it appertains to us Jews as Jews, and because it is a serious one we have no right to act upon it, few as we are here today. After all, I practically see before me an Alumni meeting with a few friends. . . . I feel confident that we can take it to our respective organizations, put it before them, and then the vote that will be taken will mean something not only to the larger organization with which we want to cooperate, but will mean something to the general world which is interested in knowing what the Jewish attitude is on the subject.[5]

The impetus for Kaplan's wide-ranging Zionist interests can be traced to his early involvement in Judah L. Magnes's prewar Achavah Club. As noted earlier, the Achavah program was partly inspired by the European agenda of *Gegenwartsarbeit* (Zionist work in the diaspora). The club served as a stimulating forum for divergent ideological and philosophical viewpoints, and for Kaplan and others, it was also their first intensive encounter with streams of Zionist radical thought. Through his participation in the Achavah Club, Kaplan became personally acquainted with the Yiddishist ideologue Chaim Zhitlowsky, the utopian theoretician Nahman Syrkin, and the Yiddish playwright David Pinsky.[6] He maintained his contact with these and other socialist Zionists throughout his lifetime.

Even though Kaplan defined and described his Zionism in various ways, he consistently sounded a core existential theme. This is exemplified in *Judaism as a Civilization* (1934), Kaplan's magnum opus, in which he employed the term spiritual Zionism to connote progressive, egalitarian, and theological aspirations:

> Spiritual Zionism cannot content itself with merely the rebuilding of Palestine. If the Jews throughout the world are to be united and creative, they must not only have a spiritual center in Palestine; wherever they live in considerable numbers they must organize themselves into vigorous communities. The associated life of a Jewish community should not be regarded as extraneous to Jewish religion. It is the very substance out of which the Jew must strive to evolve religious values. Cooperation on a communal scale is the *sine qua non* of a genuine and sustained interest in Jewish religion. . . . To raise the present status of the Jews from a disintegrated and fragmented mass of individuals into an organic unity, whether it be the unity of the Jewish people as a whole, or any part of it, is to create the conditions that make the Jewish religion possible. What the oil and the wick are to the flame, organized Jewish life is to Jewish religion.[7]

Kaplan's Zionist analysis echoes the multifaceted debate about Jewish spiritual and national identity conducted by Ahad Haam, A. D. Gordon, Martin Buber, and other leading thinkers in the early decades of the twentieth century.[8] Arguing that "the status of the Jews . . . is that of an international nation with its home in Palestine," Kaplan resolved that "only in a Jewish national home is it possible for Judaism to achieve those environmental conditions which are essential to its becoming a modern, creative and spiritual civilization."[9] Thus Kaplan insisted that the social and cultural needs of the Jewish people necessitated the rebuilding of Eretz Israel. His espousal of Zionism as a program to which all Jews could rally—including secular and nontraditional Jews—was essentially a redefinition of the cornerstone of Judaism. His insistence that the diaspora's future and communal rejuvenation depended on social and political action, particularly cooperative forms of Jewish life, reflected the values of liberal American Jews and left-oriented Zionists.

Horace M. Kallen was also at the center of the nationalist debate in elite American Jewish circles. Like Kaplan, Kallen was born into a rabbinic family from the Silesian town of Berenstadt. When he was five years old, his family immigrated to the United States. Kallen grew up in Boston and graduated from Harvard University in 1903. After a brief interlude at Princeton University, Kallen returned to Harvard and took up his doctoral studies under the tutelage of William James, George Santayana, and Josiah Royce, three humanist philosophers of international repute.[10] At Harvard, Kallen joined Harry Wolfson and Henry Hurwitz to found a Zionist student group called the Menorah Society. American Zionism was then, according to Kallen, "essentially Yiddishist," divided "between people who were beginning to become Labor Zionists and [those] who were in bitter controversy with the socialists of New York."[11] When the Menorah Society drifted from its original nationalist premise, Kallen launched the short-lived, semisecret fellowship of Perushim, made up of men and women devoted to the Zionist cause.[12] When the Perushim disbanded, Kallen joined a group of promising idealists that included Isaac B. Berkson, Hayim Fineman, Solomon Schiller, Israel Goldberg (later known by his pen name, Rufus Learsi), Morris Zeldin, and Emanuel Neumann to found Zeirei Zion Hitahdut of America.[13]

Kallen's ties to Zeirei Zion, through which he absorbed elements of Nahman Syrkin's utopian Zionist socialism, represent a watershed in his philosophical development. Enthralled with Jewish colonization efforts in Palestine, he saw in the *haluzim* (pioneers) a new ascetic vanguard, an elite not unlike the Perushim. The haluzim, Kallen declared, "ask for nothing . . . are all of a high sensibility and delicate nature. . . . To reach Palestine they will endure everything, they will stop at nothing."[14]

Of course, in characterizing the haluzim, Kallen was also speaking figuratively about his generation and Zionism as it was developing in America's progressive period.[15] To Kallen, the haluzim symbolized the ongoing Jewish struggle for social equality, dignity, and autonomy. They also supplied tangible evidence of a specifically Jewish mentality, revolutionary and humanist in orientation, whose larger goal was the elevation of humanity's universal condition. In reality, however, Kallen's Labor Zionism was less radical and less doctrinaire than that espoused by the haluzim themselves. Tempered by the American Jewish experience, his philosophical approach was devoid of the personal imperative known as *hagshamah azmit* (self-realization), which was, in fact, at the heart of the *haluz* (pioneer) ideal.[16] Rather, Kallen's orientation emphasized "Hebraism," a concept he used to combine elements of Ahad Haam's cultural Zionism and Simon Dubnow's diaspora nationalism.

To the Jews of the world it [is] . . . a program of self-help and social justice within Jewry; giving the same rights and responsibilities to both sexes, and actually trying out experiments in economic organization to abolish the exploitation of one man by another without abolishing the impetus towards individual excellence. To the nations of the world [Hebraism] . . . should carry into effect the social and spiritual ideals of the Hebrew prophets. . . . [It should] reassert the prophetic ideal of internationalism as a democratic and cooperative federation of nationalities.[17]

By affirming the centrality of Eretz Israel in Jewish life and the contributions of diaspora Jews to their lands of residence, Kallen synthesized, with his commitment to America, the political struggle for a socially just national home in Palestine. That his vision resonated with American Jewry is clear in the Zionist Organization of America's Pittsburgh Program that he drafted in 1918. Its platform called for national ownership and control of Palestine's lands, natural resources, and public utilities. It also upheld the "cooperative principle" in administering the Yishuv's affairs, a system of free public education and the primacy of the Hebrew language.[18]

Hayim Greenberg also displayed a talent for voicing the ideological agenda of his time.[19] In 1905, following the Kishinev pogrom, he coauthored a proclamation that was widely circulated by the Russian Zeirei Zion.[20] At age seventeen, Greenberg made his debut as the youngest Russian Zionist delegate at the 1906 Helsingfors Conference, where resolutions favoring *Gegenwartsarbeit* as well as equal rights for Jews and other nationalities in the Russian Empire were adopted.[21]

Although in many respects he was philosophically akin to Kaplan and Kallen, Greenberg differed significantly from them in his personal development and ideological orientation. Born in Todoristi, Bessarabia, Greenberg grew up in the twilight of the Romanov dynasty. He never received any religious training or a formal secular education, but he did possess a passion for learning and taught himself to read and write Yiddish, Hebrew, and Russian (as well as German and English in his adult years). As a result of his autodidactic proclivity and voracious reading habits, Greenberg acquired a broadly based Jewish and general education.

In the uncertain and turbulent period that followed the Bolshevik revolution, Greenberg remained faithful to a combination of Zionist and communist ideals. But he did so at enormous political and personal risk and was arrested on several occasions by the Soviet authorities.[22] His last stand in Russia was in defense of Habimah (The Stage), a well-known Hebrew theater company in Moscow. When these efforts failed, the rising tide of Jewish "cultural attrition" swept Greenberg, along with thousands of other Jewish radicals, out of the Soviet sphere.[23]

In 1921 Greenberg traveled to Berlin, joining other émigré intellectuals in this important center of Zionist activity, and there he matured as a Zionist thinker.[24] His writings reveal the influence of religious neo-Judaism, originally propounded by the German master Hermann Cohen and later developed by Martin Buber and Franz Rosenzweig.[25] Greenberg's identity was also shaped by opposition to certain prevailing trends in Jewish and Zionist thought.[26] He rejected antimodernist rabbinic sentiment as anachronistic and classical Reform as superficial. At the same time, he dismissed the rigid Zionist dogmatism of *shlilat hagolah* (negation of the exile) and posited a supportive approach to Jewish life in the diaspora. For Greenberg, Zionism was the synthesis of Judaism and national revival.

Philosophically, Greenberg was closest to Chaim Arlosoroff, a Russian émigré like himself, who completed his formal education in Berlin. Arlosoroff, a cofounder of the German branch of Zeirei Zion—which was known in Palestine as Hapoel Hazair (The Young Worker)—emerged in this period as a rising star of Zionist politics and a brilliant economist. Like Greenberg, Arlosoroff was inspired by A. D. Gordon's cosmic vision of physical toil and national redemption, especially the voluntaristic notion of *kibush haavodah* (the conquest of labor).[27] The very terminology, with its layers of unfolding meaning—*avodah*, the Hebrew word for "labor," is also the classical term for worship—tapped an idealistic vein in the radical east European Jewish milieu of the period. *Kibush haavodah* symbolized the complete transformation of Jewish life.[28]

Even though Arlosoroff drew much from Gordon's philosophy, his Zionist thinking was also substantially shaped by the scientific rigors of the German academy. Out of this admixture, he developed a synthesis of popular socialism and pragmatic Zionism, a program with which Greenberg and other diaspora members of Zeirei Zion strongly identified. In contradistinction to Gordon's vague political views and Russian Poalei Zion's doctrinaire Marxist Zionism, Arlosoroff promoted what came to be known as a "constructivist" Zionist agenda.[29] In other words, he maintained that pioneering settlement and the gradual development of Palestine's Jewish socioeconomic infrastructure would eventually enable the Zionists to make a claim for a Jewish state.[30] Arlosoroff consequently supported Chaim

Weizmann's conciliatory policies toward the British authorities, which emphasized "economic and social initiatives within the political conditions created by the Mandate."[31]

Against the background of Buber's neo-Hasidism, Gordon's Tolstoyan romanticism, and Arlosoroff's Zionist constructivism, Greenberg evolved his own understanding of Jewish life and modern society. In a 1923 article in *Haolam*, he wrote,

> We [Zionists] have neither sufficiently clarified nor explained . . . that Eretz Israel will not suddenly be acquired at a historically propitious moment, but that it will rather be built stone upon stone and layer upon layer. . . . The success and victory of our political labors, those which we have achieved and those which are yet to be achieved, are meaningless unless accomplished on the basis of positive substance as well as sensible economic and cultural values that were and are created by ourselves.[32]

Greenberg's Labor Zionism was an amalgam of political, economic, spiritual, and ethical positions. In short, he considered Jewish social regeneration to be a matter of this-worldly redemption rather than an elusive goal to be pursued at the expense of current generations. He supported the notion of an open society with an economic infrastructure designed to provide for the common welfare of its members. Yet he rejected all forms of social experimentation that required the physical or spiritual repression of the individual. Confronting the radical Russian traditions of the nineteenth century, the oppressive reality of east European Jewish life in the early twentieth century, the German Jewish intellectual debates of the 1920s, and the promise of Zionist settlement in Palestine, Greenberg forged an original and nuanced assessment of socialist Zionism. He retained, however, a firm belief in the creation of a socially just world, the importance of a Jewish national home in Eretz Israel, the vitality of Judaism in its myriad forms, and the moral imperative of individual freedom.

Like Greenberg, Maurice Samuel's formative years were spent outside the United States. Although he was born in Romania, his family emigrated to Paris where he spent two years as a child. The Samuels next moved to England, where Maurice spent his youth. As a result of his exposure to Manchester's Jewish working-class neighborhood, Samuel "became a socialist and an atheist around the age of thirteen."[33] His immigrant background and intense Jewish interests set the stage for Samuel's eventual attraction to Labor Zionism, which, he later recalled, was intuitively undogmatic:

In New York I discovered for the first time that there was such a thing as a socialist Zionist movement. . . . The Zionists I knew were anti-socialist, the Jewish socialists anti-Zionist. But more pleasing was the discovery that one could be a socialist within the general Zionist movement, which was strongly tinged with liberalism. One could, through the Zionist congresses and funds, support socialist-oriented enterprises in Palestine, and thus work for socialism at large by creating a socialist Jewish state. I did not join the socialist Zionist party. I had had enough of "inevitability."[34]

Samuel completed his education at the University of Manchester, and it was here that he first met Chaim Weizmann, Zionism's preeminent inter-war leader, with whom he closely identified. After the outbreak of World War I, Samuel emigrated to the United States, where he enlisted in the American Expeditionary Force and was stationed in France between 1917 and 1919. In the summer of 1919, Samuel served as the secretary and Yiddish interpreter for the Pogrom Investigation Commission to Poland led by the American Jewish diplomat Henry Morgenthau. This experience affected him deeply and cemented his identification with east European Jewry and the Zionist cause.[35]

I was a Zionist before I met Weizmann and would have remained one without him; I had involved myself in Jewishness, in the fate of the Jewish people, in Yiddish and in Yiddish literature, before my visit to Poland, and the involvement would have been lifelong without it; but as Weizmann deepened my response to the Zionist idea, so that strange, fortuitous, direct contact with east European Jewry, attended as it was by peculiar circumstances, added to my involvement a new element of sensitivity.[36]

Following his return to the United States, Samuel was naturalized as an American citizen, and he worked for the Zionist Organization of America between 1921 and 1928. Despite his employment as a publicist, he quickly secured a place for himself as the gadfly of American Zionist politics. He challenged the complacency of American Jewish leaders and lamented the "practical" orientation of American Zionism, reserving especially scathing criticism for the "pseudointellectual" behavior of American Zionist youth, notably the Avukah student group:

Avukah is a failure intellectually because the nice boys and girls in it are not intellectuals at all. They are merely nice boys and girls. At best, with its present constituency, it can become an educational institution exerting mild pressure on adults for funds. . . . It could extort from me the same grudging interest which I accord to that other national joke, the Menorah Society. I am a humane sort of person. But the original hope that there could arise in this country a group of intellectual students, giving a new impetus to the mind-content of the Zionist movement, has almost wholly disappeared. . . . Intellectual Zionism—whatever there is of it—must be saved by making it clear that it is alone of its kind. . . . An intellectual student Zionist movement can be of one kind only: small, spontaneous, independent; indifferent to practical affairs—which today means largely money-raising; unaffiliated with officialdom; unconscious of purpose; impelled only by intellectual curiosity combined with youthful vigor.[37]

As illustrated by this statement, Samuel was the very antithesis of an organizational or party spokesman. His vigorous assertion of Eretz Israel as the locus classicus of Jewish life and his contention that Avukah was "merely a university repetition of the Zionist movement outside: the mouthing of great spiritual words by people who are essentially indifferent to spiritual values" rankled.[38] Yet none denied the honesty, forthrightness, and courage of his penetrating analysis. In fact, Samuel's contemporaries viewed him as a Zionist tribune of surpassing moral stature.

As Labor Zionist thinkers and spokesmen, Kaplan, Kallen, Greenberg, and Samuel are best understood in relationship to one another. Moreover, their varying approaches to Jewish life reflect common tensions embedded in the American experience. Intellectual leaders committed to ideology, action, and populist concerns, their activities were highly publicized, and a wide range of individuals and groups looked to them for direction. The spectrum of Labor Zionist leadership—like similar cohorts in American Jewish history[39]—was polychromatic and provides a striking contrast to American Zionism's top leadership in the prestate period. Louis D. Brandeis, for example, the movement's patron saint and the only leader to attain international stature, has been described as "a typical Western Zionist, sharing traits common to certain emancipated Jews in Europe and America."[40] Both Brandeis's successors, Stephen S. Wise and Abba Hillel Silver, were Reform rabbis with strong ties to American Jewry's German elite. Their leadership styles, institutional bases, and ideological orientations differed considerably from those of Greenberg, Kallen, Kaplan, and Samuel.[41] Even Brandeis's chief rival, Louis Lipsky, a Zionist leader with Jewish immigrant roots, was qualitatively different from the Labor Zionists.[42]

The undogmatic Labor Zionism of Greenberg and Samuel, which was infused with a more vigorous east European sensibility than that of Kallen and Kaplan, played an important role in their relationship to the Jewish immigrant world. Greenberg and Samuel shared Kallen's and Kaplan's appreciation of American society, but they insisted that their primary allegiances were to Judaism, the Jewish people, and the Yishuv. They considered the creation of a Jewish labor society in Palestine the chief task of their generation. They also argued that "Palestinocentrism" (a term coined by the German Zionist leader Kurt Blumenfeld to emphasize the centrality of the Yishuv in Jewish life) and the social and cultural rejuvenation of the diaspora Jewish life were interdependent. "We cannot be indifferent to the problems of world Jewry in general or American Jewry in particular," Greenberg exclaimed, "because the diaspora is the reservoir from which the Jewish homeland must be fed."[43] Such a cultural-political orientation resonated among broad segments of the American Jewish public, especially leftists and liberals who were proud of their east European origins and ethnic identity.

Greenberg's and Samuel's popularity derived from their eloquent and warm appreciation of the Yiddish milieu. Both were celebrated essayists and contributed to a wide range of periodicals and journals. Samuel was a master translator and became well known in literary circles for his book *The World of Sholom Aleichem* (1943). In addition, Greenberg and Samuel were first-rate speakers, making them extremely popular in American Jewry's immigrant quarters and much in demand by local Zionist and Yiddishist groups.

Labor Zionism's leaders never attained the public stature of Brandeis, Wise, Silver and Lipsky, but they were no less influential in American Jewish life. In fact, their unusual cultural and intellectual standing, which derived from their close contact with Yiddish and Hebrew writers, European Jewish intellectuals, and the Zionist leadership of the Yishuv, contributed much to the American movement. Brandeis, Wise, Silver, and Lipsky also depended on their efforts to nurture the movement's regional leaders, the rank and file, the Jewish masses, and various Zionist parties and groups. Ideally suited to this role, the Labor Zionist leaders functioned as the movement's external interlocutors as well as its internal guides.

Greenberg, Kallen, Kaplan, and Samuel shared more than a superficially common *mentalité*, or generational outlook. Like other American Zionist leaders, they rejected the formulaic negation of the diaspora and the ingathering of the exiles as the immutable crux of Zionist philosophy. In part, this vantage point reflects a profound understanding of American society's libertarian and postemancipationist structure. Kaplan summarized this conception in *A New Zionism* (1955), which he dedicated to Greenberg:

No American Jew will subscribe to any cause that may cast serious doubt on the wholeheartedness of his Americanism. What that implies we have no less an authority, both from the American and Zionist standpoint, than the late Justice Brandeis to remind us. "An immigrant is not Americanized," he wrote, "unless his true interests and affections have become deeply rooted here." . . . It was Hayim Greenberg, a European Zionist and a naturalized citizen, and not a third or fourth generation American Jew, who, at the 1951 World Zionist Congress in Jerusalem, declared: "It would be wrong to say that Jews have not struck roots [in America]. . . . Mass emigration is not on the current agenda of American Jewry."[44]

Kaplan's fusion of Brandeis's creedal statement and Greenberg's assessment of American Jewish vitality help explain the bipolar tension of American Zionism. On the one hand, the American movement was heavily influenced by the cultural Zionist thinker Ahad Haam.[45] Israel Friedlaender, the figure chiefly responsible for making Ahad Haam's ideas accessible in the United States, was one of Kaplan's colleagues at the Jewish Theological Seminary of America, and both men were members of Judah L. Magnes's Achavah Club. Friedlaender was also deeply involved in the organized Zionist bodies of the early twentieth century. His activity in the United States put him in direct contact with Horace M. Kallen, one of Brandeis's closest advisers and the person historically credited with developing the "philosophic basis for the 1914–21 'Brandeis era' in American Zionism."[46] Scholars have noted the strong parallels between Friedlaender's early writings and Kaplan's and Kallen's later expositions.[47]

Kaplan's statement is also revealing because he singles out Greenberg as a counterweight to Brandeis. This choice demonstrates the abiding influence of Labor Zionism's moderate-spiritual wing on American Zionism's intellectual core. It also implicitly dismisses the Zion-centered militancy of the Yishuv's (later the Jewish state's) premier leadership. Kaplan was familiar with the spectrum of socialist Zionist thought, from the radical theories of Chaim Zhitlowsky, Ber Borochov, and Nahman Syrkin to the pragmatic voluntarism of Chaim Arlosoroff, Berl Katznelson, and Hayim Greenberg. That he identified Greenberg as a quintessentially American Zionist shows his awareness of the dialectical process in which he himself played a role. The Brandeis group represented the thesis, the militant socialist Zionists the antithesis, and the American Labor Zionist leaders themselves the synthesis.

The intellectual touchstone of Kaplan, Kallen, Greenberg, and Samuel was the concept of individual freedom. They argued that ideas about Jewish existence have meaning only in relation to natural conditions and human relationships. Kaplan explained his position from a religious-humanistic perspective. In *Judaism in Transition* (1936), he argued that the "God idea means the recognition of the supreme importance of those ideals which represent man's insight into his destiny" and that "the natural is not at war with the humanly desirable, but supports and sustains it."[48] Kallen emphasized the relationship between individual freedom and collective autonomy from a secular viewpoint. In a speech entitled "The Struggle for Jewish Unity" (1933), he stated that "no individual can be emancipated through, in, and for himself" but, rather, only "through his group." "The form of [Jewish] unification," he stressed, "must be integrated with the conditions of modern life. The days of the ghetto are past."[49] Samuel, meanwhile, articulated this concept in the poem "Al harei katskil" (On the Catskill Mountains):

> My uncles, father's cousins, second cousins,
> By pairs and handfuls cover the world . . .
> Some live beside the Golden Gate, and some
> Beside the Brandenburger; some, I hear,
> Are Talmud students in the Gaon's city,
> Vilna the old—and some are "Harvard men,"
> While I, who live in Babylon the New,
> Preach the return to startled Jews, and spend
> This summer in the Catskill Mountains here.[50]

Finally, Greenberg asserted that "there are no transitional generations in history."[51] The security, happiness, and fulfillment of the present generation, he contended, are inherently legitimate aims.

All four men directed their appeals to Jews who had discarded American Judaism's institutional conventions but continued to sense a lack of meaning and fulfillment in their personal lives. In contrast to American Zionism's patriarch Louis D. Brandeis, they concluded that there could be no true amalgam of their American and Jewish identities. In Kaplan's words, the individual Jew lives in two distinct "civilizations." The status of the Jews, he maintained, "is that of an international nation with its home in Palestine."[52] Greenberg went a step further than Kaplan on two counts. First, he ruled out the possibility of an "ipso facto solution of the Jewish question." Second, he posited the Labor Zionist idea as the guiding principle of modern Jewish life: "Only that synthesis in Jewish thought which is nationalist without being chauvinist, and which stands for fundamental economic reconstruction without being Communist . . . can answer the need of the disorientated modern Jew."[53]

For Greenberg and Samuel, the notion that "all Jewish roads . . . lead . . . to Eretz Israel" was both a figurative expression of Zionist goals and a personal imperative.[54] In the record of his first voyage to Palestine, Samuel summarized this metahistorical sensibility:

> I was "returning" to a land which I had never seen, nor [had] my parents' parents. I was going "home" to a place which existed for me only by hearsay, a thing told. My own life had been a replica of my people: I had been born within a thousand miles of Palestine, and since then I had wandered by devious roads of many tens of thousands, and I had never come nearer to it. And now a longing as strong as life itself drew me back.[55]

In contrast to Samuel—who along with Greenberg was first and foremost a Zionist thinker—Kaplan and Kallen were relatively ambivalent about the role of Eretz Israel in their personal lives. If we imagine Jewish life as a continuum, we would locate Kaplan and Kallen more closely to historian Ben Halpern's "typical Western Zionists."[56] Schooled in American pragmatism and progressivism, Kaplan and Kallen were, respectively, religious and secular Jewish thinkers for whom Labor Zionism's social democratic nature was especially appealing. Their foci were "Judaism as a civilization" and "cultural pluralism," and their dominant analytic framework was American society—not the Jewish question. In short, although all four shared a weltanschauung and a Labor Zionist vision, they also were distinguished by the East-West split that characterized Zionism in the prestate period.

At first glance, we might expect that these men's seemingly contradictory perspectives would have kept them from wielding much influence. In fact, owing to American Jewry's heterogeneity, their divergence from any monolithic or streamlined Labor Zionist path was a source of collective strength. Thus, for example, Greenberg was a welcome guest at the conference of the New York Board of Rabbis and the Asia League; Kaplan was frequently invited to address the American Jewish Congress as well as groups of Reform rabbis; Kallen was at home in both the Histadruth Ivrith of America (Hebrew Federation of America) and the American Philosophical Society; and Samuel was eagerly sought as a lecturer by Hadassah and American universities alike.

In general, the key to Kallen's and Kaplan's influence was, in addition to their intrinsic intellectual gifts, their relative proximity to both American Jewry's elite and mainstream American culture. Their direct access enabled them to exert considerable influence on acculturated American Jews who sought to vitalize their ethnic-religious identity.[57] Similarly, Greenberg and Samuel were closely linked to the Jewish immigrant milieu and the east European leaders of the Yishuv. Their adherents sought ways and means of integrating into the new societies that offered them hope for an unapologetically Jewish life.

All four men developed and nurtured a common American discussion that revolved around Labor Zionist values, ideals, and goals. They were keen observers of modern Jewish culture generally, and their opinions were sought by a variety of diaspora leaders. They stimulated one another intellectually, and they set the tone for the contemporary discussion of Zionism and Labor Palestine.[58] An examination of *Menorah Journal, New Palestine,* and *Jewish Spectator*—arguably the principal American Jewish periodicals of the 1930s and 1940s—are filled with their contributions. Greenberg and Kaplan even created their own intellectually and culturally stimulating journals, namely, *Jewish Frontier* and *Reconstructionist.*[59]

Their early published works, which reached a wide Jewish and non-Jewish readership, also are noteworthy. This was true not only of Kallen's *Zionism and World Politics* (1921) and *Judaism at Bay* (1932), which express his indebtedness to Jewish values and arguments in favor a Jewish national home, but also of Kaplan's *Judaism as a Civilization* (1934) and *Judaism in Transition* (1936), parts of which read like Labor Zionist tracts. Samuel, however, was by far the most prolific and widely read of the Labor Zionist leaders. In addition to fiction, he published much nonfiction including *I, the Jew* (1927), *Jews on Approval* (1932), *The Great Hatred* (1940), and *Harvest in the Desert* (1944). These books testify to his committed and articulate vision of Labor Zionism.

Of all the literary vehicles at their disposal, *Jewish Frontier,* the organ of the League for Labor Palestine, provided the central channel for conveying Labor Zionism's message to American Jews. Under Greenberg's editorship, the journal frequently published provocative pieces by himself, Kaplan, Samuel, and Kallen. In addition, Greenberg's broad interests and personal acquaintance with leading American intellectuals, including Reinhold Niebuhr, Hannah Arendt, Kurt Lewin, Will Herberg, Charles A. Beard, Norman Thomas, and Ludwig Lewisohn, helped make *Jewish Frontier* a stimulating forum of intellectual debate. The journal also translated and published articles written in Hebrew that were previously unavailable to the English-reading public. It regularly featured Palestinian contributors such as David Ben-Gurion, Berl Katznelson, Yizhak Ben-Zvi, and Zalman Rubashov (later Shazar). It took special pride in presenting literary translations, such as the poetry of Haim Nahman Bialik, Rahel Blaustein, and Nathan Alterman as well as prose by Shlomo Zemah and Haim Hazaz. On the whole, the journal's "substantive and thoughtful articles," one historian points out, "attracted the attention of many American Jews who never joined a socialist Zionist organization."[60]

In both *Jewish Frontier* and *Reconstructionist*, Greenberg and Kaplan devoted considerable attention to the distinction between Communism and democratic socialism. In the 1930s, while most liberal intellectuals were still enchanted with the Soviet Union, Kaplan and Greenberg publicly criticized Communism's authoritarian tendencies. Kaplan's critique of Communism was governed by a mixture of ethical and pragmatic considerations. For example, he organized courses on Judaism and Marxism at the Jewish Theological Seminary of America and presented a series of sermons on the topic at the Society for the Advancement of Judaism.[61] And although he was publicly negative about Bolshevism, Kaplan confessed in his diary that he nevertheless hoped "something good might ultimately come out of Russia."[62] Greenberg, however, who was personally familiar with the autocratic Bolshevik regime, was far less sanguine. In an open letter addressed "To a Communist Friend," he flatly rejected Marxism's theory of revolutionary stages and the deification of society:

> What is the sense of dictatorship—that very dictatorship which is first called the dictatorship of the peasantry and the proletariat, then merely of the proletariat, then of the Party, then of a wing of the Party, till it finally becomes the dictatorship of one man? I know all the arguments. The dictatorship is temporary, the political slavery that you have introduced is a sad necessity. These will disappear in the future, when the final goal of socialism will have been realized. But how can one transform a man into something worthless in order to endow him with worth? How can we introduce slavery for the sake of freedom, an epidemic in the interests of sanitation?[63]

Greenberg's advocacy of Labor Zionism similarly stressed the efficacy of voluntarism and the notion of hagshamah azmit. In fact, he considered Poalei Zion's reigning Borochovian determinism to be totally unrealistic.[64] During a visit to Palestine in 1935, he clarified his views before an audience of haluzim that had accused him of diluting socialist Zionism. "I would be an opponent of pioneering in Palestine . . ." he proclaimed, "if the pioneers of Palestine were considered as manure on the fields of the country. . . . But pioneering in Palestine is a voluntary task . . . and [Jewish youth] finds personal satisfaction in following its call."[65]

Kallen also played a conspicuous role in carrying the moral debate about Zionism's agenda into the realm of Jewish communal politics. His tactics and quiet diplomacy provide an interesting counterpoint to Greenberg's strategy of direct confrontation. For example, when Revisionist Zionists tried to establish a foothold in the United States—a campaign initiated by Vladimir Jabotinsky in 1920 and reinvigorated by his supporters in the early 1930s[66]—Greenberg published numerous articles in *Jewish Frontier* designed to expose Revisionism as a "sinister movement of frank Fascist hooliganism."[67] Kallen, meanwhile, seized the moral high road, insisting that what was really at stake was the fundamental principle of liberty of speech and expression. In response to Stephen S. Wise, who decried Jabotinsky's "unmistakably Fascist sympathies and his anti–Labor Party conduct,"[68] Kallen wrote:

> Yes, the report is true that I have accepted membership on the Reception Committee for Jabotinsky. . . . My reason is extremely simple. . . . As you know very well, I am opposed to Jabotinsky in terms of his basic program, but I am also opposed to denying the leader of an opposition party and the spokesman of a view contrary to mine a hearing. . . . I am therefore making a gesture, not for Jabotinsky's platform and program, but his right under a democratic conception of human relations to present his principle and program for serious consideration of all people.[69]

This encounter demonstrates, in brief, Greenberg's and Kallen's divergent attitudes toward Revisionism. It also illustrates the extent to which American Zionism, by the late 1930s and early 1940s, had incorporated a quasi–Labor Zionist sensibility as its own ethos. Indeed, it is striking, if not paradoxical, that Jabotinsky, a Zionist leader of international stature, should be soundly rebuffed by American Zionism's top leader and defended by a Labor Zionist intellectual.

Arab nationalism was another issue that attracted the attention of the Labor Zionist intellectual leadership during the interwar period. Although American Jewish awareness of Palestine's Arab community rose after World War I, especially as a result of the steady stream of American travelers to the Yishuv, the Arab riots of 1929–1930 caught most American Jews by surprise. Gripped by the Depression and faced with a rising tide of antisemitism at home, American Jews in general and Zionists in particular were wracked by disunity.

In the wake of the riots, Samuel defended the Zionist organization's authority against the challenge of the Enlarged Jewish Agency's non-Zionist leadership.[70] The Enlarged Jewish Agency was an international body whose purpose was to provide new momentum for the economic development of Palestine. The American non-Zionists were led by the American Jewish jurist and American Jewish Committee leader Louis Marshall.[71] In fact, Samuel was one of only a handful of Zionist spokesmen in the position to confront effectively the attempts by non-Zionist leaders, who controlled the purse strings of American Jewry, to soften Zionist demands for an independent Jewish national home.

An example is an instance in which James Marshall, another non-Zionist leader, sided with the *New Republic* and the *Nation*, the mouthpieces of American liberal opinion. Marshall categorically stated: "We neither need nor want a *Judenstaat*" (Theodor Herzl's original term for the Jews' state).[72] Samuel, responding acerbically, defended the Jewish people's right to cultural autonomy and independence. He exposed what he considered to be the pandering nature of Marshall and other American Jewish leaders:

> We are made sick, distorted, unnatural; we are stunted in our natural spiritual development; we are made the heir of a genuine national inferiority complex—all for the reason that organically Palestine and we are one; and physically Palestine has been taken from us. *This is the foundation of our right to a Homeland in Palestine.*[73]

At the heart of the issue, Samuel asserted, was the false presumption that Arab and Jewish national rights were mutually exclusive. He argued that this stance contradicted the U.S. government's public support for the Balfour Declaration (1917) and the Lodge-Fish resolution (1922). It also belied "the facileness and carelessness with which liberal opinion treat[ed] the [Palestine] problem." American liberals, Samuel warned, including many Jews, did "not seem capable of carrying two principles in their heads."[74]

As the Marshall-Samuel conflict illuminates, Palestine's fate was linked to public opinion. Samuel's response to this challenge was to publish *What Happened in Palestine: The Events of August, 1929, Their Background and Their Significance* (1929) and to embark on a lecture tour throughout the country. Likewise, Greenberg published a series of opinion pieces in the Yiddish press and addressed numerous audiences on the subject of the riots. (In a similar vein, Greenberg later contributed to and supported Enzo Sereni's provocative *Jews and Arabs in Palestine: Studies in a National and Colonial Problem* (1936), the first comprehensive analysis of Arab-Jewish relations in English. By contrast, Kaplan and Kallen remained virtually silent on this issue.

How can we understand and interpret the Labor Zionist response to the seminal issue of Palestinian Arab nationalism? We have seen that the Labor Zionist leadership was not monolithic and that each leader varied in his ideological orientation and strategy. Kallen and Kaplan, however, unlike Greenberg and Samuel, seemed to have reconciled the paradox of American Jewish life by distancing themselves from the nexus between Jewish culture and American politics. When the moment of reckoning arrived, as in 1929, the historical record clearly indicates their preference for theory over practice. Perhaps this isolationism enabled Kaplan and Kallen to continue to view the Jews as a quintessential American ethnic minority. Their philosophical constructs notwithstanding, they avoided political activism that might undermine their broad formulations.

Greenberg and Samuel, however, were indelibly marked by the ferment of revolutionary Jewish politics in eastern Europe. Against the backdrop of the Palestine riots and Hitler's rise to power in Nazi Germany, their principled liberalism adjusted to world Jewry's increasingly precarious condition. Their change of heart was totally unlike the adventurism of Ben Hecht and Peter Bergson, Jabotinsky's militaristic American supporters. Greenberg and Samuel were most deeply affected not by the arguments of Zionist militants but by the seeming reticence of those Western leaders whom they admired most.

An excellent example of this is the exchange of views between Greenberg and the Indian leader Mahatma Gandhi. In the late 1930s, Greenberg, like Martin Buber, carried on a public correspondence with Gandhi.[75] Distressed by Gandhi's indifference to the rising antisemitism among Muslims in India, as well as his failure to speak out against the persecution of European Jewry, Greenberg invited Gandhi to express his views in *Jewish Frontier*. In "Death Has No Terror," published in March 1939, Gandhi wrote:

> Why should [the Jews] not, like other peoples of the earth, make that country their home where they were born and where they earn their livelihood? Palestine belongs to the Arabs in the same sense that England belongs to the English or France to the French. It is wrong and inhuman to impose the Jews on the Arabs. What is going on in Palestine today cannot be justified by any moral code of conduct. . . . If I were a Jew and were born in Germany . . . I would claim Germany as my home even as the tallest Gentile

may, and challenge him to shoot me or cast me in the dungeon; I would refuse to be expelled or to submit to discriminating treatment. And for doing this, I should not wait for fellow-Jews to join me in civil resistance but would have confidence that in the end the rest were bound to follow my example.[76]

If Greenberg was troubled by Gandhi's profoundly insensitive remarks, he was stunned by the suggestion that German Jewry should practice nonviolence against the Nazis. In his own reply, "We Are Treated as Subhumans—We Are Asked to Be Superhuman," he disclosed the moral and philosophical inconsistencies of Gandhi's argument, noting that the Indian leader "failed to grasp the unequaled tragedy of Jewish existence." "A Jewish Gandhi in Germany . . ." he asserted, "could function for about five minutes—until the first Gestapo agent would lead him, not to a concentration camp, but directly to the guillotine."[77] The non-Jewish press took notice of the Indian leader's anti-Zionist statement, which was subsequently reprinted in many major American newspapers. Outside the Anglo-Jewish press, however, Greenberg's erudite critique of Gandhi's position was virtually ignored. The American media's selectivity taught Greenberg an important lesson.

An intriguing parallel is Samuel's postwar critique of historian Arnold J. Toynbee's antipathetic treatment of the Jewish people in his twelve-volume *Study of History* (1934–1961). Attributing the origins of bigotry and oppression to Maccabean Jewish society, Toynbee argued that antisemitism is something "into which Christianity was betrayed by the Judaic, not the Hellenic, element in its ethos."[78] Having descended this slippery slope, Toynbee effortlessly arrived at the conclusion that the extermination of European Jewry was a low point in German morality to be exceeded only by Zionism's "archaic" conventions.

> But the Nazi Gentiles' fall [from grace] was less tragic than the Zionist Jews. On the morrow of a persecution in Europe in which they had been the victims of the worst atrocities ever known to have been suffered . . . the Jews' immediate reaction to their own experience was to become persecutors. . . . On the Day of Judgement the gravest crime standing to the German Nationalist Socialists' account might be, not that they had exterminated a majority of Western Jews, but that they had caused the surviving remnant of Jewry to stumble.[79]

"Now what is this man driving at?" Samuel asked in *The Professor and the Fossil* (1956). The interpretation to which we are "driven" by Toynbee himself, Samuel explained, is that if the Nazis committed a grave crime in exterminating [six] million Jews, they committed an even graver one in having caused the Palestinian Arabs to suffer. . . . To this [conclusion] we are directed over and over again by Professor Toynbee's opinion of that Zionist movement which had been at work in Palestine for many decades before Hitler had been heard of.[80]

Examining their responses to Gandhi and Toynbee, we see that Greenberg and Samuel concurred in their philosophical approach to resolving the conflict between Judaism and universalism. They also recognized and challenged antisemitism. Zionism increased their self-esteem and pride vis-à-vis their own ethnic identity and culture, enabling them to confront their surroundings without being overwhelmed by them. Like Irish, Italian, Greek, and Slavic intellectuals, they claimed to be members of a full-fledged people in the process of reclaiming their heritage and national homeland. As such, they could face gentiles as equals and rejected the need to assimilate into the American national fabric.

It is also apparent that whereas Kallen and Kaplan viewed Labor Zionism as a source of cultural and spiritual strength, Greenberg and Samuel were determined to use their political skills to alleviate the plight of European Jewry and fortify the Yishuv. For example, with the outbreak of World War II, Greenberg put *Jewish Frontier* to work as a lightning rod for news about the Jewish condition in Palestine and Europe as well as a channel for information that might not otherwise reach the American public. In February 1941, he published a letter smuggled out of Palestine that "managed to slip past the censors." Drawing attention to the Palestine administration's "severe repressive measures," he condemned the Mandatory regime as " 'colonial' in the worst sense." He noted the British hostility to the Zionist enterprise and "the incredibly brutal treatment—reminiscent of [czarist] Russian police methods—which the Administration has seen fit to mete out to the so-called 'illegal' immigrants in order to insure that the White Paper remain inviolate."[81]

The publication of such information was vital to the Zionists' wartime strategy of pressuring Britain to relax its restrictions on the Yishuv. In fact, in preparation for a March 1941 meeting, Chaim Weizmann forwarded a copy of Greenberg's "Palestine Administration Indicted" to Lord Moyne (Walter E. Guinness), the British resident minister in Palestine who was later assassinated by the Stern group. Weizmann, who noted that "Greenberg is a responsible person and has considerable influence in American Labour circles," subsequently embarked on a three-month trip to the

United States "at the request of the British government, which was concerned at the extent of anti-British propaganda then rife in America."[82]

The following year, rumors of the Nazi campaign to exterminate European Jewry reached the West, and reports of the so-called Final Solution
became too numerous to be dismissed. It was Greenberg who finally broke
the silence of top American Zionist leaders, namely, Stephen S. Wise and
the ZOA establishment, who, although aware of the magnitude of the
tragedy, barely hinted in public at its scope for fear of alienating or provok-
ing the Roosevelt administration.[83] *Jewish Frontier* was the first Anglo-
Jewish journal to publish complete details of the Nazi genocide. As a result
of Greenberg's bold move, the *Frontier* set off tremors in organized American Jewish life and horrified the Jewish and non-Jewish press alike. A
month later, the U.S. State Department officially confirmed the incoming
reports of Nazi atrocities. The following February, as the truth about the
so-called Final Solution was revealed, Greenberg published an open letter
entitled "Bankrupt!" that scandalized the American Jewish leadership. The
piece was both an expression of anguish and a revealing critique of the
American Jewish condition.

> The time has come, perhaps, when the few Jewish communities remaining
> in the world which are still free to make their voices heard and to pray in
> public should proclaim a day of fasting and prayer for American Jews. . . .
> They deserve to be prayed for. They are not even aware what a misfortune
> has befallen them, and if they were to look at themselves with seeing eyes
> they would realize with shock how intolerable this misfortune is. . . . At a
> time when the American Jewish community is the largest in the world, at a
> time when the eyes of millions of Jews in Europe who are daily threatened
> with the most terrible and degrading forms of physical extermination are
> primarily turned to American Jewry, this American Jewish community has
> fallen lower than perhaps any other in recent times, and displays an unbeliev-
> able amount of highly suspect clinical "health" and "evenness of temper." If
> moral bankruptcy deserves pity, and if this pity is seven-fold for one who is
> not even aware how shocking his bankruptcy is, then no Jewish community
> in the world today (not even the Jews who are now in the claws of the Nazi
> devourer) deserves more compassion from Heaven than does American
> Jewry.[84]

As World War II and the campaign for Jewish statehood escalated,
Greenberg, Kallen, Kaplan, and Samuel assumed central positions as spokesmen for American Jewry's liberal, Labor-oriented Zionist philosophy. During the war, Greenberg served as chairman of the executive committee of

the American Zionist Emergency Council. Kallen, Kaplan, and Samuel, on the other hand, whose Zionist leadership styles were less overtly organizational—with the notable exception of their involvement in the League for Labor Palestine (later known as the National Assembly for Labor Israel)—devoted their energies to teaching, publishing, and urging American Jews to support the Labor enterprise in Palestine.

Labor Zionism's American leaders reached the apex of their influence during World War II and the years leading up to the creation of the Jewish state. For a time, Greenberg served as head of the American Zionist Emergency Council and also played a key role at the Biltmore Conference and sessions of the American Jewish Conference. Meanwhile, Kaplan, Kallen, and Samuel used their influence to shore up American Jewish support for the Labor enterprise's Jewish state-in-the-making. Despite their important contributions to these and other spheres, historians have, for the most part, elected to ignore them and the movement they guided.

The reason, perhaps, is that the Labor Zionist leaders were never fully integrated into American Zionism's organizational structure. They did not fit the paradigms of American Jewish leadership formed during the interwar period. Although Kaplan was a rabbi, his authority, like that of Greenberg, Kallen, and Samuel, did not stem from an institutional religious base. Nor were they American civic leaders whose independent wealth and influence entitled them to a place among American Jewry's self-appointed elite. Moreover, unlike Syrkin, Borochov, and Zhitlowsky, they were not extraordinarily charismatic leaders who commanded mass followings.

If their point of departure differed significantly from that of other American Jewish and Labor Zionist leaders, they were nonetheless among the most creative and vibrant Jewish thinkers to concern themselves with the Zionist program. They were also among the few diaspora Zionist intellectuals who seriously thought about the future of American Jewry. They understood the limits and potential of Labor Zionist and social democratic values in the American context. They correctly surmised that the United States, unlike other countries with large numbers of immigrants such as France or Argentina, had historically possessed many points of access for immigrants. Thus, American society offered a singularly favorable environment for Jews to press their ethnic-American interests and claims while championing individual freedom and national independence.[85] American Jews, they asserted, needed to build a secure ethnic-American identity that would serve as a bridge to American society and also a way of preserving Jewish identity within the context of modern Jewish life.

Greenberg, Kallen, Kaplan, and Samuel articulated a Labor Zionist vision whose values, goals, and ideals transcended the confines of party politics and carried considerable weight among a diverse range of American Jewish and Zionist circles. What otherwise comprised a catalog of imperatives for Zionist ideologues they viewed as an ideological road map, maintaining that only a mutually positive and creative diaspora–Eretz Israel relationship would serve the dynamic needs of Judaism and the Jewish people. According to Greenberg,

> in the final historical analysis, the State of Israel should be interested in the spiritual growth of diaspora Jewry no less than the Jews of the *galut* themselves. All Jewish roads—sooner or later, directly or indirectly, with landmarks or without them—lead to the same destination: to Eretz Israel.[86]

Greenberg, Kallen, Kaplan, and Samuel helped win broad support for American Zionism. Moreover, they persuasively argued that haluziut and the Yishuv had a claim on American Jews and American Judaism, and they succeeded in uniting American Jewish personalities of varying secular, religious, Yiddishist, Hebraist, and nationalist orientations. In this way, they were instrumental in making the Labor Zionist idea a centerpiece of American Jewish life. As a result of their efforts, they touched the lives of tens of thousands of American Jews. In print and through public debate, they garnered substantial American Jewish support for Labor Zionism.

To understand American Zionism, we must account for the appeal of the Labor Zionist idea to a wide spectrum of American Jews. Against this backdrop, the leadership of American Zionism also awaits a thorough reassessment.[87] The cohort examined in this chapter illustrates the need to look beyond the pantheon of Zionist history's so-called giants and titans and include people formerly consigned to the historiographical sidelines.[88] Kaplan, Kallen, Greenberg, and Samuel qualify as major leaders and central figures in American Zionist history who "embodied the crucial experiences and offered a personal resolution of a generational crisis."[89] They recognized that Labor Zionism's success in the United States was a matter of social and political chemistry. They were—to paraphrase the eminent social historian Jacob Katz—harbingers of a new American Zionism.[90]

6

Years of Crisis, 1935–1939

In January 1935, the first National Conference for Palestine was held in Washington, D.C. The conference, jointly sponsored by the Zionist Organization of America and several other groups, attracted representatives from fifty-two national organizations and 1,337 delegates representing approximately 1.3 million constituents. In an unusual display of solidarity, the Zionist and non-Zionist participants pledged to "set up an expert commission to survey economic conditions in Palestine and prepare a program for coordinating the work of various agencies active in the [American Jewish] economic field."[1] To avoid intramovement and interorganizational strife, the conference organizers did not discuss Jewish statehood in Palestine. Instead, they adopted several carefully crafted resolutions affirming the Jewish Agency's program for land acquisition and colonization in Palestine. They also endorsed the Huleh Valley concession, a land reclamation project crucial to the Labor Zionist program of rural development in the Upper Galilee.

Such bipartisanship did not mute the ongoing philosophical debate between advocates and opponents of Jewish sovereignty in Palestine. But it did highlight the fact that irrespective of such differences, a broad cross section of American Jews in the 1930s felt responsible for the welfare and progress of the Jewish national home.[2] At the closing session, Zionist spokesman Maurice Samuel emphasized the conference's practical and ethical considerations:

> We pledged ourselves to one thing—that the Palestine to which our pioneers were giving their lives would not be a Palestine which would be a replica of the scramble system of the rest of the world. Useless to me are words which have to do with mere social justice, unless they are implemented by those instruments which we created, and those which we recognized years ago as containing not only the national, but also the moral will. We have a labor movement in Palestine which stands in a place of moral leadership today which we would do ill to ignore. It is under the sign of

Labor Palestine and under that sign, and under no other, that you can succeed.[3]

Samuel's statement highlights the uniquely New World brand of Palestinocentrism that emerged in the early 1930s—a philosophical and programmatic approach that went beyond the philanthropic activity of American Zionist groups in previous decades. For the majority of American Jews, who were not estranged from their heritage and religion, Palestinocentrism served as a bridge between a firm belief in the vitality of Judaism in its myriad forms and the importance of a Jewish national home. In contrast, contemporary German Jews—including the Zionist leader Kurt Blumenfeld, who coined the term *Palestinocentrism*—generally viewed Zionism as "the modern way to Judaism" for acculturated central European Jewry.[4]

The growing American Jewish concern for and attachment to Palestinian Jewish society in this period was fueled by two key issues: the rescue of European Jewry and, in time, plans for postwar Jewish reconstruction. To be sure, many American Jewish groups played a visible role on both fronts. As this book argues, however, the historical record indicates that American Jewry's evolving pro-Zionist orientation was linked to the practical achievements and idealistic appeal of the Palestine labor movement. As a result, Labor Zionism's American wing found the scope and inducement to strengthen relations with old allies and develop ties with new partners.

The National Conference for Palestine was emblematic of a turning point in the relationship between American Jews and Zionism. It was also the first in a series of seemingly nonpartisan public events that signaled American Jewry's widespread preference for the Labor Zionist agenda. A month later, the momentum generated by the conference found renewed impetus in another quarter of American Jewish life when several hundred Reform and Conservative rabbis publicly endorsed the Histadrut and Labor Palestine. As noted in chapter 2, the Reform rabbis' declaration marked the first step by Reform Judaism toward the repudiation of its antinationalist Pittsburgh Platform of 1885. This process culminated in 1937 when the Central Conference of American Rabbis, under mounting pressure to alter its official stance, endorsed the Columbus Platform, which announced:

> In the rehabilitation of Palestine, the land hallowed by memories and hopes, we behold the promise of a renewed life for many of our brethren. We affirm the obligation of all Jewry to aid in its upbuilding as a Jewish homeland

by endeavoring to make it not only a haven of refuge for the oppressed but also a center of Jewish culture and spiritual life.[5]

The rabbinical pronouncement was a bellwether of the changing attitude of acculturated American Jews. It demonstrates that even formerly anti-Zionist American Jews had begun to revise their orientation in light of the recent tumultuous events, especially the Depression, the rise of Nazi Germany, and the desperate plight of central European Jewry after the promulgation of the Nuremberg laws in 1935. In short, the Columbus Platform did not overtly endorse Zionism or the *haluzim* (pioneers), but it did serve to legitimize the nationalist conceptions of Jewish peoplehood and *Gegenwartsarbeit* (Zionist work in the diaspora) in the American context.[6]

During this time, the American Jewish left was also compelled to re-evaluate its position vis-à-vis Zionism, a process that resulted in the radical political realignment of several trade unions, fraternal orders, socialist groups, and Yiddishist associations.[7] A turning point was reached with the Arab riots that erupted in Palestine between 1936 and 1939. Following the outbreak of disturbances, some key Jewish labor leaders altered their stance vis-à-vis the Yishuv and publicly announced support for the Haavarah (Transfer) agreement between the Zionist movement and Nazi Germany.[8]

The Trust and Transfer Office Haavarah Limited was created through the initiative of Labor Zionist leader Chaim Arlosoroff and was formally established in August 1933 by an agreement between the Jewish Agency and the Nazi regime. The agreement made possible the emigration of Jews to Palestine by allowing the transfer of their capital in the form of German export goods. Between 1933 and 1939, the Haavarah facilitated the emigration of approximately sixty thousand German Jews to Palestine and the transfer of more than $40 million, which was used for the immigrants' social and economic absorption.[9]

The Haavarah agreement provoked considerable controversy in the Yiddish press. The debate featured a heated exchange between Berl Locker, a Zionist spokesman with strong ties to the Jewish immigrant community, and Baruch Charney Vladeck, a socialist activist and general manager of *Der forverts* (The Forward). At first, Vladeck vigorously opposed the agreement. But the impact of the Nuremberg laws, coupled with the outbreak of Arab riots in Palestine, prompted him to conduct a fact-finding mission to Palestine in 1936. A five-week visit persuaded him to revise his views, and he subsequently became an advocate of the Jewish national home, particularly the Yishuv's cooperative sector.[10] "All this propaganda that the Jews are ruining the Arab masses economically is false," he reported, "and just as false is the contention that the Jews are a tool in the hands of British imperialists."[11]

In contrast to Vladeck's Zionist conversion, many segments of American Jewish labor viewed the Haavarah as a betrayal of the nationwide anti-Nazi boycott undertaken by Jewish union leaders and the American Federation of Labor three years earlier.[12] Nonetheless, some Jewish labor leaders did follow Vladeck's lead and rallied to the plan as an effective way of procuring German Jewish immigration to Palestine while safeguarding the refugees' capital.[13] Among those who favored the Haavarah agreement were Maurice Finestone of the United Hebrew Trades, Saul Matz and Julius Hochman of the International Ladies Garment Workers' Union, Joseph Schlossberg of the Amalgamated Clothing Workers' Union, Max Zaritsky of the Hat and Cap Makers Union, Mikhael Ivensky of the Arbeter Ring (Workmen's Circle), Alexander Kahn of the American Socialist Party, and Abe Cahan, editor of *Der forverts*.

These men, who cast a wide net over the Yiddish-speaking immigrant community, argued that the proposal's advantages outweighed its disadvantages. They warned that the plight of German Jews would only worsen without the Haavarah agreement and that the ensuing state of affairs would create enormous hardships for German Jewish emigrants. They further asserted that the boycott's economic impact was negligible and lacked widespread American support. Moreover, neither the United States nor the Soviet Union was interested in restricting or halting trade relations with Germany. Finally, in an unusual philosophical departure, the Jewish labor leaders stressed the uniqueness of German Jewry's situation and the Jewish Agency's responsibility for protecting the interests of German Jewish immigrants and workers in Palestine:

> [We] are of the opinion that owing to the extraordinary tragedy that has befallen German Jewry, the work of the Transfer is both necessary and justified. The boycott movement must be continued throughout the whole of the Jewish and Labor world; but at the same time means must be found for salvaging as many of our brethren as possible, together with their property, from the Nazi inferno. To condemn this work of the Haavarah or to boycott goods transferred through its means would amount to a boycott of the German Jews themselves and condemn them to physical and spiritual destruction.

We are convinced that now that the Transfer [agreement] has been placed in Eretz Israel under the control of the Jewish Agency, and knowing the profound interest taken in this matter by the Histadrut . . . any abuses will be eliminated and the Transfer [agreement] will continue to be used for the great rescue work and for the creation of economic positions which will bring the German Jews hope and a new life of productive activity.[14]

Fear of Communist insurgency also played a role in the American Jewish community's attraction to Labor Palestine: in a negative sense, the tragic reality of Jewish life under the Soviets drove many left-wing American Jews away from the illusory panacea of universalistic Bolshevism; in a positive sense, the Yishuv offered a viable and constructive alternative for the realization of widely shared liberal Jewish values. Zionist proponents and sympathizers believed that the Jewish social democrats in Palestine were creating a model society that the Soviets would do well to imitate. Thus in the United States, Labor Zionism strove to distinguish itself from Soviet Communism and pro-Soviet American political organizations, even though it had similar philosophical roots. Unlike the left-wing Hashomer Hazair movement, for instance, Labor Zionism moderated its ideological orientation and stressed a social democratic vision of the Yishuv as the Jewish state-in-the-making.

In the 1930s, such a position risked the ire of many liberal intellectuals who were still entranced by the Russian Revolution of 1917. For example, the "alienated" Jewish intellectuals grouped around *Partisan Review*, an influential non-Marxist literary publication founded in 1936 by Phillip Rahv, William Phillips, and Sidney Hook, generally viewed Zionism and the Yishuv with scorn and derision.[15] This group of so-called non-Jewish Jews contrasted sharply with the cohort of highly identified Jewish intellectuals who coalesced around *Jewish Frontier*, the *Menorah Journal*, and the *Reconstructionist*. These journals, each with a distinctive orientation, vigorously promoted Jewish cultural and Zionist interests while elevating the standards of Jewish journalism and the intellectual tone of Jewish public discourse.

Jewish Frontier spearheaded the campaign to avert stigmatization of the Yishuv and took a special interest in the relationship between democratic socialism and Soviet Communism. It published several critical analyses of the Soviet enterprise. Hayim Greenberg, the *Frontier's* editor, attracted a cadre of highly capable writers on the subject, including Will Herberg.[16] In a notable instance, Marie Syrkin's unprecedented indictment of the Soviet political trials of August 1935 and January 1936 caused a stir in American intellectual circles. When Syrkin's "The Moscow Trials" appeared in May

1937, the article proved to be something of a coup for Jewish intellectuals on the left. In her analysis, Syrkin scrutinized both the Soviet regime and the Communist party's proponents:

> By now everyone is familiar with the set-up. The chief figures of the Bolshevik revolution admit to a collection of crimes among which murder is the most attractive. This wholesale confession is indulged in by all of Lenin's closest associates and collaborators with two exceptions—Stalin and Trotsky. Stalin is in the Kremlin, Trotsky in Mexico, the rest are in their graves or about to repose in them. . . .
>
> Those who believe in the validity of the confessions claim that they are the results of genuine repentance. . . . After all, these are mysterious Dostoyevskian Russians with a revolutionary past, who are suddenly overcome with repentance for their sins against Russia and the revolution. . . . If they were genuine penitents who were really "confessing," we must assume that they held nothing back. How then can one explain the fact that the January trials allegedly revealed their complicity in even greater crimes than those to which they had confessed? . . . This circumstance in itself invalidates the authenticity of all subsequent confessions.[17]

Syrkin and other Labor Zionist sympathizers were strongly attacked by the American Jewish radical left. In general, the challenge issued from deracinated and alienated Jewish circles like the Young People's Socialist League, the American Bundists, and the anti-Zionist sections of the Jewish Labor Committee. Labor Zionism also waged a fierce battle with the Communists for control of the Jewish social work profession in urban centers. This struggle, virtually unknown to American Jews at the time, had a dramatic impact on the development of organized Jewish communal life in the 1930s and 1940s. Beginning in the Depression, Communists attempted to "bore from within" and infiltrate the field of Jewish social work. They organized discussion groups and played a leading role in the radicalization and politicization of several social workers' unions. In a few years, the leadership of many such clubs and unions was closely connected to the Communist Trade Union Unity League. The league, headed by a disproportionately large number of Jewish Communists, was affiliated with the Jewish People's Fraternal Order of the International Workers Order, a devoutly pro-Soviet group.[18]

Communist insurgents also attempted to gain control of the Graduate School for Jewish Social Work, a forerunner of Columbia University's School of Social Work. Under the leadership of Maurice J. Karpf, however, a Jewish educator and non-Zionist spokesman, the Graduate School proved to be a stronghold of so-called antiassimilationist forces. Karpf tacitly endorsed the nationalist activity of the school's "oppositional group" of "younger Jewish social workers," many of whom later organized the Social Workers' Chapter of the League for Labor Palestine.[19] Although the Communists assailed Karpf and the Graduate School, the Labor Zionist group prevailed. It established a firm foothold in the school that it then used to recruit pronationalist and pro–Labor Zionist social work students, many of whom were subsequently dispatched to urban centers around the country.[20] A newly organized branch of the League for Labor Palestine described the social workers' orientation:

> We see in Labor Palestine an outstanding phenomenon in modern Jewish history. It has sought to change the conditions under which Jews live. Labor Palestine has affected the political, economic, cultural and psychological status of the Jews of the entire world. As a solvent of Jewish disabilities and as a creative rejuvenating force in Jewish life, it stands unmatched. Because it can give all of us the understanding and feeling for the Jewish people which is essential to our professional and personal life, we should identify ourselves with it through the League for Labor Palestine.[21]

Sympathy for Labor Zionism also stemmed from the American Jewish community's largely negative appraisal of Revisionist Zionism. In 1935, the Revisionist Zionists seceded from the World Zionist Organization and created the New Zionist Organization, but their subsequent campaign to establish a presence in the United States was generally deprecated by liberal Jews and moderate Zionists.[22] Meanwhile, organized Jewish labor, which supported the Histadrut and the social democratic Palestinian labor parties, had only antipathy for the Zionist right wing. Indeed, many American Jews considered Revisionist Zionism no less a threat to Jewish interests than Soviet-style Communism. Even the leaders of Hadassah and the Zionist Organization of America (ZOA), though officially neutral on questions of ideology, were dismayed by the Revisionists' belligerent antisocialist and anti-Histadrut posture. Their fears were exploited by Jewish Agency leaders, especially the Labor Zionists, who vilified the Revisionist leader Vladimir Jabotinsky and his followers.[23]

Labor Zionists worked tirelessly to undermine Revisionist efforts to establish an American presence, and throughout the 1920s and 1930s, Hayim Greenberg and visiting Palestinian leaders Chaim Arlosoroff, Yosef Baratz, Yosef Sprinzak, Enzo Sereni, and Goldie Meyerson (later Golda Meir) lambasted the Revisionist cause. After Arlosoroff's assassination in June

1933—a crime initially blamed on Revisionist conspirators but never solved—relations between Labor Zionism and the Zionist right wing became especially acrimonious.

Thus Jabotinsky's visit to the United States in late 1935 prompted Greenberg to demand publicly of the Revisionist leader "not only his usual brilliant oratory, but also a sober and reasonable explanation of his relations with, and his position in, the sinister movement of frank Fascist hooliganism."[24] In another instance, Greenberg characterized Revisionism as a movement fundamentally opposed to Western humanitarian values. "The most significant trait of Fascism and Revisionism," he declared,

> is the hatred it bears toward internationalism and toward every form of friendly cooperation between one nation and another. Not for nothing does . . . Jabotinsky quote so often the old Latin proverb, *Homo homini lupus* ["Man is to man as wolf"]. . . . When we read in the Revisionist press . . . that only two courses are left to the Arab, either back to the desert or into the depths of the sea . . . that we have but one task for the next few generations, namely, to build the Jewish state, and that only after we have attained this goal, and provided we have spare time, shall we be able to worry "about dogs and cats, about Chinamen and Arabs,"—when we read this, we see in it a pathological expression of national egotism which is not only immoral, but . . . against the real interests and beneath the dignity of Jewry and Zionism. It is impossible, from a purely practical point of view, to build a Jewish national home or a Jewish state in Palestine without a minimum of cooperation with other nations or at least with certain progressive elements of other nations.[25]

Jewish Frontier waged an ongoing campaign to excoriate the Zionist right wing. The editorial board scrutinized Revisionism and often featured articles by various American Jewish opponents of Jabotinsky. Most damning of all, it published English translations of hate-mongering excerpts from the Revisionist press in Palestine, speeches from Betar youth conferences, and incriminating testimony from the hearings of the Arlosoroff murder trial.[26] Such exposés were intended to emphasize the contrast, on the one hand, between Labor Zionism and Revisionism and, at least implicitly on the other, American Jewish liberalism and right-wing fanaticism. Other American Jewish journals and liberal spokespersons also denounced the Revisionist Zionists.[27] Boston's *Jewish Advocate*, for example, pointedly referred to the members of the movement as "Revisionist Fascists."[28] Bert Goldstein, the president of Pioneer Women and wife of ZOA leader Israel Goldstein, was equally caustic. She asserted that the American Friends of

Jewish Palestine, a Revisionist front organized by Rabbi Louis I. Newman and Benjamin Akzin, was "calculated to draw Jews away from the regular channels of upbuilding work of Palestine."

> [The Revisionist group] has very deliberately and with malice aforethought duplicated the work now being done by all the national organizations, the Keren Hayesod (Palestine Foundation Fund), the Keren Kayemet (Jewish National Fund), and the Histadrut. Indeed, they have duplicated in such a way so as to bring chaos and confusion to those American Jews who heretofore have been approached for the support of those funds.[29]

Significantly, many members of the American movement's old guard also viewed Revisionism with suspicion. Some believed it to be incompatible with mainstream American Jewish interests, whereas others feared that the right wing jeopardized general support for the Yishuv and threatened to undermine the Zionist cause. For example, on the eve of the Nineteenth Zionist Congress held in Lucerne in 1935, Felix Frankfurter confided to Robert Szold, one of Brandeis's lieutenants, "Yes, I should vote as a General Zionist [at the Congress]. . . . *But*—the Histadrut is fundamentally right and the Revisionists are fundamentally wrong. Go out and see for *yourself.*"[30] Frankfurter's comment prefigured the trajectory of American Zionist politics in subsequent years.

It is evident from the Zionist Congress elections of the 1930s that the General Zionist camp was largely out of step with popular American Jewish attitudes toward Zionism and the Yishuv. This disjunction first became apparent in the elections to the Nineteenth Zionist Congress when the world Labor Zionist movement scored a landslide victory, winning 44 percent of 1.2 million votes cast worldwide. These results demonstrated Labor Palestine's hold on the imagination of diaspora Jewry, including American Jews who purchased roughly 134,000 shekels and cast 25,149 of their 55,456 votes for the Labor Zionist slate. Most surprised of all, however, were the ZOA and Hadassah, who united to form the General Zionist slate and received 19,005 votes.[31]

The predisposition of American Jews for Labor Zionism's approach to the problems of mass colonization and economic development in Palestine was so pervasive that even Hadassah feared for its organizational and political independence. In fact, the Hadassah leadership agreed to unite with the ZOA in the congress elections on the condition that the ZOA would not seek a "joint ticket" with the Labor bloc.[32] This proved to be the only effective strategy for Zionist centrists, whose ranks included several eminent American Jewish leaders, to retain their prominent political position. In the end, the General Zionist leadership hammered out a "bipartisan" and "neutral" platform that commended the haluzim but tempered the coalition's official stance on Labor Palestine. Meanwhile, the Labor Zionists organized a separate congress delegation that explicitly endorsed the Histadrut and the Mapai party's agenda. ZOA leader Robert Szold explained the centrists' conservative approach, sardonically refuting the insinuation that the ZOA-Hadassah coalition "should adjourn and go over into the halls of the Histadrut . . . and become a part of the Poalei Zion party." At the same time, he was careful to point out that despite their philosophical differences, General and Labor Zionists shared many aims and ideals.

> For my own part, I will not be driven into one camp or into another camp. For many years, my friends, I have been a General Zionist and I have thought that General Zionists had a function to perform which was a constructive function. . . . I believe today as I have always believed in the heroism and in the self-sacrifice of the *haluzim* and of the Histadrut. I believe in the further principle that we Jews come to Palestine to give work for Jewish labor, and Jewish labor on Jewish standards, with some sense of justice, and many other principles. . . . But I still think that we General Zionists have the great responsibility for carrying forward this movement. After all, when the parties come to the [Zionist] Congresses, the parties ask for this budget and the parties ask for that in the budget; and when the Congress is over and the parties go home, who is it that has the responsibility in the largest measure for raising the funds that constitute the budget of the Zionist Executive in Palestine? The General Zionists.[33]

Szold's statement, a cautionary reminder of the economic power of American Jewry's vital center, exemplifies the attitude of ZOA and Hadassah leaders. They wearied of the endless task of Zionist fund-raising and the potentially damaging effect that unchecked socialist control of the Jewish Agency and the World Zionist Organization might have on Jewish communal politics and the image of Zionism in the United States. In reality, the practical realm of Zionist fund-raising was dominated by political centrists and moderate non-Zionists. The General Zionist platform, however, was largely viewed by the rank-and-file Zionist membership as inadequate, and some even considered it a betrayal of the Yishuv. As a result, in the 1930s, thousands of individuals broke ranks with the General Zionists and voted for the Labor Zionist slate, making the latter the clear winner in the American elections.

The Nineteenth Zionist Congress, at which Labor Zionism emerged as the most powerful faction in the World Zionist Organization, forced the General Zionists to enter into a coalition with the Labor Zionists. This alliance marked the start of an effective partnership between the leadership of Labor Palestine and the moderate wing of General Zionism led by several Americans with ties to the Brandeis group. Labor Zionist leaders also used the Lucerne congress as an opportunity to restore Chaim Weizmann to the presidency of the world movement. Weizmann's return to power—part of Labor's larger effort to attain legitimacy in the eyes of diaspora Jewry—was regarded by contemporary observers as politically expedient and an important public relations maneuver. As Stephen S. Wise remarked to the novelist Ludwig Lewisohn after the Lucerne gathering: "The Congress was good. . . . I was a good boy and supported the Labor majority who insisted that they needed Weizmann, and I think they did."[34] The *Reconstructionist* elaborated on this sentiment:

> In the selection of Dr. Weizmann as the new President of the World Zionist Organization, [a] determination to break down barriers was evident. Although it has always been known that Weizmann is pro-Labor, the enthusiastic choice of his leadership by the Labor group deserves commendation, for, as a majority, they might very well have insisted upon the election of one of their own. But they realized the divisive effect that such a partisan act would have had, and heartily supported him. Zionists who had previously opposed him rallied around him, moved by the principle of "loyalty to the cause and not to a person."[35]

In the middle 1930s, as these statements indicate, the Labor Zionist program of "constructivism," effectively augmented by Chaim Weizmann's strategy of gradualism, became the World Zionist Organization's philosophical and political canon. In tandem with these developments, the Palestine labor movement swiftly expanded its vast socioeconomic network of trade unions, workers' associations, health funds, agricultural settlements, industrial enterprises, youth groups, clandestine defense forces, and cultural and educational frameworks.[36]

The results of the Zionist Congresses, coupled with the intensification of American Jewish communal politics, sharpened the terms of the public debate regarding Palestine's future. After 1935, for instance, the General Zionist movement, having had to reexamine many of its cherished positions, convened a special ZOA conference in Atlanta. Spurred by a vigorous minority that championed Labor Palestine, the meeting voted to endorse most programmatic aspects of the Histadrut and Labor Palestine.[37] The ZOA went so far as to repudiate the official stance of the World Union of General Zionists, which, although led by the moderate Polish Zionist Isaac I. Schwarzbart, was dominated by the Revisionist Zionist camp. "So far as we American Zionists are concerned," the Atlanta convention declared,

> We believe in organized labor in Palestine and in the recognition of the Jewish national home. The members and groups within such an organization of Jewish labor are to be united upon the basis of their mutual economic interests, are to have absolute autonomy in the political, social and intellectual field. This is the policy now being maintained by the Histadrut, to which not only we, but the Zionist Congress, has given its approval.[38]

Despite rising popular support for Labor Palestine, the problem of the relation of American Jewish life to Zionism continued to vex the public arena. In the 1930s, however, even those people who objected to Jewish nationalism on religious and/or philosophical grounds conceded that the Zionist movement was emerging as a powerful force in diaspora affairs. As the parameters of Jewish communal discourse expanded, individuals and groups from every walk of life began to define themselves in relation to the Jewish problem and the Palestine question. Consequently, in addition to those who identified as General, Labor, and Revisionist Zionists, increasing numbers of American Jews attached labels to themselves like "non-Zionism," "cultural Zionism," "spiritual Zionism," "philanthropic Zionism," and even "anti-Zionism."[39]

Cyrus Adler, an American Jewish Committee leader and opponent of Zionism, articulated the crux of the larger debate in a letter to Felix Warburg, a non-Zionist spokesman and influential investment banker: "As a non-Zionist, I do not at all deplore . . . the establishment of a Jewish commonwealth."

> However, the term "national home" does now and always has seemed to me a little ridiculous. It sounded like a big orphan asylum. Had the gentlemen in charge of the diplomatic negotiations of the Zionist Organization [after World War I] been bold enough to ask for the establishment of a Jewish commonwealth they might have got it; at least they would have openly stated their plans. . . . [The Zionists] have a movement. They would like to possess the souls of every Jew in every country of the world, mold his education, mold his thinking, and in fact be as it were a scattered totalitarian organism based theoretically upon a democracy which is taxed a *shekel* every

year or every other year and managed in fact by an oligarchy. A movement which conceives of itself in such a way is difficult to deal with either on legal or practical terms.[40]

Adler's assessment highlights the centrality of Zionism to American Jewish life as well as the high stakes of Jewish communal politics. He and others (notably those associated with the non-Zionist camp) continued to view the Zionist movement with suspicion, but they could not fail to notice the upsurge in Jewish national awareness that was steadily changing the character of American Jewry.

The Order of Bnai Brith is an excellent barometer of this metamorphosis. A venerable American Jewish service organization that attracted a cadre of non-Zionist leaders, Bnai Brith's biographical composition, philosophical moderation, cultural orientation, and steady politicization mirrored broad trends in American Jewish communal life.[41] At first, Bnai Brith gravitated to the moderate non-Zionist camp, "viewing Palestine as a solution to the refugee situation." But it soon found itself caught between the competing forces of the American Jewish Committee and the American Jewish Congress, which disagreed on communal tactics and policies. In 1938, the scales were tipped when Henry Monsky, a nonpartisan General Zionist, was elected president of Bnai Brith. Monsky's base of support encompassed a vast immigrant constituency that identified with the Zionist enterprise. On this basis, he carefully orchestrated Bnai Brith's cooperation with the Zionists "without changing its non-Zionist ideology."[42]

Joseph Schlossberg, a Jewish labor leader and Zionist convert, also is typical of the American Zionist sensibility of this period. "The most vital problems of the Jewish community," Schlossberg noted in 1937, "are immigration, land, labor. The Arab-Jewish issue flows from them."[43] Schlossberg argued that the "Jews are wanted nowhere" and that the successful solution of these three problems "will make Palestine a happy land for Jew and non-Jew."[44] This subtle reformulation of the Labor Zionist agenda echoes both the class-conscious weltanschauung of east European Jewry and the Brandeisian concept of noblesse oblige.

Schlossberg's assessment of Zionism and the Yishuv typified that of many American Jews in the New Deal era. With roots in the Jewish immigrant milieu and ties to Franklin D. Roosevelt's populist liberalism, American Jews increasingly believed in the power of social planning and the proposition that the national government is responsible for the welfare of its citizens.[45] In addition, the ubiquitous Zionist propaganda of that period asserted that the Zionist enterprise, under the rubric of the Jewish Agency, the World Zionist Organization, and the Vaad Leumi, would protect the interests of the Jewish people worldwide. Thus many American Jews, acting as much out of self-perception as of self-interest, envisioned a Palestine in which both Arabs and Jews would transcend interracial conflict and reap the benefits of Zionist economic and social progress. These convictions were enshrined in the canon of American Zionism by the movement's leaders—Stephen S. Wise, Louis D. Brandeis, Henrietta Szold, and Abba Hillel Silver—who viewed Labor Palestine as serving a mediatory function for different segments of diaspora Jewry, Zionism, and the Yishuv.

Against this backdrop, the Labor Zionist program received the warm endorsement of significant communal leaders who were neither specifically socialist nor nationalist in their orientation. The case of Rabbi Philip S. Bernstein of Rochester, New York, for example, typifies the outlook of many non-Orthodox spiritual leaders of the period. Bernstein esteemed the Yishuv because it "washed Jews free of their complexes and fears. . . . It has helped them face life without timidity or assertiveness, without inferiority or superiority complexes."[46] In an unusual twist, he also co-opted elements of the Palestine workers movement's class-conscious orientation:

> Labor Zionism is making a very important contribution to Jewish economic health. Today antisemitism is largely the product of economic causes. Not only in the United States, but in every land in which there is a substantial Jewish population, the Jew finds himself, owing to historic causes over which he had no control, in the precarious middle class. . . . Of all Jewish forces, Labor Zionism alone penetrates to the causes in order to change the results.[47]

Bernstein also linked Jewish economic hardships to the Reform movement's sense of universal mission:

> It is well that we Reform Jews be appreciative of [Labor's] achievement [in Palestine], for it gives substance to our ideal of a Jewish mission to bring righteousness and justice to mankind. We know how difficult it is to promote this ideal in Reform Judaism, for our congregations consist largely of business and professional men . . . who tend to follow the economic interests of their own class. Since 1933 there has been increasing timidity, verging almost on panic, about the Jews' position. There is not more but less advocacy of social justice. In Palestine alone, among consciously Jewish forces, is social justice a reality.[48]

At this ideational juncture, Bernstein parted ways with Zionist ideology. Palestine might be the center of modern Jewish life, he admitted, but it "is not the answer to the problems of world Jewry." He confidently predicted that the great majority of the Jewish people would continue to live in the diaspora. "To say that [Jews] cannot be happy in [the diaspora]," he argued, "that they must consider themselves in exile would be faithless to the universalistic ideals of Judaism and the principles of democracy."[49] In sum, Bernstein articulated a liberal Jewish perspective in which Palestinocentrism, devoid of the ideological rigidity of its European counterpart, served as a conduit to Labor Palestine. Unlike many of his avowed Zionist colleagues, he did not consider the Yishuv a hothouse of Jewish cultural and religious renewal. Nor did he regard Palestinian Jewish society as the ultimate repository or the last line of defense of modern Jewish identity. Rather, Bernstein's support for Zionism and the Yishuv was bound up in his particular vision of Labor Palestine as the quintessential Jewish national home.

With the doors of the West closed to all but a small fraction of persecuted and homeless Jewish refugees, Monsky, Schlossberg, and Bernstein joined American Zionist leaders who clamored for the British Mandatory to open the gates to Palestine.[50] In fact, the issue proved to be the centerpiece of American movement's intensive shekel campaign for the Twentieth Zionist Congress which convened in Zurich in August 1937. The network of Zionist parties and groups in the United States embarked on a massive drive to enroll new members. Ludwig Lewisohn spoke for the Zionist consensus when he declared that Jews everywhere were in danger, and he called on American Jews to unite for the sake of common action, in the form of a "popular front."

> There is one Jewish people. There is one Jewish problem. . . . The Jew who does not give to Palestine or buy his *shekel*, remote as he may seem to himself to be from both Europe and Palestine, breaks the common front of a people's necessary defense and delivers his children up to degradation and despair.
>
> *The enemy is one. The danger is one. The ruthless conqueror when he enters the sacred city which you and I have not defended will not ask: were you orthodox or liberal, were you Zionist or not, were you ZOA or Mizrahi or a member of the Histadrut, did you give to the community chest or not, were you American Democrat or Republican? He will not ask. He will come with the old, old contemptuous cry of the Middle Ages: Hierosolymn est perdita! Jerusalem is lost! Hep! Hep! cried the crusaders as they waded through pools of Jewish blood.*
>
> JEWS OF AMERICA, see to it that Jerusalem is not lost again! . . .
>
> The besiegers are at the gate of your city. Your house is on fire over the

heads of your children. Not only the houses of your brethren in Germany and Poland and Rumania. . . . Nothing less will do than the gift of yourself, your voice, your vote, your moral being. This is what buying the *shekel* means. This is what public adherence to the Zionist cause means. . . .

JEWS OF AMERICA form and sustain the popular front!

JEWS OF AMERICA sign the Declaration in support of the Jewish national home which is the symbol of your security and of the ending of your homelessness in the world![51]

In 1937, the American Zionist movement conducted a countrywide campaign to convince American Jews that purchase of the shekel was a moral and existential responsibility. Labor Zionism made use of its far-ranging contacts in the Jewish immigrant milieu and the Jewish labor movement. It also exploited the talents of a unique cohort of prominent Palestinian spokespersons. The League for Labor Palestine underwrote the cost of publicity tours to major urban centers by Shlomo Zemah, Golda Meir, Yosef Baratz, and Enzo Sereni, and it sponsored a lecture circuit of well-known "American" personalities associated with Labor Palestine, such as Hayim Greenberg, Maurice Samuel, Joseph Schlossberg, Alexander Kohanski, and Rabbi Edward L. Israel.

The common theme of these speakers was clear. Without the Palestine labor movement as Zionism's central energizing factor, they argued, no significant national venture in the Yishuv was possible. The movement had proved to be the hub around which all social, economic, and political Zionist efforts revolved. Labor Zionism's congress agenda was enunciated in "A Call to the Jewish Masses."[52] The declaration warned of European Jewry's impending disaster and Zionist demoralization caused by continued Arab rioting in Palestine. It also expressed grave uncertainty about the Royal Peel Commission sent to Palestine in 1936. The commission was charged with investigating the Arab riots and proposing ways of preventing further violence.

When the Peel Commission commenced its investigation in 1936, there was no American Jewish consensus on the issue of the Yishuv's political future. As described earlier, however, throughout the 1930s, growing numbers of American Jews and Jewish groups—including the Yiddish and Anglo-Jewish press, rabbis, educators, union leaders, and communal activists—had registered their support for Labor Palestine. Thus what the *American Jewish Year Book* referred to at the time as "the strength of pro-Labor sentiment in the United States" may, in historical perspective, be viewed as a barometer of the growing affinity of American Jews for the Yishuv.[53]

The upswing in support for Labor Palestine generally set the stage for a new phase in relations between American Jews and the Zionist movement.

It was widely assumed that the Peel Commission's report would lead to the cantonization or tripartition of Palestine into Arab, Jewish, and international entities. But American Zionist leaders cautioned that such an outcome would shrink the size of the Jewish national home.[54] Fear of potential British geographic and political constraints was based on the Zionist movement's experience of 1923 when the Mandatory ruled that Transjordan was not part of the plans for the establishment of a Jewish national home. As a result, approximately 26,000 square miles of pre-Mandatory Palestinian territory was reduced by more than half, and the larger and more fertile terrain was barred to Jewish immigration and colonization. American Zionist leaders now anticipated the remaining 10,000 square miles of territory might also be significantly reduced. Aware that British diplomacy tended increasingly to placate anti-Zionist Arab sentiment at the expense of Jewish interests, the Mandatory appeared ready to use the Peel Commission's findings once again to limit drastically the size and growth of the Yishuv.

This prospect aroused considerable anxiety among Zionists and Zionist sympathizers in the United States. In an attempt to avert disaster, the Zionist leadership moved swiftly to coordinate an antipartition lobby. Exploiting the political clout of its staunchest gentile supporters, particularly the American Christian Conference and the Pro-Palestine Federation of America (a pro-Zionist front with strong ties to organized Jewish labor), the Zionist movement launched a propaganda campaign aimed at American public opinion as well as the American and British governments. Several prominent American leaders were conspicuous in this effort, including Senator Robert F. Wagner of New York; William Green, president of the American Federation of Labor; James W. Gerard, former ambassador to Germany; Rev. John Haynes Holmes, an eminent Protestant theologian; and Rev. Ivan Lee Holt, president of the Federal Council of Churches. These men spearheaded public efforts to petition American and British officials, including President Franklin D. Roosevelt, to prevent modification of the Palestine Mandate.[55] Their efforts were largely unsuccessful.

In July 1937, American Jewish commitment to the Yishuv was put to the test when the Peel Commission formally recommended partitioning Palestine. "Half a loaf is better than no bread," the British investigators remarked in an effort to appease Jewish and Arab nationalist groups.[56] The American response was mixed and heated, with the majority of public opinion opposed to the British proposal. The controversy laid bare the disunity of American Jews and the diverse spectrum of American Jewish attitudes toward Palestine. Initially, most Zionists and non-Zionists, led by the ZOA, Mizrahi, and the American Jewish Committee, denounced the scheme as violating the guarantees of the Balfour Declaration.

Meanwhile, a significant segment of American Jewish society, including the National Labor Committee for Palestine (an extramovement framework organized by Labor Zionists), criticized the proposal but refrained from rejecting it outright. Last, Hadassah assumed a seemingly neutral stance. The organization, as Hadassah president Judith Epstein observed, remained optimistic that the "inherently unworkable" British proposal would be replaced by a better recommendation.[57]

Virtually overnight, the British proposal sharpened the terms of the partition debate and the views of Zionist groups, Zionist sympathizers, and non-Zionist participants in Jewish communal affairs. One segment of American Jews, inspired by right-wing Zionist propaganda, adhered to a set of maximalist demands. An alliance of Revisionist Zionists, for example, united around Meir Grossman's Jewish State Party and categorically refused to renounce Jewish claims to any part of Mandatory Palestine (including Transjordan). This position also won the support of the Mizrahi Party and other traditional Jews who opposed the severance of holy sites from the proposed Jewish state.

Second, an unusual combination of political bedfellows coalesced around the call for a binational solution to the conflict in Palestine. This minority group included supporters of Brit Shalom, renegade members of the American Jewish Committee and the Jewish Labor Committee, and even some Jewish Communists and Bundists. These factions rejected the dominant Zionist coalition's insistence on the primacy of Jewish sovereignty in Palestine, contending that Jewish national claims were secondary to Arab-Jewish reconciliation and coexistence. With some important modifications, this position was also shared by Hashomer Hazair and Left Poalei Zion, a radical offshoot of the Poalei Zion–Zeirei Zion party. These Marxist Zionist groups argued that mutual economic interests would ultimately bring together Arabs and Jews in a binational framework.[58] Unlike the extreme Jewish left, the latter organizations were willing to accept Zionist political demands on the basis of proportional representation within a federative structure.

Finally, the American Zionist mainstream gravitated toward the Jewish Agency leadership's strategy of not rejecting the partition plan. This approach mirrored that of Palestine's dominant Mapai Party under David

Ben-Gurion and Moshe Sharett and the General Zionist camp under Chaim Weizmann.[59] "If there is no hope of alleviating the Arab fears of future Jewish domination," explained the Labor Zionist spokesman Abraham Revusky, "and weakening if not completely abolishing Arab resistance to Jewish immigration, we must accept the partition plan, bargaining, perhaps, for minor improvements."[60] This stance also signaled a subtle but important shift in Zionist tactics, for it left open the possibility of divergent ideological and political opinions within the context of a general plan to partition Palestine. At the same time, it demonstrated that centrist Zionist interests were anchored by a fundamental assumption: the urgent need for large-scale colonization coupled with mass immigration to Palestine. Consequently, Arab needs and demands were subordinated to the overall scheme of building up the Jewish national home, a conception that dovetailed with Labor Zionism's evolving approach to Jewish self-defense and the Arab rebellion in Palestine.[61]

In the face of mounting Arab hostility and British vacillation over the future of the Mandate, the American Zionist movement, with Rabbis Stephen S. Wise and Abba Hillel Silver at the helm, settled on a practical, constructive strategy congruent with the Yishuv's policies. It was unthinkable, Silver, Wise, and other leaders reasoned, that the League of Nations would turn to another major power to assume the Mandate. Nor did it seem likely the United States would seriously consider assuming an international trusteeship of Palestine. The only sensible alternative, according to this American view, was to protest British policy and press for the most favorable partition terms. In the meantime, Zionists hoped the pressure of liberal public opinion in the West, including the vocal opposition of American Jews, would force Britain to eliminate the glaring injustices of the Mandatory policies.[62]

Paradoxically, despite the rising popular support for the Yishuv in this period, nurtured by disparate Zionist propaganda campaigns nationwide, American Jews generally chose not to join the Zionist movement. Nor did widespread concern over the Peel Commission prompt more than a small minority of American Jews to participate in the shekel drive for the Twentieth Zionist Congress held in Zurich in August 1937. In all, approximately 207,000 American shekels were purchased during the registration drive for the congress elections.[63] Although this represented a significant numerical increase over the number of shekels purchased in 1935, it accounted for only 4 percent of the total American Jewish population. In any event, the highest percentage of ballots actually cast went to the Labor Zionist bloc. In the United States, Labor won 36,450 out of 99,959 votes cast, capturing more than a third of the total vote. General Zionists were the next most successful group, with 23,810 votes.[64] The well-disciplined, independent Hadassah list, earned 20,000 votes. Although most members voted for the organization, historical and anecdotal evidence suggests that a sizable number were otherwise sympathetic to Labor Palestine. Indeed, Hadassah leaders Henrietta Szold, Irma Lindheim, and Jessie Sampter sustained close ties with the Labor Zionist movement and frequently proclaimed their sympathy with the Histadrut, the *kvuzot* (communes), and other cooperative ventures of the Yishuv.[65]

As had been the case in 1935, the results of the 1937 American elections proved politically embarrassing and problematic for the ZOA and Hadassah. So that Labor Zionists would not head the American delegation, Hadassah and the ZOA, led by Rose Jacobs and Stephen S. Wise, respectively, consolidated their mandates and formed a united General Zionist front. In this arrangement, the General Zionist camp won forty Congress delegates; the Labor Zionist group received thirty-two; and the Mizrahi Party received eighteen.[66]

This maneuver by the General Zionist leaders in the Zionist Congress elections caused Labor Zionism's proportional lead to fall from 44 percent overall in 1935 to 37 percent in 1937. Weighed in the balance, however, rather than diminishing Labor's strength, this pattern actually reflected the general increase in total shekel purchases worldwide by middle-class Jews since 1933. Indeed, the foregoing pattern was also true of the United States, where approximately 20,000 votes were cast out of 70,000 shekels sold in 1933, and roughly 55,000 votes were cast out of 134,000 shekels sold in 1935. Such statistics—compared with those for 1937 when nearly half of the 207,000 shekels purchased resulted in ballots cast—demonstrate the swift rise of American Jewish interest in Zionism. Viewed in the aggregate, therefore, the election results also reveal that Labor Zionism appealed to a substantial constituency beyond the movement's ranks. Meanwhile, the reverse was true of other American Zionist groups, which polled fewer votes than the size of their organizational membership indicated.[67] This paradox suggests that the philosophy of the Labor Zionist movement, never having more than about ten thousand members before 1939, appealed to mainstream American Jewish values and interests.[68]

In August 1937, the Twentieth Zionist Congress debated the Peel Com-

mission's proposal to partition Palestine. The commission's recommendation to "separate the areas in which the Jews have acquired land and settled
from those which are wholly or mainly occupied by Arabs" produced
intense discord among the congress delegates.[69] Despite vehement disagree-
ment over the merits of the plan, the Jewish Agency and WZO leadership's
strategy of "nonrejection" was endorsed by a majority of delegates. Whatever the Zionist movement had hitherto accomplished, Chaim Weizmann
reminded the congress, was achieved "dunam by dunam, man by man,
house by house. I am not dazzled by the name of 'Jewish State' but I regard
the offer as the first stage of a great achievement and as an alternative to
8,000 [immigration] certificates a year."[70]

Labor Zionist leaders David Ben-Gurion, Moshe Shertok, and Berl
Katznelson maintained that both the British proposal to partition Palestine
and the congress's decision rested on the fait accompli of Zionist colonization. They argued that the British plan reflected the status quo of the
Yishuv's pioneering infrastructure. The terms of the proposal, they reasoned, would no doubt have been even more favorable to the Zionist
enterprise a few years hence, but timing was essential and the Jewish people
could not wait. This view was also endorsed by the American delegation.[71]
Hayim Fineman, a Labor Zionist delegate from Philadelphia, summed up
the American group's attitude by remarking that the partition plan was not
the last act in the drama of the Jewish return to Palestine. "Ultimately, no
matter what English or Arab politicians may try to do," he declared, "the
land will belong to those who are willing to work on it."[72]

The final congress vote on the British proposal was preceded by an
address by Hayim Greenberg. The partition plan had been thrust on the
Zionist movement from outside, Greenberg claimed, and as such it was not
to be lightly disregarded. Nor could the proposal be easily accepted or
rejected. Faced with choosing between what he viewed as the lesser of two
evils, he recommended that the Zionist executive be entrusted with investigating possibilities for improving the British proposal. In the end, the
majority of delegates agreed not to reject the partition plan outright. Instead, they passed a resolution calling on the Zionist executive to negotiate
a modified proposal with the British government to be presented at the
next Zionist Congress.[73]

With the Twentieth Zionist Congress, the Zionist movement reached a
new juncture. It was clear that the Peel Commission's findings had irrevo-
cably changed the nature of the Palestine debate and that the possibility of

Jewish statehood was at hand. Not even Britain's discriminatory policies and Arab hostility could suppress the underlying current of cautious optimism that pervaded the congress's closing sessions. The World Zionist Organization resolved to accelerate the pace of Jewish development in the Yishuv, and the movement committed itself to an ambitious goal of resettling some 200,000 Jews in Palestine by the end of the decade.[74]

The debate over partition underscored the ideological fissures of the American Jewish public arena. First, as noted previously, it revealed the extent to which the future of modern Palestine had become a paramount concern of American Jews. Second, it highlighted the peculiar disjunction between general American Jewish attitudes and the political stance of the American Zionist movement. For example, a March 1938 opinion poll of 172 American Jewish leaders, representing Zionists and non-Zionists as well American Judaism's Orthodox, Conservative, and Reform branches, indicated that 86 percent (148) were for the Mandate and against partition, and only 14 percent (24) were either wholly or conditionally in favor of the Mandate. Meanwhile, at the Zionist Congress itself, the American Zionist delegation, numbering 91 of 475 delegates, split over the issue of partition, with a majority voting in favor of the Labor Zionist resolution providing for negotiations with the Mandatory. Viewed in conjunction, however, the overall shift in American Jewish attitudes represented by the poll (away from anti-Zionism and toward Zionism) and the American delegation's congress vote (away from nonpartisanship and toward Labor Zionism's activist political agenda) reflects the centripetal force of the Yishuv.

In the wake of the Peel Commission and the Twentieth Zionist Congress, the question of Palestine's future became a centerpiece of the American Jewish public agenda. Regardless of the differing philosophical and political viewpoints, a consensus crystallized around the perceived need to safeguard the Zionist enterprise and the Yishuv. Sol M. Stroock, a prominent New York attorney and non-Zionist spokesman, tacitly acknowledged this sea change at the thirty-first annual meeting of the American Jewish Committee when he introduced a resolution on Palestine. The committee, he observed, endorsed the principles of the Balfour Declaration in 1918 but "preferred since the establishment of the Jewish Agency to permit the problems affecting Palestine to be worked out and solved by and through the Jewish Agency."[75] However, he added, the Peel Commission report now made it necessary to assume a more activist stance:

We do not speak either for against the establishment of a Jewish state. We seek . . . in the adoption of any resolution or any plan that might be discussed or proposed today, the protection of the rights of Jews, including their right to settle and live peacefully in Palestine, and the responsibilities that devolve upon us—you and me and all of us here assembled, and those whom we represent—toward those Jews whose rights we in turn seek to protect.

I think that we ought to be very clear about that, so that in any discussion that may take place here it may be well understood that the American Jewish Committee as such takes no stand whatsoever upon the problem as to whether or not there should be a Jewish state or should not be a Jewish state, or whether there should be a small Jewish state or a large Jewish state. What the American Jewish Committee is called upon to consider is what we are to do . . . to protect the rights of our fellow Jews suffering from persecution and outrage in the lands of Europe in order that they may find some peace and rest, if it is possible to be found, in Palestine.[76]

In other words, Stroock not only stressed the need to ensure Jewish rights in Palestine and the diaspora, but he also implicitly legitimated the Zionist objective of Jewish sovereignty in Palestine. Previously, even during the heady period following the issuance of the Balfour Declaration, such a notion was anathema in American Jewish Committee circles.[77] On the eve of World War II, however, the committee's willingness to embrace the Yishuv served to underscore the plight of European Jewry and the growing power of the Zionists in the intertwined arenas of American and international Jewish politics.

At the same time that Zionism was gaining a firm foundation and respectability in American Jewish life, the venerable American Jewish Joint Distribution Committee (JDC) was shutting down its operation in the Biro-Bidjan territory of Soviet Russia.[78] This operation, which since 1928 had tried to create a self-sufficient Jewish republic in Biro-Bidjan as part of official Soviet policy, provides an instructive comparison with the Yishuv. In 1936 when the Stalin regime promised to permit the immigration of one thousand Jewish refugee families into the Siberian territory, the JDC and other American Jewish philanthropic groups, working together under the auspices of the Agro-Joint and the American Society for Jewish Farm Settlements in Russia, became deeply involved in the project.[79] The Soviet government never retracted its promises and encouraged American Jewish investment in the so-called Jewish republic. But the conspicuous lack of state interest in Biro-Bidjan's social and economic growth as well as the government's failure to live up to its obligations effectively halted the territory's development. In all, the Agro-Joint and the American Society for Jewish Farm Settlements in Russia sent approximately $18 million to Biro-Bidjan and Jewish colonies in Soviet White Russia, Ukraine, and Crimea. At the height of the Agro-Joint's work, the agency claimed that more than 250,000 Jews were settled on the land.[80]

The closure of the Agro-Joint's operations, after ten years of costly work, offered a stark contrast to the Zionist enterprise. Both were territories that needed to be built up and where Jewish settlers faced numerous hardships and obstacles. Palestine, however, sustained the commitment of diaspora Jews and also demonstrated considerable pioneering success. At the same time, the Agro-Joint's failure in Soviet Russia served as a stern warning to supporters of the Jewish national home, prompting American Zionists and American Jewish investors in Palestine to question British intentions toward the Yishuv. Without London's firm backing, they feared, would the Zionist enterprise go the way of Biro-Bidjan?

On the eve of World War II, the severely limited possibilities for Jewish settlement, exacerbated by the increasingly desperate plight of European Jewry, amplified the critical role of the Yishuv to Jewish survival. The various options considered by the world community for Jewish emigration, colonization, and temporary refuge in this period were stillborn. A dramatic example was the Evian Conference of 1938, an international gathering of thirty-two nations that convened to investigate "new" alternatives for re-locating central European Jewish refugees. Among them was London's offer for "immediate large-scale [Jewish] settlement" in an area known as British Guiana, a colony on the northeastern coast of South America.[81] Although the scheme initially raised high hopes, the British government soon im-posed numerous demands, thereby making it impractical. This tragic epi-sode, coupled with the ongoing restrictions on Jewish immigration to Man-datory Palestine, underscored Britain's indifference to the plight of European Jewry. Similar proposals for resettling Jewish refugees in the Do-minican Republic and the Philippine Islands also fell through.[82] The fol-lowing months brought only grave political problems, insurmountable dif-ficulties, and dashed hopes for the possibility of Jewish resettlement anywhere.

American Jewry reacted with alarm to the Mandatory's declared policy of sharply reducing the schedule of Jewish immigration to Palestine. The process had been set in motion in March 1938 when, guided by the prin-ciple of Palestine's alleged "economic absorptive capacity," the British issued a scant three thousand immigration certificates for the coming six months. The certificates were allocated to two categories of potential immigrants: two thousand "capitalists" and one thousand "laborers." In an attempt to soften this blow, each certificate holder was allowed to bring in his or her immediate family outside the quota.[83] Theoretically, this would result in the immigration of some ten thousand Jews. In reality, however, the government's action was disingenuous. Rather than assist Jewish refugees, it was intended to mollify anti-Zionist Arab forces. Indeed, the number of "capitalist" certificates fell far short of the growing need of the Jewish middle-class families in Germany, Poland, and Romania. The policy similarly discriminated against the swelling ranks of young single pioneers.[84]

By the spring of 1938, therefore, mounting public concern over the plight of European Jewish refugees and anti-Jewish British policy vis-à-vis Palestine led to the call for an American Jewish assembly to be modeled after the American Jewish Congress of World War I. The impetus for the new assembly came from regional Jewish leaders, many of whom were concerned about the apportionment of JDC funds to the Zionist cause. From the outset, the notion of such a gathering was vociferously opposed by the American Jewish Committee and the Jewish Labor Committee. These groups, which objected to using American Jewish charitable funds for overtly Zionist activities, worried that such a framework would result in de facto support of Aliyah Bet, the Jewish Agency's program of "illegal" immigration to Palestine.[85]

Rabbi Samuel H. Goldenson, the spiritual leader of the Reform movement's flagship Temple Emanu-El in New York City and a key spokesmen of the "German" Jewish establishment, denounced the proposed American Jewish assembly. "The evils which may arise from turning the Jewish people of this country from individual citizens into a solidified group or one so regarded by our neighbors are terrible to contemplate," he declared in a Sabbath sermon.

> The proper way and the more successful way of securing a greater measure of unity in the household of Israel is for the leaders in all Jewish endeavors to come together in a mutually confident and cooperative spirit and then as representatives of already existent organizations, to speak to the world at large not in the name of a solidified Jewry, but in the name of humanity and justice, freedom and equality.[86]

Goldenson's address illustrates the deep-seated trepidation with which American Jewry's elite leaders viewed efforts to create a representative communal decision-making framework. As during World War I, the very idea of such a body threatened to undermine the position of the "German" Jewish elite—derisively referred to in the Yiddish press as "the Fifth Avenue aristocracy." Meanwhile, the latter accused supporters of the proposed assembly of forsaking American Jewry's long-term needs and safety in the name of illusory goals. "An organization of all the Jews that speaks of itself as a congress or an assembly," Goldenson warned, "cannot but give support to the charge that we Jews are at bottom racially different from the rest of the citizens of the country."[87]

The Jewish Labor Committee (JLC) also resisted the call for an American Jewish assembly. Despite the recent advent of close ties between the Histadrut and elements of organized Jewish labor in the United States, the JLC viewed its own organizational authority as inviolate, and so it rejected any move that threatened to subsume American Jewish labor under a non-labor aegis. The JLC leaders also were reluctant to align themselves in such a framework with the American Jewish bourgeoisie and Jewish Communists. Taking part in an American Jewish assembly, they explained, would be tantamount to legitimizing the anti-Jewish labor positions of their opponents.[88]

But the rising tide of communal pressure could not be held back. In June 1938 representatives of the four main "nonpartisan" American Jewish organizations—the American Jewish Committee, the Order of Bnai Brith, the Jewish Labor Committee, and the American Jewish Congress—met in Pittsburgh to examine possibilities for creating a unified American Jewish strategy. The original communal referendum proposed by the American Jewish Congress contained four questions, one of which asked whether the assembly should be empowered to act as the representative agency of American Jewry in defense of Jewish rights.[89] This proposal was troubling to the American Jewish Committee, Bnai Brith, and the Jewish Labor Committee and so was changed to "Do you favor a union of all American Jewish groups engaged in safeguarding the equal rights of Jews, which shall undertake to create for the defense of such rights a single, all-inclusive agency organized on a democratic, representative basis in accordance with American ideals?"[90]

This text also proved too strong for the factions. The American Jewish Committee balked at the creation of a Jewish "bloc" and objected to any process that would result in establishing a national or political American Jewish framework. The Jewish Labor Committee, fearful of class collaboration, also opposed the proposal. Finally, the sixty thousand members of

Bnai Brith, who officially maintained a position of neutrality on the issue of Zionism, rejected the concept of a national election that could make the American Jewish Congress the chief spokesman of American Jewry. To achieve unity, therefore, the referendum was dropped, and it was decided to create a General Jewish Council that would not take up racial, national, or religious questions.[91] This agreement effectively nullified the council's original purpose of securing an overall communal strategy. As in the past, when no agreement could be reached on the boycott of Germany or the convening of the World Jewish Congress,[92] American Jewish collaboration seemed a distant prospect.

When the assembly, now renamed the American Jewish Congress, finally convened in October 1938, it proved to be a pale shadow of its historic predecessor. In fact, many American Jewish leaders considered the congress a divisive and partisan affair. Nevertheless, the hundreds of thousands of voters who participated in the June elections for the congress indicated its growing hold on the imagination of American Jewry.[93] Moreover, the congress itself served as a barometer of Labor Zionism's expanding influence in American Jewish life. Of the 375 delegates elected to the congress, 85 men and women specifically represented the Labor Zionist movement.[94]

American Jewish hopes for concerted communal action suffered another setback in November 1938 when Britain retracted the partition scheme and declared it impracticable. Shortly thereafter, London issued the MacDonald White Paper of May 1939, which placed a cap on the growth of the Yishuv and closed the doors of Palestine to Jews in distress. American Zionists were shocked and enraged by the new Mandatory policy and subsequently held an emergency conference in Washington, D.C. The gathering reiterated the need for constructive Zionist work on all fronts, including, first and foremost, the realization of Britain's commitment to establish an autonomous Jewish national home. In an unusual move, the conference censured antipartition and maximalist Zionist groups who refused to honor the decision of the recent Zurich Congress. The administrative committee of the Zionist Organization of America went so far as to pass a resolution barring all "unauthorized" Zionist political activity that undermined the Jewish Agency's negotiations with the Mandatory power. It was hoped that such a policy would strengthen those American Jewish forces that recognized the need for united political action.[95]

In September 1939, the Nazi conquest of Europe, which had begun with the Anschluss in March 1938, shifted into high gear, and Hitler's forces overran Poland. These events prompted a flurry of American Jewish communal and political activity and escalated the organizational efforts of the United Palestine Appeal (UPA), the Joint Distribution Committee, and Hadassah's Youth Aliyah program. During this time, the National Labor Committee for Palestine (NLCP), an extramovement organization that grew out of the Geverkshaftn campaign in 1936, came to the fore of American Zionist lobbying efforts. Beginning in 1938, for example, the NLCP conventions annually attracted more than two thousand delegates from a wide array of trade unions, fraternal orders, social and cultural organizations, and Hebraist associations. The delegates represented almost 750,000 American Jews, the majority of whom did not belong to either the Zionist or the Labor Zionist movement.[96] This was a far cry from the founding conventions of the Geverkshaftn in the 1920s, which drew a few hundred supporters from the ranks of Poalei Zion and a handful of Jewish workers' groups.[97]

Unlike the UPA, the JDC, and the Hadassah rescue program, the NLCP also made the social and cultural arena of American Jews a target of its political work. By 1939, the NLCP had emerged as a mainstream organization capable of inspiring and penetrating broad segments of American Jewry. Yet the NLCP's fund-raising apparatus was no match for the massive JDC and UPA drives. Instead, the group's strength lay in its ability to conduct effective educational and propaganda work and to inculcate in working- and middle-class American Jews a sense of kinship with and responsibility for the Yishuv.

As one European Jewish community after another passed under the control of antisemitic totalitarian regimes, the Jewish refugee problem grew. American Jews recognized that the only hope available to European Jewry was emigration, and they rallied to the cause of their oppressed brothers and sisters overseas. What distinguished the NLCP's rescue efforts in this period was its unique relationship with Palestine's hegemonous labor movement. The NLCP considered itself the front line of Labor Zionism's campaign in the American diaspora. The organization wholeheartedly committed itself to advancing Labor Palestine's objectives: expanding the Yishuv's socioeconomic infrastructure and supporting the "illegal" immigration of Jewish youth from European countries of distress. Like their counterparts in Palestine, Labor Zionists in the United States argued that rural settlements, industrial cooperatives, social welfare institutions, and other Histadrut-related agencies held the key to absorbing European Jews who reached Palestine's shores. As the cause of Labor Palestine became better understood in the United States, so did the NLCP's ability to attract ordinary Jews who looked to the Yishuv as an example of Jewish renaissance as well as a haven.

On the eve of World War II, the ascendance of generally liberal and pro-Labor Zionist forces within American Zionist leadership circles was clear. When, for example, the Zionist Organization of America elected Rabbi Solomon Goldman to be its new president in 1938, Labor Zionism indirectly gained an important and influential advocate on the national level. Goldman was an outspoken supporter of Labor Palestine and closely associated with the Zionist wing of the Conservative movement. (Following his tenure as ZOA president, Goldman served as the national chairman of the League for Labor Palestine.) Even his challenger Rabbi Israel Goldstein, who later succeeded Goldman as ZOA president, established strong relations with Labor Zionism. In addition, Bert Goldstein, Israel Goldstein's wife, served as the national president of Pioneer Women during this period.

The fateful year 1939 witnessed a watershed in activity on behalf of the Yishuv. Labor Zionists played a key role in mobilizing the American Jewish community without undue regard for partisan and ideological viewpoints. One such example was the National Conference for Palestine, which met in February 1939. The conference attracted a diverse mixture of American Jewish leaders. Its high profile was also derived from the participation of Robert H. Jackson, solicitor general of the United States, and Jan Garrigue Masaryk, son of Tomás Garrigue Masaryk, the first president of independent Czechoslovakia. (The younger Masaryk later served as the foreign minister of the Czech provisional government in exile from 1940 to 1945 and of the restored government in Prague after the war.) The central issue debated by the conference was the creation of a unified fund-raising campaign for Palestine and the diaspora. Advocates of the plan, a scheme that ultimately gave rise to the United Jewish Appeal for Refugees and Overseas Needs, called for the elimination of duplicated organizational efforts and communal drives. The conference also called for a new national fund-raising goal of $20 million. Reasoning that the security of the Yishuv and the Jewish people were interrelated goals, the conference endorsed the proposition that a solution to the plight of European Jewry—even a partial solution such as resettlement in the Yishuv—was in the best interests of the European Jewish refugees, Palestine, and the Jewish people.[98]

With the launching of the United Jewish Appeal, American Zionists gained access to previously inaccessible reservoirs of financial and communal resources. Similar efforts had earlier resulted in the Enlarged Jewish

Agency, a vehicle established in 1929 under the aegis of Chaim Weizmann and the American Jewish jurist Louis Marshall. The expanded agency's purpose was to bring together Zionists and non-Zionists in a cohesive framework, but it suffered from insoluble philosophical conflicts and inter-necine controversy. As a result, it gradually deteriorated and was almost defunct by 1939.[99]

By contrast, the collaborative Jewish communal efforts of the 1930s and 1940s, which resulted in a series of large-scale conferences, conventions, and events devoted to the needs of the Yishuv, were successful. Like the National Conference on Palestine, these public parleys gained the sympathy of a broad cross section of American Jewish society. They raised millions of dollars that directly and indirectly benefited the Yishuv, serving as models for the later efforts of American Jewish fund-raising giants Henry Montor, Rudolf Sonneborn, and others who assumed responsibility for the financial backing of Aliyah Bet and Haganah self-defense initiatives in Palestine.[100]

In the final analysis, notwithstanding these advances, neither American Jewry nor the Zionist movement was able to stem the tide of the Nazi catastrophe—a painful subject about which the last word has yet to be written. What is certain, however, is that the critical years between 1935 and 1939 solidified American Jewry's profound sense of Jewish peoplehood and commitment to the Jewish national home. Popular consensus crystal-lized around the Yishuv as the single best hope for postwar Jewish recon-struction. Even formerly opposing forces in the United States—like the Reform movement, the Jewish Labor Committee, and the American Jew-ish Committee—now turned to Labor Palestine to solve the dilemma of Jewish homelessness and powerlessness. American Zionists and Zionist sympathizers, on the other hand, coalesced around the Yishuv as a viable haven and also because its social democratic character seemed essential to the future of the Jewish people. Labor Zionism's role in stimulating, shap-ing, and mobilizing the nationalist sentiment of American Jewry at this critical juncture in Jewish history cannot be overemphasized.

Conclusion

The Campaign for the Jewish State

As late as 1939, in contrast to the emerging American Jewish consensus, the militant leader of the Zionist Organization of America (ZOA), Abba Hillel Silver, vehemently opposed the Zionist program of Aliyah Bet. At the Twenty-first Zionist Congress, held in Geneva in August 1939, Silver accused the Labor-led Jewish Agency and its supporters of pursuing policies that resulted in the cancellation of legal immigration and urged the movement to "refrain from desperate acts of opposition, from civil rebellion, from non-cooperation." Silver correctly alleged that Labor dominated Zionist policymaking and imposed its will on much the world movement; it controlled the building blocks of the Jewish state-in-the-making. Moreover, he argued, the Labor Zionist leaders were behaving as though a Jewish state already existed and that their policies would ultimately lead to a clash with the Mandatory.[1] Silver's attack on the Labor Zionist movement and the policies of the World Zionist Organization provoked tremendous consternation. In response, Silver was publicly castigated by Berl Katznelson, a leading spokesman of the Yishuv: "From this podium remarks were made yesterday by Rabbi Silver which I cannot permit myself to ignore. It was as if he cast a stone at our refugees on the high seas and stabbed Zionist policy in the back."[2] The majority of congress delegates, including the Americans, agreed with Katznelson's point of view. In fact, at the conclusion of a private meeting, the American delegates unanimously rejected Silver's remarks and declared that he spoke in his "personal capacity."[3]

The reactions by Katznelson and the American delegation to Silver, who was then chairman of the United Palestine Appeal, highlights the congruence of American Jewish interests and Labor Zionist policy even before the outbreak of war in September 1939. Indeed, at a time when total Zionist enrollment in the United States numbered roughly 200,000 members, or 4 percent of the American Jewish population, such support was vital to the Zionist cause.[4]

American society's receptivity to Labor Zionism was also bolstered by many gentile intellectuals. As noted in chapter 5, Hayim Greenberg, Maurice Samuel, Horace M. Kallen, and Mordecai M. Kaplan sustained contact with an array of remarkable and influential thinkers. Their efforts were strengthened by Trude Weiss-Rosmarin, Oscar Janowsky, and other Jewish intellectuals who, though not directly associated with Zionism, were generally sympathetic to Labor Palestine. Together they opened channels of communication with Charles A. Beard, Taraknath Das, Reinhold Niebuhr, Jacques Maritain, Paul Tillich, John Dewey, Carl J. Friedrich, Paul Goodman, Alvin Johnson, and Mark Van Doren, who represented an elite segment of Western society with which the Zionist movement had otherwise little contact.[5]

In this period, Labor Zionism also enjoyed the strong support of organized American labor, particularly the powerful American Federation of Labor (AFL). Although the AFL had previously demonstrated its sympathy with the Balfour Declaration and the call for a Jewish national home in Palestine, the remaining American labor organizations did not officially back the Yishuv and Zionist aspirations for independence until 1944. Before this time, however, it was not unusual for opposing workers' groups and factions within the labor movement to set aside their intra- and inter-organizational differences to present a united front on behalf of specific Histadrut-related activities.[6]

Thus with the rise of Hitler and the ascendance of American labor's anti-Stalinist forces, prominent leaders like William Green of the AFL and John L. Lewis of the Congress of Industrial Organizations (CIO) took the lead in expressing sympathy with the Palestine labor movement. The AFL's position on Zionism and the Yishuv was refined and articulated in a 1941 convention resolution:

> With a feeling of confidence and faith, the [AFL] has also given at all times a full measure of support to its Jewish membership and to Jewish organizations in the effort put forth to establish a Jewish homeland in Palestine. When the Balfour Declaration was first announced the [AFL] viewed this great statement in hopeful and gleeful anticipation. We wish on this occasion to reaffirm our endorsement of this great declaration, and propose that it be implemented to insure an early opportunity to the Jewish people to develop their national culture and homeland.
>
> We draw particular attention to the fact that the area terrorized by the

Nazis continues to expand, and that the Jewish people have been singled out by the Hitler regime for especial savage persecution. It is, therefore, all the more urgent that this suffering people, the greatest of all sufferers at the ruthless hands of our enemies of freedom and democracy should be accorded real hope and aid through a restoration of rights long overdue it—rights to a full development in Palestine. This is the least the democracy of the world can pledge in these fateful hours of humanity.

We therefore recommend . . . the hope that when this war against the barbarism of Hitler, and of black absolutism, is over, when freedom and democracy once more may breathe in peace throughout the world, that Great Britain in cooperation with the United States, and other democratic countries, will take the necessary steps to implement the Balfour Declaration of 1917 in its full meaning by facilitating further immigration and a large scale settlement of Jewish laboring masses in their national home in Palestine. Genuine equality of the Jewish people among the nations of the earth can only be advanced through restoring their national life on the soil of Palestine.[7]

This endorsement of the Jewish national home illustrates, at least implicitly, Labor Zionism's attempt to strengthen relations with important American political power brokers. It was assumed, moreover, that such support would benefit segments of American society beyond the reach of Zionist movement, including other nationally minded American ethnic groups, like the Irish and Poles, associated with organized labor.[8]

With the onset of World War II, Labor Palestine's political campaign and propaganda work became even more important. These efforts, it was hoped, would help open channels to American society through which Jewish Agency leaders could influence the public debate about Palestine's future. In the wake of the greater intergovernmental cooperation between Washington, D.C., and London, the Zionist leadership feared the Roosevelt administration would turn a blind eye to Britain's discriminatory Palestine policies. Against this backdrop, David Ben-Gurion and Chaim Weizmann in Palestine and Stephen S. Wise and Abba Hillel Silver in the United States quietly supported Labor Zionist efforts to lobby the AFL and other American labor groups whose support of the Yishuv would attract nationwide attention. Before 1943, no other Jewish faction in the United States so persistently sought to influence the American political arena by exploiting Franklin D. Roosevelt's electoral coalition.[9]

The AFL remained true to its support of Jewish national aspirations despite the protests of Arab nationalist spokesmen. Even though some AFL leaders refrained from taking a stand on the Arab question because it theoretically fell outside the purview of "pure trade unionism," most were convinced by the Labor Zionist argument that Palestine's economic improvement would foster positive Arab-Jewish relations in the country as a whole.

Meanwhile, in the Labor Zionist movement itself, different schools of thought roundly disagreed on the issue of Arab national rights.[10] The American movement as a whole, however, followed the lead of Ben-Gurion and Mapai to unite around the strategy of "combative Zionism." This policy placed the realization of a Jewish majority in Palestine ahead of accommodation with the Arabs. In the end, Berl Katznelson, Hayim Greenberg, Moshe Shertok, and other leading moralists threw their support to the mainstream policymakers but continued to insist on the just treatment of Arabs in Palestine. The latter were persuaded, in large part, by the overwhelming conviction that the time had arrived to maximize support for the Jewish national home.[11]

The question of Arab rights in Palestine was also hotly debated in the Biltmore Conference, an American Zionist gathering held in May 1942 in New York City in lieu of a wartime Zionist Congress.[12] Ben-Gurion himself originally proposed the idea of a conference that would go beyond platitudes of "Zionist unity" and instead encourage American Jews to unite behind a "common platform" for Jewish statehood.[13] The three chief issues that the Biltmore Conference addressed were the political future of Palestine, the Arab problem, and the feasibility of creating an American Zionist alliance. The first two questions had also been central to the Twenty-first Zionist Congress of 1939. At the time, Chaim Weizmann had advocated a cautious policy of constructive Zionist work within the framework of restrictions imposed by the Mandatory. But Ben-Gurion had insisted on a combative approach, including the full use of Aliyah Bet as a political instrument. In short, despite the Zionist leaders' differences of opinion, the debate of 1939 rested on the assumption of Jewish dependence on the Mandatory.

At Biltmore, the Zionist case was formulated anew. Zionist demands, which now exceeded the context of Anglo-Jewish relations, were based on American interests in the Middle East.[14] As the ZOA leader Emanuel Neumann pointed out, the political playing field was no longer dominated by either the Palestine administration or the British government; the locus of action and struggle had shifted from London to Washington, D.C. "Official Washington does not live in a vacuum. Even as we sit here, the preparation for the post-war settlement is going on in the form of discussions in official and non-official circles. In the State Department there is a special bureau concerned exclusively with . . . post-war reconstruction." Pointing out that the United States had become the new "battleground" for Zionism, Neumann urged American Zionists to respond positively to Ben-Gurion's combative Zionist approach.

> We Zionists have isolated ourselves from the vital currents of American life and American thought. We have withdrawn into our shell. . . . We have failed to integrate the Zionist problem, the problem of the Jews, the problem of Palestine, into the larger problems and wider scheme of things with which thoughtful America is now concerned; and unless we succeed in breaking through our shell and establishing a fruitful contact with these vital currents about us, we shall find ourselves stranded and isolated.[15]

During the conference deliberations, the Labor Zionists argued against whittling down Jewish claims to Palestine in order to appease the Arabs or Britain. "If Jewish immigration to Palestine depends on Arab consent," Ben-Gurion proclaimed, "there will hardly be any Jewish immigration at all."[16] He also declared that Jewish immigration to Palestine required no consent—be it Arab or British. Despite intense opposition and the highly charged nature of wartime Jewish politics, the Labor-led coalition, which included Poalei Zion and the majority of General Zionists, prevailed. The conference adopted an eight-point resolution that came to be known as the Biltmore program. As Shabtai Teveth has observed, the first six parts of the program were ideological, being adapted from Weizmann's address. Furthermore, items 7 and 8, the program's operative political concepts, were lifted directly from Ben-Gurion's policy address on the second day of the conference.

> 7. In the struggle against the forces of aggression and tyranny, of which the Jews were the earliest victims, and which now menace the Jewish national home, recognition must be given to the right of the Jews of Palestine to play their full part in the war effort and in the defense of their country, through a Jewish military fighting force under its own flag and under the high command of the United Nations.
> 8. The Conference declares that the new world order that will follow victory cannot be established on foundations of peace, justice and equality, unless the problem of Jewish homelessness is finally solved.
> The Conference urges that the gates of Palestine be opened; that the Jewish Agency be vested with control of immigration into Palestine and with

the necessary authority for upbuilding the country, including the development of its unoccupied and uncultivated lands; and that Palestine be established as a Jewish commonwealth integrated into the structure of the new democratic world.

Then and only then will the age-old wrong to the Jewish people be righted.[17]

The Biltmore program, Walter Laqueur has suggested, was not actually a policy but a symbol, "a slogan reflecting the radicalization of the Zionist movement as the result of the war and of the losses suffered by the Jewish people."[18] In fact, a plan to institutionalize American Zionist unity and establish a new federative body—a proposal submitted by the Labor Zionist leaders Louis Segal and Hayim Fineman—was effectively blocked. With the exception of the Labor Zionists, no other group was prepared to commit itself to a federative scheme. The General Zionists justified their indifference to the idea by observing that although such a framework "would undoubtedly contribute to unity in action, it is hard to overhaul a machine while it is in motion. . . . It is particularly hard to do so when it must be geared to a rapidly accelerating speed, as must the Zionist machine at the present time." Hadassah leaders similarly feared that such a federation would inadequately represent their large membership in the American context. Therefore, as a precondition to the movement's involvement, Hadassah insisted on establishing a system of representation different from that employed by the World Zionist Organization. In addition, the Mizrahi party, in its zeal to defend religious Zionist interests against the interests of secular groups, refused to entertain the federative proposal. In the end, as was the case during World War I, the Labor Zionist movement remained the chief advocate of Zionist unity.[19]

Organizational and philosophical differences notwithstanding, the Biltmore program epitomized the progress that American Zionism as a whole had made since 1917. The creation of an autonomous "Jewish commonwealth" in Palestine became the new rallying call of the movement. This was a great advancement over winning general support for the Balfour Declaration's ambiguous promise to support a "national home for the Jewish people."[20]

In the months before the Biltmore Conference, information about the persecution and mass murder of European Jewry by the Nazi regime had begun to leak out. Indeed, the very month the conference took place, the

Polish government-in-exile transmitted a report to the West (smuggled out of Warsaw by the Bund, the Polish Jewish Labor Party) describing the systematic extermination of the Jews. More information followed about fully operative death camps, nearly all of which was conveyed to American Jewish leaders. To them, however, the reports were, quite simply, unfathomable. In fact, authenticated evidence of the "Final Solution" did not reach the West until late that summer. Up to the eleventh hour, therefore, American Jewish and Zionist leaders continued to believe both that such an unconscionable crime against humanity was impossible and that the Allies would not completely abandon European Jewry. They reasoned that the full impact of their clout would be felt at the peace conference—as had been the case at Versailles following World War I.[21]

Even the editors of *Jewish Frontier*, who had close ties with Jewish workers' groups in eastern Europe, found the news of European Jewry's destruction to be beyond comprehension. Thus the *Frontier* relegated its initial report of the catastrophe to the last pages of its September 1942 issue. The following month, however, after the shocking revelations of Nazi atrocities were fully verified, the *Frontier* became the first Anglo-Jewish journal to publish comprehensive accounts of the Nazi regime's "systematic" efforts to "exterminate" the Jewish people. A "holocaust," the editors intoned, "has overtaken the Jews of Europe."[22]

The revelation of Nazi atrocities prompted widespread American Jewish anguish and mourning. It also led many to reexamine the road leading from the unfulfilled promises of the Balfour Declaration in 1917—including the subsequent years marked by occasional American congressional and presidential endorsements of the British document—to the catastrophic loss of European Jewish life.[23] Those who had counseled against Zionist assertiveness and militancy were now thoroughly discredited, and the Jewish world looked to the Zionist movement and the Yishuv as its last real hope. By default, therefore, the burden of the Zionist cause now lay at the doorstep of American Jews.

Because of American Zionism's long-standing claim to represent the national will of American Jewry, the movement's leaders aroused expectations by which they later would be harshly judged. In short, American Zionists were expected to assume responsibility for the fate of the Jewish people, a duty that other Jewish leaders and groups were unwilling to perform. Even after half a century, investigation of this complex subject is still obscured by accusations of "perfidy" and "moral bankruptcy."[24]

To be sure, a comprehensive treatment of American Zionism and the

Holocaust is beyond the scope of this book. "The fact is," as Jehuda Reinharz noted, "that during the Holocaust years American Jewry failed to convince the [American] administration to act decisively to rescue the Jews of Europe."[25] It also remains an open question how the limitations on freedom of choice and action faced by American Jews affected the decisions and policies of American Zionist leaders. But four main points may help clarify the predicament of American Zionism during this critical period:

First, antisemitism abroad and at home scared American Jews. Whether the transplanted Nazism of the German American Bund, the racism of the notorious radio priest Father Coughlin, or *Look* magazine's genteel character assassination of the "flesh-and-blood Jew" Ben Kaufman, American Jews were increasingly reminded of their marginality in American society.[26] In this context, Zionist leaders tried to mobilize popular support for the Yishuv without escalating public antisemitism or exacerbating American Jewish feelings of vulnerability and insecurity.

Second, news of the Final Solution was largely hidden from the American Jewish public until the late summer of 1942. Before then, it was generally assumed that European Jewry would somehow survive the war, a supposition based on the collective memory of American Jewry during World War I. Between 1914 and 1917, several hundred thousand East European Jews were uprooted, and scores of Jewish communities were decimated in the theaters of war. The occupying Russian, German, and Austrian armies treated the Jews with great cruelty, and Jewish communities throughout eastern Europe became utterly impoverished.[27] But these regimes never subjected the Jews to a plan of systematic extermination. Rather, "the genocide and enslavement of entire nations were the exclusive domain of Nazi Germany and cannot be ascribed to Germany in World War I."[28]

Third, during World War II, the safety of Palestine Jewry was in serious jeopardy. In February 1943, German Field Marshal Erwin Rommel's Afrika Korps scored a series of significant military offensives, breaking through the Kasserene Pass and heading north toward Tebessa. Threatening to blaze a trail to Palestine, the Allied forces, at least momentarily, appeared vulnerable and unable to halt the "Desert Fox." The embattled Yishuv, American Zionist leaders feared, was in imminent danger.[29] Moreover, the fact that no country would admit European Jewish refugees increased the urgency of the American Zionists' activity. Zionism meant saving Jews, the movement's leaders contended, and a secure Jewish national home was the best single hope of the Jewish people.

Fourth, as recent scholarship demonstrates, Franklin D. Roosevelt masterfully manipulated American Jewish public opinion during the war. In this period, two major issues preoccupied him: defeating the Axis powers and sustaining a robust wartime economy. The salvation of European Jewry, he insisted, depended on the United States' remaining strong and winning the war. Anything that detracted from these primary goals imperiled the future of the Western world. So persuaded by this argument were Roosevelt's closest Jewish advisers—Stephen S. Wise, Felix Frankfurter, Henry Morgenthau, and Benjamin Cohen—that they suppressed news of the Nazi death camps. "I don't know whether I am getting to be a Hofjude [a court Jew interceding on behalf of his people]," Wise remarked in September 1942, "but I find that a good part of my work is to explain to my fellow Jews why our government cannot do all the things asked of or expected of it."[30] In any event, American rescue activities began very late and only after the Allies had gained the upper hand. Throughout the war, Roosevelt did take modest steps to provide temporary haven for refugees. However, he did not commit substantial resources to this effort until mounting public pressure forced him to establish the War Refugee Board in January 1944.[31]

If American Zionist leaders were generally misled and tragically misguided during the war, their predicament was made possible and accentuated by the fact that they and other American Jews, like other American minority groups, eagerly placed their faith in the New Deal.[32] They fully expected that Roosevelt's compassion for the "ill clothed, ill housed and ill fed" would extend to their own unfortunate brothers and sisters overseas. In short, American Zionist leaders were simply unwilling to believe that Hitler's ravings about "the annihilation of the Jewish race in Europe" could become a reality.[33] They viewed Nazi rhetoric in much the same way as did other Jewish leaders, not necessarily as writing on the wall but, rather, as a device calculated to influence public opinion. Indeed, antisemitism was a staple of global politics in this period. Or as one Western diplomat infamously remarked, "Antisemitism means attributing to the Jews more harm than is necessary."

Moreover, the fact that American Jews generally took the Nazi threat seriously is evident insofar as the community as a whole, including the numerically small Zionist movement, contributed to war relief out of all proportion to its size. Between 1939 and 1945, for example, the Joint Distribution Committee spent more than $78 million on rehabilitation and emigration schemes in Europe, such as attempts to alleviate conditions in the ghettos, smuggle money to the Jewish underground, and persuade Nazi officials to halt the deportations of Jews.[34]

The historical record also shows that Zionist leaders in Palestine were not indifferent to the fate of European Jewry. But they were preoccupied by the Yishuv's precarious and vulnerable position as well as the daunting task of preparing for an anticipated flood of European Jewish refugees.[35] As early as 1939, David Ben-Gurion made this clear to the American Zionist leadership in a confidential cable that bluntly stated: "*We must and are prepared to bring in fifty thousand Jews weekly.*"[36]

Significantly, Labor Zionism in the United States differed from the Yishuv leadership in two respects. First, although it advocated free immigration to Palestine, it simultaneously supported the creation of Jewish refugee havens in the diaspora. That the movement did not link these demands made philosophical, if not political, sense. For although Labor Palestine continued to be the axis of the movement, the movement's American constituents were equally aware of their diaspora society's unique position and considerable potential. *Jewish Frontier* articulated this duality on the eve of World War II:

> There is something mad in the passive acceptance of Nazi Germany's right to plunder and throw out a whole sector of her population. There is something mad in the failure of civilized countries to open their doors to the victims. . . . In this chaos some footing must be found. If German Jews must flee, if the world cannot devise a means of throttling German savagery, then rescue must mean life, not a swifter death. There is one logical place for Jewish immigration at present—Palestine. . . .
>
> According to latest reports, the Intergovernmental Committee for Political Refugees [of the League of Nations] expects no change in existing immigration laws to meet the present need. . . . We must say openly and courageously to those interested in our fate: The civilized world is roomy enough to hold even 600,000 German Jewish victims. Palestine can absorb a large proportion at once; for the rest, place must be found within the gates of the great democracies. Any other course is merely an aping of great Caesar's kindness—a slitting of the throat.[37]

Against the devastating backdrop of the war, including the consequences of the failed Evian Conference, American Labor Zionists continued to urge both permanent and temporary Jewish refugee resettlement. Among the list of unrealized possibilities for havens, the Alaskan territory stands out. In this instance, the Labor Zionist movement was the only American Jewish organization to support the King-Havenner bill (S. 3577 and H.R. 5971), a proposal that was ultimately defeated in 1940.[38] Intended to open Alaska to "European refugees," the bill would have permitted American corporations to import "migrant laborers" and thereby advance the economic development of the Alaskan territory. In affirmation of the bill, Labor Zionists suggested that even limited measures be enacted to save the Jews of Europe. They argued that resettlement schemes—whether or not sympathetic to Zionist aspirations—be accompanied by concrete action. Anything less, *Jewish Frontier* noted, amounted to "a brutal joke at the expense of a defenseless and desperate people."[39]

However hopeful Labor Zionists may have initially been about the prospect of admitting Jewish refugees to the United States, the movement's energies remained focused on British policy vis-à-vis the Jewish national home. Following Britain's announcement of the 1939 MacDonald White Paper, which imposed severe restrictions on land purchase and Jewish immigration to Palestine, Labor Zionism used its extensive American contacts to press the case of the Yishuv.[40] "History . . . has imposed upon the Jewish community of America," the *Frontier* asserted, "the main burden of assistance which must now become of far greater scope than ever before."

> The Jewish community of about four and a half million in the United States possesses resources of strength and energy that have so far remained untapped. The very gravity of the situation can be made to arouse heretofore dormant springs of action and can bring to our aid the support of allies among the progressive elements outside of the Jewish community.[41]

By 1943, such independent efforts became unnecessary when the American Jewish Conference, an unprecedented gathering of organized American Jews, was called by the president of Bnai Brith, Henry Monsky. The conference proposed to unite American Jewry behind a platform for the rescue of European Jewry, the removal of restrictions on Jewish immigration to Palestine, and the reconstruction of Jewish life in post–World War II Europe. After a lengthy process of propagandizing and balloting, the conference emerged from relative obscurity to assume a position of primary importance. In all, 501 delegates representing roughly 2.25 million men and women from 64 national organizations and 375 communities comprised the democratic assembly.[42]

Monsky equated the role of the conference with that of the American Jewish Congress of 1918. "Then, too," he asserted, "there was a division of opinion as to Zionist aspirations for Palestine and as to the method of safeguarding Jewish rights in certain European countries.''[43] Today, Monsky continued,

> an even greater emergency than that of twenty-five years ago confronts us. . . . We have a vital stake in the peace that is to come. Not only have we suffered appalling destruction of Jewish life, but much of what was achieved after the first World War, in respect to the position of the Jew in afflicted lands, has been lost. . . . There is crucial need for the restoration of that lost position and for its fortification upon enduring foundations of equality and justice. The right of the Jewish people to rebuild their homeland in Palestine, recognized more than a quarter of a century ago, has now again become the subject of controversy. That right may have to be reaffirmed under conditions that will enable Palestine to serve as one of the important factors in the amelioration, if not the solution, of the Jewish problem.[44]

Monsky's statement illustrates the degree to which a quasi–Labor Zionist orientation had passed imperceptibly into the mainstream of American Jewish discourse by 1943. He even linked the conference to the American Jewish Congress of 1918, which was a prime example of earlier Labor Zionist agitation. Monsky next described the centrality of Jewish national claims in American Jewish life, suggesting that the vitality of the American diaspora was inextricably bound up with the fortunes of European Jewry and the Yishuv. Finally, he emphasized the necessity of pragmatic efforts in Palestine and Zionist political work. Only this combination, Monsky asserted, would ensure the Jewish people control over its destiny.

The fifty-seven members of the Labor Zionist delegation were among Monsky's most enthusiastic supporters. Labor was also remarkably at one with the majority of conference participants, an estimated 80 percent of whom were avowed Zionists.[45] This situation reflected the consensus that American Jews should band together, despite their differences, to chart a common course of action. In this way, it contrasted with the thunderous performances and dissension of Labor Zionist leaders at the American Jewish Congress of 1918. In fact, Labor Zionists were disproportionately represented in the conference proceedings. As a result, not only did Hayim Greenberg take the floor on several occasions—he and Abba Hillel Silver shared the spotlight by offering the closing addresses—but the conference also adopted several overtly pro-Labor Palestine resolutions.

In particular, the delegates almost unanimously agreed on the rescue of European Jewry, the importance of postwar reconstruction, and the restitution of minority political and civil rights in war-torn Europe. The Palestine proposal, however, proved to be quite controversial. Although the conference participants were predominantly Zionist, this did not mean that the delegates would endorse the notion of an independent Jewish commonwealth. Thus despite the delegates' nationalist sympathies, Zionist leaders worried lest an ambivalent resolution be adopted in the name of communal unity. The scales were then tipped by Abba Hillel Silver, whose moral position cut across ideological and philosophical lines. "I am for unity in Israel," Silver declared, "for the realization of the total program of Jewish life, relief, rescue, reconstruction and the national restoration in Palestine."[46]

In 1943, Silver supplanted Stephen S. Wise as American Zionism's foremost leader. He carried the day because he articulated the changed attitude of mainstream American Jews toward Zionism. Acknowledging the essential role of the Zionist enterprise in modern Jewish life, he called for an immediate political solution based on wartime realities. "We cannot truly rescue the Jews of Europe," Silver argued,

> unless we have free immigration to Palestine. We cannot have free immigration into Palestine unless our political rights are recognized there. Our political rights cannot be recognized unless our historic connection with the country is acknowledged and our right to rebuild our national home is affirmed. The whole chain breaks if one of our links is missing.[47]

The comprehensive program placed by Silver before the conference opened the floodgates of American Jewish consensus, and the Palestine proposal passed with only four dissenting votes. The delegates resoundingly called for "the fulfillment of the Balfour Declaration" and the reconstitution of Palestine as the Jewish commonwealth. Next, the audience spontaneously "rose, applauded and sang Hatikvah [The Hope]."[48] This event signaled a watershed for American Zionism that presently came into full view as the driving political force of American Jewish life.

Meanwhile, minority opposition to the Palestine proposal crystallized around Joseph Proskauer, president of the American Jewish Committee. Wary of the charge of dual loyalties and unhappy with the conference's populist character, Proskauer fought a losing battle to retain the American Jewish Committee's anachronistic grasp on Jewish communal stewardship.[49] Likewise, the Jewish Labor Committee, which dissented ostensibly because it refused to take a position on "the ultimate constitutional status of Palestine," feared for its authority. The organization's leaders tried to quell the growing disenchantment of members who disagreed with the Jewish Labor Committee's neutrality on the Jewish national question. The leaders also continued to fear the effect of "class collaboration" on the organization's more militant members. In the end, the Jewish Labor Committee abstained from voting, but it did call for abrogating the White Paper, safeguarding the right of free Jewish immigration, and permitting unchecked land acquisition and colonization in Palestine.[50]

The most vociferous opponent of the conference resolution was the anti-Zionist American Council for Judaism, which opposed "the effort to establish a national Jewish state in Palestine . . . as a philosophy of defeatism."[51] In response, the Central Conference of American Rabbis, many of whose members were on record in support of Labor Palestine, censured the American Council for Judaism and urged the group to disband. This position was officially endorsed by the ZOA, which joined in repudiating the American Council for Judaism.[52]

The spirit of the American Jewish Conference was bold and dynamic, and the major philosophical and political questions were debated openly and honestly. The Zionist leadership prevailed on the delegates to adopt an unequivocal Palestine resolution which, in the final analysis, was done without regard for the elusive issue of American Jewish harmony. The conference thus underscored the difference between the majority of American Jews who supported the total Zionist program of Labor Palestine and the small minority who opposed the mainstream.

After the conference, Abba Hillel Silver assumed control of the American movement's Emergency Committee for Zionist Affairs (renamed the American Zionist Emergency Council, AZEC). The council took charge of American Zionism's dual agenda of saving European Jewry and building up Palestine, functioning as the executive branch of American Zionism and working to mobilize the vast resources of American Jewry. The AZEC's chief spokespersons were Silver and Stephen S. Wise. Among other prominent Zionists elected to the AZEC, Hayim Greenberg served as chairman of the executive committee. He also was drafted to head the AZEC for a brief period when Silver and Wise were unwilling to work as cochairmen.[53] Although a definitive study of the American Zionist Emergency Council's impact has yet to be written, the weight of historical evidence suggests that the organization's efforts were tied to the political alliance between Silver and Ben-Gurion and that official American Zionism became the chief exponent of Labor Palestine's strategy for establishing the Jewish state-to-be, if not in name, then in practice.[54]

The solidification of American Zionism under the AZEC convinced the Allies of American Jewry's emergent political clout. In this period, the Zionist movement was the only group in the United States to challenge American and British policymakers who tried to drive a wedge between the Palestine issue and the Jewish problem in Europe.[55] Thus the American Zionist campaign proved to be vital to the realization of the overall Zionist program. After the war, the American, British, and Soviet governments crafted their policies vis-à-vis Palestine largely in response to Zionist claims about the Jewish displaced persons and the future of the Jewish national home.[56]

In anticipation of such a historic juncture, Labor Zionists had worked tirelessly over the years to promote the cause of unified American Jewish political action regarding Palestine. At the same time, the movement provided a direct link to American society for the leaders of the Yishuv and the Jewish Agency, a channel fully exploited by Chaim Weizmann, David Ben-Gurion, and others. Having sustained an active communal presence in American Jewish life for decades, when the moment of reckoning came, Labor Zionism was able to cast a wide net over the institutions and organizations of American Jewish life. In the event, a complex partnership arose between American Zionism and the Labor Palestine, and when the United States entered World War II and news of the Holocaust finally reached the West, American Jewish consensus crystallized around Zionism and the Yishuv as the only viable postwar solution to the Jewish problem. At this fateful juncture, the reality of Labor Palestine enabled American Jews to make shrewd political choices about the future of the Jewish people.

After 1945, American Zionism was consumed by the very revolution that had propelled it to the fore of American Jewish life. With the end of World War II, the leadership of the Yishuv and American Jewry united in the campaign to create a sovereign Jewish state. The tasks of resettling Jewish displaced persons, coordinating Aliyah Bet, harnessing the vast resources of diaspora Jewry, and lobbying the victorious Allied powers required a broad coalition of forces. State building was no longer the purview of any single group but was elevated to the level of a quasi-messianic partnership between diaspora Jewry and Israeli Jews. The new historical reality gave rise to undercurrents of philosophical moderation and communal optimism and ushered in a new era of debate and discussion concerning Zionism and American Judaism. These trends crested with American Jewry's widespread and vital public support for the establishment of the state of Israel in 1948.[57]

Notes

NOTES TO INTRODUCTION

1. Samuel Halperin, *The Political World of American Zionism* (reprint, Silver Spring, Md.: Information Dynamics, 1985), app. 5, 327.

2. Jehuda Reinharz, *Fatherland or Promised Land: The Dilemma of the German Jew, 1893–1914* (Ann Arbor: University of Michigan Press, 1975); Ezra Mendelsohn, *Zionism in Poland: The Formative Years, 1915–1926* (New Haven, Conn.: Yale University Press, 1981).

3. Jonathan Frankel, *Prophecy and Politics: Socialism, Nationalism and the Russian Jews, 1862–1917* (Cambridge: Cambridge University Press, 1981), chap. 9.

4. Arthur Hertzberg, *The Jews in America: Four Centuries of an Uneasy Encounter* (New York: Simon & Schuster, 1989), 228.

5. Howard M. Sachar, *A History of the Jews in America* (New York: Knopf, 1992), 594.

6. Ben Halpern, "The Americanization of Zionism, 1880–1930," *American Jewish History*, September 1979, 15–33.

7. See Michel Vovelle, *Ideologies and Mentalities*, trans. Eamon O'Flaherty (Chicago: University of Chicago Press, 1990).

8. *Conference Record*, September 1, 1943, 4–5, A180/69, Baruch Zuckerman Papers, Central Zionist Archives.

NOTES TO CHAPTER I

1. *Henrietta Szold: Life and Letters*, ed. Marvin Lowenthal (New York: Viking, 1942), 118.

2. Ben Halpern, *The American Jew: A Zionist Analysis* (New York: Schocken Books, 1983), 20–21.

3. See Jacob Katz, *Out of the Ghetto: The Social Background of Jewish Emancipation, 1770–1870* (Cambridge, Mass.: Harvard University Press, 1973); Paul Mendes-Flohr and Jehuda Reinharz, eds., *The Jew in the Modern World: A Documentary History*, 2d ed. (New York: Oxford University Press, 1995), chap. 3.

4. Eli Lederhendler, *The Road to Modern Jewish Politics: Political Tradition and Political Reconstruction in the Jewish Community of Tsarist Russia* (New York: Oxford University Press, 1989).

5. Jacob Katz, "The Forerunners of Zionism," *Jerusalem Quarterly* 7 (1978): 10–21; Gideon Shimoni, *The Zionist Ideology* (Hanover, N.H.: University Press of New England, 1995), chap. 2.

6. See Jonathan Frankel, *Prophecy and Politics: Socialism, Nationalism and the Russian Jews, 1862–1917* (Cambridge: Cambridge University Press, 1981), chap. 2.

7. Jehuda Reinharz, "On Defining Jewish National Autonomy: Demarcating Ideological Boundaries," in Israel Bartal, ed., *Israel Heilprin Memorial Volume* (Jerusalem: Merkaz Zalman Shazar), in press.

8. A. L. Patkin, *The Origins of the Russian-Jewish Labour Movement* (Melbourne: F. W. Cheshire, 1947), 124–135.

9. The acronym Bilu is derived from Isaiah 2:5, "Beit Yaakov lehu venilhah" (House of Jacob, come let us rise up).

10. Moshe Davis, "The Holy Land Idea in American Spiritual History," in Moshe Davis, ed., *With Eyes toward Zion: Scholars Colloqium on America–Holy Land Studies* (New York: Arno Press, 1977), 5.

11. Robert T. Handy, "Sources for Understanding American Christian Attitudes toward the Holy Land, 1800–1950," in Davis, ed., *With Eyes toward Zion*, 34–35.

12. Sydney E. Ahlstrom, *A Religious History of the American People* (New Haven, Conn.: Yale University Press, 1972), 390–397, 740, 774–784.

13. Zvi Gitelman, *A Century of Ambivalence: The Jews of Russia and the Soviet Union, 1881 to the Present* (New York: Schocken Books and YIVO Institute for Jewish Research, 1988), chaps. 1–2.

14. Gerald Sorin, *A Time for Building: The Third Migration, 1880–1920* (Baltimore: Johns Hopkins University Press, 1993), 50–51.

15. Hasia R. Diner, *A Time for Gathering: The Second Migration, 1820–1880* (Baltimore: Johns Hopkins University Press, 1993), 48, 233.

16. "Abraham P. Spitz," in *History of the Jews of Boston and New England. Their Financial, Professional and Commercial Enterprises from the Earliest Settlement of Hebrews in Boston to the Present Day: Containing a Historical and Statistical Record of Every Jewish Congregation, Fraternal Order, Benevolent Society and Social Club Together with Biographies of Noted Men and Other Matters of Interest* (Boston: Jewish Chronicle Publishing, 1892), not paginated, American Jewish Historical Society.

17. Gerald Sorin, *A Time for Building*, 56, 151–152.

18. Ben Halpern, "The Americanization of Zionism, 1880–1930," *American Jewish History*, September 1979, 17–19.

19. Jacob Kabakoff, "Beginnings of Hibbat Zion in America," in *Herzl Year Book*, vol. 6 (1964–1965), 255.

20. F25/383, Papers of Hibbat Zion in America, Central Zionist Archives (hereafter cited as CZA). The original orthography has been retained.

21. *American Jewish Year Book*, vol. 1 (1899), 36–42; *Proceedings of the Third Annual Convention of the Federation of American Zionists, June 10–11, 1900* (New York:

Federation of American Zionists, 1900), 71–90. The original orthography has been retained.

22. *Proceedings of the Third Annual Convention of the Federation of American Zionists,* 89.

23. Josephine Lazarus, "Zionism and American Ideals," *American Hebrew,* May 12, 1905, 756.

24. Quoted in Jacob Kabakoff, "Beginnings of Hibbat Zion in America," 262.

25. Moshe Davis, "The Holy Land Idea in American Spiritual History," 3–33.

26. See Jonathan D. Sarna, *Jacksonian Jew: The Two Worlds of Mordecai Noah* (New York: Holmes & Meier, 1981), chap. 4.

27. Abraham J. Karp, "The Zionism of Warder Cresson," in Isidore S. Meyer, ed., *Early History of Zionism in America* (New York: American Jewish Historical Society and Theodor Herzl Foundation, 1958), 1–20.

28. Arthur Zeiger, "Emma Lazarus and Pre-Herzlian Zionism," in Isidore S. Meyer, ed., *Early History of Zionism in America* (New York: American Jewish Historical Society and Theodor Herzl Foundation, 1958), 77–108.

29. See Arthur Hertzberg, ed., *The Zionist Idea: A Historical Analysis and Reader* (New York: Atheneum, 1984), 181–198.

30. Shlomo Avineri, *The Making of Modern Zionism: The Intellectual Origins of the Jewish State* (New York: Basic Books, 1981), chap. 7; Walter Laqueur, *A History of Zionism* (New York: Holt, Rinehart and Winston, 1972), 70–75.

31. Quoted in Arthur Zeiger, "Emma Lazarus and Pre-Herzlian Zionism," 88.

32. Naomi W. Cohen, "The Ethnic Catalyst: The Impact of East European Immigration on the American Jewish Establishment," in David Berger, ed., *The Legacy of Jewish Migration: 1881 and Its Impact* (Brooklyn: Brooklyn College Press, 1983), 141.

33. Michael A. Meyer, *Response to Modernity: A History of the Reform Movement in Judaism* (New York: Oxford University Press, 1988), 294; Jonathan D. Sarna, "Mumarim lezionut betnuat hareformah haamerikait," in Shmuel Almog, Jehuda Reinharz, and Anita Shapira, eds., *Zionut vedat* (Jerusalem: Merkaz Zalman Shazar; Boston: Tauber Institute for the Study of Zionism, Brandeis University, 1994), 223.

34. *Jewish Encyclopedia,* vol. 1 (1901), 519; Rudolf Glanz, *The Jewish Woman in America: Two Female Immigrant Generations, 1820–1929* (New York: Ktav Publishing House and National Council of Jewish Women, 1976), vol. 2, 165.

35. Nahum Sokolow, *History of Zionism, 1600–1918* (reprint, New York: Ktav Publishing House, 1969), vol. 1, 243–244; Gerald Sorin, *A Time for Building,* 141.

36. Israel Klausner, "Adam Rosenberg: One of the Earliest American Zionists," in *Herzl Year Book,* vol. 1 (1958), 232–287.

37. Jonathan D. Sarna, ed. and trans., *People Walk on Their Heads: Moses Weinberger's Jews and Judaism in New York* (New York: Holmes & Meier, 1982), 117.

38. Jacob Kabakoff, "Beginnings of Hibbat Zion in America," 255–258; Shlomo Noble, "Pre-Herzlian Zionism in America as Reflected in the Yiddish

Press," in Isidore S. Meyer, ed., *Early History of Zionism in America* (New York: American Jewish Historical Society and Theodor Herzl Foundation, 1958), 39–54; Melvin I. Urofsky, *American Zionism from Herzl to the Holocaust* (Garden City, N.Y.: Anchor/Doubleday, 1975), 82–83. On the competition between Hapisgah and Haivri, see Israel Klausner, "Adam Rosenberg: One of the Earliest American Zionists," 252–254.

39. See Shlomo Noble, "Pre-Herzlian Zionism in America as Reflected in the Yiddish Press," 39; Ofer Shiff, "The Integrative Function of Early American Zionism," *Journal of Israeli History* 15 (Spring 1994): 3–5.

40. Stephen S. Wise, "The Beginnings of American Zionism," *Jewish Frontier*, August 1947, 6; Abraham Goldberg, "Zionism in America: A Chronicle of Its Development," in Meyer W. Weisgal, ed., *Theodor Herzl: A Memorial* (New York: Zionist Organization of America, 1929), 211, 213.

41. See "Appendix: Platforms of American Reform Judaism," in Michael A. Meyer, *Response to Modernity*, 387–388.

42. Quoted in Elias Tcherikower, *The Early Jewish Labor Movement in the United States*, trans. Aaron Antonovsky (New York: YIVO Institute for Jewish Research, 1961), 333.

43. See Jonathan D. Sarna, *A Great Jewish Awakening: The Transformation That Shaped Twentieth Century American Judaism and Its Implications for Today* (New York: Council for Initiatives in Jewish Education, 1995).

44. Rufus Learsi, *The Jews in America: A History* (Cleveland: World, 1954), 235.

45. Louis Lipsky, *Memoirs in Profile* (Philadelphia: Jewish Publication Society of America, 1975), 211–214.

46. "Zionist Conference in New York," *Jewish Chronicle*, July 22, 1898, 9–10; Stephen S. Wise, "The Beginnings of American Zionism," 6–7; Melvin I. Urofsky, *American Zionism from Herzl to the Holocaust*, 88.

47. Abraham Goldberg, "Zionism in America," 211.

48. "Zionism," *Jewish Encyclopedia*, vol. 12 (1909), 686.

49. Chaim Weizmann, *Trial and Error* (New York: Harper Bros., 1949), 25.

50. Salo W. Baron, *Steeled by Adversity: Essays and Addresses on American Jewish Life* (Philadelphia: Jewish Publication Society of America), 384–385.

51. Louis Lipsky, *A Gallery of Zionist Profiles* (New York: Farrar, Straus and Cudahy, 1956), 194; Irving Howe, *World of Our Fathers: The Journey of the East European Jews to America and the Life They Found and Made* (New York: Simon & Schuster, 1976), 229–235.

52. *Sermons by Reverend Zevi Hirsch Masliansky*, ed. Abraham J. Feldman and trans. Edward Herbert (New York: Hebrew Publishing, 1926), 307–312.

53. Louis Lipsky, *Memoirs in Profile*, 22, 237–242; Stephen S. Wise, "The Beginnings of American Zionism," 7; Marc Lee Raphael, *Abba Hillel Silver: A Profile in American Judaism* (New York: Holmes & Meier, 1989), 7–9; Marc Lee Raphael, "Cincinnati: The Earlier and Later Years," in William M. Brinner and Moses

Rischin, eds., *Like All the Nations?: The Life and Legacy of Judah L. Magnes* (Albany: State University of New York Press, 1987), 31–32; Bernard G. Richards, "First Steps in Zionism," in *Herzl Year Book*, vol. 5 (1963), 353.

54. Louis Lipsky, *Memoirs in Profile*, 189.

55. *Henrietta Szold: Life and Letters*, ed. Marvin Lowenthal, 36–49.

56. Ibid., 53.

57. Jonathan D. Sarna, *JPS: The Americanization of Jewish Culture, 1888–1898* (Philadelphia: Jewish Publication Society, 1989), 49–50.

58. Quoted in Susan Dworkin, "Henrietta Szold: Liberated Woman," in Elizabeth Koltun, ed., *The Jewish Woman: New Perspectives* (New York: Schocken Books, 1976), 168.

59. Quoted in Rudolf Glanz, *The Jewish Woman in America: Two Female Immigrant Generations, 1820–1929* (New York: Ktav Publishing House and National Council of Jewish Women, 1976), vol. 1, 153.

60. Louis Lipsky, *Memoirs in Profile*, 189; Rose G. Jacobs, "Beginnings of Hadassah," in Isidore S. Meyer, ed., *Early History of Zionism in America* (New York: American Jewish Historical Society and Theodor Herzl Foundation, 1958), 231; Jonathan D. Sarna, *JPS*, 23–24.

61. See Jonathan D. Sarna, *JPS*, 88–94.

62. Michael D. Marcaccio, *The Hapgoods: Three Earnest Brothers* (Charlottesville: University Press of Virginia, 1977), 148–151.

63. Hutchins Hapgood, *The Spirit of the Ghetto: Studies of the Jewish Quarter of New York*, rev. ed. (New York: Schocken Books, 1976), 177–178.

64. In fact, American Jews responded to the Kishinev crisis quickly and forcefully; see Philip Ernest Schoenberg, "The American Reaction to the Kishinev Pogrom of 1903," *American Jewish Historical Quarterly*, March 1974, 262–283.

65. Jonathan Frankel, *Prophecy and Politics*, 473–474, 477.

66. Letter from Cyrus Adler to Louis Marshall, January 1, 1906, in *Cyrus Adler: Selected Letters*, vol. 1, ed. Ira Robinson (Philadelphia: Jewish Publication Society of America and New York: Jewish Theological Society of America, 1985), 127.

67. Naomi W. Cohen, *Not Free to Desist: The American Jewish Committee, 1906–1966* (Philadelphia: Jewish Publication Society of America, 1972), 3–36.

68. Jonathan Frankel, *Prophecy and Politics*, chap. 9.

69. Mordecai Soltes, *The Yiddish Press: An Americanizing Agency* (New York: Teachers College Press, 19), 20; Jonathan Frankel, *Prophecy and Politics*, 473.

70. For example, see "A Jewish Congress," *American Hebrew*, November 24, 1905, 890, 892; Jonathan Frankel, *Prophecy and Politics*, 473–484.

71. Quoted in Jonathan Frankel, *Prophecy and Politics*, 475.

72. Anatole Leroy-Beaulieu, "Jewish Immigrants and Judaism in the United States," *American Hebrew*, June 16, 1905, 72.

73. *Book of Genesis*, eds. M. Rosenbaum and A. M. Silberman (New York: Hebrew Publishing, 1934), 197.

74. Moshe Davis, "Israel Friedlaender's Minute Book of the Achavah Club, 1909–1912," in *Mordecai M. Kaplan Jubilee Volume*, ed. Moshe Davis (New York: Jewish Theological Seminary of America, 1953), 161.

75. *Dissenter in Zion: From the Writings of Judah L. Magnes*, ed. Arthur A. Goren (Cambridge, Mass.: Harvard University Press, 1982), 15.

76. Arthur A. Goren, *New York Jews and the Quest for Community: The Kehillah Experiment, 1908–1922* (New York: Columbia University Press, and Philadelphia: Jewish Publication Society of America, 1970).

77. Jonathan Frankel, *Prophecy and Politics*, chap. 5; Irving Howe, *World of Our Fathers*, 504–507; Melech Epstein, *Profiles of Eleven* (Detroit: Wayne State University Press, 1965), chap. 10.

78. Baila Round Shargel, *Practical Dreamer: Israel Friedlaender and the Shaping of American Judaism* (New York: Jewish Theological Seminary of America, 1985).

79. Evyatar Friesel, "Ahad Haamism in American Zionist Thought," in Jacques Kornberg, ed., *At the Crossroads: Essays on Ahad Haam* (Albany: State University of New York Press, 1983), 137.

80. *Jewish Encyclopedia*, vol. 7 (1904), 304.

81. Moshe Davis, "Israel Friedlaender's Minute Book of the Achavah Club," 161.

82. See Leib Spizman, ed., *Geshikhte fun der zionistisher arbeter bavegung*, 2 vols. (New York: Farlag Yidisher Kemfer, 1955).

83. Moshe Davis, "Israel Friedlaender's Minute Book of the Achavah Club," 170–171.

84. Ibid.

85. See Isidore S. Meyer, ed., *Early History of Zionism in America*, esp. Anita Libman Lebeson, "Zionism Comes to Chicago," 155–190; and Maxwell Whiteman, "Zionism Comes to Philadelphia," 191–218.

86. *Maccabean*, July 1905, 49.

87. Evyatar Friesel, "Brandeis' Role in Zionism Reconsidered," *American Jewish History*, September 1979, 47, n. 21.

88. Ben Halpern, introduction to Dorothy Spector, ed., *Boston Jewry and Its Relationship to Palestine and Israel: A History* (Boston: Combined Jewish Philanthropies of Greater Boston, 1973), 4.

89. Nathaniel S. Shaler, *Nature and Man in America* (New York: Scribner, 1891); William James, *Talks to Teachers on Psychology and to Students on Some of Life's Ideals*; George Santayana, *Santayana on America: Essays, Notes and Letters on American Life* (New York: Harcourt, Brace and Wohl, 1968).

90. Allon Gal, *Brandeis of Boston* (Cambridge, Mass.: Harvard University Press, 1980), 151–152.

91. Jehuda Reinharz, "On Defining Jewish National Autonomy: Demarcating Ideological Boundaries," in press.

92. Jonas S. Friedenwald, "The Intercollegiate: A Retrospect," in David S.

Blondheim, ed., *Kadimah* (New York: Federation of American Zionists, 1918), 196–197.

93. Allon Gal, *Brandeis of Boston*, 159.

94. Harry A. Wolfson, "The Spirit of Hebraism," trans. H. B. Ehrmann, in George Kohut, ed., *Standard Book of Jewish Verse* (New York: Dodd, Mead, 1917), 539.

95. Steven J. Zipperstein, *Elusive Prophet: Ahad Haam and the Origins of Zionism* (Berkeley and Los Angeles: University of California Press, 1993), chap. 2; Yosef Salmon, "Ahad Haam and Bnei Moshe: An Unsuccessful Experiment?" in Kornberg, ed., *At the Crossroads*, 98–105.

96. Sarah Schmidt, "The Perushim: A Secret Episode in American Zionist History," *American Jewish Historical Quarterly*, December 1975, 121–139.

97. Maier Bryan Fox, "Labor Zionism in America: The Challenge of the 1920s," *American Jewish Archives*, April 1983, 55; Emanuel Neumann, *In the Arena: An Autobiographical Memoir* (New York: Herzl Press, 1976), 48–49.

98. Jonathan Frankel, *Prophecy and Politics*, chap. 6.

99. Ibid., chaps. 5–7.

100. Arthur Hertzberg, ed., *The Zionist Idea*, 340.

101. Horace M. Kallen, *Zionism and World Politics: A Study in History and Social Psychology* (Garden City, N.Y.: Doubleday, Page, 1921), 3.

102. Naomi W. Cohen, *American Jews and the Zionist Idea* (New York: Ktav Publishing House, 1975), 16–17.

103. Sarah Schmidt, "Toward the Pittsburgh Program: Horace M. Kallen, Philosopher of American Zionism," *Herzl Year Book*, vol. 8 (1978), 18–36.

104. Ben Halpern, *The Idea of the Jewish State*, 2d ed. (Cambridge, Mass.: Harvard University Press, 1969), 185–188. On the Palestine Development Council, see XII:42a, Julian W. Mack Papers, CZA. On the Palestine Economic Corporation, see VI:4, Robert Szold Papers, CZA. On the Palestine Endowment Fund, see VI:10, Robert Szold Papers, CZA.

105. See Sarah Schmidt, *Horace M. Kallen: Prophet of American Zionism* (New York: Carlson, 1995).

106. Evyatar Friesel, "Brandeis' Role in Zionism Reconsidered," 41, n. 12.

107. Allon Gal, *Brandeis of Boston*, chap. 5; Sarah Schmidt, "Toward the Pittsburgh Program," 18–36.

108. Phillipa Strum, *Louis D. Brandeis: Justice for the People* (New York: Schocken Books, 1984), 232–235.

109. Allon Gal, *Brandeis of Boston*, 187.

110. See Jack Wertheimer, *Unwelcome Strangers: East European Jews in Imperial Germany* (New York: Oxford University Press, 1987).

111. Leo Shubow, "Jacob De Haas and the Boston Jewish Advocate," in *Herzl Year Book*, vol. 5 (1963), 286–287.

112. Allon Gal, *Brandeis of Boston*, 203.

113. Paul Mendes-Flohr and Jehuda Reinharz, eds., *The Jew in the Modern World*, 496.

114. "Zion Flag Week," December 1915, P-153, Papers of Benjamin Rabalsky, American Jewish Historical Society.

115. See Jonathan D. Sarna, " 'The Greatest Jew in the World since Jesus Christ': The Jewish Legacy of Louis D. Brandeis," *American Jewish History* 81 (Spring–Summer 1994): 346–364.

116. Melvin I. Urofsky, *American Zionism from Herzl to the Holocaust*, 155–163; Walter Laqueur, *A History of Zionism*, 179–181.

117. Melvin I. Urofsky, *American Zionism from Herzl to the Holocaust*, 255–256.

118. Jonathan Frankel, *Prophecy and Politics*, chap. 9.

119. Jehuda Reinharz, *Chaim Weizmann: The Making of a Statesman* (New York: Oxford University Press, 1993), vol. 2, chap. 6; Jehuda Reinharz, "Zionism in the USA on the Eve of the Balfour Declaration," 144–145; Richard Ned Lebow, "Woodrow Wilson and the Balfour Declaration," *Journal of Modern History* 40 (1968): 501–523.

120. Ben Halpern, *A Clash of Heroes: Brandeis, Weizmann and American Zionism* (New York: Oxford University Press, 1987), chap. 4.

121. Eliezer Jaffe, *Kitvei Eliezer Jaffe* (Tel Aviv: Am Oved, 1947), vol. 2, 124; Yitzhak Mihaeli, "Reshitah shel histadrut Hehaluz be-Amerikah," *Asufot*, December 1959, 109.

122. See Joseph B. Glass, "Balfouria: An American Zionist Colony," *Studies in Zionism* 14 (1993): 53–72.

NOTES TO CHAPTER 2

1. *Encyclopaedia Judaica*, vol. 10 (1971), 1331; C. Bezalel Sherman, "The Beginnings of Labor Zionism in the United States," in Isidore S. Meyer, ed., *Early History of Zionism in America* (New York: American Jewish Historical Society and Theodor Herzl Foundation, 1958), 279–280.

2. Jacob Katzman, *Commitment: The Labor Zionist Life-Style in America* (New York: Labor Zionist Letters, 1975), 37; interview with Jacob Katzman, July 21, 1988, and February 17, 1991; Leib Spizman, "Etafn in der geshikhte fun der zionistisher arbeter bavegung in die fareinikte shtatn," in Leib Spizman, ed., *Geshikhte fun der zionistisher arbeter bavegung in zfon amerike* (New York: Farlag Yidisher Kemfer, 1955), vol. 1, 137–145, 236–250.

3. Ben Halpern and Jehuda Reinharz, "Nationalism and Jewish Socialism: The Early Years, " *Modern Judaism*, October 1988, 217–248; Gideon Shimoni, *The Zionist Ideology* (Hanover, N.H.: University Press of New England, 1995), chap. 5.

4. Berl Locker, "The Zionist Socialist Movement of America," ca. 1925, 1, manuscript, Poalei Zion Papers, Lavon Institute for Labor Research (hereafter cited as LILR).

5. Arthur Hertzberg, ed., *The Zionist Idea: A Historical Analysis and Reader* (New York: Atheneum, 1981), 349.

6. Ibid., 349–350.

7. Arthur A. Goren, *New York Jews and the Quest for Community: The Kehillah Experiment, 1908–1922* (New York: Columbia University Press, 1970), 157–158.

8. This has been demonstrated in the British context; see Gideon Shimoni, "Poale Zion: A Zionist Transplant in Britain, 1905–1945," *Studies in Contemporary Jewry* 2 (1986): 227–269.

9. Anita Shapira, "Hamotivim hadatiim shel tnuat haavodah," in Shmuel Almog, Jehuda Reinharz, and Anita Shapira, eds., *Zionut vedat* (Jerusalem: Merkaz Zalman Shazar; Boston: Tauber Institute for the Study of European Jewry, Brandeis University, 1994), 301–328.

10. Jacob Katzman, *Commitment*, 41.

11. Ibid., 42.

12. Leib Spizman, "Etafn in der geshikhte fun der zionistisher arbeter bavegung," vol. 1, 199–210, 221–235; vol. 2, 326–339.

13. Jonathan Frankel, *Prophecy and Politics: Socialism, Nationalism and the Russian Jews, 1862–1917* (Cambridge: Cambridge University Press, 1981).

14. Letter from the Russian Poalei Zion Central Committee to Lazer Moshe, ca. Fall 1912, PZ-12, Poalei Zion Papers, LILR. I am grateful to Mr. Ben Barlas for alerting me to this material.

15. Minutes of the Jewish Social Democratic Union Poalei Zion, August 1, 1914, and October 18, 1914, nos. 36 and 37, Poalei Zion Papers, LILR. See also Melech Epstein, *Jewish Labor in USA: An Industrial, Political and Cultural History of the Jewish Labor Movement, 1882–1914*, 2 vols. (New York: Ktav Publishing House, 1969), vol. 1, 351–352; vol. 2, 58–59, 82–83, 269–272.

16. Arnold Kretchmar-Isreeli, "The Poal-Zion Movement [*sic*]," in *The Jewish Communal Register of New York City, 1917–1918* (New York: Kehillah of New York City, 1918), 1338.

17. Melech Epstein, *Jewish Labor in USA*, vol. 2, 351–352.

18. Arnold Kretchmar-Isreeli, "The Poal-Zion Movement," 1331; Robert S. Wistrich, "Marxism and Jewish Nationalism: The Theoretical Roots of Confrontation," *Jewish Journal of Sociology*, June 1975, 43–54; Ben Halpern and Jehuda Reinharz, "Nationalism and Jewish Socialism."

19. Melech Epstein, *Jewish Labor in USA*, vol. 1, 309–310.

20. Elias Tcherikower, *The Early Jewish Labor Movement in the United States*, trans. Aaron Antonovsky (New York: YIVO Institute for Research, 1961), 329–333.

21. Charles A. Madison, *Jewish Publishing in America* (New York: Sanhedrin Press, 1976), 137.

22. Arthur A. Goren, "The Jewish Press in the United States," in Sally Miller,

ed., *The Ethnic Press in the United States: A Historical Analysis and Handbook* (Westport, Conn.: Greenwood Press, 1987), 216.

23. These circulation figures are approximate. Even if the *Yidisher kemfer*'s actual print run was as low as 2,000, the estimate cited here would still be supported by a contemporary account of the Yiddish press stating that "every paper bought [in New York] is read by at least three people including the buyer"; *The Jewish Communal Register of New York City, 1917–1918* (New York: Kehillah, 1918), 613. The estimate used here is derived from fragmentary data cited in Dirk Hoerder, ed., *The Immigrant Labor Press in North America, 1840s–1970s: An Annotated Bibliography*, vol. 2, *Migrants from Eastern and Southern Europe* (Westport, Conn.: Greenwood Press, 1987), 594, 668–670; Charles A. Madison, *Jewish Publishing in America*, 137. It is also based on interviews with Jacob Katzman, New York City, July 21, 1988, and February 17, 1991; Abe Sachar, Waltham, Mass., March 5, 1991; and Saadia Gelb, Kfar Blum, Israel, July 5, 1993.

24. Baruch Zuckerman, "Das yidishe leben in amerike in ershtn fertl fun zvanzikstn yarhundert," in Leib Spizman, ed., *Geshikhte fun der zionistisher arbeter bavegung in zfon amerike* (New York: Farlag Yidisher Kemfer, 1955), vol. 1, 73–80; Leib Spizman, "Etafn in der geshikhte fun der zionistisher arbeter bavegung," vol. 1, 142–149, 211–215, 242–247; vol. 2, 298–304, 387–391.

25. Baruch Zuckerman, *Zikhronos* (New York: Farlag Yidisher Kemfer, 1962), vol. 1, 337–343; Leib Spizman, "Etafn in der geshikhte fun der zionistisher arbeter bavegung," vol. 1, 261–273.

26. *American Jewish Year Book*, vol. 16 (1914), 115.

27. Ibid., 117–118.

28. See S. Yefroikin, "Yiddish Secular Schools in the United States," *The Jewish People Past and Present* (New York: Marstin Press, 1948), vol. 1, 144–150; Mark M. Krug, "The Yiddish Schools in Chicago," *YIVO Annual*, vol. 9 (1954), 281–286.

29. Abraham Goldberg, "Zionism in America: A Chronicle of Its Development," in Meyer W. Weisgal, ed., *Theodor Herzl: A Memorial* (New York: New Palestine, 1929), 213.

30. Nahman Syrkin, "Keren Hayesod," *Kuntres*, vol. 67 (1920), reprinted in B. Katznelson and S. Meirov, eds., *Yalkut Ahdut Haavodah* (Tel Aviv: Hozaat Vaadat Hayalkut, 1931), vol. 2, 20.

31. "[Memorandum to] the Inner Executive Committee of the Zionist Organizations," ca. 1918, A180/65, Baruch Zuckerman Papers, Central Zionist Organization (hereafter cited as CZA).

32. Ibid.

33. Arnold Kretchmar-Isreeli, "The Poal-Zion Movement," 1339.

34. Samuel Halperin, *The Political World of American Zionism* (reprint, Silver Spring, Md.: Information Dynamics, 1985), 66.

35. *Encyclopaedia Judaica*, vol. 4 (1971), 224.

36. Yonathan Shapiro, *Leadership of the American Zionist Organization, 1897–1930* (Urbana: University of Illinois Press, 1971), 119–124.

37. Ben Halpern, *A Clash of Heroes: Brandeis, Weizmann and American Zionism* (New York: Oxford University Press, 1987), 251–253; Yonathan Shapiro, *Leadership of the American Zionist Organization*, 153–158.

38. Zosa Szajowski, *Jews, War and Communism*, vol. 1, *The Attitude of American Jews to World War I, the Russian Revolutions of 1917 and Communism, 1914–1945* (New York: Ktav Publishing House, 1972), chap. 12.

39. Marie Syrkin, *Nachman Syrkin: Socialist Zionist. A Biographical Memoir and Selected Essays* (New York: Herzl Press and Sharon Books, 1961), 160–163.

40. Translated and quoted in Zosa Szajowski, *Jews, War and Communism*, vol. 1, 521–522.

41. Diary of Private Leon Cheifetz quoted in Roman Freulich, *Soldiers in Judea: Stories and Vignettes of the Jewish Legion* (New York: Herzl Press, 1964), 38.

42. Leib Spizman, "Etafn in der geshikhte fun der zionistisher arbeter bavegung," vol. 2, 367.

43. Samuel Rodman, "Ha-Gedud Ha-Ibri," in David S. Blondheim, ed., *Kadimah* (New York: Federation of American Zionists, 1918), 29.

44. Shabtai Teveth, *Ben-Gurion: The Burning Ground, 1886–1948* (Boston: Houghton Mifflin, 1987), 126.

45. Rufus Learsi, *Fulfillment: The Epic Story of Zionism* (Cleveland: World, 1951), 204–205.

46. C. Bezalel Sherman, *Labor Zionism in America: Its History, Growth, and Program* (New York: Labor Zionist Organization of America–Poale Zion, 1957), 18; Rufus Learsi, *Fulfillment*, 205.

47. Shabtai Teveth, *Ben-Gurion*, 126.

48. On antisemitic stereotypes in the United States, see Leonard Dinnerstein, *Antisemitism in America* (New York: Oxford University Press, 1994); Jonathan D. Sarna, "American Antisemitism," in David Berger, ed., *History and Hate: The Dimensions of Antisemitism* (Philadelphia: Jewish Publication Society, 1986), 115–128; Robert Singerman, "The Jew as Racial Alien: The Genetic Component of American Antisemitism," in David A. Gerber, ed., *Antisemitism in American History* (Urbana: University of Illinois Press, 1987), 103–128.

49. Hyman L. Meites, *History of the Jews of Chicago* (reprint, Chicago: Chicago Jewish Historical Society and Wellington Publishing, 1990), 269–270.

50. *Maccabean*, May 1918, 122.

51. Ibid.

52. Letter from Benjamin Rabalsky to Jacob De Haas, ca. 1916, P-153, Benjamin Rabalsky Papers, American Jewish Historical Society (hereafter cited as AJHS).

53. On the creation of the Yidish Nazionaler Arbeter Farband, see Baruch Zuckerman, *Zikhronos*, vol. 1, 329–335.

54. Leib Spizman, "Etafn in der geshikhte fun der zionistisher arbeter bavegung," vol. 1, 256.

55. "Poale Zion Palestine Committee Financial Report as at September 30th, 1918," 10–12, A137/52, Shlomo Kaplansky Papers, CZA; Moshe Cohen, ed., *Labor Zionist Handbook: The Aims, Activities and History of the Labor Zionist Movement in America* (New York: Poale Zion Zeire Zion of America, 1939), 72.

56. Samuel Halperin, *The Political World of American Zionism*, 327.

57. "[Memorandum to] the Inner Executive Committee of the Zionist Organizations," ca. 1918 (emphasis added), A180/65, Baruch Zuckerman Papers, CZA.

58. Arnold Kretchmar-Isreeli, "The Poal-Zion Movement," 1337–1339.

59. Jonathan Frankel, *Prophecy and Politics*, 547.

60. Naomi W. Cohen, *Not Free to Desist: The American Jewish Committee, 1906–1966* (Philadelphia: Jewish Publication Society of America, 1972), 105–110, 149–153.

61. Arthur Hertzberg, *The Jews in America: Four Centuries of an Uneasy Encounter* (New York: Simon & Schuster, 1989), 217–236.

62. See Lillian Gorenstein, "A Memoir of the Great War, 1914–1924," in *YIVO Annual*, vol. 20 (1991), 167–182.

63. John Higham, *Strangers in the Land: Patterns of American Nativism, 1860–1925* (New York: Atheneum, 1973), chap. 10.

64. Leonard Dinnerstein, *Antisemitism in America*, chaps. 4–5.

65. Deborah Dash Moore, *Bnai Brith and the Challenge of Ethnic Leadership* (Albany: State University of New York Press, 1981), chap. 5; Howard M. Sachar, *A History of the Jews in America* (New York: Knopf, 1992), 411.

66. A study of the Yiddish press notes that "support in rebuilding National Jewish Homeland in Palestine" ranked first among the topics most frequently addressed by leading Jewish papers. See Mordecai Soltes, *The Yiddish Press: An Americanizing Agency* (New York: Teachers College Press, 1925), 106–107.

67. *Young Judean*, February 1920, 116–119, I–61, Jewish Student Organizations, AJHS.

68. *Young Judean*, January 1921, n.p., I–61, Jewish Student Organizations, AJHS.

69. Declaration of Jewish workers assembled at Cooper Union, April 29, 1920, manuscript, A180/65, Baruch Zuckerman Papers, CZA.

70. Gabriel Davidson, "Aspects of the Agricultural Settlement of Palestine," *Jewish Forum*, July 1920, 328, 331.

71. Samuel Halperin, *The Political World of American Zionism*, 327.

72. Anita Shapira, *Berl: The Biography of a Socialist Zionist* (Cambridge: Cambridge University Press, 1984), 117–124.

73. See Allon Gal, "Brandeis' View on the Upbuilding of Palestine, 1914–1923," *Studies in Zionism*, Autumn 1982, 211–240.

74. Chaim Arlosoroff, *Surveying American Zionism* (New York: Zionist Labor Party "Hitachduth" of America [sic], 1929), 23–24, emphasis in the original.

75. K. Weitmann, "Parzufim," in Menahem Ribalov, ed., *Sefer hayovel shel Hadoar* (New York: Hozaat Hahistadrut Haivrit be-Amerikah, 1927), 143–145.

76. Marie Syrkin, *Nachman Syrkin: Socialist Zionist*, 204–208.

77. Letter from Manya Shohat to Rahel Yanait, September 21, 1921, in Rachel Yanait Ben-Zvi, ed., *Before Golda: Manya Shohat*, trans. Sandra Shurin (New York: Biblio Press, 1989), 174.

78. J. C. Rich, "The Jewish Labor Movement in the United States," in R. Abramovitch et al., eds., *The Jewish People Past and Present* (New York: Marstin Press, 1948), vol. 2, 403–404.

79. Quoted in Hyman J. Fliegel, *The Life and Times of Max Pine* (New York: Published by the author, 1959), 22.

80. Quoted in Maier Bryan Fox, "Labor Zionism in America: The Challenge of the 1920s," *American Jewish Archives*, April 1983, 61.

81. Moshe Cohen, ed., *Labor Zionist Handbook*, 151.

82. Abraham Revusky, *Looking Forward after Twenty Years of Keren Hayesod* (New York: Keren Hayesod, 1945), esp. 8–21; Samuel Halperin, *The Political World of American Zionism*, chap. 8.

83. See Zvi Scharfstein, *Toldot hahinukh beisrael*, vol. 3, 2d ed. (Jerusalem: Reubin Mass, 1962), 50–82.

84. Leo L. Honor, "Jewish Education in the United States," in Raphael R. Abramovitch et al., eds., *The Jewish People Past and Present*, vol. 2, 164.

85. Meir Ben-Horin, "From the Turn of the Century," in Judah Pilch, ed., *A History of Jewish Education in America* (New York: American Association for Jewish Education, 1969), 111.

86. Michael A. Meyer, *Response to Modernity: A History of the Reform Movement in Judaism* (New York: Oxford University Press, 1988), 299–301.

87. Letter from Isaac B. Berkson to Alexander Dushkin, February 7, 1928, A348/139, Isaac B. Berkson Papers, CZA.

88. Letter from Alexander Dushkin to Isaac B. Berkson, February 29, 1928, A348/100, Isaac B. Berkson Papers, CZA.

89. Meir Ben-Horin, "From the Turn of the Century," 85–86. See also Samuel Dinin, *Zionist Education in the United States: A Survey* (New York: Zionist Organization of America, 1944), 14–17; and, for example, *Jewish Education*, vols. 1–7 (1929–1930).

90. Walter Ackerman, "Israel in American Jewish Education," in Allon Gal, ed., *Envisioning Israel: The Changing Ideals and Images of North American Jews* (Jerusalem: Magnes Press, Hebrew University of Jerusalem, and Detroit: Wayne State University Press, 1996), 178.

91. See Ruth Bondy, *Hashaliah: hayav vemoto shel Enzo Sereni* (Tel Aviv: Am

Oved, 1973), chap. 14. Shlomo Grodzensky's remarks also are revealing: see his "Notes on Our Youth Movement," translated and reprinted from *Der yidisher kemfer*, December 25, 1942, in J. J. Goldberg and Elliot King, eds., *Builders and Dreamers: Habonim Labor Zionist Youth in North America* (New York: Herzl Press and Cornwall Books, 1993), 85–87.

92. See Shlomo Shulsinger, ed., *Kovez Masad: mahanaiot ivrit* (Israel: Irgun Mahanot Masad, 1989), vol. 2, esp. Shimon Frost, "Kavim letoldot hamahanaiot haivrit bezfon amerikah," 17–79; Jenna Weismann Joselit, *A Worthy Use of Summer: Jewish Summer Camping in America* (Philadelphia: National Museum of American Jewish History, 1993).

93. Leo L. Honor, "Jewish Education in the United States," 166–167.

94. Judah Pilch, *A History of Jewish Education in America*, 93–96; Max Vorspan and Lloyd P. Gartner, *History of the Jews of Los Angeles* (Philadelphia: Jewish Publication Society, 1970), 212–213; *American Jewish Year Book*, vol. 38 (1936), 74–75, 85–86.

95. From a copy of the text of Solomon Goldman's opening address to the forty-second annual convention of the Zionist Organization of America, New York City (June 25–27, 1939); A406/103, Robert Szold Papers, CZA, 6–7.

96. See *American Jewish Year Book*, vol. 42 (1940), 230–278; David Rudavsky, "Nature and Extent of Secondary Jewish Schooling in America," *Jewish Education*, vol. 12, no. 1 (April 1940), 25–32; Jacob S. Golub, "Some Trends in Jewish Education," *Jewish Education*, vol. 14, no. 1 (April–June 1942), 36–37.

97. Walter Ackerman, "Israel in American Jewish Education," 176–179.

98. See Ben Rosen and William Chomsky, "Improving the Teaching of Hebrew in Our Schools," *Jewish Education*, vol. 12, no. 2 (September 1940), 97–101; Harry Blumberg, "Some Desiderated Materials in Hebrew Language Teaching in the Public High Schools," *Jewish Education*, vol. 12, no. 3 (January 1941), 166–170.

99. Emanuel Gamoran, *Changing Conceptions in Jewish Education* (New York: Macmillan, 1924), vol. 2, 122–124.

100. Zvi Scharfstein, *Toldot hahinukh beisrael*, 117–118; Michael A. Meyer, *Response to Modernity*, 300–301.

101. Leib Spizman, ed., *Geshikte fun der zionistisher arebeter bavegung in zfon amerike* (New York: Farlag Yidisher Kemfer, 1955), vol. 2; Anita Shapira, *Berl*, 120–121.

102. Manya Shohat to Rahel Yanait Ben-Zvi, January 12, 1922, in "The Letters and Papers of Manya Shohat," ed. Jehuda Reinharz and Shulamit Reinharz, in progress. I am grateful to Jehuda Reinharz and Shulamit Reinharz for making this material available to me.

103. Kenneth W. Stein, *The Land Question in Palestine, 1917–1939* (Chapel Hill: University of North Carolina Press, 1984), chap. 2.

104. Translated from *Der tog*, March 8, 1924.

105. Judith A. Sokoloff, "Naamat USA through the Decades," *Naamat Woman,* September–October 1995, 17.

106. Nick Mandelkern, "The Story of Pioneer Women," *Pioneer Woman,* September 1980, 22.

107. Thea Keren, *Sophie Udin: Portrait of a Pioneer* (Rehovot: Published by the author, 1984), 37, emphasis added.

108. Samuel Halperin, *The Political World of American Zionism,* 319–320, 327.

109. *Konvenshun deklarazya fun der pionern froyen* (1926), Naamat USA Archives.

110. *American Jewish Year Book,* vol. 30 (1928), 234.

111. *Register of Jewish Social Service Agencies in Palestine,* vol. 4: *Jewish Social Service Agencies in Haifa, Safad, Tiberias, Tel Aviv and the Colonies* (Bureau of Jewish Social Research, December 1931), 316–317, Jewish Welfare Foundation Papers, box 188, AJHS.

112. *Konvenshun suvenir-bukh fun der pionern froyen organizazya,* October 16–18, 1930, Naamat USA Archives.

113. Golda Meir, *My Life* (New York: Dell, 1975), 124–125.

114. Quoted in Judith A. Sokoloff, "Naamat USA through the Decades," 19.

115. Moshe Cohen, *Labor Zionist Handbook,* 124–125; Samuel Halperin, *The Political World of American Zionism,* app. 4, 325–326.

116. *American Jewish Year Book,* vol. 43 (1941), 584.

117. Samuel Halperin, *The Political World of American Zionism,* app. 4, 325–326.

118. Charles S. Liebman, "Reconstructionism in American Jewish Life," *American Jewish Year Book,* vol. 71 (1970), 3–99.

119. Mark A. Raider, "Toward a Re-examination of American Zionist Leadership: The Case of Hayim Greenberg," *Journal of Israeli History* 15 (Summer 1994): 133–160.

120. *American Jewish Year Book,* vol. 41 (1939), 183.

121. Based on data cited in Samuel Halperin, *The Political World of American Zionism,* 327.

122. Quoted in James West Davidson et al., *Nation of Nations: A Narrative History of the American Republic* (New York: McGraw-Hill, 1990), vol. 2, 948; see also John Kenneth Galbraith, *The Great Crash, 1929* (Boston: Houghton Mifflin, 1955).

123. The ZOA dropped from a membership of nearly 150,000 in the aftermath of the Balfour Declaration, to roughly 18,500 in 1922, to fewer than 8,500 in 1932; see Samuel Halperin, *The Political World of American Zionism,* 327.

124. Ibid.

125. On Mizrahi, see ibid., 65–97.

126. Ibid.

127. Howard M. Sachar, *A History of the Jews in America,* 460; Melech Epstein, *Jewish Labor in USA,* vol. 2, 193.

128. Deborah Dash Moore, *Bnai Brith and the Challenge of Ethnic Leadership*, 114, 168.

129. Michael A. Meyer, *Response to Modernity*, 307–308.

130. See Beth Wenger, "Ethnic Community in Economic Crisis: New York Jews and the Great Depression" (Ph.D. diss., Yale University, 1992), 18–27; Ronald H. Bayor, *Neighbors in Conflict: The Irish, Germans, Jews and Italians of New York City, 1929–1941*, 2d ed. (Urbana: University of Illinois Press, 1988), chap. 2; see also Eli Ginzburg, "Jews in the American Economy: The Dynamics of Opportunity," in Gladys Rosen, ed., *Jewish Life in America: Historical Perspectives* (New York: Ktav Publishing House, 1978), 113–114.

131. Ben Halpern and Jehuda Reinharz, *Zionism and the Creation of a New Society* (New York: Oxford University Press, 1998), chap. 7.

132. Henry Near, *Frontiersmen and Haluzim: The Image of the Pioneer in North America and Pre-State Jewish Palestine* (Haifa: University of Haifa and Kibbutz University Center, 1987).

133. Interview with Marshall Sklare, Waltham, Mass., March 6, 1991.

134. Allon Gal, *Socialist-Zionism: Theory and Issues in Contemporary Jewish Nationalism* (Cambridge, Mass.: Schenkman, 1973), 188.

135. *American Jewish Year Book*, vol. 37 (1935), 342.

136. Ibid.

137. Letter from Emanuel Gamoran to Charles Cowen, March 10, 1933, roll 1604, LZOA microfilm, American Jewish Archives (hereafter cited as AJA).

138. "Minutes of the Administrative Committee of the League for Labor Palestine," October 7, 1934, roll 1534, LZOA microfilm, AJA.

139. Ibid.

140. Charles A. Madison, *Jewish Publishing in America*, 117.

141. Editorial, "Our Stand," *Jewish Frontier*, December 1934, 5.

142. Ber Borochov, *Nationalism and the Class Struggle: A Marxian Approach to the Jewish Problem*, ed. Moshe Cohen (New York: Poale Zion–Zeire Zion of America and Young Poale Zion Alliance, 1937), 196.

143. "Our Stand," 4.

144. *The Rabbis of America to Labor Palestine* (New York: League for Labor Palestine, 1935), 5, Palestine collection, AJA.

145. Ibid., 7–8.

146. Ibid., 13.

147. Michael A. Meyer, "A Centennial History," in Samuel E. Karff, ed., *Hebrew Union College–Jewish Institute of Religion At One Hundred Years* (Cincinnati: Hebrew Union College Press, 1976), 45.

148. For an analysis of Brandeis's Zionist views, see Ben Halpern, *A Clash of Heroes*, 86–108.

149. Based on data in the following issues of the *American Jewish Year Book*: vol. 35 (1933), 192, 213, 216; vol. 36 (1934), 324, 347, 348–349; vol. 37 (1935), 303,

308, 328, 330; vol. 38 (1936), 478, 484, 507, 510; see also Samuel Halperin, *The Political World of American Zionism*, 327.

150. Samuel Halperin, *The Political World of American Zionism*, 357, n. 130.

151. *The Rabbis of America to Labor Palestine*, 12.

152. "Our Stand," 5.

NOTES TO CHAPTER 3

1. *Emma Lazarus: Selections from Her Poetry and Prose*, ed. Morris U. Schappes (New York: Emma Lazarus Federation of Jewish Women's Clubs, 1982), 35–37.

2. Quoted in *Jewish Encyclopedia*, vol. 5 (1903), 321.

3. Quoted in Heinrich Eduard Jacob, *The World of Emma Lazarus* (New York: Schocken Books, 1949), 117, 121.

4. Arthur Zeiger, "Emma Lazarus and Pre-Herzlian Zionism," in Isidore S. Meyer, ed., *Early History of American Zionism* (New York: American Jewish Historical Society, 1958), 88.

5. Ibid., 98–99.

6. Theodor Herzl, "A Solution of the Jewish Question," *Jewish Chronicle*, January 17, 1896, 12–13.

7. See Eliezer Don-Yehiya, "Hanukah and the Myth of the Maccabees in Zionist Ideology and in Israeli Society," *Jewish Journal of Sociology*, June 1992, 5–23.

8. Theodor Herzl, *The Jewish State: An Attempt at a Modern Solution of the Jewish Question* (New York: American Zionist Emergency Council, 1946), 157.

9. See Joseph Campbell, *The Hero with a Thousand Faces* (Princeton, N.J.: Princeton University Press, 1973).

10. Ibid., 30.

11. Theodor Herzl, "A Solution of the Jewish Question," 12.

12. Ben Halpern, "Herzl's Historic Gift: The Sense of Sovereignty," *Herzl Year Book*, vol. 3 (1960), 27–35.

13. Num. 32:32, *The Torah: The Five Books of Moses* (Philadelphia: Jewish Publication Society of America, 1973), 313.

14. Joshua 6:7–9, *Joshua and Judges*, ed. A. Cohen (London: Soncino Press, 1970), 27–28.

15. Walter Z. Laqueur, *Young Germany: A History of the German Youth Movement* (New York: Basic Books, 1962), 3–49; Jehuda Reinharz, *Fatherland or Promised Land: The Dilemma of the German Jew, 1893–1914* (Ann Arbor: University of Michigan Press, 1975); Israel Oppenheim, *Tnuat Hehaluz be-Polin, 1917–1929* (Jerusalem: Hozaat Sfarim Al Shem J. L Magnes, Hauniversitah Haivrit, 1982), 22–81; Mordecai Naor, ed., *Tnuot Noar, 1920–1960: Mekorot, sikumim, parashot nivharot vehomer ezer* (Jerusalem: Hozaat Yad Yizhak Ben-Zvi, Hamahlakah Lehinukh Vehadrakhah, 1989).

16. Isaiah Berlin, *Russian Thinkers* (New York: Penguin Books, 1986), chap. 6;

Kropotkin's Revolutionary Pamphlets: A Collection of Writings by Peter Kropotkin, ed. Roger Baldwin (Mineola, N.Y.: Dover, 1970), esp. "An Appeal to the Young," 260–282.

17. Jonathan Frankel, *Prophecy and Politics: Socialism, Nationalism and the Russian Jews, 1862–1917* (Cambridge: Cambridge University Press, 1981); Ezra Mendelsohn, *On Modern Jewish Politics* (New York: Oxford University Press, 1993).

18. Jonathan Frankel, *Prophecy and Politics*, 178–179, 309, 368; Michael Berkowitz, *Zionist Culture and West European Jewry before the First World War* (Cambridge: Cambridge University Press, 1993), chap. 4.

19. Jonathan Frankel, *Prophecy and Politics*, 337–338, 368; Shulamit Laskov, "The Biluim: Reality and Legend," *Studies in Zionism* 2 (Spring 1981): 17.

20. Joseph Vitkin, "Call to Jewish Youth," in *The Second Aliyah: An Anthology* (New York: Zionist Youth Council, 1955), 27; Walter Laqueur, *A History of Zionism* (New York: Holt, Rinehart and Winston, 1972), 279–281, 292–293.

21. Joseph Campbell, *The Hero with a Thousand Faces*, 31.

22. Rufus Learsi, *The Jews in America: A History* (Cleveland: World, 1954), 221–223; Ronald Sanders, *Shores of Refuge: A Hundred Years of Jewish Emigration* (New York: Henry Holt, 1988), 235–240.

23. Gerald Sorin, *A Time for Building: The Third Migration, 1880–1920* (Baltimore: Johns Hopkins University Press, 1992), 58.

24. See *American Jewish Year Book*, vol. 9 (1907), 24–430, and vol. 12 (1910), 254–280.

25. Jacob Rader Marcus, *This I Believe: Documents of American Jewish Life* (Northvale, N.J.: Jason Aronson, 1990), 151.

26. See Abraham Menes, "The *Am Oylom* Movement," *YIVO Annual* 4 (1949): 9–33.

27. "America," *Jewish Encyclopedia*, vol. 1 (1902), 504. For an example of the revolutionary immigrant ethos, see Emma Goldman, *Living My Life*, 2 vols. (New York: Dover, 1970).

28. Eliezer Schweid, *The Land of Israel: National Home or Land of Destiny*, trans. Deborah Greniman (Cranberry, N.J.: Associated University Presses, and New York: Herzl Press, 1985), 157–170.

29. For an analysis of the economic pressures faced by Jewish immigrants in the United States, see Uri D. Herscher, *Jewish Agricultural Utopias in America, 1880–1910* (Detroit: Wayne State University Press, 1981), 116.

30. Margalit Shiloh, "Nizanei raayon hamoshav—Haikar Hazair, hakvuzah haamerikanit baaliyah hashniyah," *Katedrah* 25 (1982): 79–80.

31. Eliezer Jaffe, "Yemei haaliyah hashniyah be-Amerikah," *Kitvei Eliezer Jaffe* (Tel Aviv: Am Oved, 1947), vol. 2, 124.

32. Evyatar Friesel, "The Knights of Zion of Chicago and Their Relations with the Federation of American Zionists, 1897–1916," in Daniel Carpi and Gedalia Yogev, eds., *Zionism: Studies in the History of the Zionist Movement and of the Jewish*

Community in Palestine, English ed. (Tel Aviv: Tel Aviv University and Massada Publishing, 1975), vol. 1, 9–48.

33. Eliezer Jaffe, "Yemei haaliyah hashniyah be-Amerikah," 122–128; see also S. D. Jaffe, "Kvuzat Haikar Hazair," in Braha Habas, ed., *Sefer haaliyah hashniyah* (Tel Aviv: Am Oved, 1947), 429–434.

34. For a description of the early Russian Hehaluz movement, see Jonathan Frankel, *Prophecy and Politics*, 337–338.

35. Yizhak Mihaeli, "Reshitah shel histadrut Hehaluz be-Amerikah," *Asufot*, December 1959, 109.

36. See Anita Shapira, *Land and Power: The Zionist Resort to Force, 1881–1948*, trans. William Templer (New York: Oxford University Press, 1992), 17–29.

37. Yosef Salmon, "Harav Shmuel Mohilever—rabam shel Hovevei Zion," *Zion* 56 (1991): 59.

38. Yitzhak Mihaeli, "Reshitah shel histadrut Hehaluz be-Amerikah," 108.

39. Joseph Campbell, *The Hero with a Thousand Faces*, 30.

40. Melvin I. Urofsky, *American Zionism from Herzl to the Holocaust* (Garden City, N.Y.: Anchor Books/Doubleday, 1976), 149; Allon Gal, "Universal Mission and Jewish Survivalism in American Zionist Ideology," in Jacob Neusner et al., eds., *From Ancient Israel to Modern Judaism, Intellect in Quest of Understanding: Essays in Honor of Marvin Fox* (Atlanta: Scholars Press, 1989), vol. 4, 61–83.

41. Evyatar Friesel, "Ahad Haamism in American Zionist Thought," in Jacques Kornberg, ed., *At the Crossroads: Essays on Ahad Haam* (Albany: State University of New York Press, 1983), 133–141.

42. Solomon Schechter, *Seminary Addresses and Other Papers* (Cincinnati: Ark, 1915), 99–100.

43. "Jewish Minute Men," *Young Judean*, October 1912, 20, I–61, Jewish Student Organizations, American Jewish Historical Society (hereafter cited as AJHS).

44. Jehuda Reinharz and Paul Mendes-Flohr, eds., *The Jew in the Modern World: A Documentary History* (New York: Oxford University Press, 1995), 497.

45. Israel Friedlaender, *Past and Present* (Cincinnati: Ark, 1919), xi; see also "The Problem of Judaism in America," in ibid., 253–278.

46. Israel Friedlander, "The Significance of Palestine for the Jewries of the World," *American Hebrew*, May 4, 1917, 888.

47. "A Palestinian Colony," *High School Zionist*, June 1914, 5–6, I–61, Jewish Student Organizations, AJHS.

48. Lotta Levensohn, "Jewish Arbor Day," *Young Judean*, January 1912, 4, I–61, Jewish Student Organizations, AJHS.

49. Ibid.

50. Jerold S. Auerbach, *Rabbis and Lawyers: The Journey from Torah to Constitution* (Bloomington: Indiana University Press, 1990), 125.

51. "Wild Wheat in Palestine Discovered by Aaron Aaronsohn," *Young Judean*, November 1912, 7, I–61, Jewish Student Organizations, AJHS.

52. Yitzhak Ben-Zvi's detailed description of official Turkish attitudes toward the Zionists appeared in the *American Jewish Chronicle* on June 1, 1917. He wrote: "In a conversation with Djemal Pasha concerning my own banishment, he told me, in the presence of the Mayor of Jerusalem and other officials: 'I know that you, Poalei Zion, want to tear Palestine away from Turkey. But so long as you will adhere to your present views, you cannot stay in this country.'" Ben-Zvi's description was later reprinted in *Palestine: The Organ of the British Palestine Committee*, July 7, 1917, 188–192.

53. The key themes expressed in Bialik's poem "Shir haavodah vehamlakhah" are contained in the following stanza: "Who will save us from hunger?/Who will give us our daily bread?/And who will give us milk?/To whom do we offer thanks?/To whom do we offer praise?/To labor and to work!" See *Shirat H. N. Bialik: antologyah*, ed. Haiyim Orlan (Cleveland: Lishkat Hahinukh Hayehudi Vehamakhon Lemadaei Hayahadut, and Tel Aviv: Dvir, 1971), 270.

54. According to the Talmud, the first benediction of the grace after meals was composed by Moses. It reads: "Blessed art thou, Lord our God, King of the universe, who sustainest the whole with goodness, kindness, and mercy. Thou givest food to all creatures, for thy mercy endures forever. Through thy abundant goodness we have never yet been in want; may we never be in want of sustenance for thy great name's sake. Thou, O God, sustainest all, doest good to all, and providest food for all the creatures thou hast created. Blessed art thou, O Lord, who dost sustain all." *Daily Prayer Book: Hasiddur hashalem*, trans. and ed. Philip Birnbaum (New York: Hebrew Publishing, 1949), 759–760.

55. David Ben-Gurion, "Mi yiten lanu et haarez?" *Hehaluz: prinzipen un oifgeben* (New York: Zentraler Farveltung Fun Hehaluz, 1916), reprinted in *Asufot*, December 1959, 98.

56. Vladimir Jabotinsky, *The Story of the Jewish Legion*, trans. Samuel Katz (New York: Bernard Ackerman, 1945), 30–31.

57. See Ber Borochov, *Class Struggle and the Jewish Nation: Selected Essays in Marxist Zionism*, ed. Mitchell Cohen (New Brunswick, N.J.: Transaction Books, 1984), 16–21; "Our Platform," 75–103.

58. David Ben-Gurion, "Mi yiten lanu et haarez?" 99–100.

59. *Daily Prayer Book*, 603.

60. Anita Shapira, "Hamotivim hadatiim shel tnuat haavodah," in Shmuel Almog, Jehuda Reinharz, and Anita Shapira, eds., *Zionut vedat* (Jerusalem: Merkaz Zalman Shazar; Boston: Tauber Institute for the Study of European Jewry, Brandeis University, 1994), 301–328; Jonathan Frankel, "The 'Yizkor' Book of 1911: A Note on National Myths in the Second Aliya," in Jehuda Reinharz and Anita Shapira, eds., *Essential Papers on Zionism* (New York: New York University Press, 1996), 422–453.

61. According to Hasidic tradition, each letter in the Hebrew alphabet—its name, shape, and numerical value—is singularly meaningful. See Rabbi Yitzchak

Ginsburgh, assisted by Rabbi Avraham Arieh Trugman and Rabbi Moshe Yaakov Wisnefsky, *The Alef-Beit: Jewish Thought Revealed through Hebrew Letters* (Northvale, N.J.: Jason Aronson, 1991), 108–119, 154–165, 168–178, 296–307.

62. Isaiah Rabinovich, *Major Trends in Modern Hebrew Fiction* (Chicago: University of Chicago Press, 1968), 56, 74–75, 97, 196, 223–224.

63. Anita Shapira, *Land and Power*, 33.

64. *Daily Prayer Book*, 213.

65. Yizhak Ben-Zvi later recorded that 150 persons joined Hehaluz as a result of the organizing efforts conducted in nineteen American and Canadian cities. Yizhak Ben-Zvi, "Beginnings in America," in Sima Altman et al., *Pioneers from America: 75 Years of Hehaluz, 1905–1980* (Tel Aviv: Bogrei Hehaluz America, 1981), 42–43.

66. Jehuda Reinharz, "Zionism in the USA on the Eve of the Balfour Declaration," *Studies in Zionism* 9 (1988): 131–145; Charles Israel Goodblatt, "The Impact of the Balfour Declaration in America," *American Jewish Historical Quarterly*, June 1968, esp. 455–496; Evyatar Friesel, "Brandeis' Role in American Zionism Historically Reconsidered," *American Jewish History*, September 1979, 48–52.

67. David Ben-Gurion and Yizhak Ben-Zvi, *Eretz yisroel* (New York: Poalei Zion Palestina Komitet, 1918), AJHS.

68. Michael Brown, "A Paradoxical Relationship: American Jews and Zionism," in Milton Plesur, ed., *An American Historian: Essays to Honor Selig Adler* (Buffalo: State University of New York at Buffalo, 1980), 83.

69. Oscar Handlin, *A Continuing Task: The American Jewish Joint Distribution Committee, 1914–1964* (New York: Random House, 1964), 31; see also *Palestine: The Organ of the British Palestine Committee*, February 22, 1917, 39–40.

70. David S. Blondheim, preface to *Kadimah*, ed. David S. Blondheim (New York: Federation of American Zionists, 1918), 9.

71. Ibid.

72. Samuel Rodman, "Ha-Gedud Ha-Ibri" [*sic*], in ibid., 20–21.

73. Ibid., 22.

74. Ibid., 24–25.

75. Ibid., 28.

76. Walter Laqueur, *A History of Zionism*, 294–295.

77. See Jonathan D. Sarna, " 'The Greatest Jew in the World since Jesus Christ': The Jewish Legacy of Louis D. Brandeis," *American Jewish History* 81 (Spring–Summer 1994), esp. 363, n. 58.

78. Henry L. Feingold, *A Time for Searching: Entering the Mainstream, 1920–1945* (Baltimore: Johns Hopkins University Press, 1992), 118–122.

79. Letter from Alexander Dushkin to Isaac Berkson, August 15, 1919. A348/15, Isaac B. Berkson Papers, Central Zionist Archives (hereafter cited as CZA).

80. See Judah Pilch, *A History of Jewish Education in America* (New York: American Association for Jewish Education, 1969).

81. See Jenna Weisman Joselitt, *A Worthy Use of Summer: Jewish Summer Camping in America* (Philadelphia: National Museum of American Jewish History, 1993); Samuel Grand, "A History of Zionist Youth Organizations in the United States from Their Inception to 1940" (Ph.D. diss., Columbia University, 1958).

82. Jessie E. Sampter, "Zionism in the Intermediate Club," *Young Judea Leader,* October 1919, 3, I–61, Jewish Student Organizations, AJHS.

83. *Young Judean,* February 1920, 119, I–61, Jewish Student Organizations, AJHS.

84. *Shaharut: yarhon lenearim velenaarot—The Youth,* February 1918, 4.

85. Ahad Haam, *Selected Essays,* trans. Leon Simon (Philadelphia: Jewish Publication Society of America, 1912), 171–194.

86. Leon Spitz, "American Patriotism in the Young Judea Club," *Young Judean,* February 1919, 1, I–61, Jewish Student Organizations, AJHS.

87. Ibid.

88. Ibid., 4.

89. John Higham, *Strangers in the Land: Patterns of American Nativism, 1860–1925* (New York: Atheneum, 1973), chaps. 10–11.

90. Sarah Kussy, "The Conquest of the Soil: A Visit to a Pioneers' Settlement in Palestine," *Young Judean,* February 1925, 10, I–61, Jewish Student Organizations, AJHS.

91. Ibid., 10, 25.

92. Matthew Frye Jacobson, *Special Sorrows: The Diasporic Imagination of Irish, Polish and Jewish Immigrants in the United States* (Cambridge, Mass.: Harvard University Press, 1995), 105.

93. Sarah Kussy, "The Conquest of the Soil," 25.

94. Letter from Louis Lipsky to the leaders of Keren Hayesod work in America, November 18, 1924, emphasis in original, S22/26, Press Office, Zionist Organization, Jewish Agency for Palestine Papers, CZA.

95. Ibid.

96. From an address to the Zionist Executive, September 1927, reprinted in Arthur Ruppin, *Three Decades in Palestine: Speeches and Papers on the Upbuilding of the Jewish National Home* (Jerusalem: Schocken Books, 1936), 153.

97. Derek J. Penslar, *Zionism and Technocracy: The Engineering of Jewish Settlement in Palestine, 1870–1918* (Bloomington: Indiana University Press, 1991), 90–91.

98. See "An Address delivered before 'The Non-Partisan Conference to Consider Palestinian Problem,'" February 1924, reprinted in Arthur Ruppin, *Three Decades in Palestine,* 121–130.

99. "Memorandum to the Executive Committee-Palestine Economic Corporation from Bernard Flexner," November 4, 1925, 1, A406/233, Bernard Flexner Papers, CZA.

100. Ibid., 2.

101. Ibid.

102. Ibid., 1–14; Joseph B. Glass, "Balfouria: An American Zionist Colony," *Studies in Zionism* 14 (1993): 53–72.

103. *Jewish Guardian*, March 27, 1925, 18, A185/32, Leonard Stein Papers, CZA. I am grateful to Jehuda Reinharz for providing me with this material.

104. "Is Zionism a Progressive Policy for Israel and America?—A Debate between Stephen S. Wise and Clarence Darrow," October 24, 1927, 9, manuscript, Zionism Collection, American Jewish Archives (hereafter cited as AJA).

105. Ibid.

106. Ibid., 8.

107. Ibid., 24.

108. Ibid., 29.

109. Memorandum from Louis D. Brandeis to Robert Szold, August 14, 1930, A251/329a, Israel B. Brodie Papers, CZA.

110. Memorandum from Louis D. Brandeis to Julian W. Mack, July 4, 1930, A251/329a, Israel B. Brodie Papers, CZA.

111. Ibid.

112. See the following copies of letters and memoranda in A251/329a, Israel B. Brodie Papers, CZA: Louis D. Brandeis to Joshua Bernhardt, July 17, 1930; Louis D. Brandeis to Jessie Sampter, July 21, 1930; Louis D. Brandeis to Berl Katznelson, July 21, 1930; Louis D. Brandeis to Joshua Bernhardt, July 22, 1930; Louis D. Brandeis to Arthur Ruppin, July 23, 1930; Louis D. Brandeis to Robert Szold, July 28, 1930; Louis D. Brandeis to H. Frumkin, July 30, 1930; Louis D. Brandeis to Berl Katznelson, August 4, 1930; Louis D. Brandeis to Nathan Kaplan, August 7, 1930; Louis D. Brandeis to Joshua Bernhardt, August 8, 1930; Nathan D. Kaplan to Louis D. Brandeis, September 9, 1930; and Robert Szold to Louis D. Brandeis, September 19, 1930.

113. Memorandum from Louis D. Brandeis to Robert Szold, August 19, 1930. A251/329a, Israel B. Brodie Papers, CZA.

114. Letter from Louis D. Brandeis to I. J. Lowe, August 12, 1930, A251/329a, Israel B. Brodie Papers, CZA.

115. Memorandum from Louis D. Brandeis to Julian W. Mack, July 16, 1930, A251/329a, Israel B. Brodie Papers, CZA.

116. Memorandum from Louis D. Brandeis to Robert Szold, September 7, 1930, A251/329a, Israel B. Brodie Papers, CZA.

117. See Susan Glenn, *Daughters of the Shtetl: Jewish Immigrant Women in America's Garment Industry, 1880–1920* (Ithaca, N.Y.: Cornell University Press, 1990); Sydney Stahl Weinberg, *World of Our Mothers: The Lives of Jewish Immigrant Women* (New York: Schocken Books, 1988), esp. chap. 10.

118. "Aims and Objectives of the Pioneer Women's Organization," *Pionern froyn konstitushn suvenir-bukh*, 1930, Naamat USA Archives.

119. Quoted in Judith A. Sokoloff, "Naamat USA through the Decades," 21.

120. Rachel Katznelson Shazar, ed., *The Plough Woman: Memoirs of the Pioneer*

Women of Palestine, trans. Maurice Samuel, 2d ed. (New York: Herzl Press, 1975), xv.

121. Ibid., xvi–xvii.

122. Gideon Shimoni, *The Zionist Ideology* (Hanover, N.H.: University Press of New England, 1995), 235.

123. Ben Halpern and Jehuda Reinharz, *Zionism and the Creation of a New Society* (New York: Oxford University Press, 1998), chap. 7.

124. Meyer Levin, *Yehuda* (New York: Jonathan Cape and Harrison Smith, 1931), 90.

125. J. Hoberman, *Bridge of Light: Yiddish Film between Two Worlds* (New York: Museum of Modern Art and Schocken Books, 1991), 183–184.

126. Quoted in ibid., 226–227.

127. Ibid., 253–255.

128. Based on data in "Proposal for the Organization of a Department of Propaganda through Motion Pictures and Radio Programs," 1936, P-672, Louis Lipsky Papers, box 4, file 2, AJHS.

129. *New York Times*, late city ed., November 21, 1935, 27.

130. *New York Herald Tribune*, May 21, 1931, A251/63h, Israel B. Brodie Papers, CZA.

131. *New York American Editorial Page*, May 25, 1931, A251/63h, Israel B. Brodie Papers, CZA.

132. *New York World Telegram*, May 22, 1931, A251/63h, Israel B. Brodie Papers, CZA.

133. "Palestine—The Land of the Future," *Jewish Advocate*, January 18, 1935, 4.

134. See the April 1938 series by Leo Shubow published in *Boston Traveler*, esp. April 11, 1938, 6; April 13, 1938, 1–2; April 14, 1938, 3–4; and April 15, 1938, 2, P-395, Leo Shubow Papers, AJHS.

135. *Jeremiah*, ed. and trans. H. Friedman (reprint, London: Soncino Press, 1977), 199. I am grateful to Marc Brettler, Brandeis University, and Mishael M. Caspi, Bates College, for their assistance with this biblical reference.

136. I am grateful to Sylvia Riese, Brandeis University, for sharing her firsthand impressions of the 1939 World's Fair and alerting me to the *Palestine Book*.

137. See Arthur Aryeh Goren, "*Anu Banu Arzah* in America: The Americanization of the *Haluz* Ideal," in Allon Gal, ed., *Envisioning Israel: The Changing Ideals and Images of North American Jews* (Jerusalem: Magnes Press, Hebrew University of Jerusalem, and Detroit: Wayne State University Press, 1996), 81–113.

NOTES TO CHAPTER 4

1. C. Bezalel Sherman, "The Beginnings of Labor Zionism in the United States," in Isidore S. Meyer, ed., *Early History of Zionism in America* (New

York: American Jewish Historical Society and Theodor Herzl Foundation, 1958), 279.

2. The history of Aliyah Bet goes beyond the scope of this study. Although the operation's clandestine activities began as early as 1934, its American wing did not gain momentum until the late 1930s. Kieve Skidell, Ari Lashner, and other Labor Zionist youth leaders later played central roles in such efforts. This is a subject that awaits further analysis. See Aviva Halamish, *Exodus: hasipur haamiti* (Tel Aviv: Am Oved, 1990), chap. 3; Yehuda Sela, "Pirkei haapalah shel haluzim mi-Amerikah," *Measef leheker tnuat haavodah hazionit vehasozialism* 17 (1987). For useful but uncritical accounts of Aliyah Bet, see, for example, Ruth Gruber, *Destination Palestine: The Story of the Haganah Ship Exodus 1947* (New York: Current Books, 1948); I. F. Stone, *Underground to Palestine* (New York: Boni and Gaer, 1946); David Breslau, ed., *Arise and Build: The Story of American Habonim* (New York: Ichud Habonim Labor Zionist Youth, 1961), 79–83; and Joseph M. Hochstein and Murray S. Greenfield, *The Jews' Secret Fleet* (Jerusalem: Gefen Publishing House, 1987).

3. Matityahu Mintz, "Work for the Land of Israel and 'Work in the Present': A Concept of Unity, a Reality of Contradiction," in Jehuda Reinharz and Anita Shapira, eds., *Essential Papers on Zionism* (New York: New York University Press, 1995), 161–170.

4. Charles Goodblatt, "The Impact of the Balfour Declaration in America," *American Jewish Historical Quarterly*, June 1968, 455–515.

5. Marie Syrkin, *Way of Valor: A Biography of Golda Meyerson* (New York: Sharon Books, 1955), 37, 42–49.

6. This translation from Yiddish into English appears in Moshe Cohen, "First Steps, 1911–1929," in David Breslau, ed., *Arise and Build*, 4–5. The original document no longer exists.

7. For example, see Eliezer Jaffe, "Yemei haaliyah hashniyah be-Amerikah," *Kitvei Eliezer Jaffe* (Tel Aviv: Am Oved, 1947), vol. 2, 122–128; and David Ben-Gurion, Yitzhak Ben-Zvi, and Yaakov Zerubavel, "Tnuat hahaluzim hahadashah," *Hehaluz: prinzipen un oifgegeben* (New York: Zentraler Farveltung Fun Hehaluz, 1916), reprinted in Raphael Mahler, "Lereshitah shel tnuat Hehaluz," *Asufot*, December 1959, 98–110.

8. Ber Borochov, *Class Struggle and the Jewish Nation: Selected Essays in Marxist Zionism*, ed. Mitchell Cohen (New Brunswick, N.J.: Transaction Books, 1984), esp. "Our Platform," 75–103.

9. See Matityahu Mintz, *Zmanim hadashim, zmirot hadashot: Ber Borochov, 1914–1917* (Tel Aviv: Hozaat Am Oved, Universitat Tel Aviv, Hamakhon Leheker Hazionut Al Shem Chaim Weizmann, 1988).

10. Ber Borochov, *Class Struggle and the Jewish Nation*, 91.

11. See Elias Tcherikower, *The Early Jewish Labor Movement in the United States*, trans. Aaron Antonovsky (New York: YIVO Institute for Jewish Research, 1961), 333.

12. Ben-Zion Ilan, *An American Soldier/Pioneer in Israel* (New York: Labor Zionist Letters, 1979), 2.

13. Morris Silverman, *Hartford Jews, 1659–1970* (Hartford: Connecticut Historical Society, 1970), esp. 40–44; *Encyclopaedia Judaica*, vol. 7 (1972), 1359.

14. The presence of Labor Zionist youth in Hartford in the early 1920s is noted in Morris I. Davidson, *Growing up in Hartford, Connecticut, 1908–1928* (Hartford: Andrew Mountain Press, 1987), American Jewish Historical Society (hereafter cited as AJHS).

15. The general attitude of Labor Zionist youth leaders in this period was later described as follows: "None of us . . . thought of himself as making history; none kept diaries, none even recorded systematically the sequence of events." Saadia Gelb, "The Founding of Habonim, 1930–1935," in David Breslau, ed., *Arise and Build*, 8.

16. See the record book of the Junior Poale Zion Club of Hartford (hereafter cited as Hartford record book), 83, American Habonim Archives, Yad Tabenkin–United Kibbutz Movement Archives (hereafter cited as UKM).

17. Elias Tcherikower, *The Early Jewish Labor Movement*, 333.

18. Anita Shapira, "Hamotivim hadatiim shel tnuat haavodah," in Shmuel Almog, Jehuda Reinharz, and Anita Shapira, eds., *Zionut vedat* (Jerusalem: Merkaz Zalman Shazar; Boston: Tauber Institute for the Study of European Jewry, Brandeis University, 1994), 301–328; Gershon Winer, "The Religious Dimension of Yiddish Secularism," *Judaism* 41 (Winter 1992): 80–95.

19. Interview with Jacob Katzman, New York City, July 21, 1988.

20. Several Zionist groups were active in Hartford during this period. See Morris Silverman, *Hartford Jews*, 42–43.

21. Hartford record book, esp. 61, 68, 70, 74, 79, 122, 125, 127.

22. Melech Epstein, *Jewish Labor in U.S.A., 1914–1952: An Industrial, Political and Cultural History of the Jewish Labor Movement* (New York: Ktav Publishing House, 1969), vol. 2, 409–410.

23. Hartford record book, 125.

24. Ibid., 129, 134–135.

25. Ibid., 107.

26. For example, dues of 25 cents were collected weekly, and anyone failing to pay this sum for three weeks was subject to "action . . . taken against him by the club." Sometimes the need for group discipline led to extreme proposals such as giving "the chairman absolute dictatorial power." On a different occasion, a motion was made "to impeach the chairman." Hartford record book, 32, 74–75.

27. Ibid., 111–112.

28. Dirk Hoerder, ed., *The Immigrant Labor Press in North America, 1840s–1970s: An Annotated Bibliography*, vol. 2, *Migrants from Eastern and Southern Europe* (Westport, Conn.: Greenwood Press, 1987), 673; Moshe Cohen, "First Steps, 1911–1929," 3.

29. The Hartford record book generally reflects only mild interest in Borochovism. In one instance, the journal explicitly refers to the lecture of a senior party member "on Dr. Borochov, the founder of Poalei Zionism, who recently died." Hartford record book, 132.

30. For contemporary views of the Labor Zionist movement, see A. Kretchmar-Isreeli, "The Poal-Zion Movement" [sic], in *The Jewish Communal Register of New York City, 1917–1918* (New York: Kehillah of New York City, 1918), 1331–1342; and A. Glanz, "The Socialist Territorialist Labor Party," in ibid., 1343–1351. See also Maier Bryan Fox, "Labor Zionism in America: The Challenge of the 1920s," *American Jewish Archives*, April 1983, 53–71.

31. For analyses of the role of women in the Labor Zionist movement, see Deborah Bernstein, *The Struggle for Equality: Urban Workers in Prestate Israeli Society* (New York: Praeger, 1987); Rahel Katznelson-Rubashow, ed., *The Plough Woman: Records of the Pioneer Women of Palestine*, trans. Maurice Samuel (New York: Nicholas L. Brown, 1932); Jacob Katzman, *Commitment: The Labor Zionist Life-Style in America* (New York: Labor Zionist Letters, 1975), esp. "The Woman's Role," 75–79.

32. One senior party member "favored" the Hartford club and considered it more "clever than the Kemfer club" because it included "girls." Hartford record book, 133.

33. Morris Silverman, *Hartford Jews*, 40–42, 60–61.

34. Samuel Grand, "A History of Zionist Youth Organizations in the United States from Their Inception to 1940" (Ph.D. diss., Columbia University, 1958), 214–215; David Breslau, ed., *Arise and Build*, 258.

35. M. Ben-Zvi and Moshe Zamir, "The Kvuzah of Detroit," in Sima Altman et al., eds., *Pioneers from America: 75 Years of Hehaluz, 1905–1980* (Tel Aviv: Bogrei Hehaluz America, 1981), 49; Moshe Zamir, "Dvarim shel hakhsharah haluzit behuz laaretz," manuscript, n.d., American Habonim Archives, UKM.

36. See the Detroit Kvuzah journal, 8, American Habonim Archives, UKM. I am grateful to Muki Tsur, Kibbutz Ein Gev, Israel, for making this material available to me.

37. Muki Tsur, Tair Zevulun, and Hanan Porat, eds., *Kan al pnei adamah* (Israel: Kibbutz Hameuhad, Sifriyat Hapoalim, 1981), 140–141.

38. The Detroit Kvuzah journal notes that on one occasion, items were read aloud from a publication of Polish Dror (Freedom), the east European youth movement of Kibbutz Hameuhad (United Kibbutz Movement), the largest of the kibbutz movements in Palestine. According to the entry, the Dror publication included "letters in Hebrew, Yiddish and Polish." Detroit Kvuzah journal, 5.

39. See S. Yefroikin, "Yiddish Secular Schools in the United States," in Raphael Abramovitch et al., eds., *The Jewish People Past and Present* (New York: Marstin Press, 1948), vol. 2, 144–150; Mark M. Krug, "The Yiddish Schools in Chicago," *YIVO Annual* 9 (1968): 276–307.

40. M. Ben-Zvi and Moshe Zamir, "The Kvuzah of Detroit," 49; Allen A. Warsen, *Jewish Communal Institutions in Detroit* (Detroit, 1952), 77–82, AJHS; Robert A. Rockaway, *The Jews of Detroit: From the Beginning, 1762–1914* (Detroit: Wayne State University Press, 1986), 85–88.

41. Detroit Kvuzah journal, 6, emphasis added.

42. Allon Gal, "Independence and Universal Mission in Modern Jewish Nationalism: A Comparative Analysis of European and American Zionism (1897–1948)," *Studies in Contemporary Jewry* 5 (1989): 242–274.

43. "Table 39, Yediot hasafah bagolah," *Hamifkad hasheni shel haovdim haivriim be-Eretz Israel, September 1, 1926* (Tel Aviv: Histadrut Haovidm Haivriim Haklalit be-Eretz Israel, Havaad Hapoel, 1926), 48.

44. Detroit Kvuzah journal, 5.

45. Ibid., 48.

46. Evyatar Friesel, "Ahad Haamism in American Zionist Thought," in Jacques Kornberg, ed., *At the Crossroads: Essays on Ahad Haam* (Albany: State University of New York Press, 1983), 133–141.

47. Anita Shapira, *Land and Power: The Zionist Resort to Force, 1881–1948*, trans. William Templer (New York: Oxford University Press, 1992), 121.

48. Petaluma was already the site of many Jewish chicken farmers; see Phillip Naftaly, "Jewish Chicken Farmers in Petaluma, California, 1904–1975," *Western States Jewish History*, April 1991, 231–247. Kvuzat Gordonia's hakhsharah attempt in Petaluma folded after a short while, however; see David Yaroslavsky, "Links in the Chain," in Sima Altman et al., eds., *Pioneers from America*, 35–39; and Yaacov Levin, "Kvuzat Gordonia in Philadelphia," in ibid., 46–47.

49. Joseph Brandes, *Immigrants to Freedom: Jewish Communities in Rural New Jersey since 1882* (Philadelphia: Jewish Publication Society of America, 1971), 285–310.

50. Moshe Zamir, "Dvarim shel hakhsharah," 1–2.

51. Yehuda Riemer, "Haaliyah hahaluzit mizfon Amerikah," *Hazionut* 16 (1991), 128.

52. For a contemporary argument, see Edmund Wilson, "An Appeal to Progressives," in David A. Hollinger and Charles Capper, eds., *The American Intellectual Tradition. A Sourcebook*, vol. 2, *1865 to the Present* (New York: Oxford University Press, 1989), 180–185. Useful information is also provided by Melech Epstein, *Jewish Labor in U.S.A.*, vol. 2, chaps. 10–11.

53. Ber Borochov, "Evolution and Therapeutic Movements," 81. In this essay, Borochov outlines his perception of the inherent contradictions of the capitalist system. As a result of these contradictions, he surmises, any national economy based on capitalism inevitably sows the seeds of its own destruction.

54. See Kenneth W. Stein, *The Land Question in Palestine, 1917–1939* (Chapel Hill: University of North Carolina Press, 1984), esp. chap. 2, "The Land Question, 1917–1929," 35–79; Esco Foundation for Palestine, *Palestine: A Study of Jewish,*

Arab, and British Policies (New Haven, Conn.: Yale University Press, 1947), vol. 2, esp. chap. 9, "The 1929 Disturbances and Their Aftermath," 595–660.

55. Saadia Gelb, "The Founding of Habonim," 9. Similar observations were made at the time by A. M. Koler, a Histadrut representative present in America during the 1929 crisis. See "Peulah be-Amerikah," *Hahistadrut hahaklait ufeulotehah: Do''h leveidah hahaklait hareviit, 1926–1931* (Tel Aviv: Hozaat Hamerkaz Hahaklai, 1931), 200.

56. Saadia Gelb, "The Founding of Habonim," 8.

57. Ibid.

58. Raphael Mahler, "Lereshitah shel Hehaluz," 100.

59. For anecdotal accounts of American hakhsharot in the 1930s, see Sima Altman et al., eds., *Pioneers from America*, esp. 38–39, 40–41, 46–47, 48–50.

60. Samuel Grand, "A History of Zionist Youth Organizations," 50–51, 114–115.

61. *Report of the Executive of the Zionist Organisation Submitted to the XVIIIth Zionist Congress at Prague, August 21st–29th, 1933* (London: Central Office of the Zionist Organisation, 1933), 258–260, 270–271.

62. Nahum Guttman, "Hehaluz in America," in David Breslau, ed., *Arise and Build*, 28; Samuel Grand, "A History of Zionist Youth Organizations," 217.

63. L. Glantz, "The Sum Total," *Hechaluz*, January 1934, 12, American Habonim Archives, UKM.

64. Nahum Guttman, "Hehaluz in America," in David Breslau, ed., *Arise and Build*, 28.

65. L. Glantz, "The Sum Total," 13.

66. "Resolutions Adopted at the First National Convention of the Hehaluz Organization of America," *Hechaluz* [*sic*], March–April 1934, 8–9, American Habonim Archives, UKM.

67. Israel Oppenheim, *The Struggle of Jewish Youth for Productivization: The Zionist Youth Movement in Poland* (Boulder, Colo.: East European Monographs; New York: Columbia University Press, 1989), 132–134; Ben-Zion Ilan, *An American Soldier/Pioneer in Israel*, 21–22.

68. Baruch Zuckerman, "Yugnt problemn in Amerike," *Der yidisher kemfer*, February 2, 1934, 5.

69. Ibid.

70. Saadia Gelb, "The Founding of Habonim," in David Breslau, ed., *Arise and Build*, 11; *Proceedings of the First Pegisha of the YPZA. Held at the YPZA Kvuzah, Accord, New York, August 26–September 3, 1934* (New York: Young Poale Zion Alliance, 1934), esp. Jacob Katzman's remarks, 20, Central Zionist Archives (hereafter cited as CZA).

71. Moshe Cohen, "First Steps, 1911–1929," 6; Golda Meir, *My Life* (New York: Dell, 1975), 124–126; Yehuda Riemer, "Haaliyah hahaluzit mizfon Ameri-

kah," 122–124; Ruth Bondy, *Hashaliah: hayav vemoto shel Enzo Sereni* (Tel Aviv: Am Oved, 1973), esp. chap. 14.

72. "Hamifkad haklali shel haovdim haivriim be-Eretz Israel, March 2, 1937," in *Pinkas Hahistadrut Haklalit Shel Haovdim Haivriim be-Eretz Israel*, January 1938, esp. tables 18 and 19, reprinted in Yehuda Riemer, "Haaliyah hahaluzit mizfon Amerikah," 137, n. 68. According to Samuel Grand, the first group of fifty certified immigrants, screened by the Vaad Lemaan Hehaluz, left for Palestine on the SS *Mauretania* in February 1930; see Samuel Grand, "A History of Zionist Youth Organizations," 217.

73. *Condensed Report of the National Executive. Submitted to the delegates of the YPZA Convention, Detroit, October 8–11, 1936* (New York: Young Poale Zion Alliance, 1936), 7, American Habonim Archives, UKM.

74. "Condensed Report of the 14th YPZA Convention," *YPZA News and Views*, October 26, 1936, esp. Saadia Gelb's remarks, 6, American Habonim Archives, UKM.

75. Ibid.

76. *Report of the Second Pegishah of the Young Poale Zion Alliance Held at Accord Kvuzah, Accord, New York, August 29, 1937* (New York: Young Poale Zion, 1937), esp. Ben Halpern's remarks, 3–4, CZA.

77. Ibid. Saadia Gelb later recalled that youth movement leaders "trained in the European tradition saw no flaw in a 'kid' of fourteen accepting a life commitment to a specific party program. . . . We insisted that youth be educated, motivated, inspired, activated, but not indoctrinated." Saadia Gelb, "The Founding of Habonim, 1930–1935," 11.

78. See Jehuda Reinharz, "Hashomer Hazair in Germany (I), 1928–1933," *Leo Baeck Institute Year Book* 31 (1986): 173–208; W. Glicksman, "The Haluz Ideology and Experience as Reflected in the Yiddish Novel in Poland, 1919–1939," *YIVO Annual of Jewish Social Science* 14 (1969): 270–284; David I. Macleod, *Building Character in the American Boy: The Boy Scouts, YMCA and Their Forerunners, 1870–1920* (Madison: University of Wisconsin Press, 1983), chaps. 8–14.

79. These figures are derived from Samuel Grand, "A History of Zionist Youth Organizations," 218; and *American Jewish Year Book*: vol. 32 (1930), 197; vol. 33 (1931), 251; vol. 34 (1932), 219.

80. Saadia Gelb, "The Founding of Habonim," 9–13.

81. Ibid., 14.

82. "The Founding Convention, 1935," in David Breslau, ed., *Arise and Build*, 18.

83. *Haboneh*, November 1936, 1, 1–61, Jewish Student Organizations, box 18, AJHS. The name was subsequently changed to Habonim Labor Zionist Youth.

84. Samuel Grand, "A History of Zionist Youth Organizations," 219, 238–239.

85. "Habonim Prospectus," in David Breslau, ed., *Arise and Build*, 19.

86. *Haboneh*, November 1936, 3–4, I–61, Jewish Student Organizations, box 18, AJHS.

87. Saadia Gelb, "The Founding of Habonim," 14.

88. Samuel Grand, "A History of Zionist Youth Organizations," 221–224, 238; Sophie Udin, "The Beginning," in David Breslau, ed., *Adventure in Pioneering: The Story of 25 Years of Habonim Camping* (New York: Chay Commission of the Labor Zionist Movement of New York, 1957), 16–17.

89. Ben-Zion Ilan, "Our Movement Today," *YPZA News and Views* (1937), 3. CZA; see also *Condensed Report of the National Executive. Submitted to the 14th Young Poale Zion Alliance Convention, Detroit, October 8–11, 1936* (New York: Young Poale Zion Alliance, 1936), esp. Saadia Gelb's remarks, 17, American Habonim Archives, UKM.

90. Allon Gal, *Socialist-Zionism: Theory and Issues in Contemporary Jewish Nationalism* (Cambridge, Mass.: Schenkman, 1973), 188.

91. This information is based on interviews with Jacob Katzman, New York City, July 21, 1988; Saadia Gelb, Kfar Blum, Israel, April 13, 1990, and July 5, 1993; and Kieve Skidell, Kfar Blum, Israel, April 13, 1990.

92. For a contemporary account of this conflict, see the transcript of the debate concerning Hehaluz and Hashomer Hazair which took place at the fourth Histadrut convention: "Havikuah basheelat aliyah veavodah," *Haveidah hareviit shel Hahistadrut, February 12–18, 1933* (Tel Aviv: Havaad Hapoel, 1933), 121–139, and also Eliahu Dobkin's statement, 143–145.

93. Hashomer Hazair maintained a stringent code of personal behavior. Like their European counterparts, American movement members foreswore certain "bourgeois" activities such as ballroom dancing, smoking, and cosmetics. See Ariel Hurwitz, ed., *Against the Stream: Seven Decades of Hashomer Hazair in North America* (Israel: Association of North American Shomrim and Yad Yaari, Givat Haviva, 1994), esp. 22, 57, 197.

94. Nahum Guttman, "Hehaluz in America," in David Breslau, ed., *Arise and Build*, 29.

95. Shmuel Yavnieli, "Darko hapolitit shel Hashomer Hazair," *Davar*, July 16, 1935, 1.

96. In the preface to an English translation of Yavnieli's article, the editor of *YPZA News and Views* wrote: "In this article the double book-keeping ideology of Hashomer Hazair is clearly revealed. In America, Hashomer Hazair parades under the banner of a pure and simple "scouting *haluz* organization." . . . How this argumentation reminds us of the Bundists! Have not the Bundists termed the Poalei Zion movement reactionary? Have they not maintained that our struggle for Zionism hinders the social revolution and weakens the class struggle of the proletariat?" See "Regarding Hashomer Hazair," *YPZA News and Views*, February 14, 1936, 4, CZA.

97. Ruth Bondy, *Hashaliah*, chap. 12; Clara Urquhart and Peter Ludwig Brent, *Enzo Sereni: A Hero of Our Times* (London: Robert Hale, 1967), 100–112.

98. "Letter from Enzo Sereni written before his departure from America, May 13, 1937," mimeographed manuscript, 1, 7, Enzo Sereni Papers, Lavon Institute for Labor Research (hereafter cited as LILR).

99. "Letter from Enzo Sereni," 8; Enzo Sereni's remarks on the organizational and cultural activities of the YPZA as recorded at the fourteenth YPZA Convention held in Detroit, reprinted in *YPZA News and Views*, October 1936, 4–5, CZA.

100. Ruth Bondy, *Hashaliah*, 228–229.

101. See Enzo Sereni and R. E. Ashery, eds., *Jews and Arabs in Palestine: Studies in a National and Colonial Problem* (New York: Hehaluz Press, 1936), 4a.

102. Enzo Sereni, "Towards a New Orientation of Zionist Policy," in ibid., 298.

103. Anita Shapira, *Land and Power*, chaps. 4–5.

104. Ruth Bondy, *Hashaliah*, 238–239.

105. Moshe Zemah, "Sereni keish Kibbutz Givat Brenner," in *Haim Enzo Sereni: 40 shanah lemoto* (Israel: Yad Tabenkin, Efal and Hatnuah Hakibbutzit Hameuhedet, 1985), 32–36.

106. The reference is to Vladimir Jabotinsky's concept of a nation's internal unity. The principle has two aspects: "the nation's hegemony toward both the individual and partial associations like classes." See Shlomo Avineri, *The Making of Modern Zionism: The Intellectual Origins of the Jewish State* (New York: Basic Books, 1981), 171–178.

107. "Letter from Enzo Sereni," 9, emphasis in original.

108. Ibid., 9–10. The findings of the committee read: "The charges which Hashomer Hazair brought against Sereni have their origin in various hearsay reports and words taken out of their [context] which were repeated from mouth to mouth but whose truth also is not proven. . . . *Haver* [comrade] Sereni, who is the representative of the Histadrut, had the right and the duty to come into continuous contact with all the youth movements associated with the Histadrut. Such direct and continuous contact between the representative of the Histadrut and the youth groups of Hashomer Hazair in America will do more to further the relations between them than casual meetings and private discussions of an accidental sort. Representatives of Hashomer Hazair must therefore inform their *snifim* [groups] that they must invite Haver Sereni to come to them and to visit them, and they must assist Haver Sereni in these visits. . . . We have heard from the representatives of the Hashomer Hazair reports of the condition which does not allow them to participate today actively in the *merkaz* [executive committee] of Hehaluz. In order to avoid misunderstanding, in order to strengthen the work of Hehaluz, we propose to them that they renew their efforts to find a way for themselves to participate more actively and more intimately in the *merkaz* Hehaluz." Ibid., 10–11.

109. Ruth Bondy, *Hashaliah*, 238–239.

110. "Letter from Enzo Sereni," 11, emphasis in original.

111. *Our Role in the Hehaluz: Consensus of Opinion of the National Executive regarding Our Present Position in Hehaluz* (New York: YPZA, 1937), 2, CZA.

112. Ben-Zion Ilan, *An American Soldier/Pioneer in Israel*, 31.

113. David Breslau, "The Gordonia: A Page in Its History," YPZA News and Views, manuscript, n.d., 13. CZA; David Breslau, "Under Fire, 1936–1940," in David Breslau, ed., *Arise and Build*, 37; David Breslau, *Gordonia in America. In Tribute to Yaacov Levin* (Published by his friends and pupils, 1984), 10, AJHS.

114. See the report entitled "Department of Immigration," in *Report of the Executives of the Zionist Organisation and the Jewish Agency for Palestine Submitted to the XXI Zionist Congress and VI Session of the Council of the Jewish Agency at Geneva, Elul 5699/August 1939* (Jerusalem: Executives of the Zionist Organisation and the Jewish Agency for Palestine, 1939), esp. 293, 295, 297–298, 307–311; Ben-Zion Ilan, *An American Soldier/Pioneer in Israel*, 22.

115. Between August 1937 and March 1939, only ten immigration certificates were allotted to American Hehaluz by the World Zionist Organization. *Report of the Executives of the Zionist Organisation and the Jewish Agency for Palestine*, 310.

116. Yosef Miller, "Haluziut in America," in *Haluz and Youth: A Yearbook Devoted to the Cause of Haluziut in America* (New York: Haluziut and Youth Commission of the Labor Zionist Movement, 1952), 6; Ben-Zion Ilan, *An American Soldier/Pioneer in Israel*, 23–27.

117. David Breslau, "Under Fire," 35; "Review of Twenty-Five Years," in David Breslau, ed., *Adventure in Pioneering*, 69.

118. Ben-Zion Ilan, "Our Movement Today," 2.

119. Yehuda Riemer, "Haaliyah hahaluzit mizfon Amerikah," 137.

NOTES TO CHAPTER 5

1. Benny Kraut, "American Jewish Leaders: The Great, Greater, and Greatest," *American Jewish History*, December 1988, 228.

2. Michael A. Meyer, *Response to Modernity: A History of the Reform Movement in Judaism* (New York: Oxford University Press, 1988), 326.

3. Ibid., 320.

4. Quoted in Herbert Parzen, "Conservative Judaism and Zionism, 1896–1923: A Documentary Account," *Herzl Year Book*, vol. 6 (1964–1965), 315.

5. Ibid., 319.

6. Moshe Davis, "Israel Friedlaender's Minute Book of the Achavah Club, 1909–1912," in *Mordecai M. Kaplan Jubilee Volume*, ed. Moshe Davis (New York: Jewish Theological Seminary of America, 1953), 170–171; Mel Scult, *Judaism Faces the Twentieth Century: A Biography of Mordecai M. Kaplan* (Detroit: Wayne State University Press, 1993), 106–107.

7. Mordecai M. Kaplan, *Judaism as a Civilization: Toward a Reconstruction of American Jewish Life* (New York: Thomas Yoseloff, 1934), 328–329.

8. Eliezer Schweid, *The Land of Israel: National Home or Land of Destiny?*, trans. Deborah Greniman (London: Associated University Presses, 1985), 157–212; see also Emanuel S. Goldsmith, Mel Scult, and Robert M. Seltzer, eds., *The American Judaism of Mordecai M. Kaplan* (New York: New York University Press, 1990), esp. Meir Ben-Hiron, "Ahad Haam in Kaplan: Roads Crossing and Parting," 221–233; S. Daniel Breslauer, "Kaplan, Abraham Joshua Heschel and Martin Buber: Three Approaches to Jewish Revival," 234–253; and Jack J. Cohen, "Reflections on Kaplan's Zionism," 408, 412.

9. Mordecai M. Kaplan, *Judaism as a Civilization*, 251.

10. William James, *Talks to Teachers on Psychology and to Students on Some of Life's Ideals* (reprint, Cambridge, Mass.: Harvard University Press, 1983); *Santayana on America: Essays, Notes, and Letters on American Life*, ed. Richard Colton Lyon (New York: Harcourt, Brace and Wohl, 1968); Josiah Royce, *Race Questions, Provincialism, and Other American Problems* (New York: Macmillan, 1908).

11. Sarah Schmidt, "Horace M. Kallen: The Zionist Chapter of His Life," *Reconstructionist*, November 1975, 28.

12. Sarah Schmidt, "The *Perushim*: A Secret Episode in American Zionist History," *American Jewish Historical Quarterly*, December 1975, 123.

13. Maier Bryan Fox, "Labor Zionism in America: The Challenge of the 1920s," *American Jewish Archives*, April 1983, 55; Emanuel Neumann, *In the Arena: An Autobiographical Memoir* (New York: Herzl Press, 1976), 48–49.

14. Horace M. Kallen, *Zionism and World Politics: A Study in History and Social Psychology* (Garden City, N.Y.: Doubleday, Page, 1921), 3.

15. Naomi W. Cohen, *American Jews and the Zionist Idea* (New York: Ktav Publishing House, 1975), chap. 2, "Zionism as Progressivism," esp. 16–17.

16. Ben Halpern and Jehuda Reinharz, *Zionism and the Creation of a New Society* (New York: Oxford University Press, 1998), chap. 7.

17. Quoted in Sarah Schmidt, "Toward the Pittsburgh Program: Horace M. Kallen, Philosopher of an American Zionism," in *Herzl Year Book*, vol. 8 (1978), 23.

18. Melvin I. Urofsky, *American Zionism from Herzl to the Holocaust* (Garden City, N.Y.: Anchor/Doubleday, 1975), 255–256; Sarah L. Schmidt, "Toward the Pittsburgh Program," 18–36.

19. For fuller treatment of Greenberg, see Robert M. Seltzer, "Hayim Greenberg, Jewish Intellectual," in Carole S. Kessner, ed., *The Other New York Intellectuals* (Albany: State University of New York Press, 1995), 25–50; Mark A. Raider, "Toward a Re-examination of American Zionist Leadership: The Case of Hayim Greenberg," *Journal of Israeli History* 15 (Summer 1994): 133–160.

20. *Enziklopedyah shel galuyot*, vol. 11 (1971), 295–296.

21. Paul Mendes-Flohr and Jehuda Reinharz, eds., *The Jew in the Modern World:*

A Documentary History, 2d ed. (New York: Oxford University Press, 1995), 555–556.

22. *Enziklopedyah shel galuyot*, vol. 11 (1971), 589–590.

23. Salo Baron, *The Russian Jews under Tsars and Soviets*, 2d ed. (New York: Schocken Books, 1987), chap. 14.

24. Hagit Lavsky, *Beterem puranut: darkam veyihudam shel zionut germania, 1918–1932* (Jerusalem: Hozaat Sfarim Al Shem J. L. Magnes, Hauniversitah Haivrit, 1989).

25. Robert M. Seltzer, "Hayim Greenberg, Jewish Intellectual," 33–34.

26. See Jehuda Reinharz, "On Defining Jewish National Autonomy: Demarcating Ideological Boundaries," in Israel Bartal, ed., *Israel Heilprin Memorial Volume* (Jerusalem: Merkaz Zalman Shazar), in press.

27. Shlomo Avineri, *The Making of Modern Zionism: The Intellectual Origins of the Jewish State* (New York: Basic Books, 1981), 158.

28. See Arthur Hertzberg, ed., *The Zionist Idea: A Historical Analysis and Reader* (New York: Atheneum, 1981), 372.

29. Shlomo Avineri, *Arlosoroff* (London: Weidenfeld and Nicolson, 1989), chap. 2.

30. See "Hasozialism haamami shel hayehudim," in *Kitvei Chaim Arlosoroff*, ed. Yaakov Steinberg (Palestine: A. J. Stybel, 1934), vol. 3, esp. 86–88. Arlosoroff's approach to building the Yishuv, to which other Zionist officials also subscribed, is examined in Kenneth W. Stein, *The Land Question in Palestine, 1917–1939* (Chapel Hill: University of North Carolina Press, 1984).

31. Jehuda Reinharz, *Writing the Biography of Chaim Weizmann* (Rehovot: Yad Chaim Weizmann, 1992), 16.

32. Hayim Greenberg, "Mediniyut vaavodah," *Haolam*, February 7, 1923, 70–71.

33. Maurice Samuel, *Little Did I Know: Recollections and Reflections* (New York: Knopf, 1963, 34.

34. Ibid., 44.

35. Ibid., 226–253.

36. Ibid., 256.

37. Maurice Samuel, "The Nature of Avukah," in Herbert I. Bloom, ed., *Avukah Annual of 1928* (New York: Avukah, 1928), 9–10.

38. Ibid., 10.

39. Jonathan D. Sarna, "The Spectrum of Jewish Leadership in Ante-Bellum America," *Journal of American Ethnic History* 1 (Spring 1982): 61–62.

40. Ben Halpern, *A Clash of Heroes: Brandeis, Weizmann, and American Zionism* (New York: Oxford University Press, 1987), 3, 267.

41. Melvin I. Urofsky, *A Voice That Spoke for Justice: The Life and Times of Stephen S. Wise* (Albany: State University of New York Press, 1982); Marc Lee Raphael, *Abba Hillel Silver: A Profile in American Judaism* (New York: Holmes & Meier, 1989).

42. Deborah E. Lipstadt, *The Zionist Career of Louis Lipsky, 1900–1921* (New York: Arno Press, 1982).

43. Editorial, "Our Stand," *Jewish Frontier*, December 1934, 5. The editorial was written by Greenberg.

44. Mordecai M. Kaplan, *A New Zionism*, 2d ed. (New York: Herzl Press and the Jewish Reconstructionist Press, 1959), 20.

45. Evyatar Friesel, "Ahad Haamism in American Zionist Thought," in Jacques Kornberg, ed., *At the Crossroads: Essays on Ahad Haam* (Albany: State University of New York Press, 1983), 133–141.

46. Sarah Schmidt, "Toward the Pittsburgh Program," 19.

47. For example, see Baila Round Shargel, *Practical Dreamer: Israel Friedlaender and the Shaping of American Judaism* (New York: Jewish Theological Seminary of America, 1985), 149–150, 164, 182; Baila Round Shargel, "Kaplan and Israel Fried-laender: Expectation and Failure," in Emanuel S. Goldsmith et al., eds., *The American Judaism of Mordecai M. Kaplan*, 94–121.

48. Mordecai M. Kaplan, *Judaism in Transition* (New York: Covici Friede, 1936), 104–105.

49. See Arthur Hertzberg, ed., *The Zionist Idea*, 531–532.

50. *The Worlds of Maurice Samuel: Selected Writings*, ed. Milton Hindus (Philadelphia: Jewish Publication Society, 1977), 368.

51. *Hayim Greenberg Anthology*, ed. Marie Syrkin (Detroit: Wayne State University Press), 291.

52. Mordecai M. Kaplan, *Judaism as a Civilization*, 251.

53. "Our Stand," 4–5.

54. *Hayim Greenberg Anthology*, 179.

55. Maurice Samuel, *I, The Jew* (New York: Harcourt, Brace, 1927), 159. An earlier version of this selection appeared in *New Palestine* on July 18, 1924, and is reprinted in *The Worlds of Maurice Samuel*, 51. The excerpt cited here was the more widely read of the two texts.

56. Ben Halpern, *A Clash of Heroes: Brandeis, Weizmann, and American Zionism*, 3, 267.

57. Sarah L. Schmidt, *Horace M. Kallen: Prophet of American Zionism* (New York: Carlson, 1995); Samuel Halperin, *The Political World of American Zionism* (reprint, Silver Spring, Md.: Information Dynamics, 1985), 357, n. 134.

58. Mordecai M. Kaplan, ed., *The Jewish Reconstructionist Papers* (New York: Behrman's Jewish Book House, 1936), 207–208.

59. Arthur A. Goren, "The Jewish Press in the United States," in Sally Miller, ed., *The Ethnic Press in the United States: A Historical Analysis and Handbook* (Westport, Conn.: Greenwood Press, 1987), 216.

60. Aaron Berman, *Nazism, the Jews and American Zionism, 1933–1948* (Detroit: Wayne State University Press, 1990), 17.

61. Rebecca Trachtenberg Alpert, "The Quest for Economic Justice: Kaplan's

Response to the Challenge of Communism, 1929–1940," in Emanuel S. Goldsmith et al., eds., *The American Judaism of Mordecai M. Kaplan*, 385–400.

62. Quoted in ibid., 396.

63. Hayim Greenberg, "To a Communist Friend," *Jewish Frontier*, May 1936, 17.

64. See Ber Borochov's "Program for Proletarian Zionism," in Jehuda Reinharz and Paul Mendes-Flohr, eds., *The Jew in the Modern World*, 552–554.

65. Hayim Greenberg, "Socialism Re-examined," *Jewish Frontier*, November 1941, 11.

66. Joseph B. Schechtman, *Rebel and Statesman: The Vladimir Jabotinsky Story, the Early Years* (New York: Thomas Yoseloff, 1958), 388–394; Chanoch (Howard) Rosenblum, "The New Zionist Organization's American Campaign, 1936–1939," *Studies in Zionism* 12 (Autumn 1991): 169–185; Elias Ginsburg, "Is Revision-Zionism Fascist? [*sic*]" *Menorah Journal* 22 (October–December 1934): 190–206.

67. Hayim Greenberg, "Revisionism: A Self-Portrait," *Jewish Frontier*, January 1935, 15. Other examples of Greenberg's writings are "Jabotinsky's Army Marches," *Jewish Frontier*, January 1935: 6; "The Threat of Revisionist Irresponsibility," *Jewish Frontier*, August 1938: 7–9; "The Irresponsible Revisionists," *Jewish Frontier*, November 1943, 6–8.

68. Letter from Stephen S. Wise to Horace M. Kallen, February 21, 1940, 317/16:243, Horace M. Kallen Papers, YIVO Institute for Jewish Research (hereafter cited as YIVO).

69. Letter from Horace M. Kallen to Stephen S. Wise, February 23, 1940, 317/16:243, Horace M. Kallen Papers, YIVO.

70. See Naomi W. Cohen, *The Year after the Riots: American Responses to the Palestine Crisis of 1929–30* (Detroit: Wayne State University Press, 1988).

71. Menahem Kaufman, *An Ambiguous Partnership: Non-Zionists and Zionists in America, 1939–1948* (Jerusalem: Magnes Press, Hebrew University of Jerusalem, and Detroit: Wayne State University Press, 1991), 25–29.

72. Quoted in Naomi W. Cohen, *The Year after the Riots*, 104.

73. Ibid., 105, emphasis in original.

74. Ibid., 105–106.

75. See Maurice S. Friedman, *Martin Buber: The Life of Dialogue* (New York: Harper & Row, 1960), 205–207. For Buber's open letters to Gandhi, see "The Land and Its Possessors," in Martin Buber, *Israel and the World: Essays in a Time of Crisis* (New York: Schocken Books, 1963), 227–233; "A Letter to Gandhi," in Martin Buber, *Pointing the Way*, trans. and ed. Maurice S. Friedman (New York: Harper Torchbooks, 1957), 139–147.

76. Mahatma Gandhi, "Death Has No Terror," *Jewish Frontier*, March 1939, 9.

77. Hayim Greenberg, "We Are Treated as Subhumans—We Are Asked to Be Superhuman," *Jewish Frontier*, March 1939, 13.

78. Arnold J. Toynbee, *A Study of History* (Oxford: Oxford University Press; London: the Royal Institute of International Affairs, 1954), vol. 8, 279, n. 2.

79. Ibid., 289–291.

80. *The Worlds of Maurice Samuel*, 114.

81. Hayim Greenberg, "Palestine Administration Indicted," *Jewish Frontier*, February 1941, 7–9.

82. Chaim Weizmann to Christopher Eastwood, March 10, 1941, *The Letters and Papers of Chaim Weizmann, July 1940–January 1943*, ed. Meyer W. Weisgal et al., English ed., ser. A, vol. 20 (New Brunswick, N.J.: Rutgers University, Transaction Books, 1979), 124; Chaim Weizmann, *Trial and Error* (New York: Harper Bros., 1949), 425.

83. Aaron Berman, *Nazism, the Jews and American Zionism*, 96–100.

84. *Hayim Greenberg Anthology*, 192–193.

85. Lawrence H. Fuchs, *The American Kaleidoscope: Race, Ethnicity and the Civic Culture* (Hanover, N.H.: University Press of New England, 1990), 1–6, 65–69, 73–74.

86. *Hayim Greenberg Anthology*, 179.

87. See the special issue "The Greatest American Jewish Leaders" in *American Jewish History*, December 1988, 169–200; Evyatar Friesel, "Criteria and Conception in the Historiography of German and American Zionism," *Studies in Zionism* 1 (Autumn 1980): 296–297.

88. Melvin I. Urofsky, "American Jewish Leadership," *American Jewish History* 70 (1981): 401.

89. Ben Halpern, *A Clash of Heroes*, 9.

90. See Jacob Katz's classic essay "The Forerunners of Zionism," in Jehuda Reinharz and Anita Shapira, eds., *Essential Papers on Zionism* (New York: New York University Press, 1996), 33–45.

NOTES TO CHAPTER 6

1. *American Jewish Year Book*, vol. 37 (1935), 148.

2. As early as 1931, a survey of Reform Judaism in several cities reported that Zionists were present in one out of every five Reform families. See *Reform Judaism in the Large Cities: A Survey* (New York: American Jewish Historical Society [hereafter cited as AJHS], 1931), 13.

3. Quoted in editorial, "Meeting of Washington Conference," *Jewish Frontier*, February 1935, 3–4.

4. Jehuda Reinharz, *Fatherland or Promised Land? The Dilemma of the German Jew, 1893–1914* (Ann Arbor: University of Michigan Press, 1975), 154–158.

5. Paul Mendes-Flohr and Jehuda Reinharz, eds., *The Jew in the Modern World: A Documentary History*, 2d ed. (New York: Oxford University Press, 1995), 517–518.

6. See Michael A. Meyer, "American Reform Judaism and Zionism: Early Efforts at Ideological Rapprochement," *Studies in Zionism* 7 (Spring 1983): 49–64.

7. *American Jewish Year Book*, vol. 38 (1936), 196–197.

8. Leni Yahil, *The Holocaust* (New York: Oxford University Press, 1987), 100–104.

9. *Encyclopaedia Judaica*, vol. 7 (1972), 1012–1013.

10. Aaron Berman, *Nazism, the Jews and American Zionism, 1933–1948* (Detroit: Wayne State University Press, 1990), 38–40.

11. Quoted in *American Jewish Year Book*, vol. 39 (1937), 239–240.

12. Gail Malmgreen, "Labor and the Holocaust: The Jewish Labor Committee and the Anti-Nazi Struggle," *Labor's Heritage*, October 1991, 22.

13. Henry L. Feingold, *A Time for Searching: Entering the Mainstream, 1920–1945* (Baltimore: Johns Hopkins University Press, 1992), 236–238; Samuel Halperin, *The Political World of American Zionism* (reprint, Silver Spring, Md.: Information Dynamics, 1985), 162–165; Howard M. Sachar, *A History of the Jews in America* (New York: Knopf, 1992), 512–513.

14. Letter to the Socialist Labor International, March 19, 1936; see enclosure 1 ("The German Transfer Agreement"), 3–4, A180/68, Baruch Zuckerman Papers, Central Zionist Archives (hereafter cited as CZA).

15. See Alexander Bloom, *Prodigal Sons: The New York Intellectuals and Their World* (New York: Oxford University Press, 1986).

16. See David G. Dalin, *From Marxism to Judaism: Collected Essays of Will Herberg* (New York: Markus Wiener, 1989), xiii–xxvii, 3–21.

17. Marie Syrkin, "The Moscow Trials," *Jewish Frontier*, May 1937, 15–16.

18. Zosa Szajkowski, *Jews, Wars and Communism*, vol. 1, *The Attitude of American Jews to World War I, the Russian Revolutions of 1917 and Communism (1914–1945)* (New York: Ktav Publishing House, 1972), 412–416; *The Jewish People Past and Present*, ed. Raphael R. Abramovitch et al. (New York: Marstin Press, 1948), vol. 2, 428.

19. See Maurice J. Karpf, *Jewish Community Organization in the United States: An Outline of Types of Organizations, Activities and Problems* (New York: Bloch, 1938), 145–146.

20. Interviews with Saadia Gelb, Kfar Blum, Israel, July 5, 1993; and Abe Cohen, Tel Aviv, July 22, 1993.

21. *Jewish Social Worker*, January 1939, 2, no. 1629, CZA.

22. *American Jewish Year Book*, vol. 37 (1935), 151–152; Joseph B. Schechtman, *Rebel and Statesman: The Vladimir Jabotinsky Story, the Early Years* (New York: Thomas Yoseloff, 1958), 388–394; Chanoch (Howard) Rosenblum, "The New Zionist Organization's American Campaign, 1936–1939," *Studies in Zionism* 12 (Autumn 1991): 169–185; Elias Ginsburg, "Is Revision-Zionism Fascist?" [*sic*], *Menorah Journal*, October–December 1934, 190–206.

23. Pierre M. Atlas, "Defining the Fringe: Two Examples of the Marginaliza-

tion of Revisionist Zionism in the 1930s," *Israel Bulletin Studies* 9 (Spring 1994): 7–11.

24. Hayim Greenberg, "Revisionism: A Self-Portrait," *Jewish Frontier*, January 1935, 15.

25. *Revisionists and Mizrachi, a Symposium Held in New York on Saturday Evening, February 3, 1934, at Which the Speakers Were Hayim Greenberg and Joseph Sprinzak,* trans. Maximilian Hurwitz (Milwaukee: Spiegel, 1934), 5–6, AJHS.

26. For example, editorial, "Jabotinsky's Army Marches," *Jewish Frontier*, January 1935, 6; Hayim Greenberg, "Revisionism: A Self-Portrait," *Jewish Frontier*, January 1935, 15–16; Hayim Greenberg, "The Threat of Revisionist Irresponsibility," *Jewish Frontier*, August 1938: 7–9; Hayim Greenberg, "The Irresponsible Revisionists," *Jewish Frontier*, November 1943, 6–8; Marie Syrkin, "The Essence of Revisionism: An Analysis of a Fascist Tendency in Jewry," *Jewish Frontier*, April 1940, 6–10.

27. See Vladimir Jabotinsky's statement "What the Zionist-Revisionists Want," in Paul Mendes-Flohr and Jehuda Reinharz, eds., *The Jew in the Modern World*, 594–597.

28. Editorial, "Immigration for Labor Palestine!" *Jewish Advocate*, February 5, 1935, 2.

29. Letter from Bert Goldstein reprinted in *Jewish Frontier*, December 1939, 26.

30. Letter from Felix Frankfurter to Robert Szold, ca. July 1935, A406/132, Robert Szold Papers, CZA, emphasis in original.

31. *American Jewish Year Book*, vol. 37 (1935), 150; *Report of the Executives of the Zionist Organisation Submitted to the XIXth Zionist Congress at Lucerne, August 20th–30th, 1935,* 241; *Palestine Post*, June 25, 1935, 1; *Palestine Post*, June 26, 1935, 5; *American Hebrew and Jewish Tribune*, June 28, 1935, 131, 140; *Jewish Examiner*, June 28, 1935, 1, 3; *American Hebrew and Jewish Tribune*, July 5, 1935, 145, 164. For a detailed analysis of election results, see Yitzhak Gruenbaum, *Hashekel: ezrahut zionit* (Jerusalem: Hanhalat Hahistadrut Hazionit, 1936), 19–23.

32. Telegram from Morris Rothenberg to Elihu D. Stone, April 16, 1935, P-555, Elihu D. Stone Papers, AJHS.

33. Address by Robert Szold to the Zionist Organization of America convention, 1935, n.p., A406/111, Robert Szold Papers, CZA.

34. Letter from Stephen S. Wise to Ludwig Lewisohn, September 23, 1935, Ludwig Lewisohn Papers, no. 49, 1935–1938, American Jewish Archives (hereafter cited as AJA).

35. "The Nineteenth Zionist Congress," *Reconstructionist*, October 4, 1935, 4.

36. Ben Halpern and Jehuda Reinharz, *Zionism and the Creation of a New Society* (New York: Oxford University Press, 1998), chap. 10.

37. *Jewish Examiner*, June 28, 1935, 2; "Zionists Hold Convention in Atlantic City," *American Hebrew and Jewish Tribune*, July 5, 1935, 146, 160; editorial, "It Was a Nice Convention," *Jewish Examiner*, July 12, 1935, 4.

38. Editorial, *New Palestine*, June 21, 1935, reprinted in *Palestine Post*, July 17, 1935, 4.

39. See Menahem Kaufmann, *An Ambiguous Partnership: Non-Zionists and Zionists in America, 1939–1948* (Jerusalem: Magnes Press, Hebrew University, and Detroit: Wayne State University Press, 1991), 11–22.

40. Letter from Cyrus Adler to Felix M. Warburg, July 19, 1937, in *Cyrus Adler: Selected Letters*, ed. Ira Robinson (Philadelphia: Jewish Publication Society of America and Jewish Theological Seminary of America, 1985), vol. 2, 336–337.

41. Deborah Dash Moore, *Bnai Brith and the Challenge of Ethnic Leadership* (Albany: State University of New York Press, 1981).

42. Ibid., 174–184.

43. Joseph Schlossberg, "Three Problems," *Jewish Frontier*, April 1937, 21.

44. Ibid., 21, 23.

45. Deborah Dash Moore, *At Home in America: Second Generation New York Jews* (New York: Columbia University Press 1981), chap. 8; Lawrence H. Fuchs, *The Political Behavior of American Jews* (Glencoe, Ill.: Free Press, 1956), 73–79; Monroe Billington and Cal Clark, "Rabbis and the New Deal: Clues to Jewish Political Behavior," *American Jewish History* 80 (Winter 1990–1991): 193–212.

46. *Year Book of the Central Conference of American Rabbis*, vol. 48, ed. Isaac E. Marcuson (Philadelphia: Jewish Publication Society, 1938), 287.

47. Ibid., 286.

48. Ibid., 287.

49. Ibid., 287–288.

50. Joseph Schlossberg, "In Six Countries," *Jewish Frontier*, July 1937, 22–25; Jacob Lestshinsky, "Bankruptcy in Poland," *Jewish Frontier*, November 1937, 10–14; Yisrael Gutman, "Polish Antisemitism between the Wars: An Overview," in Yisrael Gutman, Ezra Mendelsohn, Jehuda Reinharz, and Chone Shmeruk, eds., *The Jews of Poland between Two World Wars* (Hanover, N.H.: University Press of New England, 1989), 97–108; Ezra Mendelsohn, "Jewish Reactions to Antisemitism in Interwar East Central Europe," in Jehuda Reinharz, ed., *Living with Antisemitism: Modern Jewish Responses* (Hanover, N.H.: University Press of New England, 1987), 296–310.

51. Ludwig Lewisohn, "Our Popular Front—The Shekel," *Jewish Frontier*, May 1937, 32, emphasis in original.

52. "A Call to the Jewish Masses" (declaration issued by the Labor Zionist conference, April 10–11, 1937), P-672, Louis Lipsky Papers, box 8, file 2, AJHS.

53. *American Jewish Year Book*, vol. 37 (1935), 150.

54. Mark A. Raider, "Where American Zionism Differed: Abba Hillel Silver Reconsidered," in Mark A. Raider, Jonathan D. Sarna, and Ronald W. Zweig, eds., *Abba Hillel Silver and American Zionism* (London: Frank Cass, 1997), 98–100.

55. *American Jewish Year Book*, vol. 39 (1937), 236–238.

56. *Palestine Royal Commission Report, July 1937* (London: His Majesty's Stationery Office, 1937), 394.

57. *American Jewish Year Book*, vol. 40 (1938), 105–109.

58. Avraham Ben-Shalom, "A Different Point of View," *Jewish Frontier*, July 1937, 20–22.

59. Itzhak Galnoor, *The Partition of Palestine: Decision Crossroads in the Zionist Movement* (Albany: State University of New York Press, 1995), 75–76; Gabriel Sheffer, *Moshe Sharett: Biography of a Political Moderate* (Oxford: Oxford University Press, 1996), 76–89.

60. Abraham Revusky, "Facts behind Partition," *Jewish Frontier*, August 1937, 7.

61. Anita Shapira, *Land and Power: The Zionist Resort to Self-Defense* (New York: Oxford University Press, 1992), chap. 6; Shabtai Teveth, *Ben-Gurion and the Palestinian Arabs: From Peace to War* (Oxford: Oxford University Press, 1985), 178–183.

62. Itzhak Galnoor, *The Partition of Palestine*, chap. 8; Chaim Weizmann, *Trial and Error* (New York: Harper Bros., 1949), 388–398; Shabtai Teveth, *Ben-Gurion: The Burning Ground, 1886–1948* (Boston: Houghton Mifflin, 1987), chaps. 34–35; *American Jewish Year Book*, vol. 39 (1937), 290–291.

63. *Report of the Executives of the Zionist Organisation and of the Jewish Agency for Palestine Submitted to the XXth Zionist Congress and the Vth Session of the Council of the Jewish Agency at Zurich, August 1937* (Jerusalem: Executives of the Zionist Organisation and the Jewish Agency for Palestine, 1937), 40–41.

64. *American Jewish Year Book*, vol. 39 (1937), 291.

65. Michael Brown, "Henrietta Szold's Progressive American Vision of the Yishuv," in Allon Gal, ed., *Envisioning Israel: The Changing Ideals and Images of North American Jews* (Jerusalem: Magnes Press, Hebrew University of Jerusalem, and Detroit: Wayne State University Press, 1996), 71. For contemporary views, see Rose Halprin, "Portrait of Hadassah," *Jewish Frontier*, August 1937, 16–19; also the correspondence of Henrietta Szold, Irma Lindheim, and Jessie Sampter with Manya Shohat in *The Letters and Papers of Manya Shohat*, ed. Jehuda Reinharz and Shulamit Reinharz (Israel: Yad Yizhak Ben-Zvi), in progress. I am grateful to Jehuda Reinharz and Shulamit Reinharz for making this material available to me.

66. *American Jewish Year Book*, vol. 39 (1937), 291.

67. Samuel Blumenfeld, "The Zionist Situation in America," *Reconstructionist* 4, part 1, February 25, 1938, 10–16, and part 2, March 11, 1938, 10–13; Yitzhak Gruenbaum, *Hashekel*, 20.

68. Samuel Halperin, *The Political World of American Zionism*, 327.

69. *Palestine Royal Commission Report, July 1937*, 382; *Palestine Post*, August 12, 1937, 1, 4, August 15, 1937, 1, August 16, 1937, 1, 4; *American Hebrew*, August 13, 1937, 7, 15, August 20, 1937, 1, 6, 15, August 27, 1937, 1–3, 10, 12, 17, 22.

70. *Palestine Post*, August 11, 1937, 4.

71. *American Jewish Year Book*, vol. 40 (1938), 106.

72. Hayim Fineman, "The New Boundary Lines," *Jewish Frontier*, August 1937, 13.

73. *Palestine Post*, August 12, 1937, 1, 4.

74. Ibid.

75. "Report of the American Jewish Committee," *American Jewish Year Book*, vol. 40 (1938), 626.

76. Ibid., 625.

77. Moses Rischin, "The American Jewish Committee and Zionism, 1906–1922," in *Herzl Year Book*, ed. Raphael Patai, vol. 5 (1963), 78–81.

78. *American Jewish Year Book*, vol. 41 (1939), 156–161.

79. *American Jewish Year Book*, vol. 38 (1936), 199–200.

80. Henry L. Feingold, *A Time for Searching*, 176–182.

81. Bernard Wasserstein, *Britain and the Jews of Europe, 1939–1945* (Oxford: Oxford University Press, 1988), p. 46.

82. See Yehuda Bauer, *American Jewry and the Holocaust: The American Jewish Joint Distribution Committee, 1939–1945* (Detroit: Wayne State University Press, 1981), 197–199; Esco Foundation for Palestine, *Palestine: A Study of Jewish, British and Arab Policies* (New Haven, Conn.: Yale University Press, 1947), vol. 2, 950–955; Leni Yahil, *The Holocaust*, pp. 94–95.

83. *Palestine Post*, March 23, 1938, 90–92.

84. Esco Foundation, *Palestine: A Study of Jewish, British and Arab Policies*, vol. 2, 908–922.

85. Naomi W. Cohen, *Not Free to Desist: The American Jewish Committee, 1906–1966* (Philadelphia: Jewish Publication Society of America, 1972), 257–260.

86. Quoted in "Jewish Vote Seen as Threat to Unity," *New York Times*, May 29, 1938, 6.

87. Ibid.

88. Samuel Halperin, *The Political World of American Zionism*, 164–166; Esco Foundation, *Palestine: A Study of Jewish, British and Arab Policies*, vol. 2, 1117.

89. *Reconstructionist*, May 20, 1938, 3.

90. Reprinted in *Reconstructionist*, June 3, 1938, 4.

91. Menahem Kaufmann, *An Ambiguous Partnership*, 49.

92. See Louis Lipsky, *Memoirs in Profile* (Philadelphia: Jewish Publication Society of America, 1975), 398–401.

93. Menahem Kaufmann, *An Ambiguous Partnership*, 48–49; Deborah Dash Moore, *B'nai B'rith and the Challenge of Ethnic Leadership*, 184–185.

94. *Jewish Frontier*, September 1938, 30.

95. See Morris Fine, "Review of the Year 5699," *American Jewish Year Book*, vol. 41 (1939), 200; "Revisionism Redividus," *Reconstructionist*, November 24, 1939, 5; "Correspondence," *Reconstructionist*, December 8, 1939, 13–16.

96. Samuel Halperin, *The Political World of American Zionism*, 161.

97. Moshe Cohen, ed., *Labor Zionist Handbook: The Aims, Activities and History*

of the Labor Zionist Movement in America (New York: Poale Zion Zeire Zion of America, 1939), 148–153; Hyman J. Fliegel, *The Life and Times of Max Pine* (New York: Published by the author, 1959), chap. 2.

98. *Palestine Post*, January 16, 1939, 1–2; Yehuda Bauer, *My Brother's Keeper: A History of the American Jewish Joint Distribution Committee, 1929–1939* (Philadelphia: Jewish Publication Society of America, 1974), 254–255; *American Jewish Year Book*, vol. 41 (1939), 230–231.

99. Menahem Kaufman, *An Ambiguous Partnership*, 31–43.

100. Charles E. Schulman, "Fundraiser Par Excellence," in Marc Lee Rapahael, ed., *Understanding American Jewish Philanthropy* (New York: Ktav Publishing House, 1979), 97–101.

NOTES TO CONCLUSION

1. Quoted in Anita Shapira, *Berl: The Biography of a Socialist Zionist* (Cambridge: Cambridge University Press, 1984), 278; see also *Palestine Post*, August 21, 1939, 1.

2. Quoted in Anita Shapira, *Berl*, 278.

3. *Palestine Post*, August 21, 1939, 2.

4. See Jehuda Reinharz, *Zionism and the Great Powers: A Century of Foreign Policy* (New York: Leo Baeck Institute, 1994), 11–12.

5. See Carole S. Kessner, ed., *The "Other" New York Jewish Intellectuals* (New York: New York University Press, 1994).

6. Samuel Halperin, *The Political World of American Zionism* (reprint, Silver Spring, Md.: Information Dynamics, 1985), 169–170.

7. Reprinted in *Jewish Frontier*, November 1941, 3.

8. See the discussions of nationalism and national identity in Matthew Frye Jacobson, *Special Sorrows: The Diasporic Imagination of Irish, Polish and Jewish Immigrants in the United States* (Cambridge, Mass.: Harvard University Press, 1995).

9. Melech Epstein, *Jewish Labor in USA: An Industrial, Political and Cultural History of the Jewish Labor Movement* (reprint, New York: Ktav Publishing House, 1969), vol. 2, 411–412.

10. Gideon Shimoni, *The Zionist Ideology* (Hanover, N.H.: University Press of New England, 1995), 383–386.

11. Shabtai Teveth, *Ben-Gurion: The Burning Ground* (Boston: Houghton Mifflin, 1987), 666–671, 683; Gabriel Sheffer, *Moshe Sharett: Biography of a Political Moderate* (New York: Oxford University Press, 1996), 122–123.

12. See David H. Shpiro, "The Political Background of the 1942 Biltmore Resolution," *Herzl Year Book*, vol. 8 (1978), 166–177; Eisuke Naramoto, "Preparation for the Biltmore Conference: Intentions and Calculations of American Zionist Leaders, June 1941–May 1942," *Hosei University Tama Bulletin*, March 1994, 59–88.

13. Shabtai Teveth, *Ben-Gurion*, p. 815.

14. *American Jewish Year Book,* vol. 45 (1943), 206–208.

15. Emanuel Neumann, "Results of Zionist Isolationism," *New Palestine,* May 15, 1942, 14.

16. *New York Herald Tribune,* May 11, 1942, 7; *New York Times,* May 11, 1942, 6.

17. Paul Mendes-Flohr and Jehuda Reinharz, eds., *The Jew in the Modern World: A Documentary History,* 2d ed. (New York: Oxford University Press, 1995), 618.

18. Walter Laqueur, *A History of Zionism* (New York: Holt, Rinehart and Winston, 1972), 548–549.

19. Cited in *The American Jewish Conference: Its Organization and Proceedings of the First Session, August 29 to September 2, 1943, New York, NY,* ed. Alexander S. Kohanski (New York: American Jewish Conference, 1944), 251–258; *Palestine Post,* May 14, 1942, 3.

20. Paul Mendes-Flohr and Jehuda Reinharz, eds., *The Jew in the Modern World,* 582.

21. Leni Yahil, *The Holocaust* (New York: Oxford University Press, 1990), 606–608.

22. Editorial, "Under the Axis," *Jewish Frontier,* November 1942, 3.

23. Walter Laqueur, *A History of Zionism,* 551.

24. See Ben Hecht, *Perfidy* (New York: Julian Messer, 1961); Arthur D. Morse, *While Six Million Died: A Chronicle of American Apathy* (New York: Ace Books, 1967); Saul Friedman, *No Haven for the Oppressed: United States Policy toward Jewish Refugees, 1938–1945* (Detroit: Wayne State University Press, 1973); Monty N. Penkower, *The Jews Were Expendable: Free World Diplomacy and the Holocaust* (Urbana: University of Illinois Press, 1983); Rafael Medoff, *The Deafening Silence: American Jewish Leaders and the Holocaust* (New York: Shapolsky Publishers, 1987).

25. Jehuda Reinharz, *Zionism and the Great Powers,* 12.

26. See Leonard Dinnerstein, *Antisemitism in America* (New York: Oxford University Press, 1994), chap. 7.

27. Salo W. Baron, *The Russian Jew under Tsars and Soviets* (New York: Schocken Books, 1987), chap. 10.

28. Fritz Fischer, *World Power or Decline: The Controversy over Germany's Aims in the First World War* (New York: Norton, 1974), viii.

29. Alex Bein, "American Settlement in Israel," in Moshe Davis, ed., *Israel: Its Role in Civilization* (New York: Jewish Theological Seminary of America, 1956), 298–309.

30. Quoted in *Stephen S. Wise: Servant of the People,* ed. Carl Hermann Voss (Philadelphia: Jewish Publication Society of America, 1969), 250.

31. Henry L. Feingold, *The Politics of Rescue: The Roosevelt Administration and the Holocaust, 1938–1945,* 2d ed. (New York: Holocaust Library, 1970), 262–263.

32. Lawrence H. Fuchs, *The Political Behavior of American Jews* (Glencoe, Ill.:

Free Press, 1956), chap. 7; Deborah Dash Moore, *At Home in America: Second Generation New York Jews* (New York: Columbia University Press, 1981), chap. 8.

33. Quoted in *Encyclopaedia Judaica*, vol. 8 (1971), 851.

34. *Encyclopaedia Judaica*, vol. 2 (1971), 830.

35. Anita Shapira, "Did the Zionist Leadership Foresee the Holocaust?" in Jehuda Reinharz, ed., *Living with Antisemitism: Modern Jewish Responses* (Hanover, N.H.: University Press of New England, 1987), 397–412.

36. Jacob J. Weinstein, *Solomon Goldman: A Rabbi's Rabbi* (New York: Ktav Publishing House, 1973), app. 2, 248, emphasis in original.

37. Editorial, "Mirage in the Jungle," *Jewish Frontier*, December 1938, 3–4.

38. Gerald S. Berman, "From Neustadt to Alaska, 1939: A Failed Attempt at Community Settlement," *Immigrants and Minorities*, March 1987, 66–83; Claus M. Naske, "Jewish Immigration and Alaskan Economic Development: A Study in Futility," *Western States Jewish Historical Quarterly*, January 1976, 139–157. I am grateful to Bernard Reisman, Brandeis University, for alerting me to this literature. See also Rafael Medoff, *The Deafening Silence*, 67–70; editorial, "Another Alaska Bill," *Jewish Frontier*, February 1941, 5–6.

39. Editorial, "Action—Not Just Sympathy," *Jewish Frontier*, August 1939, 4.

40. For further analysis, see Kenneth Stein, *The Land Question in Palestine, 1917–1939* (Chapel Hill: University of North Carolina Press, 1984), chap. 4.

41. Editorial, "Our Duties," *Jewish Frontier*, June 1939, 6.

42. *The American Jewish Conference*, 361–362, 373–377.

43. Paul Mendes-Flohr and Jehuda Reinharz, eds., *The Jew in the Modern World*, 520.

44. Ibid.

45. Editorial, "The Conference Elections," *Jewish Frontier*, July 1943, 3; Aaron Berman, "Rescue through Statehood: American Zionists and the Holocaust," manuscript, January 1992, 23.

46. Abba Hillel Silver, "Toward American Jewish Unity," in Arthur Hertzberg, ed., *The Zionist Idea: A Historical Analysis and Reader* (New York: Atheneum, 1984), 597.

47. Ibid.

48. *The American Jewish Conference*, 177.

49. Naomi W. Cohen, *Not Free to Desist: The American Jewish Committee, 1906–1966* (Philadelphia: Jewish Publication Society of America, 1972), 256–261.

50. *The American Jewish Conference*, 94–96, 107.

51. *New York Times*, September 1, 1943, 12; see also Thomas A. Kolsky, *Jews against Zionism: The American Council for Judaism, 1942–1948* (Philadelphia: Temple University Press, 1990), 74–77.

52. *New Palestine*, September 24, 1943, 29.

53. Telegram from Hayim Greenberg to Stephen S. Wise, June 16, 1945, 125/3, Stephen S. Wise Papers, American Jewish Historical Society.

54. Mark A. Raider, "Where American Zionism Differed: Abba Hillel Silver Reconsidered," in Mark A. Raider. Jonathan D. Sarna, and Ronald W. Zweig, eds., *Abba Hillel Silver and American Zionism* (London: Frank Cass, 1997), 116–119.

55. Bernard Wasserstein, *Britain and the Jews of Europe, 1939–1945* (New York: Oxford University Press, 1988), chap. 1; Henry L. Feingold, *A Time for Searching: Entering the Mainstream, 1920–1945* (Baltimore: John Hopkins University Press, 1992), 242–249.

56. See Arieh Kochavi, *Akurim vepolitikah benleumit: Britania vehaakurim hayehudim leaher milhemet haolam hashniyah* (Tel Aviv: Am Oved, 1992).

57. Arnold Eisen, *The Chosen People in America: A Study in Jewish Religious Ideology* (Bloomington: Indiana University Press, 1983), chap. 2; Yosef Gorny, *The State of Israel in Jewish Public Thought* (New York: New York University Press, 1994), chaps. 1–4.

Selected Bibliography

ARCHIVES AND LIBRARIES

American Jewish Archives, Cincinnati, Ohio
American Jewish Historical Society, Waltham, Massachusetts
Brandeis University Archives and Libraries, Waltham, Massachusetts
Central Zionist Archives, Jerusalem
Naamat USA Archives, New York City
New York Public Library, New York City
Pinhas Lavon Institute for Labor Research, Tel Aviv
Yad Tabenkin–United Kibbutz Movement Archives, Tel Aviv
YIVO Institute for Jewish Research, New York City

NEWSPAPERS, JOURNALS, AND REFERENCE WORKS

American Hebrew
American Hebrew and Jewish Tribune
American Jewish Year Book
Davar
Encyclopaedia Judaica
Encyclopedia of Zionism and Israel
Enziklopedyah shel galuyot
Der forverts
Haolam
Jewish Advocate
Jewish Chronicle
Jewish Education
Jewish Encyclopedia
Jewish Examiner
Jewish Frontier
Maccabean
New Palestine
New York Times
Palestine: The Organ of the British Palestine Committee
Palestine Post

Reconstructionist
Year Book of the Central Conference of American Rabbis
Der yidisher kemfer

PRIMARY SOURCES

Altman, Sima, et al., eds. *Pioneers from America: 75 Years of Hehaluz, 1905–1980.* Tel Aviv: Bogrei Hehaluz America, 1981.

American Jewish Conference: Its Organization and Proceedings of the First Session, August 29 to September 2, 1943, New York, N.Y. Edited by Alexander S. Kohanski. New York: American Jewish Conference, 1943.

American Jewish Conference: Proceedings of the Second Session. December 3–5, 1944. Pittsburgh, Pa. Edited by Alexander S. Kohanski. New York: American Jewish Conference, 1945.

Ben-Gurion, David. "Mi yiten lanu et haarez?" *Hehaluz: prinzipen un oifgeben.* New York: Zentraler Farveltung Fun Hehaluz, 1916. Reprinted in *Asufot,* December 1959.

Blondheim, David S., ed. *Kadimah.* New York: Federation of American Zionists, 1918.

Bloom, Herbert I., ed. *The Avukah Annual of 1928.* New York: Avukah American Student Zionist Federation, 1928.

Borochov, Ber. *Class Struggle and the Jewish Nation: Selected Essays in Marxist Zionism.* Edited by Mitchell Cohen. New Brunswick, N.J.: Transaction Books, 1984.

———. *Nationalism and the Class Struggle: A Marxian Approach to the Jewish Problem.* Edited by Moshe Cohen. New York: Poale Zion–Zeire Zion of America and Young Poale Zion Alliance, 1937.

Breslau, David, ed. *Adventure in Pioneering: The Story of 25 Years of Habonim Camping.* New York: Chay Commission of the Labor Zionist Movement of New York, 1957.

———. *Arise and Build: The Story of American Habonim.* New York: Ichud Habonim Labor Zionist Youth, 1961.

Buber, Martin. *Israel and the World: Essays in a Time of Crisis.* New York: Schocken Books, 1963.

———. *Pointing the Way.* Translated and edited by Maurice S. Friedman. New York: Harper Torchbooks, 1957.

Cohen, Moshe, ed. *Labor Zionist Handbook: The Aims, Activities, and History of the Labor Zionist Movement in America.* New York: Poale Zion Zeire-Zion of America, 1939.

Cyrus Adler: Selected Letters. Edited by Ira Robinson. Philadelphia: Jewish Publication Society of America and Jewish Theological Seminary of America, 1985.

Daily Prayer Book: Hasidur hashalem. Translated and edited by Philip Birnabaum. New York: Hebrew Publishing, 1949.

Davidson, Morris I. *Growing up in Hartford, Connecticut, 1908–1928.* Hartford: Andrew Mountain Press, 1987.

Emma Lazarus: Selections from Her Poetry and Prose. Edited by Morris U. Schappes. New York: Emma Lazarus Federation of Jewish Women's Clubs, 1982.

Feldman, Abraham J., ed. *Sermons by Reverend Zevi Hirsch Masliansky.* Translated by Edward Herbert. New York: Hebrew Publishing, 1926.

Fossum, Robert H., and John K. Roth, eds. *American Ground: Vistas, Visions and Revisions.* New York: Paragon House, 1988.

Goldman, Emma. *Living My Life.* 2 vols. New York: Dover, 1970.

Gorenstein, Lillian. "A Memoir of the Great War, 1914–1924." *YIVO Annual* 20 (1991).

Habas, Braha, ed. *Sefer haaliyah hashniyah.* Tel Aviv: Am Oved, 1947.

Hahistadrut hahaklait ufeulotehah: Do''h leveidah hahaklait hareviit, 1926–1931. Tel Aviv: Hozaat Hamerkaz Hahaklai, 1931.

Haluz and Youth: A Yearbook Devoted to the Cause of Haluziut in America. New York: Haluziut and Youth Commission of the Labor Zionist Movement, 1952.

Hamifkad hasheni shel haovdim haivriim be-Eretz Israel, September 1, 1926. Tel Aviv: Histadrut Haovidm Haivriim Haklalit be-Eretz Israel, Havaad Hapoel, 1926.

Hapgood, Hutchins. *The Spirit of the Ghetto: Studies of the Jewish Quarter of New York.* Rev. ed. New York: Schocken Books, 1976.

Haveidah hareviit shel Hahistadrut, February 12–18, 1933. Tel Aviv: Havaad Hapoel, 1933.

Hayim Greenberg Anthology. Edited by Marie Syrkin. Detroit: Wayne State University Press, 1968.

Herzl, Theodor. *The Jewish State: An Attempt at a Modern Solution of the Jewish Question.* New York: American Zionist Emergency Council, 1946.

Hollinger, David A., and Charles Capper, eds. *The American Intellectual Tradition: A Sourcebook.* Vol. 2, *1865 to the Present.* New York: Oxford University Press, 1989.

Ilan, Ben-Zion. *An American Soldier/Pioneer in Israel.* New York: Labor Zionist Letters, 1979.

Jabotinsky, Vladimir. *The Story of the Jewish Legion.* Translated by Samuel Katz. New York: Bernard Ackerman, 1945.

James, William. *Talks to Teachers on Psychology and to Students on Some of Life's Ideals.* Reprint, Cambridge, Mass.: Harvard University Press, 1983.

The Jewish Communal Register of New York City, 1917–1918. New York: Kehillah of New York City, 1918.

Kallen, Horace M. *Zionism and World Politics: A Study in History and Social Psychology.* Garden City, N.Y.: Doubleday, Page, 1921.

Kaplan, Mordecai M. *The Jewish Reconstructionist Papers.* New York: Behrman's Jewish Book House, 1936.

———. *Judaism as a Civilization: Toward a Reconstruction of American Jewish Life.* New York: Macmillan, 1934.

————. *Judaism in Transition*. New York: Covici Friede, 1936.

————. *A New Zionism*. 2d ed. New York: Herzl Press and the Jewish Reconstructionist Press, 1959.

Karpf, Maurice J. *Jewish Community Organization in the United States: An Outline of Types of Organizations, Activities and Problems*. New York: Bloch, 1938.

Katzman, Jacob. *Commitment: The Labor Zionist Life-Style in America*. New York: Labor Zionist Letters, 1975.

Katznelson, Berl, and S. Meirov, eds. *Yalkut Ahdut Haavodah*. Vol. 2. Tel Aviv: Hozaat Vaadat Hayalkut, 1931.

Katznelson-Rubashow, Rachel, ed. *The Plough Woman: Records of the Pioneer Women of Palestine*. Translated by Maurice Samuel. New York: Nicholas L. Brown, 1932.

Kitvei Chaim Arlosoroff. Edited by Yaakov Steinberg. Vol. 3. Palestine: A. J. Stybel, 1934.

Kitvei Eliezer Jaffe. 2 vols. Tel Aviv: Am Oved, 1947.

Kohut, George, ed. *The Standard Book of Jewish Verse*. New York: Dodd, Mead, 1917.

The Letters and Papers of Chaim Weizmann, July 1940–January 1943. Edited by Meyer W. Weisgal et al. English ed., ser. A, vol. 20. New Brunswick, N.J.: Rutgers University, Transaction Books, 1979.

The Letters and Papers of Manya Shohat. Edited by Jehuda Reinharz and Shulamit Reinharz. Jerusalem: Yad Yizhak Ben-Zvi. Forthcoming.

Levin, Meyer. *Yehuda*. New York: Jonathan Cape and Harrison Smith, 1931.

Lipsky, Louis. *Memoirs in Profile*. Philadelphia: Jewish Publication Society of America, 1975.

Marcus, Jacob Rader. *This I Believe: Documents of American Jewish Life*. Northvale, N.J.: Jason Aronson, 1990.

Meir, Golda. *My Life*. New York: Dell, 1975.

Meites, Hyman L., ed. *History of the Jews of Chicago*. Reprint, Chicago: Chicago Jewish Historical Society and Wellington Publishing, 1990.

Mendes-Flohr, Paul, and Jehuda Reinharz, eds. *The Jew in the Modern World: A Documentary History*. 2d ed. New York: Oxford University Press, 1995.

Neumann, Emanuel. *In the Arena: An Autobiographical Memoir*. New York: Herzl Press, 1976.

Palestine Royal Commission Report, July 1937. London: His Majesty's Stationery Office, 1937.

Pinkas Hahistadrut Haklalit Shel Haovdim Haivriim be-Eretz Israel. January 1938.

Reform Judaism in the Large Cities: A Survey. New York, 1931.

Report of the Executives of the Zionist Organisation Submitted to the XVIIIth Zionist Congress at Prague, August 21st–29th, 1933. London: Central Office of the Zionist Organisation, 1933.

Report of the Executives of the Zionist Organisation Submitted to the XIXth Zionist

Congress at Lucerne, August 20th–30th, 1935. London: Central Office of the Zionist Organisation, 1935.

Report of the Executives of the Zionist Organisation and of the Jewish Agency for Palestine Submitted to the XXth Zionist Congress and the Vth Session of the Council of the Jewish Agency at Zurich, August 1937. Jerusalem: Executives of the Zionist Organisation and the Jewish Agency for Palestine, 1937.

Report of the Executives of the Zionist Organisation and the Jewish Agency for Palestine Submitted to the XXI Zionist Congress and VI Session of the Council of the Jewish Agency at Geneva, Elul 5699/August 1939. Jerusalem: Executives of the Zionist Organisation and the Jewish Agency for Palestine, 1939.

Revisionists and Mizrachi: A Symposium Held in New York on Saturday Evening, February 3, 1934, at Which the Speakers Were Hayim Greenberg and Joseph Sprinzak. Translated by Maximilian Hurwit. Milwaukee: Spiegel, 1934.

Royce, Josiah. *Race Questions, Provincialism, and Other American Problems.* New York: Macmillan, 1908.

Ruppin, Arthur. *Three Decades in Palestine: Speeches and Papers on the Upbuilding of the Jewish National Home.* Jerusalem: Schocken Books, 1936.

Samuel, Maurice. *I, The Jew.* New York: Harcourt, Brace, 1927.

———. *Little Did I Know: Recollections and Reflections.* New York: Knopf, 1963.

Santayana on America: Essays, Notes, and Letters on American Life. Edited by Richard Colton Lyon. New York: Harcourt, Brace and Wohl, 1968.

Sarna, Jonathan D., ed. and trans. *People Walk on Their Heads: Moses Weinberger's Jews and Judaism in New York.* New York: Holmes & Meier, 1982.

Schappes, Morris U., ed. *A Documentary History of the Jews in the United States, 1654–1875.* New York: Citadel Press, 1950.

Schechter, Solomon. *Seminary Addresses and Other Papers.* Cincinnati: Ark, 1915.

Schwartz, Leo W., ed. *The Avukah Annual of 1929.* New York: New York Chapter, 1929.

Schwartz, Leo W., John J. Tepfer, and James Waterman Wise, eds. *Avukah Annual, Fifth Anniversary Edition, 1925–1930.* New York: Avukah, American Student Zionist Federation, 1930.

The Second Aliyah: An Anthology. New York: Zionist Youth Council, 1955.

Sereni, Enzo, and R. E. Ashery, eds. *Jews and Arabs in Palestine: Studies in a National and Colonial Problem.* New York: Hehaluz Press, 1936.

Shaler, Nathaniel S. *Nature and Man in America.* New York: Scribner, 1891.

Shirat H. N. Bialik: antologyah. Edited by Haiyim Orlan. Cleveland: Lishkat Hahinukh Hayehudi Vehamakhon Lemadaei Hayahadut, and Tel Aviv: Dvir, 1971.

Shubow, Joseph Shalom, ed. *The Brandeis Avukah Annual of 1932: A Collection of Essays on Contemporary Zionist Thought Dedicated to Louis D. Brandeis.* Boston: Avukah, American Student Zionist Federation, 1932.

Sokolow, Nahum. *History of Zionism, 1600–1918.* 2 vols. Reprint, New York: Ktav Publishing House, 1969.

Spitz, Abraham P. *History of the Jews of Boston and New England. Their Financial, Professional, and Commercial Enterprises from the Earliest Settlement of Hebrews in Boston to the Present Day: Containing a Historical and Statistical Record of Every Jewish Congregation, Fraternal Order, Benevolent Society, and Social Club Together with Biographies of Noted Men and Other Matters of Interest.* Boston: Jewish Chronicle, 1892.

Stephen S. Wise: Servant of the People. Edited by Carl Hermann Voss. Philadelphia: Jewish Publication Society of America, 1969.

Toynbee, Arnold J. *A Study of History.* Vol. 8. Oxford: Oxford University Press, and London: Royal Institute of International Affairs, 1954.

Tsur, Muki, Tair Zevulun, and Hanan Porat, eds. *Kan al pnei adamah.* Israel: Kibbutz Hameuhad and Sifriyat Hapoalim, 1981.

Weisgal, Meyer W., ed. *Theodor Herzl: A Memorial.* New York: Zionist Organization of America, 1929.

Weizmann, Chaim. *Trial and Error.* New York: Harper Bros., 1949.

The Worlds of Maurice Samuel: Selected Writings. Edited by Milton Hindus. Philadelphia: Jewish Publication Society, 1977.

SECONDARY SOURCES

Abramovitch, Raphael, et al., eds. *The Jewish People Past and Present.* 4 vols. New York: Marstin Press, 1946, 1948, 1955.

Ahlstrom, Sydney E. *A Religious History of the American People.* New Haven, Conn.: Yale University Press, 1972.

Almog, Shmuel, Jehuda Reinharz, and Anita Shapira, eds. *Zionut vedat.* Jerusalem: Zalman Shazar Center for Jewish History, and Boston: Tauber Institute for the Study of European Jewry, Brandeis University, 1994.

Auerbach, Jerold S. *Rabbis and Lawyers: The Journey from Torah to Constitution.* Bloomington: Indiana University Press, 1990.

Avineri, Shlomo. *Arlosoroff.* London: Weidenfeld and Nicolson, 1989.

——. *The Making of Modern Zionism: The Intellectual Origins of the Jewish State.* New York: Basic Books, 1981.

Baron, Salo W. *The Russian Jew under Tsars and Soviets.* New York: Schocken Books, 1987.

——. *Steeled by Adversity: Essays and Addresses on American Jewish Life.* Philadelphia: Jewish Publication Society of America, 1971.

Bauer, Yehuda. *American Jewry and the Holocaust: The American Jewish Joint Distribution Committee, 1939–1945.* Detroit: Wayne State University Press, 1981.

——. *My Brother's Keeper: A History of the American Jewish Joint Distribution Committee, 1929–1939.* Philadelphia: Jewish Publication Society of America, 1974.

Bayor, Ronald H. *Neighbors in Conflict: The Irish, Germans, Jews and Italians of New York City, 1929–1941.* 2d ed. Urbana: University of Illinois Press, 1988.

Ben-Zvi, Rachel Yanait. *Before Golda: Manya Shohat.* Translated by Sandra Shurin. New York: Biblio Press, 1989.

Berger, David, ed. *History and Hate: The Dimensions of Antisemitism.* Philadelphia: Jewish Publication Society, 1986.

——, ed. *The Legacy of Jewish Migration: 1881 and Its Impact.* Brooklyn: Brooklyn College Press, 1983.

Berman, Aaron. *Nazism, the Jews and American Zionism, 1933–1948.* Detroit: Wayne State University Press, 1990.

Bernstein, Deborah, ed. *Pioneers and Homemakers: Jewish Women in Pre-State Israel.* Albany: State University of New York Press, 1992.

——. *The Struggle for Equality: Urban Workers in Prestate Israeli Society.* New York: Praeger, 1987.

Bloom, Alexander. *Prodigal Sons: The New York Intellectuals and Their World.* New York: Oxford University Press, 1986.

Bondy, Ruth. *Hashaliah: hayav vemoto shel Enzo Sereni.* Tel Aviv: Am Oved, 1973.

Brandes, Joseph. *Immigrants to Freedom: Jewish Communities in Rural New Jersey since 1882.* Philadelphia: Jewish Publication Society of America, 1971.

Brinner, William M., and Moses Rischin, eds. *Like All the Nations?: The Life and Legacy of Judah L. Magnes.* Albany: State University of New York Press, 1987.

Brown, Michael. *The Israeli-American Connection: Its Roots in the Yishuv, 1919–45.* Detroit: Wayne State University Press, 1996.

——. "A Paradoxical Relationship: American Jews and Zionism." In Milton Plesur, ed., *An American Historian: Essays to Honor Selig Adler.* Buffalo: State University of New York at Buffalo, 1980.

Campbell, Joseph. *The Hero with a Thousand Faces.* Princeton, N.J.: Princeton University Press, 1973.

Cohen, Naomi W. *American Jews and the Zionist Idea.* New York: Ktav Publishing House, 1975.

——. *Encounter with Emancipation: The German Jews in the United States, 1830–1914.* Philadelphia: Jewish Publication Society of America, 1984.

——. *Not Free to Desist: The American Jewish Committee, 1906–1966.* Philadelphia: Jewish Publication Society of America, 1972.

——. *The Year after the Riots: American Responses to the Palestine Crisis of 1929–30.* Detroit: Wayne State University Press, 1988.

Davidson, James West, et al. *Nation of Nations: A Narrative History of the American Republic.* Vol. 2. New York: McGraw-Hill, 1990.

Davis, Moshe, ed. "Israel Friedlaender's Minute Book of the Achavah Club, 1909–1912." In Moshe Davis, ed., *Mordecai M. Kaplan Jubilee Volume.* New York: Jewish Theological Seminary of America, 1953.

——. *Israel: Its Role in Civilization.* New York: Jewish Theological Seminary of America, 1956.

————, ed. *With Eyes toward Zion: Scholars Colloquium on America–Holy Land Studies.* New York: Arno Press, 1977.

Diner, Hasia R. *A Time for Gathering: The Second Migration, 1820–1880.* Baltimore: Johns Hopkins University Press, 1993.

Dinnerstein, Leonard. *Antisemitism in America.* New York: Oxford University Press, 1994.

Don-Yehiya, Eliezer. "Hanuka and the Myth of the Maccabees in Zionist Ideology and Israeli Society." *Jewish Journal of Sociology* 34 (1992).

Dundes, Alan, ed. *The Study of Folklore.* Englewood Cliffs, N.J.: Prentice-Hall, 1965.

Dworkin, Susan. "Henrietta Szold: Liberated Woman." In Elizabeth Koltun, ed., *The Jewish Woman: New Perspectives.* New York: Schocken Books, 1976.

Eisen, Arnold M. *The Chosen People in America: A Study in Jewish Religious Ideology.* Bloomington: Indiana University Press, 1983.

Elazar, Daniel. *Israel: Building a New Society.* Bloomington: Indiana University Press, 1986.

Epstein, Melech. *Jewish Labor in USA: An Industrial, Political and Cultural History of the Jewish Labor Movement, 1882–1914.* 2 vols. New York: Ktav Publishing House, 1969.

————. *Profiles of Eleven.* Detroit: Wayne State University Press, 1965.

Esco Foundation for Palestine. *Palestine: A Study of Jewish, Arab, and British Policies.* 2 vols. New Haven, Conn.: Yale University Press, 1947.

Feingold, Henry L. *The Politics of Rescue: The Roosevelt Administration and the Holocaust, 1938–1945.* New York: Holocaust Library, 1970.

————. *A Time for Searching: Entering the Mainstream, 1920–1945.* Baltimore: Johns Hopkins University Press, 1992.

Frankel, Jonathan. *Prophecy and Politics: Socialism, Nationalism and the Russian Jews, 1862–1917.* Cambridge: Cambridge University Press, 1981.

Freud, Sigmund, and D. E. Oppenheim. *Dreams in Folklore.* New York: International Universities Press, 1958.

Freulich, Roman. *Soldiers in Judea: Stories and Vignettes of the Jewish Legion.* New York: Herzl Press, 1964.

Friedman, Maurice S. *Martin Buber: The Life of Dialogue.* New York: Harper & Row, 1960.

Friesel, Evyatar. "Ahad Haamism in American Zionist Thought." In Jacques Kornberg, ed., *At the Crossroads: Essays on Ahad Haam.* Albany: State University of New York Press, 1983.

————. "Criteria and Conception in the Historiography of German and American Zionism." *Studies in Zionism* 1 (Autumn 1980).

————. *Hatnuah hazionit be-arzot habrit bashanim 1897–1914.* Tel Aviv: Tel Aviv University and Hozaat Hakibbutz Hameuhad, 1970.

————. "The Knights of Zion of Chicago and Their Relations with the Federation of American Zionists, 1897–1916." In Daniel Carpi and Gedalia Yogev, eds., *Zionism: Studies in the History of the Zionist Movement and of the Jewish Community in Palestine.* Vol. 1. Tel Aviv: Tel Aviv University and Massada Publishing, 1975.

Frost, Shimon. "Kavim letoldot hamahanaiot haivrit bezfon amerikah." In Shlomo Shulsinger, ed., *Kovez Masad: Mahanaiot ivrit.* Vol. 2. Israel: Irgun Mahanot Masad, 1989.

Fuchs, Lawrence H. *The American Kaleidoscope: Race, Ethnicity and the Civic Culture.* Hanover, N.H.: University Press of New England, 1990.

———. *The Political Behavior of American Jews.* Glencoe, Ill.: Free Press, 1956.

Gal, Allon. *Brandeis of Boston.* Cambridge, Mass.: Harvard University Press, 1980.

———. *The Changing Concept of "Mission" in American Reform Judaism.* Cincinnati: American Jewish Archives, 1991.

———. *David Ben-Gurion and the American Alignment for a Jewish State.* Jerusalem: Magnes Press, Hebrew University of Jerusalem, and Bloomington: Indiana University Press, 1991.

———, ed. *Envisioning Israel: The Changing Ideals and Images of North American Jews.* Jerusalem: Magnes Press, Hebrew University of Jerusalem, and Detroit: Wayne State University Press, 1996.

———. "Independence and Universal Mission in Modern Jewish Nationalism: A Comparative Analysis of European and American Zionism (1897–1948)." *Studies in Contemporary Jewry* 5 (1989).

Galbraith, John Kenneth. *The Great Crash, 1929.* Boston: Houghton Mifflin, 1955.

Galnoor, Itzhak. *The Partition of Palestine: Decision Crossroads in the Zionist Movement.* Albany: State University of New York Press, 1995.

Gerber, David A. *Antisemitism in American History.* Urbana: University of Illinois Press, 1987.

Gitelman, Zvi, ed. *A Century of Ambivalence: The Jews of Russia and the Soviet Union, 1881 to the Present.* New York: Schocken Books and YIVO Institute for Jewish Research, 1988.

———, ed. *The Quest for Utopia: Jewish Political Ideas and Institutions through the Ages.* New York: Sharpe, 1992.

Glanz, Rudolf. *The Jewish Woman in America: Two Female Immigrant Generations, 1820–1929.* Vol. 1, *The Eastern European Jewish Woman.* New York: Ktav Publishing House and National Council of Jewish Women, 1976.

Glass, Joseph B. "Balfouria: An American Zionist Colony." *Studies in Zionism* 14 (1993).

Glenn, Susan. *Daughters of the Shtetl: Jewish Immigrant Women in America's Garment Industry, 1880–1920.* Ithaca, N.Y.: Cornell University Press, 1990.

Glicksman, W. "The Haluz Ideology and Experience as Reflected in the Yiddish Novel in Poland, 1919–1939." *YIVO Annual of Jewish Social Science* 14 (1969).

Goldberg, J. J., and Elliot King, eds. *Builders and Dreamers: Habonim Labor Zionist Youth in North America*. New York: Herzl Press and Cornwall Books, 1993.

Goldsmith, Emanuel S., Mel Scult, and Robert M. Seltzer, eds. *The American Judaism of Mordecai M. Kaplan*. New York: New York University Press, 1990.

Goodblatt, Charles Israel. "The Impact of the Balfour Declaration in America." *American Jewish Historical Quarterly*, June 1968.

Goren, Arthur A. "Jews." In Stephan Thernstrom, ed., *Harvard Encyclopedia of American Ethnic Groups*. Cambridge, Mass.: Harvard University Press, 1980.

———. "The Jewish Press in the United States." In Sally Miller, ed., *The Ethnic Press in the United States: A Historical Analysis and Handbook*. Westport, Conn.: Greenwood Press, 1987.

———. *New York Jews and the Quest for Community: The Kehillah Experiment, 1908–1922*. New York: Columbia University Press, 1970.

Gorny, Yosef. *The State of Israel in Jewish Public Thought: The Quest for Collective Identity*. New York: New York University Press, 1994.

Grand, Samuel. "A History of Zionist Youth Organizations in the United States from Their Inception to 1940." Ph.D. diss., Columbia University, 1958.

Haim Enzo Sereni: 40 shanah lemoto. Tel Aviv: Yad Tabenkin, Efal, and Hatnuah Hakibbutzit Hameuhedet, 1985.

Halperin, Samuel. *The Political World of American Zionism*. Reprint, Silver Spring, Md.: Information Dynamics, 1985.

Halpern, Ben. "The Americanization of Zionism, 1880–1930." *American Jewish History*, September 1979.

———. *The American Jew: A Zionist Analysis*. 2d ed. New York: Schocken Books, 1983.

———. *A Clash of Heroes: Brandeis, Weizmann and American Zionism*. New York: Oxford University Press, 1987.

———. *The Idea of the Jewish State*. 2d ed. Cambridge, Mass.: Harvard University Press, 1969.

Halpern, Ben, and Jehuda Reinharz. "Nationalism and Jewish Socialism: The Early Years." *Modern Judaism*, October 1988.

———. *Zionism and the Creation of a New Society*. New York: Oxford University Press, 1998.

Handlin, Oscar. *A Continuing Task: The American Jewish Joint Distribution Committee, 1914–1964*. New York: Random House, 1964.

Herscher, Uri D. *Jewish Agricultural Utopias in America, 1880–1910*. Detroit: Wayne State University Press, 1981.

Hertzberg, Arthur. *The Jews in America: Four Centuries of an Uneasy Encounter*. New York: Simon & Schuster, 1989.

———, ed. *The Zionist Idea: A Historical Analysis and Reader*. Philadelphia: Jewish Publication Society, 1997.

Higham, John. *Strangers in the Land: Patterns of American Nativism, 1860–1925.* New York: Atheneum, 1973.

Hoberman, J. *Bridge of Light: Yiddish Film between Two Worlds.* New York: Museum of Modern Art and Schocken Books, 1991.

Hoerder, Dirk, ed. *The Immigrant Labor Press in North America, 1840s–1970s: An Annotated Bibliography.* Vol. 2, *Migrants from Eastern and Southern Europe.* Westport, Conn.: Greenwood Press, 1987.

Howe, Irving. *World of Our Fathers: The Journey of the East European Jews to America and the Life They Found and Made.* New York: Simon & Schuster, 1976.

Hurwitz, Ariel, ed. *Against the Stream: Seven Decades of Hashomer Hatzair in North America.* Israel: Association of North American Shomrim and Yad Yaari, Givat Haviva, 1994.

Jacob, Heinrich Eduard. *The World of Emma Lazarus.* New York: Schocken Books, 1949.

Jacobson, Matthew Frye. *Special Sorrows: The Diasporic Imagination of Irish, Polish and Jewish Immigrants in the United States.* Cambridge, Mass.: Harvard University Press, 1995.

Jones, Maldwyn Allen. *American Immigration.* Chicago: University of Chicago Press, 1960.

Joselit, Jenna Weissman. *A Worthy Use of Summer: Jewish Summer Camping in America.* Philadelphia: National Museum of American Jewish History, 1993.

Kabakoff, Jacob. "Beginnings of Hibbat Zion in America," *Herzl Year Book.* Vol. 6, 1964–1965.

Kaisar, Ilan. "Mobilizing American Jewish Liberals to Support Labor Zionism." *Journal of Israeli History* 15 (Autumn 1994).

Katz, Jacob. "The Forerunners of Zionism." *Jerusalem Quarterly* 7 (1978).

Kaufman, Menahem. *An Ambiguous Partnership: Non-Zionists and Zionists in America, 1939–1948.* Jerusalem: Magnes Press, Hebrew University of Jerusalem, and Detroit: Wayne State University Press, 1991.

Keren, Thea. "Sophie Udin: Portrait of a Pioneer." Privately published master's thesis. Hebrew University of Jerusalem, 1984.

Kessner, Carole S., ed. *The "Other" New York Jewish Intellectuals.* Albany: State University of New York Press: 1995.

Klausner, Israel. "Adam Rosenberg: One of the Earliest American Zionists." *Herzl Year Book.* Vol. 1, 1958.

Kochavi, Arieh. *Akurim vepolitikah benleumit: Britania vehaakurim hayehudim leaher milhemet haolam hashniyah.* Tel Aviv: Am Oved, 1992.

Kolsky, Thomas A. *Jews against Zionism: The American Council for Judaism, 1942–1948.* Philadelphia: Temple University Press, 1990.

Kraut, Benny. "American Jewish Leaders: The Great, Greater, and Greatest." *American Jewish History,* December 1988.

Laqueur, Walter. *A History of Zionism.* 2d ed. New York: Schocken Books, 1989.

————. *Young Germany: A History of the German Youth Movement.* New York: Basic Books, 1962.

Laskov, Shulamit. "The Biluim: Reality and Legend." *Studies in Zionism* 2 (Spring 1981).

Lavsky, Hagit. *Beterem puranut: darkam veyihudam shel zionut germania, 1918–1932.* Jerusalem: Hozaat Sfarim Al Shem J. L. Magnes, Hauniversitah Haivrit, 1989.

Learsi, Rufus (Israel Goldberg). *Fulfillment: The Epic Story of Zionism.* Cleveland: World, 1951.

————. *The Jews in America: A History.* Cleveland: World, 1954.

Lederhendler, Eli. *The Road to Modern Jewish Politics: Political Tradition and Political Reconstruction in the Jewish Community of Tsarist Russia.* New York: Oxford University Press, 1989.

Liebman, Charles S. "Reconstructionism in American Jewish Life." *American Jewish Year Book.* Vol. 71, 1970.

Lipsky, Louis. *A Gallery of Zionist Profiles.* New York: Farrar, Straus and Cudahy, 1956.

Lipstadt, Deborah E. *The Zionist Career of Louis Lipsky, 1900–1921.* New York: Arno Press, 1982.

Macleod, David I. *Building Character in the American Boy: The Boy Scouts, YMCA and Their Forerunners, 1870–1920.* Madison: University of Wisconsin Press, 1983.

Madison, Charles A. *Jewish Publishing in America.* New York: Sanhedrin Press, 1976

Mahler, Raphael. "Lereshitah shel tnuat Hehaluz." *Asufot*, December 1959.

Malmgreen, Gail. "Labor and the Holocaust: The Jewish Labor Committee and the Anti-Nazi Struggle." *Labor's Heritage*, October 1991.

Marcaccio, Michael D. *The Hapgoods: Three Earnest Brothers.* Charlottesville: University Press of Virginia, 1977.

Mendelsohn, Ezra. *On Modern Jewish Politics.* New York: Oxford University Press, 1993.

————. "The Russian Roots of the American Jewish Labor Movement." In Deborah Dash Moore, ed., *East European Jews in Two Worlds: Studies from the YIVO Annual.* Evanston, Ill.: Northwestern University Press and YIVO Institute for Jewish Research, 1990.

————. *Zionism in Poland: The Formative Years, 1915–1926.* New Haven, Conn.: Yale University Press, 1981.

Menes, Abraham. "The *Am Oylom* Movement." *YIVO Annual.* Vol. 4, 1949.

Meyer, Isidore S., ed. *Early History of Zionism in America.* New York: American Jewish Historical Society and Theodor Herzl Foundation, 1958.

Meyer, Michael A. "A Centennial History." In Samuel E. Karff, ed., *Hebrew Union College–Jewish Institute of Religion At One Hundred Years.* Cincinnati: Hebrew Union College Press, 1976.

————. *Response to Modernity: A History of the Reform Movement in Judaism.* New York: Oxford University Press, 1988.

Mintz, Matityahu. *Zmanim hadashim, zmirot hadashot: Ber Borochov, 1914–1917*. Tel Aviv: Hozaat Am Oved, Universitat Tel Aviv, Hamakhon Leheker Hazionut Al Shem Chaim Weizmann, 1988.

Moore, Deborah Dash. *At Home in America: Second Generation New York Jews*. New York: Columbia University Press, 1981.

———. *Bnai Brith and the Challenge of Ethnic Leadership*. Albany: State University of New York Press, 1981.

Naor, Mordecai, ed. *Tnuot Noar, 1920–1960: Mekorot, sikumim, parashot nivharot vehomer ezer*. Jerusalem: Hozaat Yad Yizhak Ben-Zvi, Hamahlakah Lehinukh Vehadrakhah, 1989.

Near, Henry. *Frontiersmen and Haluzim: The Image of the Pioneer in North America and Pre-State Jewish Palestine*. Haifa: University of Haifa and Kibbutz University Center, 1987.

Oppenheim, Israel. *The Struggle of Jewish Youth for Productivization: The Zionist Youth Movement in Poland*. Boulder, Colo.: East European Monographs, and New York: Columbia University Press, 1989.

———. *Tnuat Hehaluz be-Polin, 1917–1929*. Jerusalem: Hozaat Sfarim Al Shem J. L. Magnes, Hauniversitah Haivrit, 1982.

Patkin, A.L. *The Origins of the Russian Jewish Labour Movement*. Melbourne: F. W. Cheshire, 1947.

Penslar, Derek J. *Zionism and Technocracy: The Engineering of Jewish Settlement in Palestine, 1870–1918*. Bloomington: Indiana University Press, 1991.

Pilch, Judah, ed. *A History of Jewish Education in America*. New York: American Association for Jewish Education, 1969.

Rabinovich, Isaiah. *Major Trends in Modern Hebrew Fiction*. Chicago: University of Chicago Press, 1968.

Raider, Mark A. "Jewish Immigrant Farmers in the Connecticut River Valley: The Rockville Settlement." *American Jewish Archives* 48 (Fall–Winter 1995).

———. "Pioneers and Pacesetters: Boston Jews and American Zionism." In Jonathan D. Sarna and Ellen Smith, eds., *The Jews of Boston*. Boston: Combined Jewish Philanthropies of Boston and Northeastern University Press, 1995.

———. "Toward a Re-examination of American Zionist Leadership: The Case of Hayim Greenberg." *Journal of Israeli History* 15 (Summer 1994).

———. "Where American Zionism Differed: Abba Hillel Silver Reconsidered." In Mark A. Raider, Jonathan D. Sarna, and Ronald W. Zweig, eds., *Abba Hillel Silver and American Zionism*. London: Frank Cass, 1997.

Raphael, Marc Lee. *Abba Hillel Silver: A Profile in American Judaism*. New York: Holmes & Meier, 1989.

Reinharz, Jehuda. *Chaim Weizmann: The Making of a Zionist Leader*. Vol. 1. New York: Oxford University Press, 1985.

———. *Chaim Weizmann: The Making of a Statesman*. Vol. 2. New York: Oxford University Press, 1993.

————. *Fatherland or Promised Land: The Dilemma of the German Jew, 1893–1914.* Ann Arbor: University of Michigan Press, 1975.

————. "Hashomer Hazair in Germany (I), 1928–1933." *Leo Baeck Institute Year Book.* Vol. 31, 1986.

————. "On Defining Jewish National Autonomy: Demarcating Ideological Boundaries." In Israel Bartal, ed., *Israel Heilprin Memorial Volume.* Jerusalem: Merkaz Zalman Shazar. In Press.

————. *Writing the Biography of Chaim Weizmann.* Rehovot: Yad Chaim Weizmann, 1992.

————. *Zionism and the Great Powers: A Century of Foreign Policy.* New York: Leo Baeck Institute, 1994.

————. "Zionism in the USA on the Eve of the Balfour Declaration." *Studies in Zionism* 9 (1988).

Reinharz, Jehuda, and Anita Shapira, eds. *Essential Papers on Zionism.* New York: New York University Press, 1995.

Ribalov, Menahem, ed. *Sefer hayovel shel Hadoar.* New York: Hozaat Hahistadrut Haivrit be-Amerikah, 1927.

Rosen, Gladys, ed. *Jewish Life in America: Historical Perspectives.* New York: Ktav Publishing House, 1978.

Rosenblum, Chanoch (Howard). "The New Zionist Organization's American Campaign, 1936–1939." *Studies in Zionism* 12 (Autumn 1991).

Sachar, Howard M. *A History of the Jews in America.* New York: Knopf, 1992.

Sarna, Jonathan D. *A Great Jewish Awakening: The Transformation That Shaped Twentieth Century American Judaism and Its Implications for Today.* New York: Council for Initiatives in Jewish Education, 1995.

————. " 'The Greatest Jew in the World Since Jesus Christ': The Jewish Legacy of Louis D. Brandeis." *American Jewish History* 81 (Spring–Summer 1994).

————. *JPS: The Americanization of Jewish Culture, 1888–1898.* Philadelphia: Jewish Publication Society, 1989.

————. "The Spectrum of Jewish Leadership in Ante-Bellum America." *Journal of American Ethnic History* 1 (Spring 1982).

Scharfstein, Zvi. *Toldot hahinukh be-Israel bedorot haahronim.* 2d ed. Vol. 3. Jerusalem: Reubin Mass, 1962.

Schechtman, Joseph B. *Rebel and Statesman: The Vladimir Jabotinsky Story, the Early Years.* New York: Thomas Yoseloff, 1958.

Schmidt, Sarah L. *Horace M. Kallen: Prophet of American Zionism.* New York: Carlson, 1997.

Schoenberg, Philip Ernest. "The American Reaction to the Kishinev Pogrom of 1903." *American Jewish Historical Quarterly*, March 1974.

Schulman, Charles E. "Fundraiser Par Excellence." In Marc Lee Raphael, ed.,

Understanding American Jewish Philanthropy. New York: Ktav Publishing House, 1979.

Schweid, Eliezer. *The Land of Israel: National Home or Land of Destiny?* Translated by Deborah Greniman. Cranberry, N.J.: Associated University Presses, and New York: Herzl Press, 1985.

Scult, Mel. *Judaism Faces the Twentieth Century: A Biography of Mordecai M. Kaplan.* Detroit: Wayne State University Press, 1993.

Sela, Yehuda. "Pirkei haapalah shel haluzim mi-Amerikah." *Measef leheker tnuat haavodah hazionit vehasozialism* 17 (1987).

Seltzer, Robert M. "Hayim Greenberg, Jewish Intellectual." In Carole S. Kessner, ed., *The "Other" New York Jewish Intellectuals.* Albany: State University of New York Press, 1994.

Shapira, Anita. *Berl: The Biography of a Socialist Zionist.* Cambridge: Cambridge University Press, 1984.

———. "Did the Zionist Leadership Foresee the Holocaust?" In Jehuda Reinharz, ed., *Living with Antisemitism: Modern Jewish Responses.* Hanover, N.H.: University Press of New England, 1987.

———. *Land and Power: The Zionist Resort to Force, 1881–1948.* Translated by William Templer. New York: Oxford University Press, 1992.

Shapiro, Yonathan. *Leadership of the American Zionist Organization, 1897–1930.* Urbana: University of Illinois Press, 1971.

Shargel, Baila Round. *Practical Dreamer: Israel Friedlaender and the Shaping of American Judaism.* New York: Jewish Theological Seminary of America, 1985.

Shiff, Ofer. "The Integrative Function of Early American Zionism." *Journal of Israeli History* 15 (Spring 1994).

Shiloh, Margalit. "Nizanei raayon hamoshav—Haikar Hazair, hakvuzah haamerikanit baaliyah hashniyah." *Katedrah* 25 (1982).

Shimoni, Gideon. "Poale Zion: A Zionist Transplant in Britain, 1905–45." *Studies in Contemporary Jewry* 2 (1986).

———. *The Zionist Ideology.* Hanover, N.H.: University Press of New England, 1995.

Shpiro, David H. "The Political Background of the 1942 Biltmore Resolution." *Herzl Year Book.* Vol. 8, 1978.

Shubow, Leo. "Jacob De Haas and the Boston *Jewish Advocate.*" *Herzl Year Book.* Vol. 5, 1963.

Soltes, Mordecai. *The Yiddish Press: An Americanizing Agency.* New York: Teachers College, Columbia University, 1925.

Sorin, Gerald. *A Time for Building: The Third Migration, 1880–1920.* Baltimore: Johns Hopkins University Press, 1993.

Spizman, Leib, ed. *Geshikhte fun der zionistisher arbeter bavegung in zfon amerike.* 2 vols. New York: Farlag Yidisher Kemfer, 1955.

Stein, Kenneth W. *The Land Question in Palestine, 1917–1939.* Chapel Hill: University of North Carolina Press, 1984.

Syrkin, Marie. *Nachman Syrkin: Socialist Zionist. A Biographical Memoir and Selected Essays.* New York: Herzl Press and Sharon Books, 1961.

Szajkowski, Zosa. *Jews, Wars and Communism.* Vol. 1, *The Attitude of American Jews to World War I, the Russian Revolutions of 1917 and Communism (1914–1945).* New York: Ktav Publishing House, 1972.

Tcherikower, Elias. *The Early Jewish Labor Movement in the United States.* Translated by Aaron Antonovsky. New York: YIVO Institute for Research, 1961.

Teveth, Shabtai. *Ben-Gurion and the Palestinian Arabs: From Peace to War.* Oxford: Oxford University Press, 1985.

———. *Ben-Gurion: The Burning Ground, 1886–1948.* Boston: Houghton Mifflin, 1987.

Urofsky, Melvin I. "American Jewish Leadership." *American Jewish History* 70 (1981).

———. *American Zionism from Herzl to the Holocaust.* Reprint, Lincoln: University of Nebraska Press, 1995.

———. *A Voice That Spoke for Justice: The Life and Times of Stephen S. Wise.* Albany: State University of New York Press, 1982.

Vovelle, Michel. *Ideologies and Mentalities.* Translated by Eamon O'Flaherty. Chicago: University of Chicago Press, 1990.

Wasserstein, Bernard. *Britain and the Jews of Europe, 1939–1945.* New York: Oxford University Press, 1988.

Weinberg, Sydney Stahl. *The World of Our Mothers: The Lives of Jewish Immigrant Women.* New York: Schocken Books, 1988.

Wenger, Beth. "Ethnic Community in Economic Crisis: New York Jews and the Great Depression." Ph.D. diss., Yale University, 1992.

Wertheimer, Jack. *Unwelcome Strangers: East European Jews in Imperial Germany.* New York: Oxford University Press, 1987.

Winer, Gershon. "The Religious Dimension of Yiddish Secularism." *Judaism* 41 (Winter 1992).

Wistrich, Robert S. "Marxism and Jewish Nationalism: The Theoretical Roots of Confrontation." *Jewish Journal of Sociology,* June 1975.

Yahil, Leni. *The Holocaust.* New York: Oxford University Press, 1987.

Zipperstein, Steven J. *Elusive Prophet: Ahad Haam and the Origins of Zionism.* Berkeley and Los Angeles: University of California Press, 1993.

Index

Aaronsohn, Aaron, 45, 82, 88
Abel, Senior, 18
Achavah Club, 18–21, 29, 150
Adas Zion Anshe Kowno, 9
Adler, Cyrus, 18, 150, 183–84
Afula, 28, 103
Agriculture, 25, 54–55, 56, 103, 104, 107, 108; *haluzim* as farmers and, 81–82, 83, 107. *See also* Cooperatives; *Hakhsharot* (training farms); *Kibbutzim; Kvuzot* (communes); *Moshavim*
"Agriculture in Old Palestine," 83
Agro-Joint, 194, 195
Ahad Haam (Asher Ginzberg), 17, 19, 20, 23, 24, 77, 97, 132–33, 151, 152, 159
Ahavath Achim Anshe Usda, 9
Akzin, Benjamin, 180
Alaska, proposed Jewish refugee resettlement in, 211–12
Alexander II (Czar of Russia), 6
"Al harei katskil" (On the Catskill Mountains) (Samuel), 160
Aliyah Bet, 125, 196, 201, 202, 205, 216
Aliyot, 127, 138; Aliyah Bet and, 125, 196, 201, 202, 205, 216; Second, 72; Third, 92, 133; youth movement and, 125
Alliance, 13
Alterman, Nathan, 163
Amalgamated Clothing Workers' Union, 175
American Alliance for Labor and Democracy, 37
American Bundists, 177
American Christian Conference, 188
American Council for Judaism, 215
American Daughters of Zion, 9
American Federation of Labor (AFL), 37, 175, 188, 203–5
American Friends of Jewish Palestine, 179–80

American Hebrew, 18, 80
American Jewess, 11
American Jewish assembly, 196–98
American Jewish Committee, 5, 150, 165, 183, 184, 189, 193–94, 196, 201, 214; American Jewish assembly and, 197; American Jewish Congress and, 27–28; formation of, 18; German Jews and, 43
American Jewish Conference (1943), 4, 170, 212–15
American Jewish Congress (1918), 2–3, 4, 32, 161, 184, 197, 198, 212–13; American Jewish assembly and, 197; Mizrahi Party and, 36–37; 1914–1918 campaign and, 27–28, 29, 35; Poalei Zion Party and, 35–36, 37
American Socialist Party, 175
American Society for Jewish Farm Settlements in Russia, 194, 195
American Zion Commonwealth, 28, 102
American Zionist Emergency Council (AZEC), 170, 215–16
Amerikantsy, 6
Am Olam (Eternal People) movement, 6, 74
Anglo-Jewish press, 11–12, 167; *Jewish Advocate,* 26, 116, 179; *Jewish Frontier,* 30, 64, 65–66, 67, 148, 162–63, 164, 166, 168, 169, 176–77, 179, 208, 211, 212; *Jewish Spectator,* 148, 162; Labor Palestine and, 187; *Menorah Journal,* 148, 162, 176; Nazi genocide and, 169; *New Palestine,* 148, 162; Saul Raskin in, 116; *Reconstructionist,* 148, 162, 163–64, 176, 182
Anti-Defamation League, 44
Antisemitism, 12n, 29, 72, 111–12, 164–65, 168, 209; after World War I, 43–44, 98, 130; Bund and, 127, 189, 209; *Dearborn Independent* and, 43, 98; Holocaust and, 169, 207–11, 216; immigration quotas

About the Author

Mark A. Raider is assistant professor of modern Jewish history in the Department of Judaic Studies at the University at Albany, State University of New York.

He is principal coeditor, with Jonathan D. Sarna and Ronald W. Zweig, of *Abba Hillel Silver and American Zionism* (London: Frank Cass, 1997). His articles have appeared in the *Journal of Israeli History*, *American Jewish History*, *American Jewish Archives*, *The Jews of Boston* (1995, edited by Jonathan D. Sarna and Ellen Smith), and *Jewish Frontier*. He is currently completing an edited and annotated anthology of writings by the Zionist thinker Hayim Greenberg and a guide to Zionist materials in the holdings of the American Jewish Historical Society.

Breinigsville, PA USA
08 March 2011
257219BV00001BA/2/A